Jazz Dialogues

Jon Gordon

Cymbal Press

Jazz Dialogues
© 2020 Jon Gordon. All rights reserved.

Published by Cymbal Press, Torrance, CA USA
cymbalpress.com

This and other Cymbal Press books may be purchased at cymbalpress.com. Volume and education discounts are available.

ISBN
Paperback: 978-0-9994776-6-3
Hardcover: 978-0-9994776-7-0

MUS025000   MUSIC / Genres & Styles / Jazz
MUS055000   MUSIC / Essays
MUS050000   MUSIC / Individual Composer & Musician
BIO004000   BIOGRAPHY & AUTOBIOGRAPHY / Music

All marks are the property of their respective owners.

Publisher: Gary S. Stager
Cover: Yvonne Martinez

1

Table of Contents

Introduction – Jay McShann

Heathrow Airport, London – August 1987

"Yeah man, Bird was a stylist, you know?"

I just nodded my head, amazed to be talking to the guy that gave Charlie Parker his first big gig.

I was coming back from performing at my first major jazz festival, sitting in Heathrow Airport in London, sharing a bottle of Aquavit with the great Kansas City Blues piano player, Jay McShann. We had just played some gigs together at the Oslo Jazz Festival. I was pretty scared at the start of the week, but he, Doc Cheatham, and the other greats I got to play with there were very kind and supportive, and helped me to feel like they weren't going to fly me home after the first concert, which, based on my own assessment of my playing, I'd thought was a real possibility!

He was 71, and I was 20. He was waiting for his flight. I'd just been bumped off of mine because a wealthy passenger was willing to pay a first class fare for a coach seat. Somehow, on a full plane with hundreds of people, it turned out to be my coach seat. They called my name over the intercom, asked me to take my things with me, promised me I was "Not being taken off the flight" and that my seat was "Not being given away." As the scene unfolded, the great clarinetist, Kenny Davern, who had been very kind to me that week and was seated near me said, "Worst case scenario you'll spend a couple a' days in one of the most beautiful cities in the world, and they'll pay for your hotel!" As I walked towards the exit door of the plane with one of the women who worked for Pan Am, I thought, "Yeah! That's the spirit. Stay positive! What's the worst that could happen?" As we stepped off the plane, a businessman in a suit walked past me onto the plane with a briefcase. The door was quickly closed behind him, and while I was standing there, jaw agape, five feet from the plane, it immediately began to roll away from us.

I looked at the flight attendant and loudly said, "What the hell!?" She quickly apologized and said, "I'm so sorry for having to lie to you, but I had to for my job." She then explained that he'd offered to pay the first class price for a coach seat and that I'd need to get another ticket reissued in another area of the airport, but that there was another flight in just five hours. Lucky me!

However, after waiting in line for over an hour, the gentleman, as it were, who worked for Pan Am and waited on me, laughed when I showed him my ticket. He explained that it was not in fact a ticket but a coupon. This may have been because the festival was sponsored by Pan Am, and they must have issued some of these coupons as tickets as part of their support of the festival. As such, according to him, it was now worthless. No ticket could be reissued to replace it. I then asked about a hotel for the night, as Kenny Davern had mentioned. He laughed again, and this time told me to get off the line and stop wasting his time.

Now I was panicked. I said, "How do I get home!?"

He responded by shouting, "I don't know and it's not my fucking problem! You have to buy a new ticket, but every flight we have to New York is fully booked for the next four weeks. Now get off the fucking line before I call security!"

I had no idea what to do at this point. I figured all I could do was go back to the ladies who worked at the gate where I'd been and tell them what had happened. I walked back there in a kind of shocked daze, found them and informed them of what I'd just been told. They looked horrified! One of them said, "Oh my goodness! That's terrible!" Another woman said, "We're so very sorry for all this! We feel awful. Really!" Then the first lady said, as she looked at a screen, "I am seeing that he's correct, this next flight is fully booked… and he's probably right that they're mostly full in the coming days and weeks. But if someone doesn't show for this next flight, we'll get you on it, ticket or not!"

Luckily for me, one guy didn't show! (This was pre-9/11, clearly it would never have happened afterwards.) My suitcase ended up still being at Kennedy Airport in baggage claim when I got there, so it all worked out. But the one big positive from all this stress and worry was seeing Jay seated nearby my gate, sitting and talking with him, and drinking Aquavit as we waited.

"Yeah man… cats nowadays don't understand. They don't know what it means to be a stylist. They might play their horns and all that. But man, you gotta have a sound, your own approach. Pres was a stylist. Bird was too. Basie. All them cats, know what I mean?"

"Uh, yeah," I said as I nodded my head. But in fairness, I really didn't. I'd never heard the term stylist before that conversation. It got me thinking, as he mentioned some more names.

"Ben Webster, Hawk, Johnny Hodges, Art Tatum. That's how cats were back in my day man, you know?" I nodded my head again and smiled, feeling somewhat less stressed out about getting home as the Aquavit was slowly starting to take effect.

"I'm not saying that everybody was that great. But musicians tended to have their own thing more than guys do now. Lots of cats, everybody really. You could tell it was them right away when they played a note or two, you know? 'Cause they had their own style. A sound, an approach, the way they played the changes."

I was slowly starting to get it.

"You sound good Little Bird." he said, referring to Charlie Parker's nickname, Bird. "I hear you playin' Charlie Parker, and that's good. But what you got to do now is find your own style, see?"

I was very honored by his kind words. And I was just happy to have a chance to talk to Jay. But I realized he was exactly right in what he was telling me I needed to do. We talked for about an hour before his plane was ready to take off, but this part of the conversation was the most memorable, and something I often like to talk about with students. And this chance meeting, such as it was, was a part of a pattern that kept occurring to me from the age of sixteen to my mid-twenties. I kept meeting, talking to, and sometimes even playing with these great musicians. And the thought that came to me at the time was, "This has to be happening for a reason. I'm trying to figure out this 'modern stuff' that I'm intrigued by, and trying to learn how to play like Joe Henderson, John Coltrane, Alan Holdsworth, and Joe Lovano—but I keep finding myself with Doc Cheatham, Benny Waters, Roy Eldridge, Mel Lewis, Eddie Locke, Dick Katz, Danny Bank, Benny Carter, Clark Terry, Flip Phillips, Eddie Chamblee, Barney Kessel, Joe Williams, Red Rodney, Milt Hinton, Roland Hanna, and Dick Hyman, among others. I better really listen and take to heart what these guys are telling me."

Many were in their seventies or eighties. Benny Waters was almost ninety when I got to meet and play with him. (He told me that he took a nap and ate ice cream every afternoon for over fifty years at that point. Seemed like that regimen was working out pretty well for him!) Although I was young, I already knew enough to realize that they weren't makin' 'em like that anymore! I knew I was damn lucky to meet and work with these guys, and I wanted to try to learn as much as I could from them. Not only for myself, but also so I could try to pass on some of what they were teaching me to my students someday.

At times in this book, I'm speaking to the musicians as a friend, peer, or student. But I often come back to just feeling like a fan in many of the stories and interviews. I always tell students, there are a lot of different ways you can make a contribution in this music. It's hard to get consistent, creative opportunities as a jazz musician. It was never easy, and it was harder for the Black musicians who created this music than most of us in this day and age could ever imagine. But the one thing I always felt about these experiences of meeting and talking to these great musicians was a sense of responsibility about passing on what they showed and taught me. It's second-hand, yes, but my students and future generations of musicians aren't going to have the luxury of showing up on a gig and getting to meet and play with many of the musicians mentioned here, and the generation or two (or three) before I came on the scene.

This book is my attempt at trying to pass on some of what they showed me and spoke to me about. It's a collection of brief talks, quotes, and stories from the road over the past 35-plus years, along with some more in-depth conversational interviews from the past 15 years or so. In the interviews in particular, my hope was to get the musicians to talk about their formative experiences in the music—their family connections to it, first experiences listening and playing, a great teacher or mentor, their inspirations, all the things that made them who they are. While not directly asking: "So how'd you find your own thing, make your particular contribution to the music, and become a stylist?" it's a kind of subtext that underlies the intention of the questions. The interviews are a combination of in-person talks, video chats, phone calls, and email correspondence. The stories and quotes should be self-explanatory.

I hope that students and fans of jazz and its history will enjoy and learn something from the interviews and stories here. They're very diverse and involve very diverse musicians and contributors to the music from the 1920s to the present day, and recount events that in some cases go back almost a hundred years. Some of the stories and interviews are very pointed and focused, while others are looser. My hope is that there's a balance between the two, and that students, fans, and readers will find different lessons and inspiration from these stories and interviews that will help enhance their appreciation for America's music, jazz.

Eddie Locke
New York City – 2005

JG: Well, I'm here in Eddie Locke's apartment.

EL: Yes!

JG: Sitting across the hall from the first apartment I ever had in Manhattan, thanks to you and a cat-sitting arrangement for your neighbor, Joan, that you hooked me up with for a couple years when I was in college. I met you through a high school friend at Performing Arts that you were teaching. You're an incredible person, player, teacher, and inspiration. So, let's start at the beginning. Tell me about growing up in Detroit in the '40s with all those great musicians!

EL: Well, it's funny you'd ask. I was just looking at a book called *Paradise Alley Days*, all about Detroit. All the things going on when I was raised there, a lot of entertainment, music. Someone just asked me last week, "How come so many great musicians came from Detroit?" It was a great environment. It's not just studying, it's the environment that created that. People being together all the time and sharing thoughts on the music.

The musicians that came here to New York were good, but there was a lot of good ones that didn't leave, older guys, so we heard good music. There was a lot of work there because of the auto factories. I came up during the Second World War. So, there was a lot of places to play and you can't beat that. I don't care how much music you know, if you you're not playing it, it's not going to happen. You gotta play it, on the job! What you learn in school or practice sometimes don't work when you get on the job! Anybody that plays an instrument knows that! [Laughter] *Yeah*! You have this master plan you gonna do! But when all those other elements come involved…

BOTH: [Laughter]

JG: So when did you start playing drums?

EL: When I was really little, I had a brother that was very sick. I was the baby of four boys, he was next to me. He was sick a lot, he was in the hospital all the time, and he died at eleven or twelve. You could die of a fever then, they didn't have antibiotics. He was in and out of the hospital most of his life. We'd ride three different buses to get there and back. At one of the bus stops there was a music store with a drum set in the window. I was like five. I told my mom I wanted it, and she got it for me. My older brother tore it up one time. It was like paper kinda. But I kept going with it.

When I was twelve or thirteen she got me a real Gretsch drum set. Five dollars down and like a dollar a month. And that's when I started. And I just played. I never studied no music or had any influences. I just loved the drums! So, I was beating on 'em… beating the hell out of them in my living room. There's a picture in there, a friend of mine, Hank Moore. He's a tenor player I played with as a kid. He's in Atlanta now. We talk periodically. He called me up and said, "You know what Locke? You always could swing!" [Laughter] He said, "You didn't know what you was doin'. But you always could swing!" I said, "Well, that's a good start for a drummer!"

BOTH: [Laughter]

EL: You know, I saw the actor that played Elijah Muhammad in *Malcolm X* on something recently, Al Freeman Jr. He was teaching at Howard University. The guy interviewing him said, "You're such a great teacher!" He said, "Well, no I'm not. You really can't teach anyone anything. You can create a great environment, and you'll learn!" More than somebody keeping telling you what to do! And that's what Detroit was! Every day you could go and play.

JG: Who were some of the musicians there that influenced you and were part of that environment?

EL: Well, it wasn't so much of an influence so much as sharing. Especially for me. Because technically I didn't know anything about the music! Nothing. But the older guys used to hire me because I could keep the time, for what they were doing. And there was always a singer and a dancer. But then, I started to meet musicians like Barry Harris, 'cause he didn't live far from me.

And I was working with Earl Van Dyke. I don't know if you know him. But they made this movie about all those guys like him that worked for Motown that nobody ever knew... and they never got any money either! He lived on my block. He had a little band. They called us, "Earl Van Dyke and His Hungry Five!"

JG: Ha! And I'm sure you lived up to the name!

EL: Yeah. And one time, Barry Harris had his little band. He lived near me. This was when we were in high school. We didn't go to the same school, but it was close. It was at the Paradise Theater, just like the Apollo. They had amateur shows and we were on the same show. That's when I first became aware of Barry. We had our band, Earl Van Dyke. We had this guitar player. A big jovial guy, last name was Brown. He didn't play nothin' but the blues. But people loved him! He'd just stomp and laugh, people loved him! We had two saxophones.

Barry had his group. I'll never forget, they played this tune, "Bottoms Up," like "Flyin' Home." [Sings it] I don't know what we played. Barry always asks me to tell this story, "Tell 'em the story Locke!" I said, "Man, Barry, we killed you!" We were the finalists. When we got through, they hold that thing over your head and the people clapped. So, they held it over our head, the people clapped.

But when they held it over Barry's head the people went *crazy*!! We thought, "Well, they weren't *that* much better than us!" Turns out, they raised the lights, the whole audience was from his high school! They're wearing the school colors and sweaters!

JG: So he brought in some ringers!

EL: Yeah! It was just a sea of kids from his school. So, I tease him about that. And then later on, there was a guy named Joe Brazil. He must have some amazing stuff... he moved to Seattle. He used to tape everything! Elvin would be there, Tommy Flanagan, everybody, you know? I wish I could find him.

JG: Wow, the Jones brothers, Tommy, Barry, Kenny Burrell, Pepper Adams, all there.

EL: Kenny went to my high school.

JG: What year did you come to New York?

EL: '54. I came with Oliver Jackson, we had this dance team.

JG: Bop and Locke!

EL: Yeah! He went to the same high school as me, but I'm two years older than him. But he was a very studious kind of guy, and really advanced. I didn't start studying until I came to

5

New York, really. I just played. See, I tell students that now. To have natural talent for a young kid is dangerous. Because that only works for a little while. It can cause you not to practice and things like that. So, I didn't know what I was doing. But I went, got me a book, could play all the scales in both hands on the piano, and Coleman Hawkins was a big influence on me for that.

JG: When did you meet Jo Jones?

EL: When I first came to New York. And me and Oliver *lived* with him! Pappa Jo Jones was the one really opened my eyes as to what the drum was really all about. Not only me, Max Roach, Roy Haynes, a whole bunch of people. He understood the drum, the functions of the drum better than anybody. You know, Roy Eldridge, Coleman, Pappa Jo... I was just a lucky guy to wind up there! Kenny Washington says he always wants to interview me and ask, "How did you wind up with all those old guys rather than the beboppers?" I said, "I don't know how it happened. But God works in strange ways."

But it was school for me. I learned a whole lot of things other than just music. I learned about living your life, which is a big part of what you're gonna be. And that was just such a blessing. Jo Jones never showed me nothing, never picked up a stick, never, nothin'. I asked Max Roach, Roy Haynes... did he ever show you anything? They all said, "Never!" He used to always just say, "Watch me!" I remember I asked him one time, "Jo, how should I hold my drumsticks?" You know what he said to me? "ANY WAY YOU CAN PLAY WITH 'EM!"

BOTH: [Laughter]

EL: But those guys, they had some insights, and they shared, they shared... I just had a song recorded for the first time ever, on one of Earl May's records. Frank Foster wrote the liner notes, and he wrote such a beautiful thing about my song I had to call him up. Such a great writer and arranger like he is? I mean, that blew my mind. But all this came because I was with Coleman Hawkins. I learned more about music—he knew more about music than anybody I was ever around—*music*! More than anybody I was ever around. I mean, the whole spectrum. He was classically trained. I mean, everybody knows what he did with "Body and Soul!" Still a classic today! For him to do what he did at that time with that song, in that period, that's just amazing.

But he was encouraging! I'd sit at his piano at his place and play just a triad, and he'd say, "Yeah Locke!" And he wasn't trying to be funny. He was encouraging. And the book is right up there, [points to top of his piano] he made me get it—*Piano Favorites*, classical short pieces. I took the book down at his house and he said, "You can learn one these Locke, one of these chordal Chopin pieces." And you know, I actually learned how to play it. Because he believed that I could do it. That's what I was talking about with the *environment*! You know?

JG: Yeah, when someone you really respect looks at you and says, "I know you can do this," it means the world.

EL: Yeah! That's right. So, what he wanted to do, because he's funny like that, if Tommy or Barry or Monk was up here, he'd say, "Locke, come over there and play that piece on the piano! Now he's a drummer! Can you do that!" [Laughter] That's why I loved him!

JG: When I think about the associations you had...

EL: Jo Jones, Roy Eldridge, and Coleman Hawkins! Those are my three musical fathers. That's just luck. I say it to myself all the time. How much luckier can you be? And they all loved me, in different ways. You know what I'm saying? I used to ask, especially about Coleman, because he was such a musician! I mean, of a level that was like, I couldn't even imagine. He was the most schooled of all of them. But I used to ask Roy, "Why does Coleman like *me* so much?" Because it was really baffling to me. I mean, *all* the great drummers that were in New York at that time. It used to blow my mind! You know what I'm saying?

I'll never forget, it was one of the early times I was playing with him at the Metropole, Roy was on it, with Tommy Flanagan and Major Holley. Another drummer, a great drummer, I won't mention his name, who I greatly admired, was at the bar. I guess he asked Roy and Coleman if he could play. Coleman came up to me and asked me, "Locke, can he come up and play?" I said, "Yeah!" I mean, I admired him myself! The fact that he even asked me, you know, that kinda respect? I mean, just that I was there I was happy! But before we went back and played the next set, you know what he did? He came up to me and said, "Locke, no, you come on back and play. 'Cause I like what you're doin'!"

God, do you know what that did for me? The fact that man said that to me and had that kind of belief in me? You know, I've said many times, if I never play again, playing with those guys, musically, I'm fulfilled! I mean, I played with those guys together, separately. It was just like… 'cause I'm playing better now than I've ever played in my life. And I think, "God, I wish I could go back and play with those guys now!" But life doesn't work that way.

JG: Man, I have to interject, the energy I see in you, whether you're teaching an eight-year-old kid, or what I saw in you the other night with Frank Wess at Smalls!

EL: Oh, that was unbelievable for me!

JG: I mean, hearing you guys was so inspirational. I called up everybody I knew. I called up Bill Charlap and found out he'd been there that night too and we were both so blown away by it! It's so great to be able to tell students about that. It's like when I told students to go hear Doc Cheatham about ten years ago when I was doing some teaching at Manhattan School of Music.

EL: That's right!

JG: Because you're not going to hear anyone play like that again. And it's the same with Frank Wess, and with you. The way you approach the drums, the way you play time, the way you play brushes! Billy Hart told me he wanted to take brushes lessons with you.

EL: You know who I gave lessons to? Did I tell you this story? The guy from the New York Philharmonic! That blew my mind! I had to sit down when I got that message on the phone. He said he had a card I gave him over twenty years ago! And he said he always admired what I could do with the brushes. I mean he's technically excellent, he's the principal percussionist in the orchestra. But he's just as nice as he could be! And he said, "Man I've always admired the way you play the drums!" But it all goes back to what those older guys told me. That's one thing that Jo Jones told me. He said, "You're not Max Roach! You're not Buddy Rich! You're Eddie Locke! You gotta figure out how to play like Eddie Locke!" And that's a hell of a thing to lay on somebody, you know why? 'Cause you always got this other thing going on in your head, you know what I mean? And when I started thinking about that, I said, "Well *damn*, who am I?" [Laughter] 'Cause that's what you gotta find. And that's when you get to that place where you belong.

JG: So now you can't lean on the people whose music you love as much.

EL: That's *right*! And who are you!? And that made me realize, when you find that spot… it's a hard thing to do. Whatever it is, 'cause everybody's got something in there. Everybody. And you find that, it's gonna be good! It might not be no whole lotta notes, it may not be no great melodies… but whatever it is that you have in you, is good. You had that when I first met you.

JG: Oh, thank you.

EL: You strayed and come back every now and then.

JG: [Laughter]

EL: No, I mean it! I would never have brought you over to play with Roy Eldridge. 'Cause I loved those guys! I knew they knew about music! 'Cause you couldn't bullshit around them! You understand? When I you took you over there, I wanted him to hear you, and he loved you! And he loved that part of you that I loved when I heard you. The natural you. The natural you is great. But not only you, me too! And that's what Jo Jones told me. But it's hard to come to those grips with those kinds of things with your own self. That's the hardest thing in the world to do!

JG: Well, that was such a great gift you gave to me, Eddie, when you had me play with Roy.

EL: Well, listen! He never forgot that. And *his* reaction was even better that what I expected! 'Cause he called his agent up. Did I tell you that story? His agent called me up and said, "Roy says he's got another quartet with a horn." I said, "What?" He said, "Yeah, he says he's got this little saxophone player." I said, "He's not *his* saxophone player, that's *my* saxophone player!" I said, "He's got a lotta nerve!" And I called Roy up and told him too! [Laughter]

He said, "Well you don't know nothin' anyway!" That's the way he talked… [Laughter] But he died before he got the chance, but he was really gonna use you!

JG: Man, that would've been unbelievable. The thing that was so amazing, I remember you talking about it before I met him. But there are certain people that are larger than life. Their spirit and their hearts are so big… I'll never forget that day. He came in late, he walked in the back door, started yelling at you, "Locke you gave me the wrong damn directions again…" You started yelling and laughing at each other. He came up on the bandstand, stomped off a blues, sang two choruses, and sang his ass off!

EL: That's right!

JG: He turned around, pointed the mic at me and shouted at the top of his lungs, "BLOW!" And it scared the *shit* outta me! [Laughter] I thought I was gonna jump three feet up in the air!

EL: But it was beautiful! His energy, the love!

JG: Oh yeah!

EL: I'll tell you what, I played with all these guys. I never played with *anybody* that LOVED to play as much as him… that LOVED the music as much as him! Never. That's why they called him Little Jazz. Dizzy said, "That's why they called him Jazz. Nobody else they ever called Jazz." He loved performing. He loved it better than anybody I ever been around. And all his peers, they said that!

JG: I want to ask you about another great association you had, with that great trio with Roland Hanna and Major Holley.

EL: Oh yeah! Oh man, Roland Hanna, I miss him so much! I got a tape here, I don't know what I'm gonna do with it. His wife let me have it. You know, me and him played back in Detroit together. I been knowing him a long time.

JG: Wow, Roland, and Tommy, and Hank, and Barry…

EL: Well, he always tells you, I got a tape of him talking about it. Barry taught him how to play changes, 'cause he wanted to be a classical musician. And he went to Barry to learn how to play changes. Barry's been teachin' forever! Roland always talked about it. And the other part of Detroit that I loved... you got all these piano players, all from Detroit, they were all very close, but they don't play nothing alike! But that's what jazz is supposed to be!

JG: Came up the same time, same place, but all total originals.

EL: You know what I'm tryin' to say? That's the part of what's happening to jazz now that I don't like. Just who you are is gonna be good! He's got that, now you find something to do. 'Cause you're going to be better at it! You like all those piano players, but they're all so different in how they think about the music, but it's good!

JG: I only got to play with Roland once. He was amazing, and very kind.

EL: And his harmonic sense! He was really a genius with that. And I loved playing with that trio so much.

JG: Well, thanks for everything Eddie!

EL: Thank you, you're welcome!

Coda

One of my favorite stories that Eddie told me (in part because it came with dozens of photos) was about the times he used to go over to Coleman Hawkins apartment. In the latter years of his life, Coleman didn't go out much. Eddie was determined to make sure he had company and support. So, several times in those years he went over to Coleman's place, and on a number of occasions Monk and Cannonball Adderley came too! They cooked him his favorite meal, red beans and rice. Eddie had dozens of photos from those nights. Monk never forgot that it was Coleman who championed him and got him his first big break, hiring him for his first recording session. Monk always wanted to let Coleman know how much that meant to him. Just to see all those guys together in those photos, and to hear Eddie talking about those times and the respect and admiration they had for Coleman was amazing!

Cab Calloway
Oslo, Norway – August 1987

At the 1987 Oslo Jazz Festival, at the end of the week of concerts, the folks that ran and promoted the festival invited the musicians and sponsors of the festival to a special party. We were going to take a boat down the Oslofjord that Sunday evening to close out the week. We played a jam session at the Grand Hotel in the early afternoon. At around 7:00 or so, we walked a few blocks down to the harbor to get on a boat that would take us to the party. There were many great musicians at the festival, but the clear headliner that week was the great Cab Calloway. Cab had an amazing career! Playing the role of "Sportin' Life" in Porgy and Bess, touring America and the world as a major star for decades. He was now about eighty, but no less grand in his manner.

That week he'd headlined a number of major concerts, singing out in front of a seemingly terrified band of good Norwegian players. And he sounded great! What a voice! But when he wasn't happy during the gig he'd hold the mic away from his face, while he shouted at the top of his lungs between lyrics, "Come on you no playin' sad mother fucker's, SWING!" Then on mic, "Heidy Hi, Hi, Ho..." then off mic, "Put some life into it you pansy ass, no good..." The funny thing was, he was almost louder shouting off mic than he was singing into it! The audience seemed too shocked and embarrassed to react very much though. However, when he met the mayor and other political and money folks afterwards that bankrolled the festival he was all charm. And he was quite nice to me ("How are you, young man?") and all the other musicians.

On this last evening, unbeknownst to me, we were all being taken to a special island that featured traditional Norwegian culture, homes, and a party with Norwegian food and drink, including Aquavit. I'm not sure if Cab had had it before or not, but he definitely had quite a bit of it that night! In fact, we all did.

We were in a large and very old wooden cabin that we were told dated back several centuries. One of the cabin's most striking features on the outside was that the roof had quite a lot of grass growing on it. I'd never seen that before, and thought it was a kind of natural insulation. The beautiful dark wood inside of the cabin was illumined not by electrical lights, but by candle and gaslight. We sat at long dark wooden tables that were soon filled with food and surrounded by roaring laughter, singing, and great stories.

Towards the end of the night, the great Cab Calloway, the guest of honor and big star of the week, sitting at the head of one of the long tables, stood (somewhat slowly and shakily) and smiled his huge beaming smile. He raised his glass, and through the sheer power of his charisma, presence, and a life of theatrical experience, immediately silenced the large room of several dozen people, as he began, "Friends... my dear... dear friends! We cannot thank you enough for the kindness, hospitality, and love that you've shown us. It is truly overwhelming, and I... and we... thank you, from the bottom of hearts!" "Hooray!" "Yea!" "Three cheers for Cab!" went the cry of those assembled. Cab again grabbed their attention by quickly going on with his powerful, booming voice before most could wet their whistle, saying with great passion and intensity, "Because you... are some of the finest people it has ever been our pleasure to meet and work with... anywhere! Because you see, I've been all over the world! Been everywhere there is to be in this world. Been knighted by queens and met and performed for the crowned heads of Europe!"

A quieter but somewhat hopeful hooray went up, trying to bring an end to the toast, but Cab was not to be deterred. "But never... I say, neeeever... have we been treated with the love, the dignity, the respect, that I... that we..." Cab seemed to pause slightly, to perfect silence and rapt attention in the room, and then went on more quietly, with a darker, earthier, gravel sound to his voice, and the rhythm of a great Shakespearean actor, "For today, you have... given us... a... kind of... a..." And as Cab said this, he slowly started to fall back into his seat, in literal slow motion. He continued to make softer, mostly unintelligible sounds, "eh... this... and... uh..." which slowly drifted off to a whisper, and as he got softer, the audience laughter slowly grew louder as we came to realize that he was in the process of slowly passing out mid-toast!

The audience laughter grew to a roar, culminating with his butt hitting his chair at which point he seemed to be out cold, although he somehow managed not to spill his drink in the process! There was a giant cheer at the summation of Cab's partial toast, with plenty of stories, eating, and drinking continuing for another half hour or so. I never knew whether he was faking it or not. He was quite a character, a brilliant actor, and could've been pulling our leg. But he seemed pretty well out of it for the rest of the night. When we left, a group of folks carried Cab back out onto the boat, and got him back to the hotel.

Maria Schneider
New York City – 2006

One of my favorite gigs I ever had was a steady Monday night at Visiones in New York City with Maria Schneider that ran for about five years from 1993–98. I wasn't a regular in the band, but I was there quite a bit in those years and did several other gigs and tours in the years since. I got to know her and her music well. I realized when I first worked with her and heard her music on a jazz cruise in the fall of 1991 that she was a really important contributor. She, like many other friends over the years, is someone I always rooted for. She had already collaborated with Gil Evans and Sting when I'd met her. She'd go on to work with David Bowie and many great jazz and classical musicians, and win several Grammy awards. By the time we did this interview she'd become a huge star, and I was very happy to see her music begin to get the attention it deserves.

JG: So I'm sitting here in Maria Schneider's apartment, one of my favorite people and musicians. The first thing I noticed when I came in was this picture of you. You look like you're a teenager back in Minnesota, with some friends or family members…

MS: Yeah, that's high school. Somebody just gave me that when I went home. We were skiing I think.

JG: Ha! It looks like you're fifteen or sixteen. I usually start by asking about those earlier years. So, tell me about Minnesota and getting into music.

MS: Well, I think that some people look at me and say, "I can't imagine how you came up, doing what you do, coming from where you come from." On the other hand, I think there's a certain beauty to it. I grew up with no preconceived notions of what's cool, what's hip, you know? I was exposed to real early jazz because of a piano teacher named Evelyn Butler who'd been a stride piano player in Chicago. And the only reason she'd moved to Windom, Minnesota was because her husband and son died within a month of each other, and her only surviving relative was a daughter who married a man in Windom. So, this really extraordinarily talented woman was there, and she gave me lessons. But her style of playing was really old, so I thought that jazz had kind of died beyond stride and early swing. I really didn't know there was a whole history beyond that, until I got to college. And then, somebody lent me some records and I started to listen to a lot of things.

In a way it was great because there was no jazz program there, so I just studied things on my own and kinda put things together for myself. And the pieces that came together were first of all coming from the harmony of standard tunes. 'Cause I loved Cole Porter and Gershwin and everything like that growing up. And then also I think about the pop music I listened to growing up. Like the 5th Dimension, Jimmy Webb tunes, and Simon and Garfunkel. And the horns in all that music at that time! Pop music was very horn oriented at that time. And then classical music, I was very into Copland and Ravel. So, all these things came together in sort of a mishmash kind of a way. Where maybe if you were in some kind of hipper place, you'd be more apt to come up within a genre, find your slot, and you'd find all the experts in that, and they'd help guide you. I had no guidance in a way.

JG: I think some of the stuff that's most real and true for me, of what I hear in music relates to the same kinds of things that you found on your own: classical music I heard at Performing Arts High School, jazz records friends played for me... and I think we were exposed to some great pop music... Hendrix, Stevie Wonder...

MS: Oh it was! Carole King... there were so many great songs back then. There's a really good book that I read, on the shelf there, *Always Magic in the Air*, about the songwriters, the duos...

JG: The Brill Building?

MS: Yes. Do you know about the book?

JG: No, but I know that was a place where songwriters were.

MS: Yeah, it's all the different people that collaborated in it there, and it's *so* fascinating. How these different people were there every day, trying to churn out hits. And they were writing so much. Also, psychologically what happened to them when the music changed suddenly, and Bob Dylan came on the scene, and the Beatles, and suddenly there were these deep lyrics and not teenybopper kind of tunes. It's a great book, you should read it.

JG: It's funny you mention Jimmy Webb. When I was very young, my mother used to play a couple of Frank Sinatra records and some Glen Campbell. And I recently bought some Glen Campbell recordings for those Jimmy Webb tunes that are so great.

MS: Oh yeah! "Galveston?"

JG: Yep.

MS: [She sings it] One of the most beautiful songs, I love it! There's a great record of him doing his music. He's playing piano on it, he sings, there's a few other instruments here and there, but basically bare bone songs. I always love to hear people do their own material, even if they're not the greatest singer or player. 'Cause you just sense what's important in the song. You hear what they love in the song, what's essential by what they emphasize.

JG: Yeah, that's very true... that brings a few things to mind. I sometimes feel that the most real, good music I make is at the piano. But I can't play the piano.

MS: Oh yeah.

JG: It's when I'm alone in a room, and I'm realizing something I'm writing, or a concept, and I feel like, that's really me. That's the most honest. It's not shaped by an instrument I play well. It's sort of like what you're talking about, growing up without some preconception of what you're supposed to do. When you're playing an instrument you've worked on there's language there, shapes under our fingers or in our minds. And we try to be as free of that as possible. But sitting at an instrument, like the piano, that's not your own, with just barely enough technique to get at the music is sort of interesting.

MS: Yeah it is.

JG: There's a series of eight CDs I found recently of Bartok playing his own music. Really great to hear that!

MS: Cool! Oh, and speaking of classical music I love Bernstein too!

JG: Yeah, me too! On that note, I saw as I came in that you have a commission by the LA Philharmonic?

MS: Well I do, but it's to write a piece for my band, by the LA Philharmonic Association. It was premiered at Walt Disney Concert Hall, and Esa-Pekka Salonen, the conductor, also a composer, came and talked to me, along with Diane Reeves. They both commissioned it. She's been the artistic director of their jazz programming. She's so great! So amazing! She heard the last CD we made and suggested it.

JG: I'd love to hear her on your music!

MS: Maybe someday, that would be great.

JG: What was the piece?

MS: "Aires De Lando." An air of Lando. Lando is a Peruvian kind of music and rhythm. It feels like it's in 6. [She sings an excerpt from it] It feels like this [she sings and snaps]. But the audience feels it and claps in 12/8 over the top of it. It's like the magic eye thing where all the sudden this other image comes up. That's what it's like where all the sudden you feel this other time feel and say *whoa*! But they feel it that way naturally. I went to Peru and started working with these musicians. I came back and started writing something, and it had a little bit of the feeling of Lando. But the thing that I was writing was coming out in multi-meter, I was just hearing that way.

So, then I was working with Jon Wikan. He's a drummer, also plays cajón. He'd gone down to Peru several times and studied this. So, we worked on how to put the Lando over it. And I realized if you have three bars of 5/4, five times three is fifteen, so it's divisible by three. And if the clapping is subdividing the eighth note, fifteen times two is thirty, so ten rounds of this [clapping], is like three rounds of 5/4 like this [clapping again]. It goes over the bar and takes a lot of bars to catch up again. Then it closes with a 6/8 and everybody's like [clapping in 6/8]. And then, Jon realized and said, "Maria, the 5/4, 4/4 works," because I had all this 5/4, 4/4, 3/8 stuff. And I said, *right*! Because it's nine, and goes into eighteen. So, it's six rounds of this. Throughout the piece we had all these meters going over the top. And on top of that we had Scott Robinson and it was un… believable! It's unbelievable! I was thinking it was kind of boring, and then I got a recording of it from LA. I'm so focused on counting and keeping us all together. But if you just listen to it the meters feel very natural and you just sit back and listen to him and it's just mind blowing. I saw Scott do a duo gig recently at Cornelia Street that was one of the greatest concerts I've ever seen in my life!

JG: I saw the previous set that was solo—incredible!

MS: But the thing that was so amazing, he was reading from his wife's math dissertation, he'd pick up an instrument, like slide soprano sax, then the timpani! It was so structurally fun and interesting, but the harmony was so beautiful! That's the thing I love about him so much! He's such a combination of the absurd. Like someone who can make sculpture from junk that's so organic and beautiful in the end. It's like he's a collage and takes all these different instruments and creates a collage, but never in a forced way. He makes real beauty out of it, his language and materials and sensibility…

JG: He's kind of a genius…

MS: Yeah.

JG: As I always say of him, He plays the entire history of jazz and all music and all these instruments…

BOTH: But always sounds like himself! [Laughter]

JG: The thing that I always found so moving about my intro to your music… there are certain musicians that do something to me, they're very varied. Your music is like that. It just takes you somewhere and grabs your heart in a way that's so profound. I think of pieces of yours that I love—"Last Season," "My Lament," "Green Piece"—and where your music has gone now. I want to ask you about the people and events that have inspired some of your pieces and impacted you.

MS: Well, I think first of all when I sit down and write, what happens to me, when I sit down and come up with a sound, I'm looking for sounds that somehow feel like they have a personality that can grow and be something very unique from the other pieces. What happens to me then is that very often when I get into the piece, the sound will bring me back to something—a person, a place, an experience. So, when I start to think of that experience it helps develop the sound. It's almost like the sound is like a radio signal that brings this experience out, and then I use that and it all kind of works together. And then I describe these pieces to people when we play them and say it's about this or whatever. But the truth is, I didn't intellectually set out to write a piece about such and such a person or thing. But the piece organically came out of me, and I believe that experience. Because all the sudden I'm transported to that. So, it's kind of involuntary. Sometimes people say, "Oh, you should write a piece about this thing in your childhood," but I can't predict what those things are. It comes in its own time, or sometimes things that I never thought about just come up.

JG: Like "Dance You Monster." I always laughed when you described the Paul Klee painting it was inspired by before we played it.

MS: But when I first started it, I was going to call it Killer Bees. Which also I remember as a child. Then I saw the painting and started steering it around that, but the original title was Killer Bees! [Laughter]

JG: I remember them talking about that!

MS: Oh, god! In *National Geographic* magazine!

JG: *They're coming up from South America!!*

MS: Oh god! Between that and worrying about nuclear war and every other fool thing that came along, and Red Dye No. 2!

JG: We've had a lot of fear installed in us over the years, it difficult to process all that…

MS: As a child…

JG: Even as a grown up! [Laughter]

MS: Yeah.

JG: Lastly, one of the things I enjoy about you is the diversity of stories and events that influence your music. There's serious, romantic, heartfelt, deep stuff, and then there's the story about "Tork's Café!" Could you tell that story?

MS: Well, [Laughter] I inadvertently did something I shouldn't have done.

JG: Why am I getting such good tips from these truck drivers for just passing on my friend's number?

MS: Well, I just played that in Windom and didn't tell the story, the family who owned the place was there. But I don't think I can tell that story anymore or here.

BOTH: [Laughter]

JG: Thanks so much Maria!

MS: Thank you!

Jan Garbarek

Rainbow Studio, Oslo, Norway – 1988

After playing the Oslo Jazz Festival again in 1988, I was supposed to do a record for Gemini/Taurus Records, a small Norwegian company run by Bjorn Petersen. Along with my bags (including all my clothes and music for the recording) getting lost for five days, the piano player had to be replaced at the last minute because of illness. I had also just changed instruments, and there would also be some snags in the studio. The assistant erased a take we were going to use and then we had an hour a few days later to make up for a ten minute take we'd lost—a tough first recording experience at age 21.

But it was a great studio, Jan Erik Kongshaug's Rainbow Studio. Many of the great E.C.M. records were recorded there. The piano was supposedly Keith Jarrett's favorite. When we arrived for the first of our two days in the studio, Jan Garbarek and Manfred Eicher (who ran E.C.M.), were finishing up some editing and mastering on Jan's latest CD at the time. They needed some more time, or at least Manfred did. My producer, Bjorn Petersen, was not happy with this and tried to negotiate something to compensate us for the time delay before we could record my project.

But Jan came out and sat and talked to me for over an hour. It was great! I was happy for the delay and that it turned out that way.

I asked him for a lesson, and he replied in typical self-deprecating Scandinavian fashion, "Oh, I am not good enough to teach anyone anything." I was amazed at his humility. He was one of the more important and influential jazz musicians to come out of Europe, and a very important and distinctive voice on the saxophone. I'd heard him on some Keith Jarrett records, as well as some of his own.

I said, "Jan, you have such a personal sound and concept, and the projects you do are so original. The recording with a children's choir, or the solo saxophone recording on a beach with a wind harp. How did you come up with your sound and some of these recording concepts? What inspires you?"

He replied, "Every day, I get up and listen to Ben Webster and Johnny Hodges. And my all-time favorite saxophonist is Eddie Lockjaw Davis."

Wow! That blew my mind. Lockjaw was Eddie Chamblee's favorite too. Eddie Chamblee was one of my musical fathers back in New York, along with Eddie Locke and Phil Woods. Eddie and Jan couldn't have been more different. But Jan went right to the tradition, and got so much from it, and created something totally different! Just like Jay McShann had talked about. A lot of times back then and since, I've met young musicians who thought that the tradition could limit them in some way. But Jan showed me that there was nothing at all limiting about going to the traditions of this music.

Ken Peplowski

Japan – 2013

JG: So, Ken Peplowski. First of all, I've got so much respect for you and what you do. When I was 19 and you were 27, we met working in Loren Schoenberg's band. You're now 39 and I'm 53. I don't know how that happened exactly. You're a great saxophonist and musician. But in my opinion, you're the greatest living jazz clarinetist in the world. And the great Danny Bank agreed as well and told me one night on a gig with Loren Schoenberg's band in '86 or so, "Ken's the greatest clarinet player in the world." And that's pretty amazing coming from him. Have I blown enough smoke at you to start the interview?

KP: [Laughter] Well, just to blow some back… you know, it's funny in New York. There are so many different paths you can go down, so many circles of musicians. Unless you live there it's hard for people to grasp the concept that you can have people that you consider your friends and colleagues and never see them for long periods of time. But I never forget. I remember all the guys that play good. The thing in everybody's playing that I admire is when your playing is an extension of you. If you're an honest player, that's what grabs me. No matter what the context, I want guys that show up, give of themselves and get into the spirit of the music, no matter what it is, and that's what you do.

JG: Well I appreciate that, thanks. To me, it's a learning experience to go into various situations. I love hearing the history of the music in people's playing and I certainly hear that with you. On this tour it's Benny Goodman music, Fletcher Henderson arrangements, and some others. But when you play that extended solo on "Sing Sing Sing" you can go any direction. It's just you and the drums, and the sax section just looks at each other and smiles every night.

KP: Well, that's great. I'm doing it half for myself and half for the band. I'm not trying to impress the band members. I'm trying to completely open up and whatever comes into my head—whatever happens, happens. In a way, that might impress the band members, when everything's flowing like that and you're creating something different. I could just play over A minor and do a real cliched thing. But if I'm going to do a job like this, within these musical parameters, I just don't want to play musical dress up.

In fact, my way of researching when I go into a long gig like this is by not listening to Benny Goodman. All the tempos, the phrasing stuff, I've changed a lot of things from how he did it to how I want, but that's out of respect to him, because it was a malleable music to him too and he never thought of it as nostalgia. It was just great music to him, and he thought about those charts and edits to make over a long period of time. I think, though no one can speak for him, but I think he respected musicians that came to the job with respect for him and the music but didn't try to imitate him. He didn't want the drummer to try to play like Gene Krupa! Then it just sounds like a bad parody.

By the same token, if somebody calls me to do something I wouldn't normally do, like a more Coltranesque thing or an avant-garde thing, I just use what I've got and put myself into that music. You have to be yourself in a slightly unfamiliar setting. They've called you because you must have something to offer. All you can do is be the best yourself you can be, that's it. If you try to do something else it's going to sound forced and false. And I have to sometimes remind myself of that when I'm in a slightly different setting, and just play my own way and try to find a way into something different.

JG: I feel the same way. You can't over think it. The only thing that works is where you're just in the moment. Eddie Chamblee, one of my musical fathers, told me his musical and life philosophy was essentially, "Fuck It!" It sounds simplistic, but particularly in a musical context with what we do as jazz musicians, "Fuck It," let go of judgment, be in the moment.

KP: One thing I've learned is to also think of recording that way. A recording is literally how you performed on that day. If you remember that and not get too hung up about it... you have to get some distance and try to listen as though it were someone else's record instead of worrying about every single note and micro-managing it. And also, as you get older—I'm not getting older of course—but you are and I've noticed this in *you*. [Laughter] But as you get older, you just tend not to care so much about what other people think.

JG: That's a good point. Dick Oatts told me one time when we were on a gig together, "At a certain point you just stop worrying so much about whether it sounds good, and it's just better, because you're more in the moment and you're not judging yourself." On a similar note, I sometimes talk to students about the process of composition and arranging because it allows you a different kind of creativity than just being in the moment as we need to do as players. You can think about music the way a sculptor or painter or playwright does, and you can deal with it for months or years and make changes to it over time, along with the in-the-moment process, like Jackson Pollock throwing paint on the canvas.

KP: That's my goal at times with standards. I revisit songs that I've done for a long time and am still chipping away the sculpture of that song. I think about people that have inspired me, Benny was one, Sinatra, Bud Powell. Sometimes it's great to step away from tunes and come back with a new concept. But Lee Konitz has been playing "Pennies from Heaven" for...

BOTH: Seventy years! [Laughter]

KP: But it's fresh every time.

JG: Yes.

KP: You notice on my gigs, for example, if we're playing older music, I never ask anybody to do anything stylistically. You're all smart players. If you love what you're doing, you find a way in and to make it your own. The solos played now couldn't have been played in 1939. That's a great thing. It's a way of treating this music so that it's not a nostalgia piece.

JG: You and Jon-Erik Kelso just hipped me to this live version of Benny on "Stealing Apples" that's incredible. And that was the arrangement we did with Loren's band.

KP: Was that at the Cat Club?

JG: Yes! So many great players! Mel Lewis, Eddie Bert, Bobby Pring, Britt Woodman, Eckert...

KP: Dick Katz...

JG: That arrangement and your solo really blew me away when I first heard it. So, I did want to ask you about how you got into music and the clarinet.

KP: Well, I fought with my family about just about everything. My dad was a conservative cop in Cleveland. I went the other way. But the only liberal quality in my family other than my outlook, was music. They really liked to listen to all kinds of music. Maybe that whole generation was that way. As an aside, I find it interesting that now a lot of younger people are strangely conservative that way. Maybe they're conservative in other ways as well. But they just limit themselves to a certain thing, though they have many more choices than we had.

JG: I wonder if it's because they feel overwhelmed by the choices? Miles said something about that in an interview in the '80s. There's more music to be aware of, to assimilate now, to find your own thing than there was when he was coming up.

KP: Could be. And there are scientific studies showing that people's attention spans are getting shorter. So, they're a little intellectually lazy now too, and they don't take the time to seek out other things. Just because they're swamped with Twitter and everything else. But anyway, I remember my family went to see *A Hard Day's Night* in the theater in 1964. I was born in 1959 and was five years old. I still remember the girls screaming. And back then I thought, "There's something in this that I want to do." Also, from an early age I liked to make people laugh. I got up in front of the class and made kids laugh. I'd make up jokes, routines actually. So, there's something in there. I just like that connection with an audience. I was shy otherwise, but it was my way of making friends. To some degree I still am actually and often just stay holed up in my room on these kinds of tours

JG: Me too. Well, this band and most of the bands I've worked with, it's a great bunch of people and that really helps.

KP: It is. And you do feel relaxed with them.

JG: It makes you want to reach out more, instead of just sitting in my room and eating a meal bar.

KP: Yeah, me too! Exactly. Back in New York we rarely go out, we just like to stay home a lot. So, going back, when I was a kid, I had all kinds of problems with my home life, but I learned how to use art as therapy from an early age. I was a voracious reader. I liked to draw cartoons, and I loved music, though I hadn't played it. As a kid I always thought that I was self-aware. That doesn't necessarily mean smart. But I could talk to myself, reason with myself, and think to myself with all the problems at home, "Someday I'm going to get out of here so I can deal with this." I had a couple friends in school, not many. But if I could make kids laugh, I'd reach out to them. I was popular, but I didn't socialize much. But, from an early age, I wanted to be a writer, an artist, or a musician. Now, my father was an amateur musician.

JG: What did he play?

KP: Well, he first tried to play trumpet, gave it up in frustration, and then gave it to my brother who was two years older than me and became a trumpet player. Then he tried to play clarinet. He gave that up in frustration, I got the clarinet. But if I'd been the third son, I'd be an accordion player today! [Laughter] Thank God for that, because that was his next instrument!

JG: This would be a very different kind of tour…

KP: Yes. You know, Polish community. I loved the clarinet from the beginning. I guess I was ten or eleven when I started. Within a year, my brother and I had a polka band, playing at weddings and dances, going on local TV shows. He was two years older, that sibling rivalry, you know? And he was a hot shot when we were growing up and I wanted to be as good as him or better right away. This was interesting too, this breaks all the rules.

My father would sit and watch us, arms crossed, making us practice, critiquing us. And that destroys many people. But I kept thinking "Fuck You!" Or the equivalent when you're eleven. But I thought, I'm gonna try to get so good that he can't say anything to me, and, I'll be outta here. And as soon as I started playing in a public forum, weddings, and dances, that was it for me. Playing music for a living. Instantly I knew that was my path. My father incidentally, never, ever, paid me a compliment. Ever.

JG: Wow.

KP: Up until literally when he was on his death bed. And then he said he was proud of me. But I headlined in Cleveland with Terry Gibbs on one half, I was on the other, with the Cleveland Jazz Orchestra. It was 1985, '86. And my father's only comment was "You squeaked on the second song." I'd just walked off to a standing ovation.

JG: Wow.

KP: So that was that. But I just turned it inward and put it into my music. Which has been the greatest therapy for me in my life.

JG: Probably for most of us, right? I found a lot of people along the way that said, "Music saved my life." You realize what a blessing it is. Here we are in Japan, we get to express ourselves, see the world, and share our love of music through playing, writing, teaching...

KP: And with all of those ways, you do feel once in a while that you may have moved somebody. You learn how to satisfy yourself too. But it does mean something to get that reward, or acknowledgment, or just the good feeling that you've made an impact on somebody else.

JG: Well, in most places outside of the states, people are really appreciative of music.

KP: Well, it means something to them too, it's not just a functional thing, like listening as background music while you're doing something else. And you know, everybody that ever said they don't care about the audience, bullshit! If that was the case, you wouldn't be in a public forum. You'd just sit in a room and not do a thing or try to submit it to anybody. Everybody cares. Miles Davis cared. Why did he dress that way if not to impress people?

JG: I agree. So, who were teachers that were very important to you?

KP: I was very lucky to have some great teachers in junior high and high school. I had this one band director in junior high. And I don't know if he really believed in me or if he was frickin' lazy, I don't know. [Laughter] But he had me write and arrange one of those school pageants with multiple performers for the whole school orchestra. I knew nothing about writing like that!

JG: How old were you?

KP: Oh my god! This was eighth or ninth grade.

JG: How did you do it?

KP: I got a book on arranging. I read about the ranges of the instruments. I would spend hours and hours at home reading. I taught myself how to play piano, in a backwards way. I learned the notes. I used to stack and write notes on top on one another without knowing what to call the chords, C7, etc. Then I learned the theory later. But in a way that's a good way to learn because you're learning by ear, intuitively. It probably didn't sound good, but I did it! I wrote an arrangement of "Smoke on the Water" by Deep Purple. [Laughter]

JG: Wouldn't you love to have that released! Ken Peplowski's arrangements of your favorite rock hits of the '60s!

KP: Yeah, greatest shits... I wrote some Stevie Wonder thing for the jazz band.

JG: Great!

KP: But real encouraging teachers! They were so hip for their time in Garfield Heights, Ohio.

First of all, they would encourage us to play our own solos, to bring in things. We would listen to records. I had this teacher, Thomas Husack, we were playing Don Ellis arrangements in junior high school!

JG: That's amazing.

KP: Because they believed that we could do it, and we did it! Now I go to schools and they can barely get through "In the Mood." It's unbelievable. It wasn't all talented kids, but somehow, we rose to the level of where they thought we could play at. I had another guy in high school like that, that let me be free to do my thing. I was always a pretty good student, A's, B's... I'd get out of classes to go to the music room and play piano all the time. Here's another weird thing—maybe because of my reading lots of books—I could always just sight read anything. Don't ask me why. I'd never practice my lesson, but I'd play like crazy, practicing everything but my assignment, and then go and sight read my lesson. I spent so much time in the band practice room. I even got good at forging the band director's signature on notes excusing me from Spanish or math class, and they'd always buy it! But I was always doing something—the music for a school play or something.

JG: Did you have a great private teacher?

KP: I did by high school. This guy was the clarinetist with the Cleveland Ballet. By this time, I'd been playing saxophone too. 'Cause the necessity of playing weddings and dances, you graduate to saxophone as well, everybody does this. I think I got a tenor and alto at the same time and was going back and forth. And I loved that for the different texture. Even back then, I never thought of myself as a doubler, and I never have. I just try to approach the instruments as two different entities, and what's different about each of them and not find shortcuts. Anyway, so this guy, my private teacher, Al Blazer...

JG: What a name...

KP: Yeah, I know. Kicked my ass! He was so tough! Literally reduced me to tears. And again, like the experience with my father, except he basically told me I was playing wrong, wasn't breathing right. He basically tore apart everything and had me start over again. He told me from the first lesson, "Hey, you're unbelievably talented, but I'm going to be really tough on you." And he was! And again, I just went, I'm gonna try to fuck this guy up, and started practicing the lessons. He was an interesting guy.

Just to skip forward... I went to Cleveland State University, just to keep studying with him, 'cause he was *such* a great teacher! But his students in college, if they didn't give him anything and didn't give a shit and weren't even trying, he'd send them out for sandwiches, that kind of thing. But me, he continued to be really tough on me, and man I'll be forever grateful to that guy.

JG: What did he have you work on? Was it a lot of the classical repertoire?

KP: Mostly classical repertoire.

JG: Have you performed much of that? I'm sure you could go out tomorrow and play a whole night of that.

KP: I wish that were true. But I do like to play that music and sometimes do. I actually recorded with a symphony in Bulgaria. We did the Darius Milhaud concerto, a great piece of music. Not widely known or recorded. And we did the "Lutoslawski Dance Preludes"—great pieces.

JG: Wow, I'd love to hear that, I'm a big Lutoslawski fan.

KP: I'll send it to you. I also had a conception of doing Ornette Coleman's "Lonely Woman" on that record, and I wanted to have the orchestra improvise too.

JG: I love getting classical players to improvise! They don't know they can do some stuff until they do it. You tell them, "You know the scales, it's just two chords, go for this here," etc.

KP: On this one, we gave them little passages. I brought a quartet over with Greg Cohen, and the conductor would cue one of these passages at random, out of time… based on what we were doing. That was my way into that. And it worked well actually. We talked about this the other day. I've got a few people I like to work with. I let them do the writing, but I sketch out the ideas. It was my concept, but Greg Cohen wrote it. Regarding classical music, I really have to work hard at it. Last year I did a concert with Ted Rosenthal. And I put a movement of the Poulenc clarinet sonata on my last record, with Ted.

JG: Well I'm on that record with you of James Chirillo's piece.

KP: The concerto.

JG: I knew and loved James' writing but didn't know his through composed stuff and really loved the piece. You sound great on it, and it reminded me a bit of Stan Getz on *Focus*. I thought it was a great vehicle for you and was great to hear you in that context.

KP: My guy, before Benny, was Jimmy Hamilton. And the reason I loved him is because he had one of the most beautiful sounds of all time. He could have easily played in an orchestra. He had that beautiful, classical, round, sound—loved it! And on clarinet, no matter what style of music you're playing, why do you have to sacrifice the sound, tone, and pitch just because you're playing jazz? I hear so many people play clarinet, and they try, for lack of a better term, to play "funky" like the great New Orleans clarinetist George Lewis. And he was great, but that was his thing. All these schooled players, trying to sound unschooled, trying to play saxophonistic, dropping their beautiful sounds, all those scoops that don't quite get back up to pitch… you have to cut that in half on the clarinet and use more grace notes. But Jimmy Hamilton had that wild exotic semi-classical sound on all that stuff that Duke and Strayhorn wrote for him.

JG: Some of the stuff on the suites.

KP: Oh my god! That really grabbed me! Even before Benny.

JG: Since we're talking about your favorite clarinet players…

KP: Well all of Duke's guys. Barney Bigard, Russell Procope, Jimmy Hamilton… the whole world of Ellington. I just thought, this is what jazz is all about.

JG: And clarinet is so essential in Ellington's music.

KP: Yeah. But even on tenor, listening to Ben Webster, Paul Gonsalves, even Jimmy Hamilton playing a kind of R&B based tenor in a way… what variety of sounds and approaches! Johnny Hodges… I always tell people, the whole history of jazz is there in Ellington, more than anybody else. So those guys, Duke's clarinet players. There was a whole school of the New Orleans guys… Edmund Hall, Albert Nicholas, Pee Wee Russell, Jimmy Noone… but mostly Benny, Duke's clarinet players. And then everybody else that I listened to was sax and piano players.

JG: But the other day you also mentioned on your short list… John Carter.

KP: John Carter! Oh, that guy! Oh *yes*! Well, I was always intrigued by Ornette's music. You and I have talked about this. I think he's one of the most melodic players of all time.

JG: Yeah. You hear a lot of history in his sound, approach, and the way he plays melodies.

KP: I'm a sucker for melody. I'm not saying that's the only approach, but that grabs me. And Ornette has that, in my mind. And John Carter… I think I heard him on the radio, probably in Cleveland. He had a quartet that modeled itself after Ornette, with Bobby Bradford on cornet, bass and drums. I apologize that I forget their names. But very much modeled after Ornette's band, similar songs, form, everything. A beautiful sound on clarinet! Again, he kept this great sound, even while playing more avant-garde free jazz. He was also a good saxophonist too. Later, he did some experimental things with synthesizers. I took some electronic music courses where there were no keyboards, just waves of sound.

JG: Theremin or something?

KP: No, just old-fashioned knobs and electronic sounds, and coming up with compositions based on that, no notes. John Carter did records like that. I always found that fascinating. He was another guy that opened up a whole word of possibilities for me.

JG: So, how long were you in college?

KP: Two years at Cleveland State. But then I played a jazz festival with a quartet. It was me, the Teddy Wilson trio, and the Tommy Dorsey band.

JG: You played with Teddy!?

KP: No, though I did sit in with him once. There was a place in Cleveland, Chung's I believe. The piano player there, Larry Booty, would bring in these more traditional musicians.

JG: Another great name…

KP: Yeah, sounds like a… oh well… [Laughter]

JG: That's for a different podcast and book… [Laughter]

KP: Larry would always have me sit in with these guys, like Art Hodes, Ralph Sutton, Kenny Davern, years before I got to New York. Somebody gave me a picture of me sitting in with Kenny one time, I was like eighteen. So anyway, I was at this jazz festival in Cleveland with Teddy Wilson's trio and the Dorsey band, and they needed a lead alto player and offered me the gig. And Buddy Morrow who led the band at the time told me he'd give me a clarinet feature each night, fifteen minutes with a quartet. So, I played on that for two and a half years before moving to New York.

By that time, it was 1981, so I was 22. Buddy convinced me to move to New York. The money wasn't good, like all those bands in those days. But if you were making signs that you wanted to leave they'd give you a slight raise. And Buddy called me into his room and said, "I know you wanna leave. I could give you another raise. But I'll tell you what. I'll make it easy for you. I'll gladly let you go. If you promise me that you'll go to New York, and not go back to Cleveland and be a big fish in a small pond."

JG: Wow! Good for him!

KP: Oh my god! So, I did. He made some phone calls on my behalf. Nothing panned out. Because the last of the old guard studio guys were very protective of their turf. But it was nice of him to do it. I knew only a couple of people, Mark Lopeman being one of them 'cause he'd moved there before me.

JG: He was from Ohio too?

KP: He was, but he was from Akron. But he was also in the Dorsey band, and that's how we met. And Lopeman called me to sub in Loren Schoenberg's band one time, very last minute, fifteen minutes before the rehearsal. But then, I'm sure you had the same experience I did—

you do one of those rehearsal bands, and you meet fifteen, seventeen guys right away, and the world starts opening up to you. Somebody calls you to do a bad wedding someplace. But in those days—I always tell this story—my first wedding job was Mel Lewis, Milt Hinton, Steve Kuhn, Bucky Pizzarelli, and the other tenor player was Buddy Tate!

JG: Wow!

KP: Kind of a weird band, but an interesting band.

JG: What a learning experience!

KP: But we're playing somebody's wedding! And those gigs were plentiful back then. And you'd just go through songs. Didn't matter what you played as long as you played the right groove. You were learning how to swim by being thrown into the water. And because I had a reputation as a clarinetist too, I got called to sub at Eddie Condon's and Jimmy Ryan's. I didn't really know that repertoire. I was listening to Sonny Stitt, Oscar Petersen, Benny too. But the whole traditional thing I didn't get into until after I moved to New York, by necessity. But those guys were so nice to let me… I'd sit there and try to follow these frickin' songs that had three or four parts and key changes… but they'd let me solo last, so I'd have a fighting chance at hearing these changes.

JG: Tell us about some of the musicians you played with at these clubs.

KP: Well, first of all, Roy Eldridge was holding court at Ryan's. Singing, not playing any more. I remember the West End Cafe, Jo Jones was there, Sonny Greer, Russell Procope, Vic Dickenson, Dick Wellstood…

JG: He's another guy I wish I could have heard live and played with.

KP: Oh my god! What a mind, in every way, on and off the bandstand.

JG: The first time I met Kenny Davern, I got hired to play as a soloist at twenty at the Oslo Jazz Festival. And luckily for me everybody took me under their wing. Kenny and I got friendly right away. And within about an hour of meeting and playing with him, we went for a walk in Oslo, we sat down and he told me about Dick having passed. He said to me, "You can't believe what you just missed! This was my best friend, both musically and personally." And just the other day I heard some Dick Wellstood that I didn't know of, and that was some of the greatest stride playing I've ever heard.

KP: And a real original! Always just sounded like himself. So, there was that whole wave. Milt Hinton, Dick Hyman, who was so good to all of the younger players. He brought us into the studio scene to the consternation of all the other guys there. But I played on some of those Woody Allen soundtracks that Dick did. He hired me for all of his concerts. I think it gave him a boost to play with some younger guys. It certainly gave me a boost, getting to play with him. And then I started doing these jazz parties.

Again, I got in at the tail end of all those great players—Al Grey, Joe Bushkin, Buddy Tate, Gus Johnson, Flip Phillips, who became like a father to me—we were really tight! When my first son was born, he made a clock for him with his name made out of an old *DownBeat* plaque of his. And I got Flip's practice box. He had this beautiful, hand-made carved box that he used, with all of his reeds and a tape that he used to like to practice along with. One side was Lester Young, the other side was Sinatra.

JG: Wow.

KP: Yeah. And he used to play along with that stuff. These guys, you'd show up on a gig and there's Mel Lewis, Hank Jones… there's Phil Woods, Al Cohn. I was shitting my pants, you know, scared to death. And they were, for the most part, pretty accepting, as long as you didn't make an ass out of yourself. I kept having to tell myself, "Just don't get nervous, do your thing." I played with Jimmy Rowles a couple times. I was really intimidated by his playing. I just loved it so much, his great sense of harmony. I wish I could go back and play with him now because I felt like I was too self-conscious playing with him.

JG: Yeah, I felt that way a lot of times, I know what you mean. I think I got the tail end of what you're talking about. I got to meet and play with some of the guys you mentioned. And I think that's one of the reasons that I'm very appreciative of all the various scenes I work and move in, and it's also one of the reasons why I wanted to do this book project. Students don't have the luxury of walking in and hearing, meeting, and playing with guys like that.

KP: Or playing songs you never even heard the titles of before!

JG: Exactly. I always tell students, go and be around these guys if you can, it's just an education.

KP: It is, and also, a lot of times there's a glibness around students. I don't think I was, or you were either. I think they listen to someone of an older era, like Buddy Tate, or Doc, or Zoot. And because with all of our knowledge in hindsight, of course we could duplicate their solos, their notes, a lot of players think that makes them unsophisticated, or easily duplicated and doesn't have validity. Incidentally, Michael Brecker *loved* those older players. Students don't get the beauty and the simplicity. Yes, we can play those notes, but that's because they came up with it first, dummy! Were it not for them, you wouldn't be standing on that foundation!

JG: Yeah, we stand on their shoulders. If something seems technically attainable some young players will think, "I know those notes, I can imagine doing that." But they could never play them *how* they played them or play a ballad the way Buddy Tate did. Or approach one note the way Gene Ammons did. And I think that's the seasoning the next generations of younger players needs to understand. The longer you play this music, the more you realize what there is to learn.

KP: It never ends, and it shouldn't.

JG: I mentioned to some students the other day, it's like someone's dropped you in the middle of the Pacific Ocean and you say, OK, let's just swim that way… it's just vast and endless. So, trying to give some indication of that to younger players, the history, the meaning of it—it can only be a bit of a doorway. But if you follow the threads, the same way that you did, in Cleveland, and followed your passion and the people and music that inspired you, it just gets deeper and wider, and all the sudden you just realize, I'm in the middle of this infinite thing, and I'm just incredibly blessed to be around the kinds of people you mentioned playing with.

KP: Buddy Morrow said something that stuck with me forever. He said, you should always try to play with people better than yourself, and never get into a place of just hiring people that are comfortable to be with, like an old pair of shoes. You want to be challenged. You want somebody that shakes you up. Even this band, I like to pick a band that's fun and does the music, but does it their own way. So, I'll take any situation within… well, even without reason. And a lot of things are scary. But I'll get in there. And all I can do is just be myself and not worry about what other people think. I always tell other musicians—sometimes they think you don't want to do side projects for them or be a sideman. But I love that! It's something new and different. I can find my way into this other music. I also love playing behind singers.

JG: Well that's a lost art form in itself. Playing with and behind great singers, hearing it done in a great way. To your previous point, I had a great time playing a week with you at the Blue

Note this past January, all those arrangements that Mark Lopeman did. Again, Benny Goodman is a doorway for you to get out here and to a lot of different things. But playing all those contemporary arrangements on that music was great. It was a great band—Lew Tabackin, Terrell Stafford, Willie Jones III, Monte Croft, Ehud Asherie. That's a perfect example of what you're talking about. Whatever you're doing, bringing it into the current moment, keeping it fresh.

KP: I like playing with Martin Wind and Matt Wilson a lot lately. I use different piano players, Ehud Asherie, Ted Rosenthal. Those guys have a great attitude towards music and are willing to go in any direction at all. They're very open and I love that. They get what I want to do. There's an assumption that guys who play a lot of mainstream jazz or standards-based jazz, that you just want them to keep time and comp tastefully. I don't want that. I always tell the rhythm section, I just want you to react to the music, and then the drummer can play as much as he wants if he's doing that. There's a difference between being busy in an annoying way and reacting to the music and playing the music.

JG: Let me ask you if you remember this. We did a tour of the Midwest with Loren's band in 1989 for two weeks, doing a lot of Benny Goodman actually. There was one marquee that read, "Tonight, LIVE, Benny Goodman!" I thought, well, that's gonna be a little tough to pull off. But we came back to New York and played the Cat Club. It was maybe towards the end of the time of when they had a swing dance night there. Mel Lewis was on drums, and he hadn't made the tour with us, it was just a day or two after the tour.

Very rarely in my life have I ever had this crazy transcendent kind of feeling on a bandstand. Loren started to count off the band, 1, 2… 1, 2, 3, and somewhere between 3 and 4, I heard the ring of a cymbal, and it just all the sudden felt like we were on a hovercraft, just somehow floating. That whole first set! My memory of Mel when he played is that he normally kind of had a poker face. But that whole first set I kept looking back at him and he was smiling like crazy! I kept looking around at guys asking, "Do you feel that?!" And they all said, "Yeah!" Do you remember that night?

KP: I remember a lot of nights like that with Mel and having that same feeling actually.

JG: And he wasn't limited…

KP: Not limited at all.

JG: Yeah, by anything at all. Any context, whether with Thad, or Lovano…

KP: And he always sounded like Mel Lewis. He had that beautiful sound, that different sound. But you could tell, again, when he played something, he liked it, he enjoyed it. He enjoyed those charts too. Loren never asked Mel to do anything other than to be himself.

JG: I got to play with Mel in a few contexts at that time, and he said to me when I was nineteen, "It's really good that you're getting the experience at your age of playing for dancers." And so immediately you're not just in the mindset of "I'm an artist!" You're in the mindset of one of the functional rudiments of the music. Of course, you're always trying to be an artist! But it's a dance music, it should never lose that.

KP: Right, no matter what the music is.

JG: If you're listening to Bird, or even late Trane, you still hear and feel that and the blues.

KP: That's how you move people, sometimes literally, but even in a theater. You're reaching out to what is a core element within everybody. Mel had the same ability that Ray Brown did. I worked with him a little bit. You'd count off a tempo, but they'd put it where they wanted it.

But you couldn't argue with them. Because it was so right, and so strong, and you just went, "Oh yeah, that's where I should have counted it off."

JG: Yeah. To kind of sum up, what's on the horizon for you?

KP: Well, I'm so happy with the record I just did. I feel like it captures everything I do. I'd like to do more gigs that capture that.

JG: And I just saw an amazing review of that recording!

KP: Yeah! And that reviewer, he really did get it! You know, I recorded a Beatles song, a Beach Boys song—I wasn't trying to be hip—those songs are forty, fifty years old. But it's stuff that I love. I'm trying to play things that reach out to me and that I can make my own.

JG: Well, Brad Mehldau and The Bad Plus are recording things like that, why not? Wasn't Duke's highest compliment to describe music or musicians that were beyond category?

KP: Yeah. And when I listen to music, I listen to everything. The frustrating thing for me, and all of us to some extent, is that I feel so proud of my records. I spend about a year planning them. But I can't then parlay that into gigs where I present that music without the strong support of a record company or an agent. I don't have a way to get gigs doing the kind of music that I'm recording that I love. So, we're all making all these compromises along the way to keep working and yet try to stay true to what you want to do. More and more now promoters are taking the easy way out and doing "The music of…" or "Tribute to…" instead of just letting us do our thing.

JG: Well Wynton's made recordings with Willie Nelson and Eric Clapton.

KP: Well, everybody does that to some degree. But I wish I could get on the Euro circuit a little more. The only clubs I can do that at in New York are Kitano and Smalls, and neither pays very well. If I play Dizzy's or the Blue Note I've gotta come up with a kind of theme for them.

JG: Well, I have no doubt that the next step for you is to have that kind of freedom to do what you want. It's certainly deserved.

KP: I remember Lee Konitz telling me—he'd just won some Danish jazz prize—"All you have to do is live long enough!" But I don't want to wait until I'm too old to not play my best. I just wish they'd meet me halfway and say, "Oh wait, this guy can play, let's let him do whatever he wants to do."

JG: Tell us about the most recent record.

KP: It's Matt Wilson, Martin Wind, and Ted Rosenthal. I called it *Always the Bridesmaid*. Somebody asked me one of those questions that only makes you feel bad, "You're in those polls every year but you're always third or fourth… how do you feel about that?" What can I do about that!? I don't have a machine to pay publicists… anyway, the recording is just songs I'm working on. I did a couple of duets with Martin Wind, a McCartney song, "For No One," a Harry Nilsson song. On the record before this I did a free version of George Harrison's "Within You Without You." And we did a weekend at Smalls in preparation for the recent CD. I wanted to record without booths or separation.

JG: I *love* that.

KP: I used Malcolm Addy—who recorded James Chirillo's "Concerto at Avatar"—though Malcolm works as an independent. We had three sessions booked, but we got it in three hours. I wanted an Edward Hopper painting, and they got it for the cover. One reviewer said this "is a manifesto against perfection" and I couldn't have put it better. That's my thing. I want that human element in the music, where you can hear and feel people breathing.

JG: I'm completely there with you.

KP: I'm not against machines. But I find that most of the music I dislike is, for lack of a better term, corporate music. Whether it's pop, country, jazz… it's music that pretty much is written by committees. They sit around and say, "What do we need?" and then it's too sterile.

JG: Oh, it's just horrific. So, what will the next recording be?

KP: The next record will be an extension of this current one. I do honestly feel that each is better than the one before and I'm proud of my records. I don't listen to them once they're done.

JG: But it is very meaningful to have a body of recorded work that you feel good about. I want to end where we started. To me I think you're the greatest living jazz clarinetist in the world.

KP: I've got a gun on him.

JG: Is now a good time to ask about a raise?

KP: [Laughter]

JG: But I mean it. It's very rare to say that in this music, there are so many great artists. But it's important to me to say, especially in light of you saying "Geez, I wish I could do the music I'd like to do." But to me you're one of the really important guys in the history of the clarinet in jazz. So, I just wanted to put that out there, so thanks for doing this.

KP: Oh, it's a blast. Really fun. I enjoyed it.

JG: And when you're trying to sleep tomorrow on the bus, I'll just keep talking at you like this until you say, "Would ya stop now? Would ya go away?"

KP: [Laughter] No, but now you got me talking again, I can't stop… no, but next year, I'm actually doing a couple jazz camps for the first time. I'm doing John Clayton's thing in Port Townsend. And I've got a week in Hayes, Kansas at a jazz camp. I like doing that and giving my own perspective on improvisation. Ultimately, I try to get students to be their own teachers and give them things I've honed over the years to get to that.

JG: Well I'm sure you'd be great at that, and I hope we get to do some of that together too.

KP: Thanks.

Tim Hagans
New York City – 1989

One night in 1989 I went to hear Joe Lovano at Visiones. The band was Judi Silvano on vocals, Scott Lee on bass, and Tim Hagans was on trumpet. (I couldn't remember who the drummer was that night but Tim thought it was either Jeff Williams or John Riley on drums, both of whom are great players I got to know and play with some then and since.) I was one of only a few people in the club and the only person at the bar. I was shocked, because to me, Lovano was, and is one of the most important musicians of his generation, and most of the time I went to see him the clubs were packed. Tim Hagans came down from the bandstand and sat at the bar on the break, and I introduced myself to him and started up a conversation.

I knew that he was one of the great young trumpet players on the scene, but I quickly learned that he was also a really nice guy. He was very kind and generous to me that night in the twenty minutes or so that we talked. We got to know each other better from playing in Maria Schneider's band some in the early–mid '90s, and I called him to play on a couple of recordings of mine during that period. One of the things that sticks with me the most from that conversation is something he told me he'd had to work on.

"You know man, the hardest thing for me, and for many of us I think, is trying to figure out how to stay inspired and motivated when you don't have work, and an opportunity to play in a creative context of some kind on a regular basis. There were times that I thought I was just going to have to give up the idea of playing and try to get a regular teaching gig at a school some place. It's better now. But it's still not easy. But if you can figure out a way to stay with the things that inspire you, the music, the people, the art—whatever it is that does it for you—then you've got a better shot of being ready when you actually do get the chance to play. As opposed to trying to get to that place within yourself once you get the gig."

That was a great lesson Tim taught me that night. I certainly have had long periods without fun, creative work. It's really tough. But part of the challenge is making sure you have the experiences and people around you to keep you inspired, and that you get out to hear music live. That way you're connected to that inner flow you need to access to be able to play and be creative.

Mark Turner

Brooklyn – 2007

We start by sitting at Mark's kitchen table at his home in Brooklyn and telling jokes and funny stories. I always enjoy getting Mark to laugh, as he seems, and can be, very serious. But he's got a goofy side too. Also, Mark's wife Helena had baked cookies!

JG: By the way, Helena's chocolate chip cookies are *killing*!

MT: I told you man! They're the bomb, right?

JG: Oh my god! Wheat allergy aside, I just had to plow on heroically in spite of it all, 'cause these are just so good!

MT: They're totally crunchy too!

JG: Well, a lot of times, when I do these interviews, I ask people where they come from and what their background is musically. But I thought to start on more current things and ask you about what you're doing now. So, what are some of the things you're listening to that are inspiring you these days? And what are some of the projects you're working on?

MT: Well, in terms of music I'm listening to, I'm actually not listening to much. If I'm listening these days it's either to some gigs I've done or been on, or someone's recording I'm on. Just like critically listening, but not so much listening for leisure. Some, a little bit. Just pointed, little things, but nothing really consistent. Partially because, you know, as your situation is, my time is limited and I usually don't have time to just chill and listen. And I usually don't bring anything on the road with me like that. I haven't had a Walkman or a laptop or anything in years.

JG: No iPod?

MT: No iPod, nothing like that. I'm totally low-tech.

JG: Well, I know what you mean. I'm not listening as much for the kinds of reasons I did in high school, college and soon after. I play a lot of music for students, so that's a kind of re-visitation of certain music and principles that I love. I find it a challenge to listen to much of my own stuff. I had to do a lot of that for ArtistShare recently, between the project you wrote notes for, and then the other playing and teaching content. After six weeks of that I felt like I needed to be whisked off to some kind of mental ward… even more than usual.

MT: [Laughter] I hear you.

JG: But do you find you need to get out of that headspace as well?

MT: I do. But you know what? I haven't been in it too much in terms of listening to my own projects because I haven't done one in years.

JG: Well, may I just interject at this point?

MT: [Laughter] Yes.

JG: Can I just say, if that's not an artistic crime I don't know what is. If I ever get rich and have a label or something, you're my guy! Let me just say, I first met you... I guess it was with the Geoff Keezer, Kenny Rampton, Steve Armour big band in '94.

MT: Yeah, I remember that. I do actually remember that.

JG: We both soloed on "Softly."

MT: Exactly. I do remember that. Strange that I remember that with all the stuff we do.

JG: Well, I felt like I made an impression personally because, while we didn't hardly say a word other than "hi" to each other at the two or three rehearsals, and I'd barely heard you play, and you do tend to be a rather quiet fellow...

MT: [Laughter]

JG: So even just the idea of getting you to do an interview...

MT: [Laughter]

JG: So anyway, when we finished the take, I looked over at you and said something like, "Holy *shit* man! Who are you!? And where are you from? And... *wow!*" I just knew the first time I heard you that you were really one of the special improvisers in the world. And you're one of my all-time favorite tenor players. I guess we're at a place where appreciation for certain musicians and artists is very far away from what the public gets exposure to. Hopefully over time things will be appreciated more deeply. But the musicians know. Obviously, people that call you for gigs and recordings like Ed Simon, George Colligan, Kurt Rosenwinkel. You must have done so many sideman dates in recent years. Do you have any idea how many you've done?

MT: I don't know. Yeah, I mean, like you, like the rest of us, tens of dates...

JG: Well, the musicians know and appreciate your voice and concept. So, there was an article in *The New York Times* a few years ago about you. That's one way for more people to know about what you're doing. I didn't see it but I heard about it. How did you feel about it?

MT: Well, I have mixed feelings about any of those things. On an objective level it's good to have something written about you. And if it's generally favorable that's nice. If it's good for myself and my family, I'm into it. I feel good about it in that instance. Subjectively, I take all that stuff with more than a grain of salt. It's some guy's opinion. And even his opinion can change with the wind, sorry to say, like all of them. And also, since they're writers, their knowledge of the music, compared to people that I respect, who are musicians, who really know the music, is minimal, compared to your knowledge or any of the other musicians I know. So, what they say about it really doesn't mean that much to me. Because in terms of my goals and the criteria which someone can judge, to me, theirs is quite low, compared to my comrades. So, if it's just another article which does general good for me and others, fine. But I don't take it that serious to be honest.

JG: I remember talking with Joe Martin about how the music you and Kurt are doing together is some of the most important music happening. I just don't understand why you guys aren't on all the major festivals and in all the *DownBeat* Critics Polls.[1]

MT: Well, you know, that stuff is so arbitrary.

JG: Well, to me it's just a kind of misplaced understanding of where the music is and what it's about. Like, I hate to see these people that say nothing great has happened in jazz since 1965. That could not be more wrong.

---

1   That did change over time.

MT: I totally disagree. There is so much happening. I think many of us are less concerned with schools of thought, in terms of whether you play free or avant-garde, or straight ahead. I think most of us see all those traditions equally. In the sense that, for example, people will think of something that's on the free side, they'll think of it literally as avant-garde and say that's the music of the future or whatever. But something that's clear forms or rich in harmonic construction of some type, mainstream, whatever you want to call it, some people might say that that's not as forward thinking. I think many of us think both those "schools of thought" are already thirty years old in a sense. And they're equals, as far as many of us are concerned. They're both things that happened, two traditions. And we can take from them equally as we want from them. And I think that alone is a difference from the past. And I think many critics aren't hearing it. They just can't hear it to be honest. Most of the people that get it are in our generation, musicians and non-musicians. Most of the people that come to hear us, I mean us in a larger sense, are young people.

JG: Well, you know, your music does something that all my favorite music does. It reflects the history of the music, but in a such a personal, present way, that it's just completely contemporary and fresh. I think of some of the two saxophone gigs we've done in recent years and how fun and inspiring they are. Your pieces "Lennie Groove" or "Iverson's Odyssey"—the structures, the line writing, the counterpoint—it's just brilliant, just great. One thing that I wanted to address with you that I've always felt was a big part of shaping what you're doing is meditation. I wondered if you could speak to that a bit.

MT: Oh, yeah. Well, I've been more consistent at some times than others. I practice meditation from a Buddhist tradition, so it's not a secular tradition. So, there's the whole philosophy behind it, but meditating, and the philosophy or Dharma behind it, have helped me to be less shaken by the ups and down of events. It's just the nature of the world. What so and so says about the music, whether someone loves it or hates it. If you're sitting there, there are going to be a certain amount of people who love you and what you do, a certain amount of people who hate what you do or who you are, or are totally ignorant of you and don't even know who you are. And that's always going to be the case no matter what. So, worrying about how much you have control over what so and so thinks is totally unnecessary and irrelevant. So, it teaches you all these various things about that. Just about following the path and not worrying about all the ups and downs. Being concerned about what you're owed or not owed, justice or injustice, all this other stuff. So, the main thing about meditation for me is that it just calms the waters. It helps you to understand a little bit more about your own mind. I could keep going on, but basically that's what helps me the most in terms of music.

JG: Well, it seems to me to contribute a lot. You're always incredibly grounded, present, and relaxed. So, ideally, that's how we'd like to be musically and in the rest of our lives.

MT: Absolutely.

JG: So, to whatever extent that's naturally who you are, or that your inner work with meditation has solidified that, to me, it's a big part of what comes across. And I think it's a part of the foundation and depth that I and others feel coming through. I read some books in recent years by the Dalai Lama that I really liked. I remember he talked about how you can get to a place where you can still the mind enough that non-ordinary phenomena can be perceived.

MT: Yeah, you can definitely get to that place.

JG: But the interesting point to me that he made is, that's not where you want to be. It's a stopover that one shouldn't want to spend time with, and it's ultimately a trap or distraction.

MT: Yeah, it's heavy. But it's true, that after some meditators have a spent a lot of time with it, they can start to gain paranormal powers. I forget the names of them. But basically, you can get to the point that you can read other people's minds, know their thoughts, see the future, hear and see things from a long distance, walk through walls.

JG: Well, with some of those obvious kinds of physical phenomena, like walking through walls, levitating, there are reports of that in various spiritual traditions. St. Teresa of Avila was said by some to levitate during deep prayer. There's also a catholic priest named Padre Pio.

MT: Yeah, right.

JG: You're familiar with him?

MT: Oh yeah. You see him all over Italy every time I go. Any restaurant or kiosk there's often a picture or placard of him.

JG: One story I heard (from a recording by Caroline Myss), was that he appeared to some Allied bombers during World War II, in the sky, and told them, in their minds, not to drop their bombs where they'd planned to, and that it was just civilians that would be hurt. He sent them to an empty field away from the village and they dropped the bombs there.

MT: Wow! Whoo!

JG: So, this is the story, not sure of the reality, but these are intriguing possibilities to be sure. I've had some interesting metaphysical conversations with musicians over the years. I'm thinking about doing a book on that some time. On another note, that reminds me of those pictures I saw of your father and your grandfather who were in the military. I know you wrote a song for your maternal grandfather.

MT: Right. "Yam Yam."

JG: Could you talk a bit about your grandfather and your family and background?

MT: My biological father's side of the family is from Louisiana. My mother's side of the family is from the Midwest—Indiana and Ohio.

JG: What part of Indiana?

MT: Gary, and another small town, it'll come to me. I grew up in L.A. mostly. I lived in a few different places from ages one to four. Because my father, who was in the military, died when I was one and a half. So then, my mother remarried when I was four and we moved to L.A.

JG: Was your dad in Vietnam?

MT: He actually didn't end up going. He was about to go but was in a plane crash. He was a navigator and engineer. And my maternal grandfather, the one I wrote the song "Yam Yam" for—I called him Yam Yam because he called me the Yam Yam man—he was an aviator from his teens on. I think he was sixteen or seventeen when he bought his first plane.

JG: Wow! That's amazing. How did he have the money to buy a plane at that age?

MT: He was a super driven guy. He died a multi-millionaire. And he started out poor, working class, and he was a seriously bad dude. He worked. He had a motorcycle too. He was kind of a daredevil type. I forgot what job he had, but he saved money and bought a plane. So, he flew in the late '20s and early '30s when flying was kind of a new thing, and it was freer then. Once he had the plane he also made money by doing fairs, doing aerobatics and things.

JG: It occurs to me that, as an African American at that time, being that flying was so new, he must have been a kind of trailblazer in that sense as well.

MT: Yeah, he was one of the few at first just to be able to do it. Obviously, at that time, the difficulties—you can't fly in this field, you can't take this plane here, all these obstacles. But he did it anyway. And he got to fly where most wouldn't have been able to. Later on he became an engineer to some extent and was building his own planes. So, when I was a kid growing up, I used to go see him and he was always flying and building a new plane. So, we'd make models.

JG: Wow!

MT: [Laughter] He'd have the car in the garage and a plane he was working on in the garage.

JG: Incredible!

MT: [Laughter] He was always welding and stuff, making planes. I took it for granted.

JG: Did you learn how to do any of this?

MT: I didn't learn how to fly. I just learned about aviation and airplanes.

JG: Where was he living then when you'd visit him?

MT: He lived in Xenia, Ohio. My grandparents lived there my whole life. They're both gone now. He was also an educator so he made his living that way. He was president of Sinclair University and vice president of another university, I can't remember that one. And then, during World War II, he was one of the flight instructors for, I forgot the name, but the division of African American Army/Air Force, and he was one of the instructors for that. The first Black people allowed to fly in combat.

JG: Incredible!

MT: So, he taught them how to fly, and a few other instructors. So that was written for him.

JG: Is there any relation to the Tuskegee Airmen?

MT: That's what it is, thank you for reminding me. That was it, he was at Tuskegee. My mother was born there.

JG: Did you see the recent movie?

MT: I saw part of it.

JG: I did too and it reminded me of your tune and your grandfather. It's amazing to me to imagine what people actually experienced. I don't know how people endured what they did. Such an inspiring life he had. What he overcame and accomplished. We're certainly not a fully evolved society in terms of dealing with all that.

MT: No. I don't know if that's ever going to change. But I certainly have it a lot better than my grandparents did. And my parents too.

JG: Did you ever know Eddie Chamblee?

MT: No.

JG: He was one of my musical fathers. I used to play with him on the Saturday brunch gig at Sweet Basil for years, from age 17 to 25. He was married to Dinah Washington, had some hits with her. He played with Lionel Hampton, Basie, the Harlem Blues and Jazz band. But I remember him telling me about one time being the only Black musician in a band. The bus pulled up at a hotel he couldn't stay at, and he had to walk two miles in the middle of the night, in winter, in Nebraska, to the nearest hotel he could stay in. It was minus twenty degrees out. He told me he couldn't uncurl his hand until the next morning, it was so frozen from carrying his horn. He told me, 'That's how I got treated. But you're always welcome to come here and play with me.'

MT: That's deep.

JG: I know, right? So, tell me, how did you get into music?

MT: My parents weren't musicians, but they played a lot of music in the house. And my biological father had a lot of jazz records that we had in the house. So, the first jazz records I listened to were his. He had a few of those Sonny Stitt and Gene Ammons records.

JG: Oh man! [Laughter]

MT: Sonny Stitt was his man. He played alto in high school.

JG: Wow.

MT: So that's how I was introduced to it. My mother still had his records after he was gone Also, my stepfather had some jazz records too. So, they happened to both love music and jazz. There was always music going on all the time—Al Green, Stevie Wonder, The Ohio Players, all kinds of stuff like that. And they also had *My Favorite Things* by Trane. There was another '50s compilation of Trane where he played "Stardust." Sonny Rollins, *The Bridge*. I didn't realize it at the time, but looking back on it they had a lot of nice records. They had a bunch of Dinah Washington records, some Cannonball. They had a lot of good stuff. That's how I knew about it.

JG: When did you start playing?

MT: I started playing clarinet in fourth grade. I was nine or ten.

JG: The pain instrument.

MT: [Laughter] Exactly.

JG: The medieval torture device

MT: I know. But I loved it. I didn't really continue to play it.

JG: Well, you played clarinet on one of my records.

BOTH: [Laughter]

MT: Well, I know, but, I can't say I played it, I sort of got through it.

JG: You know, Maria Schneider's first instrument was clarinet too. And sometimes I sub in her band. We did a concert at Hunter College a couple years ago with Bob Brookmeyer, there was one piece that called for another clarinet part. She sat next to me and played it, and we're not sure which one of us was worse. You know, my hand issue from the injury I had in '99, makes the clarinet the hardest instrument for me to play on because rather than hitting keys you have to cover those holes, and so it really limits what I can do. I had just put in a couple years of study on the flute before I had the injury and I'd hoped to do the same on the clarinet, but I haven't been able to since the injury. But playing next to Maria…

MT: That must have been precious. [Laughter]

JG: You know, if I do say so myself… [Laughter]

MT: Come on! That's great!

JG: The two of us huffin' and puffin' and squawkin' and squeakin'…

MT: [Laughter]

JG: Yeah, I think precious is probably the right way to put it. And you on clarinet on my record *Witness*.

MT: I'm sorry... I apologize.

JG: Are you kidding? Nothing to apologize for! So, you started on clarinet. When did you get into the saxophone?

MT: I moved to alto around middle school. And then tenor in high school.

JG: I'd like to hear some Mark Turner on alto!

MT: You don't wanna hear that. I can't play it at all now. But you know, there was a stage band, the whole LA stage band thing. I don't know if that happened on the East Coast as much. On the West Coast and the Midwest there's a big jazz educator big band thing. It's a whole other level, very out.

JG: I know, it can be strange.

MT: It's very strange, very out. I just want to say, the only reason I knew something about and heard about the fathers of this music is because of my parents.

JG: I know!

MT: They just slept on so many people they wouldn't even mention. They never mentioned Duke Ellington, Miles, nothing about Trane or Sonny Rollins.

JG: Let me ask you about two people I'm sure they talked about. Stan Kenton...

MT: That's *right*!

JG: And Maynard Ferguson.

MT: There you go! But what about the people that came before? Not even one word. That was out man!

JG: I know!

MT: Come on man! That was out, man! I think that was some deliberate shit. I can't get with that. They knew what was happening. They didn't want to give it up.

JG: I think there were many people that did and some were just completely ignorant and know nothing about jazz.

MT: But there were people that did know and now that I'm older I know that they knew, and they didn't say anything?

JG: Oh yeah, I agree. See, a lot of people don't want to talk about issues like this and race. When I really got it about this is when I went to college. When I went to Manhattan School of Music, they didn't have an undergrad jazz major yet. And the person running the program didn't know anything about jazz. And it was that same shit you're talking about. And none of the teachers were African American.

MT: There you go.

JG: And they used to talk about wanting to teach a club date class.

MT: Exactly man! [Laughter]

JG: It was *insanity*! One of my musical fathers was Eddie Locke, I don't know if you know him. He played for years with Roy Eldridge and Coleman Hawkins.

MT: Wow, you've been raised by some interesting people.

JG: Well, I'm very lucky. But Eddie Locke told me one time he got an award from Barry Harris. He gives a lifetime achievement award to a different person at the end of this yearly concert he does at Symphony Space. Eddie had never gone, though he'd known him since they were kids in Detroit. And Barry said, "Eddie, you gotta promise me you'll come this year, you never come to my concert and it's right in your neighborhood." Eddie said, "I promise I'll be there this year." They get to the end of concert and Barry gets up and says, "This year I'd like to give my lifetime achievement award in jazz to my old friend Eddie Locke!" Eddie was shocked! He said he just broke down in tears. He loves and respects Barry so much, and he grew up with all those amazing musicians in Detroit.

But see, here's something that I really love and respect about Eddie. Eddie is a truth teller. He got up there, thanked Barry, sort of gathered himself, and then said, "Hey! How come Barry isn't running one of these jazz programs at one of these schools?" And man, his three musical fathers were Pappa Jo Jones, Roy Eldridge, and Coleman Hawkins.

MT: Wow man, that is deep!

JG: You wanna talk about having some stories!?

MT: You know, that lineage, that spiritual lineage, that comes with keys to the craft too.

JG: Yeah, the oral tradition.

MT. Yeah, but you know, that blessing. It's a blessing too, it's a part of it, that's passed. That's a missing link for me. I feel like I've gotten what I have learned from records and my peers. I've known some older musicians, but very few, not that many.

JG: Well I feel very blessed, for sure. I think for some people, and myself, it's been a thing where I was a bit hesitant to strike out in my own direction at times because some of those older cats that I loved, if I did that, might say, "Man! Why you getting so avant-gardey on me!"

MT [Laughter]

JG: Literally. I heard that, OK? Just like that.

MT: But that's deep though.

JG: It is.

MT: I can get with that though.

JG: But that speaks to what you were saying earlier. It's not about the stylistic choices you're making. It's more about the integrity with which you're doing whatever you're doing.

JG: Definitely, sure.

JG: And just to finish up the point about jazz education—there is something wrong with all that jazz education stuff that we got and that's still around in some places.

MT: Yes.

JG: And there is an incredibly strong racist strain of thinking in there.

MT: Totally.

JG: It's frustrating and annoying and it needs to be more about the real music. Maynard Ferguson was great, and a great friend to my mom and her husband Bob Gordon.

MT: No, nothing against his musicianship. He was great too. But what about the others that were great?

JG: There's just an awful lot of music missing there.

MT: A lot that's missing.

JG: I saw you were teaching at Manhattan School of Music?

MT: Oh, that was just a little bit, maybe seven years ago. I wouldn't mind doing something like that again. You know, one other point on that. First of all, at least in California, with that jazz ed format, I was just surprised by how little was mentioned about various people on various instruments. Or even if you're playing big band, they might mention Count Basie, but never Duke Ellington. And plenty of other bands that we know that aren't mentioned, at all. This is a big band here. Like, not even a listening session!? You're at these little collegiate or high school festivals. How about a listening class? A half hour! Ten minutes! These are the records you should listen to. You can buy them here. Or we'll give 'em to you!

JG: Amen.

MT: It doesn't even have to be that long, just a little bit, I mean… [Laughter]

JG: When I go to these colleges I always play music for them, 'cause they haven't heard it.

MT: And just to reiterate, once I was on tour, and we went out to the Midwest, and we did a clinic. And there were a bunch of big bands playing, and you're supposed to make comments on a tape recorder, you should do this, that, time, sound, all this mess, right? So, first of all, I totally disagree with it, partially because I was in those things and I didn't learn anything from it. Not from the comments, just from playing in the band. So, later on you're supposed to make comments to a specific band, right? So, I didn't know this was happening. I went to the gig but didn't know there was this educational component to it. If I'd known I would've refused, or said I'd like to be involved but do something else. So, I was thrown into this.

I was in with one of the bands, starting to talk to them. I said, "The trio…" and they didn't know what I was talking about. So, I said, "The piano, bass, and drums—you guys have to get your thing together. If you're not together the rest of the band won't be together." So, they had no idea what I was saying. The band director hadn't said anything to them about what a piano trio is or anything. So, we go through all these issues, about plenty of things I expected them to know. I thought this guy was leading a jazz band, so I just went straight to the point. So, later a letter comes back. I don't know if it was me, it was probably me, about what a jazz education is, blah blah blah. And it says for example, I was talking to the piano trio and it said he had to tell them what a piano trio was. So, if he hadn't told him at that point, what was he doing for the whole year?

JG: [Laughter] Right.

MT: So, what's the deal? Anyway, it was just out, you know? So, I would've sat them down and said, "You have to listen to these things." Not dealt with any of the charts, because all the bands sounded the same, they had the same issues. There were just a few things that could've made all those bands sound better. Just a few simple things. Once a week listen to a little music, read a little history. The rhythm section, learn how to play together. The piano player, learn to play a few voicings, comp a little bit, learn about how to get a feel. Just little things that no one said anything to them about. Nothing!

BOTH: [Laughter]

MT: I couldn't believe it! Like… what is this man!?

JG: Well, I guess that's what happens when people who don't know a whole lot about music start teaching it. It's not nice to say…

MT: But it's true!

JG: You know, Charles McPherson told me when I was a kid that if the bass player's quarter note wasn't happening, nothing can happen over that.

MT: That's it.

JG: So, I sometimes say to young players, "Let's just start by trying to feel the quarter note together between the bass player and drummer." We'll slowly add upbeats on the ride cymbal, try to find where that is. Then in the band, get them to feel 2 and 4, and then the upbeats of 2 and 4. Then you've got a shot at something.

MT: That's it, just work on the time, quarter notes, do that, get that together.

JG: Forget about technique.

MT: Also, forget about playing these weird collegiate charts by somebody from North Texas. I hate to say it. But what is that mess man!?

JG: [Laughter] Mark Turner is going off! I'm just loving this! The world must see the other side of this stoic Buddhist Monk! [Laughter] What is that mess!?

MT: [Laughter] I mean, *come on man!* Anyway, I just thought it was ridiculous.

JG: A few years ago I got called to do a masterclass at a school. They had really good people running the program. I did a gig or two, worked with some students, did a masterclass with their top band's sax section. They had five big bands, but they told me they had no jazz sax teacher. They had forty jazz saxophone students but no jazz saxophone teacher.

MT: How can that be?

JG: That's what I'm saying. The position opened up a couple years later and I looked to apply and they said they thought they had it wrapped up.

MT: Well, why not… well, anyway go ahead.

JG: Well, I think they're trying to legitimize their stuff via paper and degrees.

MT: Right, true, there's a lot of that shit.

JG: But then there's, "But I got to play with this person and that person." But that oral tradition that you were talking about is not what's respected there in academia, but it's what they need.

MT: It's definitely what they need.

JG: If you were paying $40,000 a year or more to get a jazz degree wouldn't you want that?

MT: Oh hell yeah! Absolutely. It's irresponsible if you don't. If you're payin' that much money? You better be able to play when you get outta that shit!

BOTH: [Laughter]

MT: You know what I'm sayin'?

JG: Yeah, again, it's misplaced priorities and a misperception of what the music is. So, you made a point earlier…

MT: Well, I just have to go back. What do you mean they have it wrapped up? After you applied? How many saxophone players are they gonna get on your level? That ask to come to their school? Come on man! [Laughter]

JG: Well, that's nice of you to say.

MT: I mean…

JG: Again, I think it speaks to the fact that they…

MT: So they got some dude that isn't really playing? I hate to say it.

JG: I don't know, it might have been an in-house thing. I was gonna commute out to start.

MT: Yeah man! Come on!

JG: I could've really used the work. I've got two kids, you know how it is. I'm guessing they wanted someone who'd be there twelve months a year and I can understand that. But they need to have real players at those schools, especially if people are payin' that kinda money, you know?

MT: In my opinion they'd be better off with someone that's extraordinary coming, even semi-annually or whatever, rather than someone mediocre that's there all the time.

JG: Yeah.

MT: Come on! Don't you think?

JG: I do.

MT: If I was in school and I had some guy drop some shit on me that was killin' and happening? That was dropping it on me like that a few times a year, as opposed to some guy who's just there? Come on! That's the shit that makes the difference. The rest of the time you're practicing in between. That's the real shit.

JG: Well, what I said to them was…

MT: If they wanna miss out on it that's on them!

BOTH: [Laughter]

JG: Mark is totally going off! Again!

BOTH: [Laughter]

JG: I love it!

MT: You know man!

JG: Mark is just laying it down! This is so great! Just blasting away at the silent image! "These motherfuckers are full a' shit!"

BOTH: [Laughter]

MT: Well come on man! I mean, come on, how many alto players are they gonna get like you asking to come to their school? Whether you feel that way or not, how many? Not many.

JG: Well, that's nice of you to say. I don't know. Well, in this day and age when it's so hard to work, I think there are a number of musicians who'd want that. I have no idea who they got.

MT: You can count the number on your hands man. I mean, whatever, maybe they can't hear it, or don't understand it, but how could they miss that shit? Well, anyway, that's what I think.

JG: Well, I appreciate what you're saying. And I'd like to think that I've done enough stuff to be considered for something like that. But at the same time, why isn't Barry Harris, or Eddie Locke, or Charles McPherson in a position like that?

MT: It's the same reason.

JG: Oh, in this top sax section, they all played classical saxophone mouthpieces. And they were playing a Thad Jones soli.

MT: Wow.

JG: There was a small audience there, no rhythm section. But I told them "Guys, there's no brass or rhythm section, and I can't hear you." I'm not someone who's always advocating for playing loud, and I've had my own struggles where I worked too hard with that and created more problems than it was worth. But this is a Thad Jones sax soli, not the Ibert concertino. And I said, "I don't want to say anything to contradict what you're learning in your lessons. But if you're going to play those mouthpieces you're going to have to really work hard to get enough sound to sing out over the band on this." They got as much sound as they could. Then I said, "OK, now let's go back and try to deal with the time." They were just so far away from the music.

MT: Of course.

JG: Well, just to go back and reiterate something I said early on. I've been saying to Scott Robinson for years, "I want the world to know what kind of a genius you are." You're very different kinds of musicians, and you're making very different kinds of contributions.

MT: Yeah, yeah, he's *bad*. He's *superbad*!

JG: But to me, when I look at you, and Kurt Rosenwinkel, which to me is some of the most important music happening in the last ten to fifteen years, I just want the contribution you're making to be realized. And when I think about some of the things we've done together, on my projects or others, there are very few things I'm proud of. Like that free thing we did with Billy Drummond.

MT: I remember that.

JG: And when I think of calling you, it's not even like, I need tenor. It's your voice I'm looking for. And it does seem to me like you're playing a good bit, with your own thing, with Fly, with Billy Hart, with Kurt, and others, and I'm really glad for that.

MT: Sure, I'm working enough. I'm happy to play. I'm working enough to make a contribution to our living here. You know, I'm not disappointed. If I stopped today and something happened I could never play again I'd be happy. I mean, there's certainly still a lot to discover on the instrument. But I'm not disappointed. If there's anything not happening it's on me. And besides, who knows what other people are gonna think? It's something you can never influence. It's always someone else's decision, if they want you to play, they want your band, want you as a side person and all those other outside factors which you can't really influence that much.

JG: Well, I just wanted to end up with an acknowledgment of what we talked about earlier. All those external things don't really matter. I think that the truth does will out in time. I think of what Phil Woods told me at my first lesson. "Man, the music just goes quietly on about its business." And I feel like that statement is very represented by you and your music and your contribution. And I'm honored that would do this interview. And it's good, I've got you recorded laughing...

MT: [Laughter]

JG: And throwing down the gauntlet at jazz education! I got a side of Mark that people don't often see. So, I'm lovin' that shit, for posterity's sake.

MT: [Laughter] That's some funny shit!

JG: You're a scholar and a gentleman sir. Thanks for everything.

MT: Likewise man.

Hank Mobley
Don Sickler's Studio - 1985

In late November or early December of 1985, when I was eighteen, I got a chance to meet Hank Mobley. I'd gotten back from a six-plus week trip to Europe about a month earlier, and I'd asked Don Sickler if I could teach a lesson at his studio where I sometimes rehearsed with him in a few different groups. He was nice enough to tell me I could.

Afterwards, as we sat in his office next to the studio, he said, "You know, Hank Mobley's staying with us." I paused, knowing Hank's name, but not yet really knowing his playing, and trying to recall what recordings I'd heard him on. As I did so, Don said, "You don't know Hank Mobley?!"

I said, "Well, I know who he is, but I don't think I know his playing well enough."

He said, "Wait here." A minute later, after he'd gone back into the apartment behind the studio, he and Hank walked into the office and Don introduced us. I stood up and shook his hand. There was a kindness, gentleness, and humility about him that I sensed. Then Don said, "Man, you gotta know Hank Mobley! Just wait a minute, I'm gonna put on the three tenor record that Hank did with Trane and Johnny Griffin!"

Hank reacted as though he'd been punched in the jaw, raising his hands to cover his face, reeling slightly to his left and leaning back against a wall of seemingly endless records that surrounded us, like a boxer leaning back against the ropes and moaned, "Oh god, no! Please don't play that record Don. Those guys kicked my ass so bad!" Don said, "Hank, you played great on it too!" Don looked hard at me and said, "But with all that stuff they played, he still played *his* thing. Hank Mobley is a melody player, man. He's a *melody* player!"

I was thinking about what that might mean as the record began. I thought about the contrasts in the three great player's styles, as I stood there next to one of them. Hank smiled as he listened to Trane and Griffin. But he held his head in his hands when his solo came up, shaking his head, seeming almost near tears. When the song ended, he smiled, somewhat sadly and wearily, still seemingly disappointed in his playing. But he was very kind to me when we spoke.

He passed away the following year. In the interim, I started to understand what Don meant about his playing and what it means to be a melody player.

A few months after this chance meeting with Hank Mobley, my friend Kevin Hays came over to the apartment I was house sitting at the time in Eddie Locke's building. He brought the record, *Miles Davis - Live at the Blackhawk*, that Mobley was on. He told me he was listening to it every day and that I had to hear it. When we got to the cut "Bye Blackbird" at the top of one of Hank's choruses, Kevin sang the line that Hank was improvising. And at that moment, I *really* got what Don had told me! It was such a great melody! Hank really *was* a melody player, playing something that could easily have been a song in and of itself, as opposed to something technically impressive or just outlining the chords or substitutions. It completely opened up a new concept of how to think and play as a jazz musician and seemed to me to transcend ego in a way that I think we all strive for over time. So, it really meant a lot that I learned about that concept from Don, meeting Hank, and hearing him on records, thanks to Don and Kevin.

Bill Easley

Japan – 2013

JG: So, here I am with my buddy, Bill Easley, on tour in Japan, at the front of the bus…

BE: With the best view… yeah… they know who the important people are.

JG: [Laughter] So, man, it's always great talking with you. And like a lot of people we know in music, you're one of the great storytellers I know. So, I thought I'd ask you about your history with your family in music, coming up in Olean, New York.

BE: Tell you the truth, it wasn't a choice. I was just born into it, being a fourth generation musician. My mother and father had a band. My father came to town in 1928 and met my mom. They had a band from then to the '60s. My maternal grandmother had graduated from a conservatory in Meadville, Pennsylvania, and her father was a band master and played all the instruments. My grandmother's brother, Dar, played the saxophone. And my mother's brother, also named Dar, played sax, so I'm a third generation sax player.

JG: When did you start working?

BE: I started working with them at thirteen, and I joined the union in 1959. We played dances, proms, Sons of Italy, Lions Clubs. TV was new and live entertainment was the norm, so people went out for their regular fix of joy.

JG: So through your teens you're working with your folks. Tell us about eventually coming to New York, taking classes at Juilliard, and getting involved in the jazz scene there.

BE: Well, since I'd started young, I knew thousands of tunes as a result. So, I had a great foundation to build on when I got to New York at eighteen. Naturally, like most people, you follow your instincts, you look for a place to sit in and play. I remember the first day, walking around in Harlem, seeing signs for clubs on 132nd St. I thought that would be my first stop. But actually, my first stop was getting on the subway and going down to Ponte's music store on 46th St. to get a Berg Larsen tenor mouthpiece to replace the one I'd borrowed from my brother-in-law. When I first started, I only played clarinet because my parents had a sax player. I'd also bring some bongos and play those a little. But then I started playing tenor sophomore year in high school and became a regular in the band at that time. I'd decided I wanted to play the clarinet after seeing *The Benny Goodman Story*. And the years I put into that clarinet has opened a lot of doors for me.

JG: You're one of my favorite clarinet players and an incredible tenor and alto player.

BE: Well, it started with clarinet, then tenor, but eventually when I was drafted into the Army and stationed in Fairbanks, Alaska, I started playing alto, on an army horn they had there. When I came home on leave the local music store owner in Olean had an alto that had been pawned to him by Charlie Ventura. He'd spent some time playing at Pauls' Steak House in our town. So, he sold it to me for $250. And then when I went back to Alaska I started to pick up the flute, and that also ended up opening up another big door. When I eventually ended up getting called to work with George Benson it was on the strength of the fact that I played a little flute.

43

JG: What was it like transitioning to the scene in New York?

BE: Yeah, I was sitting in, finding jam sessions. There was a club on 152nd and Broadway called the L Bar, later called Chick Morrison's Lounge. Chick was a drummer who played in a hotel downtown, this was '64–65. I lived on 145th and St. Nicholas. I had a friend who was a drummer, Robert Callender. We would go there and play every night just like we worked there. After my savings ran out, I got a job working nine to five at First National City Bank. Plus, I'd go to school a few nights a week, then I'd be at this club every night. It was an organ club. There were a number of clubs in Harlem and throughout the country at that time that had a B3 organ. There was a guy there named Eddie Clark and we'd go in and just sit in. It was just like our regular gig. That was my first place to sit in in New York. But then I started working with a guy named Ross Carnegie. This was back in the day when you had ballroom dances, and he sometimes had several in a night. I met some great musicians working with him, like Harold Ousley, Chris Woods, Jimmy Buchanan, Charlie Persip, who'd be playing these dances. Ross would have three to four gigs on a given night and he'd make an appearance at all of them. I remember when Malcolm X was killed at the Audubon Ballroom. I'd just played there the prior Friday or Saturday night. So, there were a lot of ballrooms and society dances.

JG: You mentioned that that period of your life or soon after you caught the tail end of that ability to work on a regular basis in a creative context. And just prior to that you talked about meeting and working with Lockjaw, Stitt, and Ammons.

BE: Well, that was little bit later, but just after this period of playing with Ross Carnegie, I got my first road gig playing with a kind of a rock and roll band called Sonny Allen and the Rockets. I'd played a few little gigs with them in town. It was a four to five piece band with three girl dancers and singers. So, Sonny called me at the bank one Monday morning. His sax player hadn't shown up and he needed me to quit my job and go on the road that day! And he promised me $75 a week on the weeks I *didn't* work! They were leaving that afternoon for Hazelton, Pennsylvania. I was only making $65 at the bank. I told my foreman that I had gotten my big break in show biz. I knew that normally it would be proper to give two weeks' notice, but I had to leave that day as this was my *huge* break.

They were waiting for me at 145th St. to leave town. I ran home, packed my bags, and met them. There was about nine of us in a station wagon. Before we got over the GW Bridge, I happened to mention to one of the girls that I'd quit my job. She said, "You quit your *what*!?" Turned out hard times were ahead. So that was the start of some serious dues paying that lasted from that point… probably right up until now!

BOTH: [Laughter]

BE: So we went out on the road, and now I was a full-time musician. This was early '65. And so, naturally we worked a couple weeks, and that's when I discovered pawn shops and Dinty Moore beef stew… and survival techniques. There was a club on 155th and St. Nicholas Place, a trendy jazz club in those days called The Showplace. It was a small bar. On weekends they had an organ trio, exotic dancers, and comedians. But during the week they had a regular organ player, Freddy Drew, brother of the great pianist Kenny Drew. So, I would go in and sit in with Freddie. And there was an elderly bartender there named Blackie who took a liking to me and knew I was out of work and said, "Man, I'm gonna get you a gig!"

He took me out the next Thursday to a place in Queens called the Colonial Inn, which was another organ trio room. There was an organ player named Bob Graham, Walter Perkins played drums. I went out there and they liked me right away. I was young, personable, and could play. At nineteen I had a steady three-night weekend jazz gig in New York. It took two trains and two buses to get there. I can't remember how I got home. But it was like utopia to be in New York at that time and have a steady job. That's where I met people like Eddie Lockjaw Davis, Billy Mitchell, Eric Dixon—all the guys that lived out there—C.I. Williams, Harold Minerve (later lead alto with the Ellington band).

One night I get there early, setting up my horn. This guy's sitting at the bar. It was just he and I and the bartender. He asked me what time the band hit. I told him, 9:00. He said, "You wanna taste?" I said, "Yes, I'd like a Coca-Cola." He gave me a strange look, and then said, "What's your name?" I told him. He held out his hand and said "Eddie Davis." I looked at him and said, "Eddie Lockjaw Davis!?" He said, "Yeah." Naturally I was excited. Of course, I knew his playing. So, to make a long story short, around the second set he went out and got his horn to sit in. But by this time, this is my house, my crowd, and these are my folks. Naturally, being young, I was respectful and polite, and would play a little bit, and let him just take the floor. But all of my fans were a little disappointed because of my reluctance to jump into the battle. They'd come up and say, "Sic 'em!" which I knew better. But by this time, I'd already experienced a little bit of hardship, having been out of work. And survival tells you that nobody's gonna take your job, no matter *who* they are! So, I upped my competitive spirit. I think that was a high peak of my career. I think I may have played better that night than since. But ironically it just happened to be when he was about to go home and put the horn in the case. So, the next night, the story around the club was that I ran Lockjaw off the stage.

BOTH: [Laughter]

BE: But I knew better.

JG: Tell me about getting to be friends with Stitt.

BE: That was later. After I came out of the Army and was with George Benson. Yes, I got to know Stitt and also Gene Ammons. Stitt took me under his wing. He was encouraging, supportive and helpful. Anybody that knew Stitt knew he was competitive and confident. He would look at me and say, "Bill Easley, you're a pretty good young saxophone player… but I… am a *master!*" And I could only say, "Yes Sonny!" And even to this day when I hear him, I must say I'm still chasing Stitt.

JG: One of the all-time greats, on alto and tenor. Not many guys were great on both.

BE: The tenor was more of a work horn, especially with organ groups. It was the norm in an organ group, more so than alto. But Fathead played great tenor and alto, but more tenor live. James Moody, his big hit was on the alto, but later years played more tenor. At a certain point you just don't want to carry them both around. I certainly don't.

JG: Tell us about your association with George Benson.

BE: I came out of the Army in '67, but there's a story before that that deals with divine intervention and the voice in my head. Anyone that's been in this business for any length of time would have to say that the main way to move forward is to follow your own instincts and listen to your own inner voice. Nobody can tell you how to survive in this business, you can't do it like anybody else. You have to find your own journey to survive. Now, having been in New York prior to being drafted, I had some working experience. But the one thing I knew I had going for me prior to going into the Army was youth. There was no marketing strategy of "Young Lions" back in those days, but it did work in my favor. I had a good foundation at an early age. But I worried, "What am I going to do when I come out of the Army as an old man of 21?" No more youth crutch.

I was stationed in Fairbanks, Alaska, in the 9th Army Band. On my way back from a furlough, I stopped in Seattle, Washington. Miles Davis was working at a club called the Penthouse. The personnel in the band at that time was Wayne, Tony, Ron, and Herbie. Hearing them live was a shocking ear opener. What they were doing at that time was amazing. It was really a new point in the development of the music. My plan was to go into the club in my army greens, listen to the first set, and then on the break I was going to go up to Miles and introduce myself and say "Hello Miles, My name is Bill Easley and I play the saxophone," and Miles was going to say, "Really!? Man, why don't you go get your horn and come sit in!" That was my plan. Made sense beforehand.

I took my seat, took my hat off and put it under my chair. When they hit, it was like some people came from another planet. It was like an out of body experience. The freedom and adventurousness of the music was way over my head. At some point I got out of my seat and stood right in front of the bandstand the first set. I was just out of my mind. I didn't know where I was, or who I was. When they finished, it was a feeling of exhilaration and exhaustion. I was emotionally drained. The voice in my head said, "Get back in the hotel and get *under* the bed! Go *hide* somewhere. Just lay under the bed." I remember trying to get out of the club, but I couldn't find my army hat. So, I'm frantically looking around under tables. Finally, I feel these piercing eyes staring at me. I turn around and see at the end of Miles' outstretched arm, my hat. Miles says to me in his raspy voice, "Is this what you're lookin' for?" I grabbed my hat and *ran* out of the club!

BOTH: [Laughter]

BE: I was totally devastated. Up to that point I thought I was a musician. But I was really devastated at the level of music I heard that night. I had no clue what it was. It took me a few days to get over it when I got back to Alaska. I was afraid to take the horn out of the case. But then, the voice in my head said, "You gotta get with a *giant!*" In other words, I had to play with someone who was at a much higher level than I was. And that manifested itself when I got out of the Army. I left Fairbanks in November of '67, I was with George Benson by January of '68. That was a great period of time. I met everybody during that time. We'd be on festivals or concerts that Monk, Miles, or Duke were on. We played the Village Vanguard one week, opposite Herbie's octet. I met Joe Henderson, who was very nice to me. Another time we worked opposite Bill Evans' trio. To say the least, I was in some pretty high cotton. I worked for George for two years, I left him in January of '70. I lived in Pittsburgh for a while when I left George.

JG: When did you start working with Isaac Hayes?

BE: Well I was in Pittsburgh for two years. It was after that. I had a trio with Gene Ludwig out there and worked local clubs there with him. I also did some road gigs in Virginia or Buffalo. Trenton, New Jersey is the club where we worked opposite Stitt and Gene Ammons, after close to two years, around October of '71. Not much work in Pittsburgh at the time. I thought about going back to New York, but somebody said, "Why don't you go to Memphis?" Sounded like a plan.

JG: What years were you there?

BE: '71–80. I got there on a Tuesday with $20 in my pocket and didn't know a soul in that town. By Friday I was working seven nights a week, $10 on Monday through Thursday, $20 on Friday to Sunday. That went on for two years of basic survival. Then I got hired by The Isaac Hayes Movement, and I went from $96 a week to $175–200 a night. And that was a pleasant discovery that you could actually make money playing music, and I've never recovered.

JG: Tell us about the musicians in the Memphis scene at that time.

BE: Well I got to know James Williams in the first couple weeks I was there. He knew that I knew a lot of standards. And he'd knock on my door just unannounced, often during that period to talk about tunes. So, we'd sit out on the porch and go over tunes. Every week he'd learn two, three standards. I grew up playing them at dances and country clubs. But the business had changed, and guys weren't learning tunes in his generation the same way. So in later years, after he became James Williams, he always introduced me as one of his Memphis teachers.

JG: Weren't you on a record of James' in the '80s called *Alter Ego*?

BE: Yes, I was, but his first record was *Flying Colors*, with me, Slide Hampton, Billy Pierce, and the rhythm section was Sticks Baker on drums and Sylvester Sample on bass.

JG: He was one of the nicest guys ever and it was a shame to lose him so early.

BE : Yeah, he sure was. But as we were leaving for this tour of Japan on November 23rd, they just gave him a brass note on Beale St. in Memphis.

JG: Oh, that's great! Was Harold Mabern still in Memphis when you where there?

BE: No, guys like Harold, Frank Strozier, and George Coleman had left long before I got there, in the '50s or early '60s. But I did get to know them when they came back to Memphis. There were also some important local musicians, a keyboard player named Honeymoon Garner, a sax player named Fred Ford. Some of the blues players that I met when I first got there played at a club called Paradise, where B. B. King and Albert King and others played. They had a house band there. I went there and heard blues players like Fat Sonny, and a lady alto player Evelyn Young, and that's when I heard the real down-home blues. I thought I could play the blues prior to that. George Benson would fuss at me, and yell at me on the bandstand "Play *funky*!" And I would think, "Well, I am in fact playing quite funky!"

BOTH: [Laughter]

BE: But you have to realize that he'd been with Jack McDuff, and in one of the great organ groups of that time with George, Joe Dukes, and Red Holloway. So, I didn't know about that. I was trying to play as many notes as possible, as young players did post-bebop. One of those great blues players would take one note and swing you into bad health! I didn't know how to do that back then. And I didn't even understand what George was asking me to do until years later. But when I first heard Fat Sonny and Evelyn Young a light went on in my head. I'd heard it on records. But it was a different kind of thing hearing it live. The core of Memphis was that Mississippi Delta blues. It's the main ingredient of Memphis music, the blues. And I got a ten-year taste of it.

JG: What years were you with Isaac Hayes?

BE: I went with him about 1973. It was a few years I was with him. But there'd be periods where we'd be off for six to eight months while he was making a movie in L.A. But then I was making all the recordings at Stax. And Willie Mitchell took me under his wing so I was recording at Hi.

JG: Who was Willie Mitchell?

BE: He produced a lot of records, including all the Al Green records. I was only on one, the Memphis Horns did most of those. But he'd ask me to put the horn sections together for his dates. But one Al Green record had me on a little alto solo, "Keep Me Crying." Willy would always sing that solo to me any time he saw me in later years.

If you ever heard the song "The Memphis Blues," it talks about the hospitality of the South. And the moment I got there, that town just embraced me. Memphis just put its arms around me from the moment I got there. When I went by Willie's studio the first few days I got there he came out and talked to me liked we'd known each other for years. He was a big wheel, but really down home and warm. In other words, not pretentious. Very open and friendly, and I liked the feel. And that's why I stayed as long as I did. Plus, I was making a good living.

JG: Tell us about Phineas Newborn.

BE: I could go hear him at this club, Gemini, and Phineas played there regularly. But when I met him, he was recovering from a nervous breakdown. He started playing around Memphis again a few nights a week. I, and all the young piano players, James, Mulgrew Miller, and Donald Brown would just soak it up. But by this time in 1973 I've got a brand new '73 Audi with a sunroof and 8-track tape, with my bell bottoms and high-top shoes and 6-foot afro. And there were nights that he would really demonstrate what a genius was. I would come by and give Phineas a ride home. I remember asking him one night as I drove him home, what he wanted at this point in his career, being such an amazing musician, what he'd like to do now. He thought for a moment and said, "I'd like to have a car like this!" And it was a revelation for me in terms of values, and what people strive for.

And not only that lesson, but with someone like George Benson, when an artist has a chance to make money, other musicians have a tendency to put him down, or say that he's sold out. They said that about Cannonball. And he said, "Sell out? I wish somebody would tell me how to! Isn't that the ultimate goal?" There's a different thought in today's world. But the early musicians that created the music didn't have other outlets or chances to make a living. That's how this music evolved in the first place, out of necessity. My own family didn't become musicians to be hip or cool, but because they were bright people and it was one of the few opportunities open to them. You had very bright, intelligent people going to an art form. And if you really think about how it evolved in one hundred years' time, that's faster than any period of time in past history. Technology and communication were also factors of course, radio and TV.

JG: I loved Benson's hits of "Masquerade" and "Broadway" before I knew anything about music. And there was great popular and artistic success with groups led by Cannonball or Wayne and Zawinul with Weather Report.

BE: Well, the press or critics, if they put it down it affects how people perceive it. Take Miles, who changed music three or four times, and what he did in the later period of his life. He wanted to continue to get to the masses and the youth. He was trying to maintain that audience, and a lot of people put him down. But he was successful and he didn't have anything to prove to those people. He did what he wanted to do. The bottom line is to evolve and hopefully succeed.

JG: I think of *Bird with Strings*, and how some people perceived that, but that's some of my favorite Bird. And Bird said, play something beautiful, to the people. Or what Benny Carter told me, that he loved Sanborn as an alto player. And Gil Evans did too. So, by 1980 you're back in New York, working with Lincoln Center, The American Jazz Orchestra, the Carnegie Band, The Smithsonian Jazz Orchestra, Broadway...

BE: Broadway and steady work brought me back to New York. Steady work and benefits. I turned down Blakey, Horace Silver, Basie, and Dizzy for steady work and benefits. I have some regrets—you give up one thing to gain another and may have sacrificed some artistic growth.

But I still worked with Jimmy McGriff, Jimmy Smith, Roland Hanna, and had a foot in the jazz arena, but no regrets really because the business has diminished quite a bit over the years. I may not have established the name that would have created more work later. But it's an art form in itself to keep the horn in your face and to continue to work and make your living doing this. When I look back, I think it's a miracle that I've done nothing but put air through these pipes since 1959. Fifty-four years, with just a few little months of nine to five, so I have no regrets.

JG: Well, it's always seemed to me that you've had, and have, a great career. A very diverse career, that most of us would aspire to have.

BE: Well, I'm still trying to figure out the next page and chapter.

JG: The various worlds that you've been in, and the experience you bring—other musicians know that and feel that, and it's that stuff you're not gonna learn in school.

BE: Well, a craftsman is more likely to make a living than an artist. So, you have to look at yourself as both. A craftsman goes to work and does what's needed on that particular night.

JG: Well I know that the coming years will continue to be great ones for you. It's always a pleasure to hear you, work with you and talk to you! And as we've taken to saying in recent years on our Japan tours, I'll see you at breakfast!

BE: That's right.

Doc Cheatham

Flying between London and Oslo – 1988

Doc Cheatham was an incredible trumpet player. Born in 1905, he truly lived the history of jazz in the twentieth century, as perhaps few others did. You can even briefly see and hear him, playing obligato, behind the great Billie Holiday, on the classic *Sound of Jazz* video, where she sings, "Fine and Mellow." If you only ever see one video in the history of jazz, see that one! The three greatest and most important tenor players in the first half of the twentieth century are featured—Coleman Hawkins, Ben Webster, and Lester Young, along with Roy Eldridge, Mulligan, and others. And Pres' solo on that! The look on Billie Holiday's face while he plays. My god. If that doesn't get you, nothing will.

I first got to play with Doc in my teens by sitting in with him a few times on Sunday afternoons at Sweet Basil. I had played regularly with Eddie Chamblee there on Saturdays, and at one point got invited to play a bit with Doc as well.

In 1987, when I was twenty, my friends Bjorn and Mona Pedersen, who'd met me on a Saturday at Sweet Basil, had gotten me hired on the Oslo Jazz Festival, which they helped to book. The first concert I did was with Doc, Al Grey, Jay McShann, Benny Waters, and a Norwegian bass player and drummer. I was petrified and really didn't know what I was doing in such company. And while I thought I sounded like crap, those guys were very kind and supportive to me that night and all week, and it meant so much. And as a kid that first year, I was actually, to my surprise, a big hit at the festival.

The next year, '88, I played the festival again. I saw Doc in the late afternoon when I arrived at JFK airport, about two hours before our flight to London. When I said hi and mentioned we still had over two hours before our flight, he said, "Man, I got here about 9:00 this morning." Musicians often prefer being early to avoid the stress of being late! Doc and I sat next to one another on the next flight that connected from London to Oslo. He was about six feet tall, quite thin, and was always dressed impeccably in a sharp suit. He had a way about him, a dignity to him, that was of an earlier age. A true Southern gentleman.

Soon after we took off, Doc looked out the window to his left, then looked at me on his right, and nodded back towards the window and said, quietly but intensely, "Man… they got some bacon down there in England that'll *blow* your mind! You ever try some a'dat bacon?" I told him that I had in fact! He went on, "Damn, that's good!"

He sometimes chewed a hickory stick and was doing so as we spoke. He reached into his jacket pocket and pulled out a trumpet mouthpiece and said, "Yeah, this is a mouthpiece that Pops gave me in New Orleans in 1922." Wow! For a lover of jazz, looking at one of Louis Armstrong's mouthpieces was a thrill for me.

"You know, I don't know if I ever played it! But I'm gonna play it on the gig tonight."

I remember playing with Doc that night, standing next to him, realizing he was playing one of Louis Armstrong's old mouthpieces. He held the trumpet up high, as always, pointing the bell nearly straight up, seeming to play to the heavens. He smiled when he sang, "Squeeze Me" and "Just a Little Girl" with a quiet grace, charm, and mastery. And I thought, how lucky am I?

Scott Robinson

Jacksonville Airport, Florida – 2007

SR: Do you have one of those sputnik things? [Referring to the shape of the mic I used.]

JG: Yeah, I think I showed you that when we got together last time. I thought you'd like it since it looks like some kind of spaceship. I'm sitting here in Jacksonville Airport with one of my favorite musicians on the planet, Scott Robinson. Just a kind of amazing, funny, and brilliant guy. What other words would describe you Scott?

SR: Tired. [Laughter]

JG: We played a gig with Maria Schneider last night.

SR: Yeah, I had to leave my house at 5:00 a.m. yesterday. We came here, went straight to sound check and all that.

JG: No food at the hotel.

SR: Well, it was a choice of an hour to eat or an hour nap. And there was a barbecue place and some of us went there.

JG: Oh that's right.

SR: But that meant I didn't get any sleep. So, I got up at seven this morning or something like that. I'm a little sleepy but it's alright. We had a two-hour bus trip.

JG: A musician's life. Well, I hardly know where to begin with you because there's so much to talk about. You're a guy that plays sixty to seventy instruments, completely sounds like himself on any of them. And does this in any music in the entire history of jazz, and reflects a kind of genius that I think is unparalleled…

SR: You might be overstating that. [Laughter]

JG: So, how did you get started in music?

SR: My brother kinda got me started because he was older than me by four years. And he started playing the trumpet, playing my father's old trumpet. He was interested in my dad's old records, 78s. There were a few interesting things in there. So, he got started in music, and I couldn't sit around and watch somebody have that much fun and not wanna get involved in it.

So, from the beginning, the idea that somebody could pick up an instrument and blow into it and make music and get a bunch of people together and form a band and play… that really appealed to me right away, as soon as I saw that something like that was possible. Before I even took up an instrument, I tried to form a band. This was the end of fourth grade. In the fifth grade we could take instrumental instruction once a week at the elementary school. So I went around and told all my friends, I said, "Look, next year we can start instrument lessons. Let's start a band. You wanna be in my band?"

JG: That's great.

SR: And I was really amazed, shocked, and horrified that some of my friends said no. "No, I'm not gonna do that." What do you mean? We can start next year. "No, I wasn't going to do

51

that, I wasn't gonna take up an instrument." What!? I couldn't believe it! I couldn't believe that someone would choose not to play music. I sort of never got over it. I still can't believe it in fact. But I've come to accept it. [Laughter]

JG: That some people will choose not to play music if given the chance.

SR: Right. So, my elementary school band never got off the ground. The first of many failures in the music business. [Laughter]

JG: So here you are nine or ten years later, playing with Nicholas Payton, Maria Schneider...

SR: Nine or ten years later?

JG: Well, twelve or thirteen...

SR: We're talking about the '60s here! [Laughter]

JG: Well, I have to say that one of my joys in recent years is, and I've been saying it to you for ten years, "I want the world to know!" But I really genuinely feel that way with you.

SR: I appreciate that.

JG: I really mean it. And I've just been glad to see you working in all these different great contexts. I remember we did a gig with Bobby Short a few years ago at the Carlyle Hotel, and you were playing bass saxophone. And man, you just played your *ass* off! And you know, I liked Bobby, I enjoyed a lot of things about the gig. But it was a challenge to know how to be myself sometimes on that gig, as it can sometimes be on certain gigs. And one of the great things I see in you is, I've never seen you not be relaxed and who you are in any musical context. And I think your access to that, to me, is a big key to why you sound great in any context.

SR: Well, I appreciate that. The Bobby Short gig was kind of stifling, it was a show really. I did it for one season.

JG: Me too.

SR: It was good experience but then I had to move on. Because, I'm not really cut out for show type of work. The sameness of it.

JG: But you're the only guy I ever heard do that there.

SR: Well I'd have to break in and say, I definitely heard John Eckert do that there. He's one of my heroes.

JG: Yes, you're right, I was just thinking of John after I said that. He really sounded great down there, there's no doubt. But I've heard you stand up and play incredible clarinet solos in big bands, do things on flute. I mean, theremin, mellophone, pocket trumpet. One night we talk about a lot is that one night we had that jam session with you and me and Lovano at the Oslo Jazz Festival.

SR: Oh, that's right!

BOTH: That was so much fun! [Laughter]

SR: That was great. I wish I had a tape of that.

JG: Oh man! It was Jay Leonhart on bass. I don't remember who the drummer was but whoever it was it felt good. And Jay has such a great beat.

SR: Yeah, I don't remember who played drums.

JG: I think it was a Norwegian guy, or somebody from Europe we didn't know.

SR: Well we hit it hard, I remember that. It was full out. I remember it was loud. Every once in a while it's good to do that. Just really blow your brains out, and like, wrestle the music to the ground. [Laughter] It reminds me of how we were in college.

JG: Yeah! And I remember, it was so funny, towards the end of the last set. You always have this bag on your person or close to you, and you'll pull out some mystery instrument. [Laughter] So I played, then Lovano played… Lovano! One of the great improvisers in the history of the music. So, just as Lovano finished, you pulled the trumpet out of the bag and got up to the mic and Lovano said, "Now wait a second, that's not fair!"

BOTH: [Laughter]

SR: Yeah, 'cause we were doin' three saxophones and he was playin' so much tenor, you know.

JG: Yeah, hard to know what you can contribute after that. But you always can. In any context. It's amazing. I remember Bill Charlap called me up about a year ago and said, "There's a musician playing a solo concert tonight. You *must* come with me!" I said, "Who is it?" He said, "Guess." I said, "Rollins?"

SR: Same initials.

JG: He said, no. I waited a few seconds and said, "Scott?!" He said *yes*! I said, "What's he playing?" He said, "I don't know but I'm going!" And we went down to Cornelia Street. How many instruments did you have set up?

SR: Oh… I couldn't begin to tell you. That's the kind of thing I used to do in the Boston days. I hadn't done that for a long, long time, where I just set up a *forest* of stuff. [Laughter] Gongs, I had a set of tuned electrical doorbells. All kinds of crazy stuff, plus various horns, slide saxophone. I remember I had alto clarinet, contra bass sax. I had a set of car horns with a transformer to power them. [Laughter] Tuned chromatic cowbells, timps…. the VW bus was full to where I couldn't see out the window. [Laughter]

Every once in a while I have to do that, just go way over the top. Just set up this thing. And then you have this whole forest of sound. And you just kind of traipse around in the forest. That's how it feels. You just pluck this little fruit or that leaf. And create a whole kind of tapestry of sound.

JG: And one of the organizing ideas behind it was your wife's math dissertation, right?

SR: Well, yeah. There were two parts of the concert. The second part of the concert was duo with my friend Jules Thayer, who's my best partner for completely free, improvised music. He's it for me. When we get together, certain music happens only then. But the first half was the centerpiece of the thing, and that was the solo piece, about an hour, and it was narrated. So, I went out and bought a clip-on wireless microphone so I could narrate the thing. And I spent a lot of time with my wife's doctoral dissertation with non-linear systems, computational sciences. I boiled it down.

You know, I'm interested in taking scientific materials and approaching them for their aesthetic value. I'm not a scientist, I'm not a mathematician. Though occasionally I'll use certain mathematical ideas in my composition. But my wife's work, she's a PhD mathematician. It's far beyond my ability to comprehend. But I can treat it from an aesthetic viewpoint. And the dissertation consisted of text, interspersed with mathematical material. So, the text would describe the parameters of things, or certain materials that were being introduced into the mathematical system or the dynamic system.

Then there would be blocks of mathematical gobbledegook, sort of demonstrating this. Then there'd be more text, like, "Now we take this dynamic system and we introduce noise into the system…" stuff like that. That's the type of language that's used. And I'm reading this and I'm saying…

JG: If that's not singin' your tune I don't know what is!

SR: I can take systems and introduce elements and stuff like that. So that's what I did. I pulled the text out with the parts that resonated with me from an aesthetic viewpoint. Then I took the blocks of mathematical material that supported those textual components, and I replaced that information with musical information.

JG: It was brilliant.

SR: My wife was there in the audience, and she didn't know anything about it. She knew that I'd been working for weeks on this piece. And I had reams of paper laying around. But I was always able to put it away when she came in the room, so she had no idea what the nature of the piece was going to be. So I said before the first note, "We have a dynamic system…" and as soon as I said those first words she realized immediately what I had done.

JG: Well, your music not only encompasses all these instruments and the entire history of jazz and other music, but it also encompasses an incredible humor, and has a spectrum that is so special. I just don't know of another musician who does what you do in that way. There's also a kind of a fearlessness to it. You'll deal with ideas and see possibilities in things that I think most people wouldn't. We were in Europe a few years ago and you were describing a piece you were working on for a concert at the New School, a kind of heroic character?

SR: Oh yeah, that was Doc Savage. Doc Savage was a pulp magazine hero from the 1930s. That was for the Jazz Composers Collective in New York. And I did a series or suite based on nine titles of Doc Savage pulps. The titles were very evocative, *Secret in the Sky*, *The Man Who Shook the Earth*. I hear a lot of music when I read titles like that. That's something I'd thought about for years and years. I've always got dozens of schemes and plans for projects. And every once in a while I see one of them through. And I did manage to see that one through. That was pretty complicated stuff. I've got to get that recorded.[2]

JG: I spoke to people that were there and they said it was unbelievable! And I was disappointed I wasn't able to make it.

SR: You probably would've gotten a kick out of it.

JG: Oh man, I would've loved it. What are some projects you're working on now?

SR: Oh man, I've got so many things that I've kind of started but haven't seen through yet. Time is so short. Sometimes I feel like time is the enemy. But one of the things that I've been kind of pecking away at is a series of chamber music compositions for large instruments. I call that "Immensities for Large Instruments." [Laughter] I'm kinda working on Immensity Number 4.

JG: What's the instrumentation?

SR: Well, they're all different, each one is a different small chamber music setting for larger instruments. Number 1 is a quartet—bass flute, bass sax, bass clarinet, bass marimba. Number 2 is a duo with contrabass, sarrusaphone, and piano. Number 3 is two contrabass clarinets, contrabassoon, and two basset horns. And Number 4 is bass trombone and timpani,

---

2   The entire Doc Savage suite, enlarged to twelve pieces, was recorded as *Bronze Nemesis* on the Doc-Tone label.

including a couple of giant contra bass timpani that this guy made himself. And there'll be others, bass sax and other groupings. I want to do one with a cathedral organ. So, I really want to get those recorded and make a CD.[3]

JG: As you're saying that I'm reminded, I know you did a C melody sax record. I guess the most well-known C melody player was Frankie Trumbauer. Lester Young and Bird both talked about listening to him. I remember hearing you in those kinds of contexts. We did a concert with Charlap that involved a Bix Beiderbecke tribute where you played "Singin' the Blues." And then you're also involved with multiple groups led by Anthony Braxton and are very inspired by Sun Ra. Which might seem to be worlds apart for some people, but for you it's not. I guess the reason it feels important to bring that up is, finding the connections between seemingly disparate things feels really compelling and important to me. Does that make sense?

SR: Yes. Well, you know what it is? I like to see people create their own worlds. That's what it is for me. It's pure creativity. If you're a really creative person, if you're an original person, you kind of create your own world. Those are my big heroes, the people who've done that. You mentioned Sun Ra. Hermeto Pascoal is another one. He sort of does everything. He plays all these different instruments. He writes amazing music that transcends all genres and boundaries, and he gets all these people together at his house and he rehearses for days and days. He just creates his own universe. I just love to see that. And there are people in all disciplines that do that. That say, "I'm gonna take this, this, and that and create my world." I just love seeing that. Braxton has done that for years.

So those are the people that really inspire me and those are the people that borrow freely from everything and do what they want to do with it. And that's the antidote to sameness. Because without those people, the ever-encroaching tide of sameness will just roll over us all. 'Cause it's out there right now beating on the windows trying to get in. Sameness is the enemy. I mean, look at it—Arby's and Wendy's. It's like we're paving over our country. This country is the seat of so much invention and creativity, and it's amazing. But it seems like we're running away from that just as fast as we can. It's like we're just giving our nation over to the forces of sameness.

JG: Man, the last two minutes of what you just said really nails it and speaks to what I and so many others see in you. It really comes down to how you live your life. I've heard people speak about that in spiritual circles—creating your own universe. That may make it sound more mysterious than I mean. But I think that's a key. And not to be limited by anything. It's just a great example. How you are and the way you live your life and the way you create your music is a great example of not only how to be a musician and live your life, but to be an architect.

SR: That's a good word, architect. When people study with me I always end up using that word. I give a lesson very rarely. But it's about how you shape things, how you put things together to serve your purposes artistically and otherwise.

JG: Bernstein said that music was the greatest representation of someone's inner architecture. I always liked that. And I think what you just said about the encroachment of sameness and really being the creator of your own kind of life is a big key. I guess there was a time when people got the impression, if I hang out and drink and do drugs then that's a freeing kind of tool. Eventually folks learned the hard way it really wasn't. But to me it's more about your intention and how you think.

---

3   As of 2020 Scott has recorded Immensities Numbers 1, 3, and 8. Number 5 will be next, and he vows that someday that album will exist.

SR: Yeah, drugs and substance abuse is really a way of retreating from the world rather than creating one. More of a retreat. The really creative world is tougher than that. It's more work.

JG: Yeah it is. And you have to be present in it.

SR: Yeah, it's a lot more work. Well, you know, you should come by some time because I built my studio that I dreamed of for years.

JG: You did? That's great!

SR: I've got all these instruments piled up. I can't even get at half the stuff. Now I've got a place where I can set things up and it's really nice. I can do recordings out there now. I'm going to start doing sixty-piece orchestras all by myself, one piece at a time.[4]

JG: Amazing.

SR: So I'm hoping to enter the next phase of really being able to do some of the stuff I'm hearing in my tiny mind but I didn't have the wherewithal to achieve. I mean, where am I going to get seventeen theremin players and six bass flutes and four marimbas or something.

BOTH: [Laughter]

SR: But if I do it myself one part at a time, I can have that. And the technology today makes it easy to do it. So, I finally built my laboratory, as I call it, ScienSonic Laboratories. And I'm going to start puttin' out CDs again, like I did in the early '80s, though that was LPs. But it's a good time for the do-it-yourselfer. On the one hand we've got this corporate sameness that's trying to stifle everything. On the other hand, certain technological advancements, and the decline of corporate influence in the arts has in a way made it go the other way, and made it a good time for the individual artist. Look at somebody like Dave Douglas. He's got his own label and he's doing things all the time now. Maria's selling scores online, there's all this downloadable stuff.

JG: Well it's forcing us to, to your point, create our own world artistically rather than relying on anyone else. Because companies think "Well, we can't make any money on this kind of music so we're not interested in dealing with it." Whether it's good, bad, creative, ground-breaking, new. Instead they're thinking, "Let's find somebody and sort of shape them into a money-making machine for us." In the meanwhile, folks like you, Maria, and others are like, well, since nobody's going to do it for me, I'm going to do it here.

SR: Little Red Hen.

JG: [Laughter] Exactly! Of all the things I've done on my ArtistShare site, the thing I've enjoyed the most is these interviews. I don't understand why I look in *DownBeat* and I don't see an interview with you, Charles McPherson, or Mark Turner. So, I can do them myself! There's a lot of older guys I'd like to interview too. I'd like to interview Frank Wess. I already did one with Phil Woods and Eddie Locke.

SR: Yeah, Eddie's a character, and he's got some good stories to tell!

JG: That's for sure! But I think this is another way of creating our world, and for me to say, "These are artists that I think are important and that people should know about. And their voices should be recognized and acknowledged." And on that note my friend, it's always a pleasure. Looking forward to the next gig and recordings.

---

4   At the time of this publication in 2020, he's more than a year into that project, and it includes more than 75 instruments. He expects it will take him more than a decade to complete.

SR: Well thanks. Thanks for chatting with me. And you know, maybe one of these days I'll get around to having some kind of site, doing something like what you're doing, so then you can come and yack on my site.

JG: [Laughter] Sounds like a deal. Thanks Scott.

SR: Sure.

Eddie Bert

Umbria Jazz Festival, Italy – 1997

Eddie Bert was a great trombonist and a great guy. He looked very young well into his seventies. He was short, with reddish brown hair and ruddy cheeks that you'd expect to see on a kid just coming in from playing in the snow. I first met and played with him while I was still in my teens. At that time he was in his sixties. He'd played with everyone in the history of jazz over the preceding forty years or so, and had also taken amazing photographs to document many of those gigs and recordings. He had lots of stories, as you might imagine, though he tended to be on the quiet side.

I did a European tour with him one time. All Eddie brought was his trombone, a small brown leather briefcase, and a light tan colored suit that he wore each day with a sort of odd fabric. But it was designed to be washed, hand-dried, and then worn the next day, so that's what Eddie did for two weeks. His main motivation was to carry as little as possible so they wouldn't take his trombone away from him when he was getting on the plane, as I came to understand extremely well.

I remember him asking me one day on tour, "Hey Jon, did you ever hear my friend Davey Schildkraut play?" I thought for a moment and said, "Yeah, I think so. Isn't he on that Miles Davis record with Lucky Thompson, with "Solar" on it?" "Yeah, that's him! He's a great player, but he's so down on himself. He kinda drives himself crazy a little bit sometimes. He was one a' the great alto players, ya know? But he's playin' mostly tenor these days. Says it doesn't drive him quite so nuts. But back in the day he was one a' the best around. In fact, Dizzy tried to hire him in the '50s after Bird passed, you know? He loved Davey. He called him and said, 'Hey Davey, I want you to join my band. Whaddaya say?' Davey said, 'Oh Dizzy, I'm so honored. I can't thank you enough for thinking of me. But I'm not good enough to play with you Dizzy!' Dizzy said, 'Why sure you are! I wouldn't call you if you weren't. Come on, take the gig!' Davey said, 'Gimme a year to practice Dizzy. I gotta get ready to play with the likes of you. Just gimme a little more time, OK?' Dizzy chuckled and said, 'Well, alright. If you say so. I can't make any promises. But if there's an opening I'll try you again some time.'"

Then Eddie told me, "A couple years later, Dizzy was gettin' ready to go on the road for a while and he was puttin' a band back together you know?" He smiled and chuckled before going on, "So Dizzy calls Davey again!" Eddie laughed. "But wouldn't you know it? Davey turned him down again! This time I think Dizzy was a little annoyed. But Davey told 'im, 'Dizzy, I just want to get good enough before I go out on the road with you, you know? I want to be at my best and I'm not there yet.'"

Eddie said to me, "I told 'im at the time, 'Davey, what's a matter wit' you?'" and then he laughed. And when he stopped laughing, he said, "But you know, Dizzy thought enough of Davey's playing that he called him a third time! Dizzy said, 'Now look Davey, no more 'a this humble crap. OK? I want you to join my band. No more waiting. None a' that. Alright?'

But Davey still said, 'Dizzy, I'm sorry, but I'm just not good enough to play with you.'

Dizzy said, 'Davey, this is it. If you don't take the gig now, I'll never call you again.'

But Davey just repeated, 'I'm so sorry Dizzy. I'd love to play with you, but I'm just not good enough.' Dizzy just hung up on him."

Eddie said, with a more serious tone and look, "Can ya believe it? Turned down Dizzy! How do ya do that? But he could a' *really* been great, if only he'd given himself a chance and not been so down on himself. I don't care *what* you think! If Dizzy Gillespie says, 'You're ready'... *you're ready!*"

There's a lesson there for sure... the main takeaway to me, along with Eddie's advice, "If Dizzy thinks you're ready..." is to remember how much you grow from playing with great players! Always give yourself a chance!

Phil Woods

San Juan, Puerto Rico – 2006

JG: Well, here I am with…

PW: Jon! Nice to see you with the iBook! Whadya wanna talk about?

JG: Oh… everything.

BOTH: [Laughter]

PW: Well I been knowin' ya a long time. I remember one of the first lessons. I gave you all that shit to do. Write a rondo, analyze Stravinsky… I think I was hung over and didn't feel like teaching. So, I sent you in the back. I figured this guy'll be back there for about three hours. You were back in fifteen minutes and had it all done. I said, hey, wait a minute now, this cat is very special. You know I've always thought that.

JG: Wow, thanks man.

PW: When you play… when people ask me, who do you listen to, you're the first guy I mention on the alto. You're the guy that's carrying it. If anybody's going to carry it forward, I believe it's you.

JG: Wow…

PW: You do some stuff that I've never heard anybody do. And you're one of the greatest alto saxophone players in the world today, in my opinion. And I've played with everybody, man.

JG: Wow…

PW: So I'm gonna go right to the core. You wanna talk about music, you're one of my heroes, man.

JG: Oh my god! Man!

PW: You're pure and you can play, man… and I'm not just sayin' this because you gave me a thousand dollars for the interview!

BOTH: [Laughter]

JG: Wow, well, my goodness… someday I can tell my grandkids you said this…

PW: Or just play it for them!

BOTH: [Laughter]

JG: Exactly! Well, thank you so much.

PW: Well, it's from my heart. I'm so glad you're going high-tech, and doing ArtistShare, finally getting a chance to take control of your recording destiny. That's so important.

JG: Yeah.

PW: Copyrights and the contractual stuff that has to be done. You have the mind to get to the core of that. Hopefully you'll be my age and you'll have your annuity.

JG: Hopefully.

PW: I wish I'd known this when I was your age. Sometimes we get so wrapped up in making music we forget about that other stuff. I signed a contract when I was 24. Somebody said, "You wanna make a record?" I said, "Yeah! Sure!" That's the way it is. But those days are over. We have to control our destiny. And I think with the computer you can do it. Brian Lynch has a great new project that I was a part of with ArtistShare and it's wonderful!

JG: Yeah!

PW: I loved taking part in that. I'm going to do a similar thing with my website.

JG: Oh good!

PW: I've got a bunch of patrons, fan club type thing. You pay a few extra bucks and get discounts and all that. And many of them are coming up with a thousand bucks to make a new quintet record.

JG: Beautiful!

PW: So anyway, I'm so proud of you. Whenever your name comes up, I say, that's my best student.

JG: Awww... man...

PW: And you played your ass off last night too baby!

JG: Well, god... I hardly know what to say to such incredibly overwhelming compliments. But, you know, standing on stage with you, I was writing about it yesterday. Just what it's like to stand next to you and play. And I remember what Benny Carter said to me at the cruise we did for the tribute to him in '94. He said to me that week, "You know, to me, in the whole history of the horn, Phil is *the* alto player. The way Phil plays the alto, that's the way the horn *should* be played! He is *the cat!*" Man, coming from Benny Carter!?

PW: Well, that's my hero. I heard from somebody that when my name came up with Benny that he said, "Phil's a great saxophone player but more importantly he's also a great musician!" And that's who Benny was—composer, arranger, lyricist. Spoke four or five languages. Understood food, wine... but a lot of the younger musicians... they don't realize that you gotta be a cultured human being. It's an art, man. At one point when it was entertainment people were dancing to it you could make a buck. It was still an art but wasn't called an art so much. It walked that peculiar tightrope between entertainment and art. Now it's relegated to an artistic fossil in some respects. It's taught in every university but there are no gigs! There's three gigs and you got 10,000 students. But I knew that when I was fourteen years old, that there'd have to be some sacrifices.

JG: Right.

PW: If you wanna play with the circus band or be in the pit, that's great! If you wanna be a working musician, that's great! But whenever I talk to cats, I talk to them artist to artist. If you wanna be an artist and do something about the world? Then you've got to learn something about where other people live. Spend some time in Europe, Japan... travel, learn about that, learn a bit of a language...

JG: These are things you told me. The stuff you learn in school is great, and you need that, but it's also what you're talking about.

PW: That's what the old cats told me.

JG: Charles McPherson said it to me too, "You've got to be a human being!"

PW: Yes.

JG: "You can't just live in the practice room."

PW: And you gotta keep fire in the belly too, forever! Any damn fool can sound great at twenty, thirty, or forty. But Benny Carter taught me, how you gonna sound at ninety? Now that's an accomplishment! See, I was the last generation that learned at the feet of the masters... like Art Blakey, Dizzy, Monk, Charlie Parker. I learned so much from just observing Bird, a few conversations and playing a couple jam sessions. I mean, Benny Carter to me is the personification of what an artist is all about. Never made any headlines, no scandals. Just quietly tilling the vines of his field and making the best wine, you know? Well-read, literate, knows painting, cinema, poetry...

JG: Yeah, such a brilliant guy.

PW: There's so much to it that they don't give you in school. You have to get it and sample it in life. When you're in Paris go to the Louvre, but also go the subway station and play in the street. Do it all man, do it all!

JG: I had a great trip in '85, took a semester off from college and traveled around Europe for seven weeks. I stayed with some people I knew and at some youth hostels.

PW: That's why you're who you are.

JG: It helped me immensely. I learned so much.

PW: You're tempered in the kiln of reality. Reality is not four guys jamming in a garage on "A Night in Tunisia," [Laughter] forever carrying a *Real Book* around. That whole thing bores the hell outta me. Be an artist, man! But be prepared... I mean, if you've got a choice between being a brain surgeon and an alto man, go over to brain surgery baby! [Laughter] I mean, I think it's only for guys who have no choice. When I was fourteen I had no choice. If you're entertaining a choice, it's not for you.

JG: I know.

PW: And having all this education is a false viewpoint. A university should reflect the needs of society. We don't need these many jazz musicians. We're makin' too many lawyers but they always get a gig. But saxophone players? There are 2,000 tenor players a year and three gigs.

BOTH: [Laughter]

JG: I know!

PW: And their idea of a standard is "Footprints." [Laughter] I say, name one George Gershwin tune and they go, George who? I mean, *really*!

JG: Right. They don't really know the history of the music... their understanding of jazz starts around 1960.

PW: Do you know Astor Piazzolla? Elis Regina? Jobim, Nuevo Flamenco... don't just be that myopic! I mean, when I went to Juilliard there was no jazz program, there were no jazz schools. So, I tried to catch up with all the classical cats. In my keyboard class I played "Dance of the Infidels" on the piano. I got put in third-year piano. The guys that played first violin couldn't play Come to Jesus in the key of C.

BOTH: [Laughter]

PW: They had to start at the beginning. Keyboard is important!

JG: Absolutely!

PW: But also of importance is family life! You know, the idea of raising a family. Be prepared, man. I mean, you're either not working, sitting on the couch, your old lady is working a part-time job and you're taking care of the kids and that's not good. Or you're on the road all the time and they never see you. This has to be dealt with. Plus, the scuffle of trying to make the rent this week, you know? I mean, you gotta have the fire in the belly to deal with that. If you have to, you go dig post holes like I did. You know? Without saying nobody understands me. We understand, dig the hole!

BOTH: [Laughter]

JG: I know what you mean, my kids are seven and five.

PW: But you knew this going in.

JG: Exactly. You know, it's funny, I never played with Art Blakey, but I talked to him a couple times. He came and sat next to me at the bar at Sweet Basil once. I was eighteen, and he said, "How you doin'!? You workin'?" I told him, no, not too much. He said, "The people who go to work every day and sit at a desk forty hours a week are the ones really payin' dues out here. We're blessed to be doing what we're doin', always remember that."

PW: Amen.

JG: He didn't know me from Adam. I didn't have my horn, nothin'! He just came up and just started talking to me, it was amazing!

PW: That's the tradition. The tribal, oral tradition of sharing with the cats, that's where I learned.

JG: Yeah! I love that!

PW: Dizzy and Art Blakey kidnapped me one time. I was working at Birdland. I was drinkin' too much. I was unhappy, and I was really maudlin. They threw me in a cab, Bu and Diz, took me out to Dizzy's house and sat me down and said, "Man, now what's your problem!?" I said, "Oh man, well, you know, I'm not getting anywhere, I'm playing for strippers and stuff." Dizzy said, "Well maybe if you cleaned up your act and got yourself together you might be somebody!" I said, [imitating himself half crying] "Well, do you think I can make it, man? I'm a white guy, and it's a Black art form." Dizzy said, "*Time out!* Wait a minute now, wait a minute!" Art was sitting there nodding his head, but Dizzy was carrying the ball. He said, "Charlie Parker didn't just write his music for Black people. He played it for the world. It's a gift to everybody in the world! And Phil, if you can hear it, you can have it! And remember, you can't steal a gift!"

BOTH: Wow! [Laughter]

PW: I said, "Do you think I can make it?" They said, "Yeah, clean up, get on the right path."

JG: Wow.

PW: Man, I mean, these two icons of American music, takin' time out, to straighten out this honkey maudlin fool!

JG: [Laughter]

PW: But I never forgot that, you know? All through our life, we're the only tribe that if somebody comes along that plays better than we do we don't try to discourage them, we try to help them. You know? Like when Cannonball came to town and Jackie McLean and I both said, "Oh *shit!*" But we *loved* him! What other business if somebody's threatening your position are you going to try to help him? Jazz is the last of the pure forms of work, art. But the tribal thing, the sharing, the camaraderie, the honesty between the players, that's… I think we're the last to do that in my book.

JG: You know, I just consider myself so lucky. My three musical fathers are you, Eddie Locke, and Eddie Chamblee. With Eddie Chamblee, I just walked in off the street on a Saturday afternoon at seventeen, my friend's mother took me there. I'd only been listening to the music for about a year. I hardly knew what to play. He said, "You come on up and play as much as you want." I played there almost every Saturday for seven years! With Jimmy Lewis who'd been in the Basie Band, and Belton Evans and Ernie Hayes that played with King Curtis.

PW: Not household names, but *heroes*!

JG: Yeah! These cats that really lived the music. And so many guys of that generation that had open arms to me. Eddie Locke…

PW: Well they heard what you were doing, and they could tell you could play. A pro can tell.

JG: I'm just so thankful. When I was sixteen and Jay Rodriguez played me *Song for Sisyphus* and *Music DuBois*, those records became my bible. I had this moment of realization, "This is why I play the saxophone!" I just knew. I've got to track this guy down, and I will bother him until he either physically accosts me or lets me come take a lesson with him. It took me about a year—I was studying with Caesar DiMauro, who you knew and we both know was great. But for about a year I just focused on trying to get a lesson with you. Where I was at in my life as a kid, I needed that more than I can put into words. All I can say is, thank God you finally kinda looked at me and threw your card down on the table and said, "Can ya play!? Well it doesn't matter, you gotta pay me anyway! Call my wife!"

BOTH: [Laughter]

JG: I went, "Hooray! He threw me out of the office at the Blue Note but he's gonna give me a lesson!"

PW: Yeah, we had some good ones too.

JG: And some of your comedic lines on tape from then that will go down in infamy. Like, "OK, play a chord with your right hand on the piano… *good*! Now play a note on the alto with your left hand that goes with that… *good*! OK, Now stick a broom up your ass and sweep the floor!"

BOTH: [Laughter]

JG: Or when you threw ESP at me. We were reading out of a book of Wayne Shorter's tunes, and I didn't know what altered dominant meant. It's full of altered dominant chords. Every time we got to E7 altered I just stopped playing and you put your face in my bell like—hello, anybody home down there!?

BOTH: [Laughter]

JG: The first two lessons were great. But the third lesson was the day after Budd Johnson had died, and I learned how much he meant to you. We spent about 24 hours together. It was incredible.

PW: We met on Quincy Jones' band, 1959, and we started talking about Tom Wolfe. We talked about some of his writing, I never forgot that. And we were close after that. Guys like that were so good to me. I just remembered Ernie Wilkins and Quincy Jones when Dizzy's band was in South America, they looked up Villa Lobos. I didn't know who Villa Lobos was, but they looked him up. They were, as writers, going to the source of where their being was. You gotta find where your source is, the fountain and the source that's gonna feed that. That's what we do every time we play or meet new players. And the tribe is very strong because of that, you know? The oral tradition. Not so much the book learning part. You can go to any school in America or now in the world and major in jazz. But it still happens on the bandstand, or in the van.

BOTH: [Laughter]

PW: In the early days with the quintet we drove everywhere! We never rehearsed but we talked it over. "Last night on that thing, Steve and Bill on that shout chorus let's try this." Man, that's musicianship. You just talk it over. Then the next night it's still there. That's the African part. It's not written down on paper. You gotta absorb it. Monk said, "You gotta hear it!"

I gotta go pack!

BOTH: [Laughter]

PW: I showed Bill Charlap how to pack. You fold it neatly, and then roll it up in a ball... and shove it in a bag!

BOTH: [Laughter]

PW: Ask him about that technique next time you see him!

JG: I will! Thanks so much Phil, for everything.

PW: I love you.

JG: I love you too.

Danny Bank
Queens NY – 1994

Danny Bank was one of the greatest instrumentalists I ever met or played with. In my opinion he was the greatest baritone saxophonist in terms of how he played the instrument, that I ever heard live. He got the greatest sound on the baritone I ever heard. He could play lead baritone, over an entire big band, in a way I've never heard before or since, while still sounding beautiful, without any strain or harshness to his sound. I remember a guest conductor at the American Jazz Orchestra saying that Danny was a continuation of the Harry Carney tradition (Duke Ellington's great baritone player), and I think he was as well.

Danny was a founding member of the New York Saxophone Quartet (a classical ensemble), and played with countless great jazz and classical musicians. He was an incredible doubler, playing all the single reeds and flutes masterfully, and—along with Milt Hinton and Ron Carter—was probably one of the most recorded musicians ever. He and Milt estimated that they were on over 9,000 records from their incredibly prolific studio days. Danny was also a rough customer when it came to chess! I was never very good at chess, but often enjoyed playing, and losing to Danny after our semi-regular sax quartet readings that we did with Loren Schoenberg and Chris Fagan at Danny's apartment in Queens in the '90s.

Danny was also a long-time member of the NBC Orchestra under Leopold Stokowski, usually playing bass clarinet. On occasion there would be guest conductors, and some very impressive ones at that. Stravinsky conducted some of his music with the orchestra for several broadcasts. One time, as they were rehearsing Stravinsky's most famous piece "The Rite of Spring," Danny decided he would talk to him, and ask him a question about his music.

"Maestro, I noticed that you notated this passage in a very complex time signature. I thought that perhaps there was a specific reason for this. It seems as though it could have been written and read in a more common time signature."

Stravinsky responded, "Yes! You are exactly right. I did do this purposely." He raised his index finger on his right hand, leaned in towards Danny and said animatedly, "I always want to keep my musicians on their toes!"

That really made me think. Stravinsky is one of the most important composers of the twentieth century. One of the greatest ever, really. And it was important to him to have his musicians on the edge of their seats to create the feeling he wanted. That was an important part of his "conception" in the realization of his music.

Billy Drummond & Ben Monder

Ottawa Airport – 2006

In the late '90s and early 2000s Billy Drummond invited me over to his house to play duo a few times. I'd met Billy at Augie's in the '80s and was blown away by him as a drummer and musician. To me he's one of the great drummers of the past few decades and someone who I've always been inspired by and admired. At one point when we were talking during those duo sessions at his house, he mentioned how much he loved Ben Monder's playing. I'd also met and played with Ben at Augie's in the '80s.

Ben is a true original, a modern stylist who's always been one of my favorite musicians to work with, and who came to wider prominence after being featured on David Bowie's final recording, *Blackstar*. I'd worked with each of them in a number of different contexts, and we'd played together some as well. Billy talking to me about Ben led to us talking about putting this group together as a trio. We played some gigs in New York City at the Jazz Standard, The Bar Next Door, and then at the Ottawa Jazz Festival. We also spent a day recording in 2005 at Red Rock Studios in Pennsylvania, and that came out on two different CDs. This talk was on the way back from the 2006 Ottawa Festival.

JG: I'm here at the airport with Ben Monder and Billy Drummond, two of my favorite musicians. We just had a really fun gig at the Ottawa Jazz Festival as a trio. Where are you from Ben?

BM: Westchester.

JG: How did you get into music?

BM: My dad got me into playing violin at an early age, as he was an avid hobbyist. So, I guess I started violin at eight or nine. Then after three or four years of that I realized that playing the violin was one of the more uncomfortable things a human being can do to themselves, so I switched to guitar.

JG: What part of Virginia are you from Billy?

BD: Newport News.

JG: When did you start playing?

BD: When I was four. Like Ben, my dad was a drummer, not professional, but a music lover with a great jazz record collection. Early on I was just kind of influenced by him because music was around the house. And I got turned on to Max Roach and Art Blakey and those kinda guys, early.

JG: When did you start playing jazz?

BD: Kinda from the start. Although when I was a kid I was in pop bands. We played music by bands that played soul music, like Kool and the Gang and that kind of stuff. But I was always fascinated with the kind of music that my dad listened to, which was the Blue Note kind of stuff—Jimmy Smith and Horace Silver. And I was into Buddy Rich because he was on TV. I still love him. But when you're a kid you're really drawn to the flash. And he was on TV!

BM: Did you ever see the clip of the seven-year-old kid doing a Buddy Rich solo on *The Tonight Show*?

BD: I have it, yeah.

JG: When was that?

BM: I think it was '92, Carson was still the host. The kid was seven. It was pretty ridiculous.

JG: I remember in the '80s into the early '90s, seeing Clark Terry on *The Tonight Show*. And John McLaughlin on that show playing "Cherokee," maybe about fifteen years ago. I saw Branford on *Letterman* playing "Giant Steps" too. You don't see that as much now unfortunately. Billy, we talked the other day traveling, about some of the gigs you did with Joe Henderson. Can you tell us about some of those gigs?

BD: Well, I didn't play with him that long or that often, but I had a few experiences with him. To me there's really nobody that's like that anymore. There are people that play great. But he was a one-of-a-kind type of a guy. The way he talked and carried himself. I mean, there's nobody like that. I imagine there's some personalities out here, but he was great. Playing with Sonny Rollins too was another amazing experience. I wish I could go back now and do a lot of those things again at this age after this amount of time out here on the international scene a little longer. I mean, playing with Horace Silver, that was very early in my time in New York. So, I had a different kind of headspace. You're younger, you just been in town a little while. You think differently now than you did then.

I wish I could come back to it with a different kind of attitude. In those instances, with Sonny and Horace especially, my attitude was I wanted it to be what I wanted it to be. As opposed to just coming in there and doing what I should have done with the utmost professionalism. But hindsight is twenty-twenty. It's hard to know that back then. It's like when you're a teenager, you think you know it all and have all the answers. But you don't know Jack! [Laughter]

JG: I know so many other musicians have said the same thing, including Max Roach, Rollins...

BD: Well, but you hear Max on those early records with Bird and think, man, you really had it together! Max was incredible! And Rollins... this guy was just... sometimes I look back on it and think, I can't believe what I was in the midst of, and didn't *really, really* know. Maybe if I'd really let it sink in it would have been too intimidating. You think about all that he's done, and all the saxophone that he's played. And all the music, and improvisation and all the creative things he's done. It's just incredible.

JG: Man, I think about hearing Rollins live... the one time I did. Or the many times I heard Joe Henderson live and was so blown away by it. I'm just glad I can talk to you about playing with those guys. The first time you hear the recordings you don't always get it, at least that was often true for me as a kid. But seeing them live!

BD: A lot of people are like that. I have students that never heard Billy Higgins live. And they don't get it. Because they feel like—he's not doing anything. And maybe that's the point. You know, you don't have to be rolling around the drums and playing in odd time signatures. Doing 5 against 6 against 7 or whatever, it doesn't have to be that all the time.

JG: Oh, he was incredible! His ride cymbal, his feel.

BD: His whole thing, man.

BM: Somehow the concept of feel has gotten lost in the shuffle. So you don't learn how to play with people.

BD: Yeah, it's all, "Look at *me*" stuff!

BM: 'Cause it's too elusive. You can't learn that in school. It's the most frustrating thing about coaching ensembles. They know the tools and the scales, but the feel…

JG: Well, Ben, speaking of feel, you work often with a special musician, a complete original on the drums and in terms of feel, and that's Paul Motian.

BM: Well he can actually play swing. Almost very traditional sounding. He just doesn't choose to do that all the time. He first called me in like 1992. And of course, I was barely doing anything. He says, "It's Paul Motian," I was like, yeah right. But it was a group with three guitars, which it is again, almost fifteen years later. The first gig was the night they thought there would be riots in New York, it was right after the LA riots. There was maybe twenty people there. I didn't hear from Paul for like another ten years. Somehow, I got back into the band.

Unfortunately, he doesn't travel anymore, so he plays the Vanguard once or twice a year, that's about it. But since his heart operation he doesn't get on a plane. Up until the age of seventy he flew as much as anybody could. He was such a road warrior. If he wants to be in semi-retirement he's earned it. He's also one of my favorite jazz composers. I don't think he gets enough credit for that. His tunes are just incredible, very personal.

BD: How does he write? Where does he write them at?

BM: The piano. He tinkers around at the piano. He claims to not know much about harmony. He just kind of plays around at the piano so in a way it's very pure. Then he comes up with chords he thinks might fit and it's always just great. Just *perfect*, these ideas that he has. And they're very distinct. You can always tell a Paul Motian song, his way of turning a melody.

BD: One of my favorite records is called *Les Voyage*, with Paul, J. F. Jenny-Clark, and Charles Brackeen—just a trio— bass, drums, and saxophone. It's one of the most beautiful records I've ever heard. It's just fantastic, on ECM in the '70s. They did two, one was with David Izenzon on bass and called *Dance*.

BM: Yeah, that's right.

BD: Man these are just… did that ever come out on CD? *Dance* did I think, and there's a couple cuts from *Voyage* on those ECM collections where the artists pick out their favorite cuts. If you ever get a chance you should get that. And Charles Brackeen, I don't know where he is now, but he's a fantastic saxophone player. He was married to Joanne Brackeen. He's fantastic. His soprano sound is incredible! He's got this kind of whimsical sound… who's that guy who the animals follow around?

JG: The Pied Piper?

ALL: [Laughter]

BD: Yeah! He's got that kind of whimsical sound that really just pulls you in. That's a great record. And Paul's tunes are incredible on there. "Folk Song for Rosie," have you ever played that with him Ben?

BM: No I haven't. He's got so many tunes.

BD: It's fantastic, man, I can't say enough about the record.

BM: One of my favorite records is *Psalm*, the quintet record with Billy Drewes and Lovano.

And later Jim Pepper played in the band after Drewes. There's a tune on there, this great tune, kind of like a rock tune, called "White Magic." I always thought the music they were into… you know, the music was so transportive. I was young and impressionable and it felt like they were into some heavy shamanistic stuff. And then a few months ago Paul was explaining how he got the title of the tune and he said it was inspired by a laundry truck.

ALL: [Laughter]

JG: Wow, this is great, this is a whole bunch of music I'd love to check out!

BM: All those quintet records are great. Also, all the trio records with Lovano and Frissell…

JG: Oh yeah, those I know, they're great.

BM: My favorite is the first one, *It Should've Happened a Long Time Ago.*

JG: Well, the one I know the best is *Monk in Motian,* I've always loved that record! And that brings us around to the genesis of this trio. I know we did some quartet gigs with Doug Weiss on bass. And Billy's always said to me, "Man I love Monder." Ben and I have known each other for twenty years, back in the Hillside days in Connecticut. And even before that at Augie's back in the '80s. And then recently hearing you and playing with you in Maria Schneider's band really inspired me to write some music for this context without bass. There's so much music that you create, it feels like an orchestra. All the colors you get into on the guitar, it's just amazing.

BM: [Long pause] Thanks Jon…

ALL: [Laughter]

JG: Would you care to expand on that?

BM: No, that's enough on that subject.

ALL: [Laughter]

JG: But those Paul Motian trio records was the first time I thought a group like this was possible.

BM: Man, I'll tell you, that first record kept me sane on the road with Jack McDuff. I was 23 or 24 at the time. I hadn't done a lot of playing with any masters. He pretty much had you think that his music was the entire universe. And all you do is, you're hanging around this guy that's telling you you're nothing, you don't deserve to play music. And I had my Walkman and this record, and thankfully there was also this other thing I could relate to. But the bright side is everything's easier after that. There are no tough tours after that.

JG: [Laughter] Well, I'm sure we've all had a few tough gigs like that, we can go into more detail some other time.

BM: That'll be when I interview you. You know, people want to know about Jon Gordon… the man.

JG: [Laughter] Well, I'm doing all kinds of journals and lectures on ArtistShare as I get started with this site… so, I'm way ahead of you! I'm so self-involved you wouldn't believe it! I've got that more than covered! For decades! I'm pretty sick and tired of myself! But it's a learning experience. I'm checking out other people's sites and you try to figure out what you might be able to contribute. But sitting and talking with guys like you is great. That's what inspires me and that I hope inspires other people. You guys have so much to offer, so thanks for doing this!

BD: You're welcome!

BM: Are we done?

JG: No, not quite. I think I'm going to put the mic over by the kid that's been screaming the whole time for a while longer.

BM: See? This is what traveling's all about.

JG: Thanks guys!

Art Blakey, Charles McPherson, & Igor Stravinsky

Art Blakey, to the audience at Sweet Basil, New York City 1985 – "The music comes straight from the creator, through the musicians, to you."

Charles McPherson, New York City 1987 – "At some point I realized that it wasn't just about Sonny Rollins' trio at the Vanguard, great as they were. As I sat there and watched them and listened to them, I realized that something else was going on. Something deeper... something was coming through them."

Igor Stravinsky – "I am the vessel through which Le Sacre Du Printemps passed."

Charles McPherson

Phone call, La Jolla Calif. to New York City – July 2019

JG: Hey Charles!

CM: Hey Jon!

JG: So you were talking about an upcoming recording at Rudy Van Gelder's. I just had a great experience there with Maureen and Don Sickler. I had too hard a reed when I started that day, so I went to an old soft reed at the last minute.

CM: Well, I think you made the right decision going with the softer reed, just between us, on saxophone stuff and alto in particular. I think the template should be how soft can the reed be and still play it instead of how hard the reed should be. How well can I play and project and everything else with a softer reed and then make your adjustments, with a very non-pressure embouchure. There's an art to playing that softer reed… with no pressure. There's no pressure, no squeeze on that at all, not at all. And put power through there without it closing up on you. No tension on that bottom jaw and lip at all. You might have an idea of a drawstring around the mouthpiece, a few dimples, like how Bird looked.

Stitt was a hell of a saxophone player. I remember I played a gig with him. He really did know what he was doing! He said, "Let me play your horn!" He was kind of arrogant. He played one note and said, "Oh no! That'll never do. Your setup is way too hard." He said, "Play mine." I played one note and he snatched the horn out of my mouth! He didn't wanna let me play more than one note! He said, "OK, that's enough. I just wanted to let you know how easy my setup is, and you think about that." I'd played with him earlier in the set. I never would've thought his reed would've been that soft playing next to him. He told me, "You have to learn how to play a softer reed, play in tune, and control it." Once you learn how to do that you do not have to have a 3 or 4 reed, just get that mouthpiece that does that for you. I couldn't believe how easy it was to play his setup. I bet that softer reed recorded better for you.

JG: Absolutely! I've always found that. And you get a quicker response too.

CM: When you're playing a gig live you want to project over the drummer and room noise. Plus, a lot tends to be critical with that. We're worried about being too wimpy. Tenor players are never worried about that. You have a good setup and put air through it on the tenor you'll get a sound. And it's easier to get a flow on the horn, it's less resistant. It's easier to connect their ideas, they don't have anything to worry about. They don't have to have an expensive New York Meyer, that's it.

JG: Well, when we met, you opened my eyes on so many levels, including about all this horn stuff. I met you on one of the first jazz gigs I ever did in the spring of 1984 when I was a senior in high school. You came into Augie's and came up and talked to me, and were so kind and supportive. Later, you stayed with me a couple times in Eddie Locke's building in '86 and '87. And those two times were like extended master classes on the saxophone, music, composition, life… I just learned so much! But I wanted to start by asking you about coming up in and around Detroit.

CM: OK, well this would be like early '50s. I was very fortunate. We moved from Joplin, Missouri in 1948 when I was nine. My mother already had relatives in Detroit. I just happened to live right down the street from Lonnie Hillyer [trumpeter], and he was my age. And I was also just down the street from The Blue Bird, a famous local jazz club. Now, at nine I'm not playing music at all. Lonnie wasn't either. We were just friends playing in the street. Later, at twelve, thirteen I got in the band in junior high school. I played trumpet first, and flugelhorn. I wanted to play saxophone but other kids were playing the other school saxophones so there were none available. Lonnie was playing trumpet. Then, about a year later, at thirteen, I got an alto. My mom bought one. But now I'm doing what I really want to do.

I still didn't really know a lot about jazz. We had a couple records, everyone did in those days. I started getting books on Johnny Hodges. I knew who he was because Duke Ellington was famous. So, I'd look at the books and listen to the records 'cause they were interesting to me. Then there was this tenor player who was like a year older than me who told me, "You oughta check out this cat Charlie Parker." I didn't know who he was, how he looked, anything. So, not long after that I was in a candy store with a jukebox, and I see Charlie Parker on there. And I said, "Oh! This is the guy he told me about." So I put the money in, and it was Charlie Parker playing "Tico Tico," I'll never forget it. And when I heard that, at thirteen or fourteen, it's like, "That's it!"

Now, I didn't know anything about ii-V-I's, harmony, nothing. I didn't know much about jazz at all. I knew nothing. But when I heard that, immediately it resonated with me. I understood it! To me it was like, man, whoever this guy is, this is it! So, then I started investigating, who is this guy? And then I found out he's just one member of a whole group of musicians that kinda play like this. And Bird is sorta the Dude. But you got Dizzy, Clifford Brown, people like Stan Getz, Chet Baker, Max Roach. You just got this whole group of young players that are playing that way. From that point on its like, OK, now I want to learn everything about everybody that plays this way! Now, at fourteen or fifteen, I find out that this club down the street from me features this kind of music, all the time! And man, when I found that out, I was like OK, I'm fifteen, so I can't go in. But I hang out outside and listen. Now here's who the house band was. Elvin Jones on drums!

JG: Wow.

CM: Pepper Adams on the baritone.

JG: Wow. [Laughter]

CM: Thad Jones on trumpet! Barry Harris on the piano.

JG: Wow.

CM: And there were different bass players, sometimes it was Paul [Chambers] or somebody else.

JG: Wow!

CM: And at one point, the owner let me come in with my parents, on a Sunday afternoon. I'm like fourteen or fifteen, and I could not believe it!

JG: Wow!

CM: And from that point on I'm there every night. People like Pepper Adams and Billy Mitchell worked there all the time. This was the period when Miles was living there for a couple years almost, and this was his home, at the Blue Bird. Miles was at the Blue Bird every night, playing with Pepper, and Elvin and Barry Harris. And this is the kind of stuff I heard at fourteen and fifteen.

JG: Wow!

CM: So I sat in one time around then. Lonnie too. I didn't know anything about the changes or anything, Lonnie was a little further along than me because he had a piano. But we sat in and could play the melody on "Star Eyes," good. But when it came to soloing it was total gibberish, I had not a clue what chord changes were. Barry said, "Do you know anything about changes?" I told him, "No." And he just happened to live around the corner, five minutes from me. So, there it is, down the block from the best club in town, five minutes from this great musician, especially for showing people harmony. He said, "You gotta know harmony, you can't play this kind of music without it." And he showed me, about dominant 7ths, etc. He kind of held open court at his house. He had a nice gig at night, a steady gig for the last three, four years then, the bread was cool. Barry would just practice all day. But his house was like open court for musicians in Detroit. So, Sonny Red, Roy Brooks, Paul Chambers, anybody coming through town, they'd come over to his house.

I remember hearing Sonny Rollins there… John Coltrane too. He was working with Miles. I remember he came in, he gets a chair, sits down near to Barry at the piano, and says to Barry, "OK, what are you working on these days? I'm tired of playing like I play. I'm getting so all I'm playing is licks. What are you doing? How are you thinking about harmony?" I remember Barry saying, "Well, I got a couple students." (I was like his main student, I was so close to him geographically.) "I'm trying to find a way to teach people as fast as possible so that they're playing as soon as possible. And I'm finding that this whole thing with ii-V-I… it's really V-I. And the ii is necessary for the piano player to play… and the bass player. But for horn players that are learning, they don't need to be as concerned about the minor ii chord and be more worried about the V, and that's where you're gonna go anyway. And the V has all the harmonic goodies with the upper extensions. So, instead of thinking A minor to D7 and worrying so much about A minor, know that it's there, know the notes that give you more of a minor sonority. But really be thinking more of the dominant of where you're going. And if you're playing two beat changes by the time you take a breath the ii chord is gone. So the V is it."

Trane seemed to be very impressed with that. And Barry said, "You can play 1 3 5 of the dominant over the ii chord, and that will sound exotic, and sound good." And if you listen to Trane, not long after that, he was doing that with modal stuff with Miles over a chord for sixteen bars. Classic Trane is playing the dominant chord over that minor 7. Now if you go to the piano right now and play an A minor in your left hand and the D7 in your right, as long as its above middle C, you'd get that sound we're talking about. It's a classic Trane sound. It's really playing the dominant 7 over the ii chord. You get this exotic sound, and the extension.

Trane was one of these guys who was a real seeker, and I think he took that from Barry and ran with it. He did that with lots of things and people and made it his own and found his own thing with it. And I heard Barry play "Countdown" and "Giant Steps" one time, and he played it *good*! And I don't hear people play those tunes like that. He's playing it like "I Got Rhythm" and just playin' the right shit. You don't have time to go to the 9th and 11th, it won't sound right. Guys are afraid to take a breath. If you do you only have one beat to outline something. Then you play it like an exercise or an etude and you end up doing the same shit over and over again. Trane didn't keep playing it live too much. Once you learn to do this, what's next? Ain't nowhere to go. Except, try holding notes to find common tones. And then playing with the rhythm.

Let's put it this way. If Sonny Rollins played "Countdown" or "Giant Steps," with his rhythmic schematic and the way he plays, then you'd hear what I'm talking about. It's different from Trane, and a thousand tenor players. And it's a lot harder to play it like that, syncopated, with the rhythm like that, starting phrases in different places, curve balls all over the place, breathing anywhere in the form, and remember where you are, hold a note here and there, then run. That's hard, man. I heard Barry play it that way. I said, "Man!"

But anyway, that was the musical climate in those days. You had Thad Jones, who played well! And Pepper Adams, played well! You can't beat Pepper! Frank Rosolino was there too. There's a bunch of people you never heard of that played good. Miles Davis when he first came to Detroit, he didn't show nobody nothing. In fact he got his ass kicked by Thad and people like that. And people like Frank Foster were there, before he joined Basie, he played *good*! Those early records with Art Farmer! He sounded like on the level of early Trane. So that environment, man… and in Detroit, in those days, to be considered hip… you'd have to not only be able to play and understand people like Bird… you'd have to understand people like Stravinsky and shit.

JG: Yeah!

CM: And Hindemith… Bach… you'd have to have that whole shit. And not only that, you'd have to be a person who could talk about philosophy, Nietzsche, and Schopenhauer. I'd listen to people like Barry and Pepper Adams and other people that'd come over, and sometimes the conversation wouldn't be about music at all. They'd talk about Cubism, painting, Edgar Varese, all this. It was like, Jesus Christ! So, to be considered hip, you'd need to know literature, Marc Chagall… you'd have to know all that to be what we'd call a *hip mother fucker*. And *then* you could walk around like you were hip.

JG: [Laughter]

CM: And if you couldn't play they'd run you off the bandstand. You couldn't be like "Well, this is what I feel!" If you were coming up there with nonsense they'd be like, "Look, you got to get with people your own age, shed, learn how to do the shit better, and then come back here. But get your ass offa the bandstand." And they would tell you that! And the audience would too! You would not be able to go in those places with some pretentious bullshit. They'd be like, "Get the fuck outta here!" And that's it, and you would, and you'd go back and do it.

JG: Everything you're saying about the environment and Detroit and Barry, Eddie Locke used to talk to me about that all the time. And everything you're saying about being not only a jazz musician, but to become a full human being, and an artist, that's what Phil Woods used to say. Whenever he got to be around the guys that he admired the most or the few times he was around Bird, those are the kinds of conversations he heard him have, and that had such an impact on him. He'd talk about art and languages.

CM: Yeah, he was a real intellectual. He wasn't just a saxophone player, there's a lot more than that. You know, Shelia Jordan is from Detroit. She told me that when she met Bird and those cats they all used to hang out at Gil Evans' pad in New York in the early '50s. Bird, Gerry Mulligan, Miles would all hang out there. She said Bird was the one that told them, "Don't just listen to music. Go to the art museum, learn how to identify great painters and know their works. Listen to Stravinsky and Hindemith." And another guy Bird talked about was Honegger. He said, "If you really wanna play this shit, you gotta learn about all art and how it connects." She said, "We didn't have a clue that this was how you're supposed to think of this stuff. We thought it was just music. But he knew this back in the '40s. And he's the one that told us, "You need to stretch your consciousness. You gonna play this music you gotta have something to play about. It ain't about playing chords, it's about playing life."

Another thing she said that was interesting too, about the whole racial thing in Detroit, is that it was a little bit different from other places. The Black and white musicians in Detroit that were into the new music, they were the kind of people that, "Man, if you can play this shit here, and you're interested in it, I don't give a fuck what color you are." You are a member of the exclusive fucking club. And they thought of each other that way. And kinda, the Detroit cats during that period they played with each other. There was no polarity, it wasn't that! Pepper Adams played with Elvin Jones. They were in the Army together. You had that going on in Detroit too. And Sheila told me that. She said the Detroit cats were different. And musically I notice this—the one thing the Detroit cats have, musically, is a strong sense of melodic logic! Philadelphia has its people, every city has its shit with great things. But the one thing Detroit had, is that them motherfuckers *really* knew how to put that shit together! And I'm talkin' about logic, where it's seamless connecting that shit up. Everybody from Tommy Flanagan to Pepper Adams to Barry Harris and everybody else. That's one thing you will notice that they really had some logic to their thing. And that's unique, that that's there.

JG: Wow, that's great insight. I remember something you told me as a teenager. "If you never heard Bird or Trane live, you never heard them. Because the records never captured them."

CM: That's exactly right. And Bird even more than Trane, because Trane lived longer and the technology got better. And you could play longer, you didn't have three minutes for a take in the modern era. And Trane lived longer in the modern period and more people got to hear him. But there's a whole slew of people that didn't get a chance to hear Bird, but you'll never know what that was like because the records do not show that. And that's why people will talk about Cannonball and I love Cannonball. But see, I'm old enough to have heard Bird and Cannonball in the same room. Not together, but playing in the same room. But see, I can hear that shit. Believe you me, there is no comparison. When I heard Cannonball, if you didn't get close and he wasn't in the mic you would not hear him that well. I could hear Bird a block before I got the gig. The difference in the attack and the power was like, the difference between a cat shooting bullets and a cat not doing that. Now see, that doesn't show up on records. You hear Bird in person, and you hear that it's like, "Oh, Jesus Christ!" And I heard Bird, and Sonny Stitt and Cannonball all in the same room. And believe you me, man, as wonderful as all them cats are, when I heard Charlie Parker, the rest of them cats are like children, talented children.

JG: Wow!

CM: I'm telling you. First of all, the sound, totally superior! The attack, the articulation, *totally* superior! And, I mean that's hard, because Cannonball could really articulate, and so could Sonny Stitt! Man, when Bird played that B natural on the horn, his attack on that, it would pop a glass, and you won't get that on the record. So, when you heard that, and the sound is that strong without him over blowing, he truly is who he is, no bullshit.

JG: Wow! I wanted to ask you briefly about working with Mingus.

CM: Well, I learned a lot from him, especially about writing. He was hard to play with some-times because he was getting older when I worked with him and I could tell some nights he didn't want to play and would find an excuse to stop the gig. His ballad writing in particular was really interesting to me, harmonically. I know he liked me a lot. He loved Charlie Parker and he loved Duke Ellington. He didn't like anybody else too much. Except him. He was very arrogant. But I did learn about writing. And I did learn how to project with him. And you had to burn with him. And he was an interesting character as a human being.

JG: Well, I can see a correlation with his music and your writing. I've always been such a fan of your writing. It sounds like you have a new project coming up of your music?

CM: It's ballet music that I wrote.

JG: Great! That music I haven't heard yet, I'd love to. But I grew up on "A Tear and a Smile," "Illusions in Blue," "Manhattan Nocturne," and those tunes of yours. I love your writing so much. I was so inspired by that music. And also, that Jazz Masters thing, you gotta be in that, man. In the history of the instrument, and the guys I've heard live in my life, I've never been more impacted by anybody on the alto than you. And you're such a special contributor on the alto, I so want you to be acknowledged that way.

CM: Well, thanks man. I've always said that you were one of the younger cats who understood the language, early on, early, when you were a kid, and I let you know that.

JG: Well, man, that meant a lot! And just the fact I got to hang out with you! I learned so much about so many things! You're the guy that taught me as much as anybody that this is an art form. You've got to deal with spirituality, art, it's not just the horn and ii-Vs. You're such a brilliant and deep person and some of the most impactful and inspiring conversations I had as a young person were with you. So, thanks so much Charles, for everything!

CM: Thanks Jon!

Jackie McLean, Milt Hinton, & Ben Riley

The S.S. Norway – 1991

In 1991, I subbed with the American Jazz Orchestra for a rehearsal one day with the band when they were preparing a concert at Cooper Union that honored Mel Lewis, that he also played on.

The sax section that day was Dick Oatts, Joe Lovano, Rich Perry, Danny Bank, and myself. We all traded on the famous Bill Holman arrangement of "Just Friends"—I was thrilled to play with those guys! Afterwards, Rich Perry told me he was recommending me to John Fedchock and Maria Schneider for a jazz cruise gig. One thing led to another, they called me for the gig, and my girlfriend Liz and I flew down to Miami a couple months later to do the cruise.

When we arrived at the airport in Miami, I saw Jackie McLean waiting at the baggage carousel and introduced myself. He couldn't have been nicer! But he told me he was a bit torn about the week, because he and his wife Dolly were "Invited Guests" of the cruise, as opposed to being hired. So, it was a nice vacation for them, but the implication was, "Hey, bring your horn, make the jam sessions!" Jackie told me, "Man, I'm sixty years old. I can't be comin' out here and playin' for free! So, I didn't bring my horn, but I really miss it!" I told him, "Well I'd be honored to lend you mine if you want to use it this week!" He said, "Really Jon? Well man, that's very kind of you. I have my mouthpiece with me, but if you could lend me the horn and neck strap that would be great." (So that's what we did at a couple of jam sessions that week, which was a thrill!) Then he said, "Hey, why don't you join my wife Dolly and I at dinner tonight?"

"Wow, thanks Mr. McLean, we'd be honored!"

What neither of us knew at the time was that wherever they sat you on that first night would be where you'd sit for the week. So, who joined us? Milt and Mona Hinton and Ben and Inez Riley—the stories!! I'd met and played a bit with Milt before that, and a bit after as well. To me, he was just a kind of archetype of what jazz musicians of his generation were like—kind, generous, supportive, and caring. He was an all-time great jazz bass player, and one of the most important photographers in jazz history as well, having documented decades of performances and recordings with some of the greatest jazz musicians who ever lived.

Earlier that year, Phil Woods and I had done some two-alto gigs at the Oslo Jazz Festival, and Milt came out and heard us. He told me, "Sounds beautiful man, keep doing what you're doin'." I'm sure he knew I was pretty nervous, and trying to stretch a little bit to try to play something personal next to Phil. Because trying to play straight ahead bebop alto standing next to Phil Woods made you feel kind of like—was this trip really necessary? But Milt was digging that and telling me, "Yeah man, go ahead" even though that wasn't the style and language you'd think of with him. But that impressed me so much.

Every time I talked with him or played with him it was just a joy. And his wife Mona was incredible! So many of those musicians of that generation that I knew had incredible wives that were amazingly supportive! It ain't easy dealing with a musician's schedule. But they did it and made sure their husbands were loved and cared for along the way. I remember one time, during a jam session that week, Mona brought me a glass of orange juice on the stage and said, "Bring this to Milt! And tell them to give him a break! They can't be workin' him like this on these 25-minute tunes with no break!"

Milt told us that his family was a part of the Great Migration around the start of the twentieth century, where many Black families moved North from the South in search of work. They'd moved from Vicksburg, Mississippi in 1919 and made Chicago their home. Milt had a paper route that he'd work with his dog, Sparky. But by 1923, at thirteen, he got a job as part of a bootlegging operation through his uncle. He said he'd go to work at around 4 or 5 a.m. He'd take his books, his violin, which he was studying, and do various jobs for his boss, including working on the deliveries to speakeasies before school from a truck. This was during Prohibition, of course. At one point while Milt was doing this job, King Oliver had a five-month residency at The Royal Gardens Theater, where they delivered to, and Louis Armstrong was in the band! Milt saw and heard the band in the wee hours from the window on several mornings when they made their deliveries. He also mentioned getting to meet and speak to Armstrong some.

At one point during this period, the truck that Milt worked on was in a terrible accident. Milt was seriously injured and was in danger of losing a finger. The guys he worked with rushed him to the hospital. But when they got there, the surgeon refused to operate on him and save his finger because he was Black. He said he'd just cut his finger off, but he wouldn't sew it back on to save it. According to Milt, the guys he was working with called Al Capone and let him know what was happening. And Milt said that Capone, or one of his lieutenants, showed up at the hospital and said, "You *operate!*" And he *did!* Milt told me, "If that hadn't happened, and they hadn't saved my finger, I would have never had a career as a musician."

He told us about playing for years with Cab Calloway's band. Often his wife Mona would join them on the road, as they went town to town by bus. And in certain towns, if there were no hotels that would allow Black people, they would have to go into town to find rooming houses in Black neighborhoods for the band members. Mona would often do this. Sometimes she'd go door to door at regular homes and explain their situation. She'd organize and negotiate the costs for rooms and meals for the band. Mona said that often people were happy just to help them and honored to host musicians that worked with the famous Cab Calloway.

Some years after that period, in 1952, there was a day that Milt was standing outside of the musician's union in New York. He'd always had plenty of work before. But Cab wasn't working very much anymore. It had just gotten too expensive to take a big band on the road. Milt's wife Mona also wasn't working. And he said, "It was the first time in my life that I didn't know how I was gonna pay my bills that next month."

He saw a guy walking down the street towards him, waving at him. He recognized him as a friendly comedian he'd worked with and accompanied many times in the previous years at bars and burlesque shows, mostly at dives just across the Hudson River in New Jersey. He told us, "Man, he was just the nicest guy! He loved the music and the musicians, and we really liked him too. He had some nights that he struggled when I knew and worked with him. In fact when I knew him he couldn't get arrested! But if he had a bad night, he'd come down off the stage, apologize to the band, and somebody'd put their arm around him and say, 'Aww man, that's alright. Come on, lemme buy you a beer!'" Well, that comedian was Jackie Gleason! So, Jackie sees Milt and says, "Hey Milt, how ya doin'? How's the family?" "Oh, hey Jackie. Yeah, well, we're doing OK. How about you?"

"Milt, you're not gonna believe it! I got this big show on CBS!" Milt was definitely surprised because he always remembered Jackie struggling with his act. But he figured he must have really gotten it together to get such a great gig. Jackie was becoming well known by this time, but not yet nearly as famous as he would soon become. His original show was on the Dumont network in 1950. "But how about you Milt? What's going on with you?"

He told him, "Well, to tell the truth, both Mona and I are out of work. Cab's not really working right now. It's the first time anything like this has happened to us. And I really don't know how we're gonna pay our bills."

Jackie said, "Wow. Really Milt? Well, listen, I'm on my way over to the studio right now to do a recording with Bobby Hackett." That recording may have been *Music for Lovers Only*, the first of ten gold records that Gleason produced starting at that time. "I can get you in the band! Where's your bass?"

Milt said, "Wow, well, I think I can get a bass from somebody here at the union. But can you really do that?"

Milt liked Jackie, but he was not the best comedian he'd worked with and was having trouble believing that even if he'd gotten a show on CBS that he had that kind of power.

Jackie said, "Sure! It's my record date. I can do anything I want!"

So, Milt went back into the union, got a bass, and they walked over to the CBS studio together.

Milt said, "I was the only Black person in the building. There wasn't a security guard, nothing. We get up to the studio, and Jackie walks into the middle of things and says loudly, 'Hey guys! This my friend Milt Hinton. He's one of the great jazz bass players in the world! He's gonna be in the band!'"

A guy walked over to them and spoke quietly to Jackie, but Milt could hear him.

He said, "Jackie, I wish I'd known about Milt a few weeks back. But we hired the band back then. The budget for a band is all used up."

Jackie said, loudly, "Hey, whatever you gotta do. He stays. He's in the band!"

The guy, who Milt figured was the contractor, said, "Jackie, honestly, this isn't about race or anything like that. But there's just no money. We already have a bass player."

Jackie said, "OK, now we got two."

The guy said, "Really, if there was anything I could do, I'd do it."

Then Jackie leaned in towards the guy and said, more quietly, but forcefully, "Either he stays, or *you go!*"

Milt said, "And just like that, I was in the band for the record date. As the result of that, I was one of the first Black musicians to work regularly in the studio scene in New York. So, it helped open up the door for all these other Black musicians that could now do theater, movies, and TV. But that was all thanks to Jackie Gleason!"

Jackie and Ben had loads of other stories, including several about Monk. Ben had played with Monk as his first call drummer for many years and had such great stories about those times!

Ben said, "I'd played with Thelonious in New York some. But the first time we had to go out of town to a gig together he told me to meet him at this car rental place. We were going to be driving to like, Boston or Philly or someplace. So, we meet there, we get the car, and I said to him, 'So, do you want to drive, or you want me to drive?'"

Thelonious said, "I'll drive." Ben thought, "OK, I can relax, one less thing to worry about."

They got in the car, Thelonious started the car, and tore out of the parking spot burning rubber!

Ben said, "Man, it felt like he was doing 90 before we got out of the parking lot! We careened out into the street and almost hit a car. There was a concrete divider in the road, and on the other side of the road there were two police cars. They saw all that and their lights and sirens went off. But they were in stop dead traffic and on the other side of that divide, and there was no shoulder for them to try to get to and to head towards an exit and try to track us down. I was screaming for my *life*! 'Stop the Car! Stop the Car!! Please! Stop the Car! I'll Drive! Please! Let Me Drive!'"

Monk said, "You wanna drive?"

"YES!" Ben shouted!

"You sure?" Monk asked.

"Yes! Please!"

"OK," Monk said.

"So, Thelonious slowed the car down, pulled over, and we switched seats, and I drove. And I resolved to myself, I'm *never* gonna let that happen again! And so, all the years I played with him, I *never* let him drive again!

So, one night, twelve years later, we're driving back to New York from an out of town gig someplace. It's the middle of the night. I look in my rear-view mirror. Monk and Nellie are asleep in the back seat. And I kind of chuckled to myself remembering how he drove that one time on my first road gig with him… and then it hit me! I'd seen Thelonious drive just fine on occasion in the years in between! But I never thought to let him drive again on a gig. So as long as he hired me, he had a driver as well as a drummer! And I realized, he'd played me! Damn! I was just stunned. Because he was crazy like a fox! Sometimes he'd play up his strangeness if it served him. And I was sure he'd done that on that first road gig with me. And it damn sure worked! But I still never let him drive again, even after realizing he'd probably set me up!"

I remember telling my girlfriend at the time, "We're getting more of an education than most jazz students get in four years at college!"

At the end of that week, as we were leaving the cruise, the cruise line tries to sell you photos from the week. There was a great one of the eight of us at our table! But it cost $20, and frankly, I just didn't have it. But I always regretted not buying it! I'd occasionally see Ben in later years. One time, Steve Wilson and I played the Savannah Jazz Festival, and Ben was kind enough to do the gig with us. He also had a septet for some years with guitar and no piano playing Monk's music, and I subbed on a few gigs. And I saw him later at the Monk competition a few times.

One year I played in the house band for the drum competition and Ben was one of the judges, so we saw each other there and had dinner together a couple nights. On a few occasions he'd tell me, "You know Jon, I got that photo of all of us from the cruise out on my coffee table in my living room. A friend of mine came over and saw that the other day and said, 'Hey Ben, that's a nice photo! There's you and Inez, the Hintons, Jackie and Dolly McLean… but hey, who's that little white guy?' I told him, 'Aw, he's nobody!'" And cracked both of us up! But he also liked to make fun of himself, and quickly added, "But it could be worse Jon… you could be like me and look like Grady from *Sanford and Son*!" And cracked us both up again! I heard him mention that a few times to make fun of himself. The first time he told me he had that photo and I said I didn't manage to buy a copy he made fun of me for not figuring out a way to get it. I asked him a couple times when he brought up the photo, "Hey Ben! Do you think I could come over and borrow and scan that photo sometime?" "Hmmm, we'll see Jon, we'll see…" and then laughed some more.

Bill Stewart

East 17th St., Manhattan, NY – 2008

Bill Stewart is one of the great drummers of the past thirty years or so, and I got to meet and play with him at Augie's in the mid to late '80s. With his Midwest vibe and red hair, he resembled a young Ron Howard. He was kind enough to make some gigs and recordings with me in the '90s and 2000s, and he's always amazing and inspiring to play with.

He played for a about a year in Maceo Parker's band, the famous saxophonist from James Brown's band. At one point during that time James was scheduled to do an HBO special, but he was in jail until 2 days before the show was scheduled. So, he hired Maceo's band to rehearse the day before and do the gig. Bill told me, "He had these movements he'd make to show me what he wanted me to do. Left elbow might be hi-hat, right might be bass drum. At one point, in between tunes he looked over at me and said, 'Hey, Drummer! Man, where you from?' Bill replied, 'Iowa.' James said, 'Iowa!! Ain't no funk there!' while the whole band cracked up."

JG: So, Bill Stewart! To me one of the most important jazz drummers, clearly, of this generation. So, as I was saying to you on the phone, there are just a lot of musicians that I want people to know more about, and you're certainly one of them. So, why don't we start in Iowa. That's where you grew up, right?

BS: Yeah.

JG: How did you get into music?

BS: I grew up in Des Moines, Iowa. I got into music because my parents were both musicians. My mother was a choir director. She directed choirs in schools and churches. My dad was a trombone player that played some jazz. He played quite a bit of jazz actually. But also, he taught music in schools. So, between the two of them and their record collection and everything I was exposed to a lot of music. It was never like work or anything. My parents were never like, "You're gonna do this" or something. I just enjoyed it. That's probably the reason you'd want to get into music, I think. My grandmother also taught piano in Des Moines. So even my father's family was musical.

JG: Was there any jazz in Iowa when you were there?

BS: Yeah, my dad played jazz, he had some gigs around town when I was younger. There was a big band that worked fairly regularly. There were some small group situations too. And then when I got into high school, I started working a little bit myself. There were a handful of musicians and a few gigs. Not too many. Not enough to allow too many to people pay their rent without doing something else.

JG: So you came to New York and studied at William Paterson College in New Jersey? Who did you study with?

BS: I studied with Eliot Zigmund for one year. Then I had lessons with Horace Arnold for two years. The other person I saw at that time was John Riley, who subbed there for a few lessons.

JG: I think that's around the time I got to know you and first hear you at Augie's, maybe around 1986 or '87 or so?

BS: Maybe by '87. Somewhere around there.

JG: There are certain musicians that I think of and remember as having this incredible growth spurt. Kevin Hays, a friend of ours, was one of them. I remember him sitting in and doing gigs with us back at Augie's and Mikell's. Do you remember Mikell's, on the Upper West Side?

BS: Yeah, sure.

JG: Well, he just seemed to me to have made this kind of precipitous jump in his growth during those gigs. And I noticed and remember the same kind of things with you when I heard you then. I remember in 1988 I played a gig with Red Rodney, and Garry Dial who'd gotten me on the gig as a sub said to me, "Man, have you heard Bill Stewart? He's really playing unbelievable!" And it was around that same time that I noticed how great you were playing, where it seemed to me like there was this incredible growth spurt in what you were doing. Maybe I just hadn't heard you as much before, but it sure did seem like you were growing like crazy. I remember around that time, you, Peter Bernstein, and Larry Goldings started a steady night at Augie's.

BS: Yeah, it was Thursdays.

JG: Right. I remember occasionally one of the three of you would call me to do the gig. I maybe did five or six with you guys, that I remember fondly. But I just remember it was amazing watching your growth at that time, individually and as a band. Did it feel that way to you, or do you attribute this perception I had to anything in particular or just working?

BS: Well, all along during that period I was just working on what I was doing. Before that and after that as well. I don't exactly know when the starting point was when you first heard me. But I was doing a lot of practicing during that time. I probably didn't have as many gigs when I first got there and was practicing a lot. But I was also starting soon after to get some experience on gigs in the New York area. So, I bet my experience of starting to play with musicians is probably what led to that growth you might say.

JG: So it was probably around that same time that I took a lesson with Joe Lovano, that was really amazing. He's somebody I always refer to as consistently inspired and inspiring. And then I remember seeing you not long after that actually working with him. I wondered if you could speak to that association a little bit.

BS: I first met Joe when he was teaching at William Patterson College. So I would have met him in '85 or '86. I think I first met him when he subbed for Eliot Zigmund for one lesson Eliot couldn't make. So, they decided, let's put all the drummers with a sax player, that sax player being Joe, who's also a drummer. So, I had a lesson with Joe, that's how I first met him. And it was just he and I playing duo. He'd stop and say a few things and we'd play another song... I still have a cassette of it somewhere.

JG: Wow...

BS: [Laughter] So, shortly thereafter I was on some gigs as a sideman with Joe. One or two different things. Soon after he called me for a gig or two. I worked with him some, with his bands. And then soon after that with John Scofield.

JG: And how did you meet John?

BS: At least partially through Joe. I think maybe a few people had recommended me to John, along with Joe, but Joe had for sure. But John had also produced a record of Joe's, *Landmarks*.

JG: That's right, yeah, that's a great record.

BS: Thanks. I think when John heard me on *Landmarks*, that might have been when he called me. Also, Mark Johnson was on that record, so he ended up hiring us both to play with him during that time.

JG: Was that when you did the record *Meant to Be*?

BS: Yeah.

JG: Oh, I love that record! That cut "Chariots!" But the whole record is great.

BS: Yeah, thanks.

JG: Also the record, *What We Do*.

BS: Yeah, that was after Mark, and Dennis Irwin was on that.

JG: I remember hearing that band at Sweet Basil in the early '90s.

BS: Yep!

JG: And I just thought that was some of the best, most important music happening at that time.

BS: That was fun.

JG: I remember the first time I heard "Camp Out."

BS: You got the reference. [Laughter] Is that "Hello Muddah?"

JG: And sure enough it was!

BS: [Laughter]

JG: You also did something kind of funny like that on your first Blue Note record.

BS: "Mayberry."

JG: [Laughter] For those of you that don't know what Bill looks like, he does resemble a young Ron Howard a bit. Now, what was your first recording as a leader?

BS: I did a record for a Japanese label called Jazz City, and it was called *Think Before You Think*. I think it was done in August of '89.

JG: I remember playing that tune the record is named for. Is it a 10 bar tune?

BS: A 9 bar tune.

JG: Well that's something I've always admired about you, you're a great composer. That tune we recorded of yours...

BS: "Soul's Harbor."

JG: The writing on the two Blue Note records—the one with Steve Wilson and Seamus, and the one with Lovano and Eddie Henderson.

BS: Exactly.

JG: Both of which I think are great. I think Tim Hagans told me that you, him, and Kevin Hays got signed to Blue Note at around the same time. But somehow the company policy just devolved and those records didn't get the kind of attention they should have.

BS: Yeah. Soon they became out of print as well.

JG: Yeah, well that was the thing. And Bob Belden had mentioned that to me as well, how record companies seem to sometimes do that for no reason.

BS: Yeah.

JG: After the Jazz City record, was there anything before the Blue Note records?

BS: No, so there was about a six-year break.

JG: And then you did the record with you, Larry Goldings, and Kevin Hays. I remember you called me to ask me for the number of a producer we knew.

BS: Oh, yeah!

JG: We had done something together not too long before that. So, I called up the producer and said, "Man, Bill Stewart is amazing. You gotta go with this." And he said, "Well, what kind of band is that? He's got two piano players and no bass. Why would he want to do that? No one's ever done that before!" And I just thought, OK, he may not get this.

BS: Yeah!

JG: So who did you sell that to?

BS: I didn't sell it. I ended it up putting it out myself. I sell it on the CD Baby website. Sometimes if I have them with me I sell them on gigs as well. So that CD went that route. But, you know, with the state of the record companies and everything, everyone can make and put out their own CDs. I mean, at least you have control of what you're doing, and the music ends up being what you want it to be, rather than a compromise.

JG: Yeah, well I know in my own process, I've had takes get lost, takes released I didn't want released, had a cover put on that I didn't want. In fact, that's one of the CDs you're on with me, *Currents*. I lovingly refer to the look of the cover as Scottish Moods…

BS: I know that one! [Laughter]

JG: Waves crashing on rocks through a rainbow filter.

BS: That almost looks like one of those things that looks like it's moving as you're looking at it. What do you call those things?

JG: Yes! [Laughter]

BS: You know what I mean.

JG: Yeah, you need 3D glasses to get the whole experience.

BS: [Laughter] Yeah, it's a little bizarre.

JG: Well, I had another photo I wanted to use. The producer said no, sent me a series of other options, and that's the one I said, "Please don't use that one, the others are OK." But it is nice with the whole ArtistShare thing. I get to do this, present my music the way I want. It can be more expensive than having a label, but that's not what presenting our music is about anyway.

BS: Yeah, especially if you're making money as a sideman, teaching and the other ways that musicians make a living.

JG: The most important thing is to get your music out there.

BS: Yeah, that way you grow as an artist.

JG: By the way, I just have a question. [I go to the piano and play the start of a tune of Bill's that I remember.] That tune just came back to me as we were talking, what's the name of that?

BS: That's the bottom part of a tune of mine called "Space Acres."

JG: Yes! That's another great tune of yours. I think people know you as an incredible drummer, but they may not know as much about your writing and I think that's an important contribution of yours as well.

BS: I'm trying to get it out there.

JG: How did you get into composition?

BS: I was interested in composition as soon as when I first started college at the University of Northern Iowa. I took a composition course there. Not in jazz composition, it was more like an introduction to twentieth century classical composition. So, we listened to things of that sort. There was some analysis, but also everyone was writing in the class. Then when I got to William Patterson College I had some composition lessons with Dave Samuels. It took me a while to get something happening with it. My first record there was only one original. But then by '95 when I did *Snide Remarks* for Blue Note, at that point I was getting right to it. So, I guess somewhere in the early to mid '90s I started to do more composing. And I play the piano at home, you know.

JG: Do you sit at the piano as part of your practicing every day?

BS: I do play the piano quite a bit when I'm home. Sometimes I think I play the piano more than the drums when I'm home. And when I compose I usually do it at the piano.

JG: I've worked at the piano over the years, taken some lessons in school and after. What I find for myself and tell students, and I'd like to get your opinion on this, is that when I sit at the piano, I feel almost no judgment. I feel free of the ego issues around, how do I sound, how is my reed?

BS: [Laughter]

JG: I have no expectations of myself. I just think it's nice to sit at an instrument where it's just about music, and you don't have to prove anything to yourself. And there's a freedom there that I think can be helpful with composing.

BS: I think I would agree with that.

JG: I think sometimes that can happen to musicians who pick up instruments later in life. I've known a few people that I've seen do that. Steve Davis played bass at one point. Mike Karn went from tenor to bass. John Webber was doing gigs on guitar for a while.

BS: Guitar! Yeah, I remember that.

JG: I remember hearing a few guys do that and being really impressed. I can't imagine doing that and gigging on another instrument. But I can definitely see something freeing about that.

BS: I think so too.

JG: What kinds of projects are you doing these days? I know you have a long-term association with the Kevin Hays Trio with Doug Weiss.

BS: Yeah, I do that from time to time. I still do a fair amount of stuff with John Scofield. Usually with a trio with Steve Swallow these days. We did a fair amount of that this year. There's a record that came out of that group on Blue Note a couple years ago. I've probably done more of that than anything else recently.

JG: The trio with Larry Goldings and Peter Bernstein?

BS: Yeah, that was usually known as the Larry Goldings Trio. We haven't done that as much because Larry moved to L.A. and he's been playing with James Taylor. So, we really haven't played all that much. However, after a long layoff, we did play a week at the Vanguard in January. That was great. It was really fun. We hope to do that again, and maybe do some other stuff too. I am doing a little tour coming up in about ten days with my own trio with Larry Goldings and Kevin Hays. We're doing eight gigs in nine days.

JG: Where will you be?

BS: There are three gigs in Spain—San Miguel, Barcelona, and Madrid. Then we play Nice, Freiburg, Germany, Paris for two nights at the Sunside, and then Lausanne, Switzerland.

JG: Great. I wanted to ask you, didn't you do a duo record with Bill Carrothers a few years back?

BS: Yeah, when did we do that? I think that was in the late '90s.

JG: Was that sort of a joint project or was it more Bill's?

BS: It came out as Bill's thing. It was on Bill's label. I don't know what was going on with my recording contract with Blue Note at that point. It was kind of over I think. It was released as Bill's record, but it was really a duo.

JG: Yeah, it seemed like you guys had a really great connection musically.

BS: Yeah! Yeah. I really enjoy playing with Bill. He's got a lot of interesting harmonic things happening, as well as really good rhythmic ears.

JG: Yeah, he seemed conceptually to have something that works great with your music. I've never heard him live, just on recordings. Is he on both your Blue Note records?

BS: He is, on the two Blue Note records.

JG: Well Bill, I really appreciate you coming by. I look forward to playing again. I think we played at Fat Cat, was it like last year in the spring, in May?

BS: That sounds about right.

JG: Well, I look forward to the next time. It's always an honor and a pleasure to get to do it.

BS: Always a pleasure for me.

JG: Thanks, man.

BS: Thank you.

Art Blakey

Sweet Basil, New York City – 1985

In late 1985 or early 1986 I was sitting at the bar at Sweet Basil. I was eighteen or nineteen. Art Blakey and the Jazz Messengers were playing and I tried to hear them whenever I could. I sometimes could get in for free down there because I often sat in on the Saturday brunch gig with Eddie Chamblee, so the folks that worked the door and the bar knew me there. At the end of the first set, as I was taking a sip of my club soda and cranberry juice, somebody hit me on my back, very hard! I was kind of in shock! I put down my drink, looked behind me, and there was Art Blakey! He loudly said, "Hey man! You workin'?!" I'd never met or spoken to him before, and had no idea why he was talking to me. I didn't even have my horn with me, and couldn't figure out how he knew I was a player. I just said, "Uh, no sir." He responded, "Well, just remember, we're lucky to be doin' what we're doin'. We're blessed. Those people going to work five days, forty hours a week, sittin' at a desk, they're the ones that are really payin' dues. Don't ever forget that!" He sat and talked to me for several minutes and I was really honored and thrilled to talk to him. And he was very kind and supportive. But I could not for the life of me figure out why he'd decided to talk to me or how he knew I was a jazz musician!

About twenty years later I told that story to Don Sickler, on a train coming back from Washington, DC. He cracked up! He said, "I know how he knew you! He was at my office a couple times next to the studio where you used to rehearse with the Young Sounds. (That was a group of young musicians put together by the union that Don ran. We rehearsed at Don's place on 28th St.) There were a lot of great musicians that I'd have in the office while you rehearsed, and I'd just part the blinds enough for us to see you guys playing without you seeing us." I laughed and said, "Well that finally solves that! But it's good we didn't know who was in there watching us, we would've freaked out!" Don agreed!

Jon-Erik Kellso
Japan - 2013

JG: So Jon-Erik Kellso, four years ago was the first time we met and I got to know your playing. And one of the things that I love about what we do is that we move in these different circles. I think the first thing I'm going to put in this book is a talk I had with Jay McShann. He introduced me to the concept of being a stylist. He told me, "Man, in my day, guys were stylists." And when I think of you, Jon, I think of that word.

JK: Oh, wow. I take that as a high compliment. Thank you.

JG: Absolutely. I think you really understand that concept in a deep way.

JK: Well, you could definitely call me an old school kind of a guy and player. And I guess that was more common among the old school players. To me the highest compliment a player can get is to have an instantly recognizable sound and style. And I think of that as one of the real high achievements of a jazz musician or any kind of musician. We all know of guys that you can recognize in two or five notes, or one note. Even if they're not your favorite player you've got to give it up to them. That means they've got a style, are a stylist, have a recognizable voice. And that's always been a goal for me. But, just to be considered among the stylists, that's a nice compliment.

JG: Well, I mean it. Listening to you play on the plunger on "Sometimes I'm Happy," I feel, that's you! Talk about how you got into music.

JK: I started playing trumpet at age ten. I had told my dad I wanted to play trumpet. And he said, "Oh really? I used to play trumpet. Lemme go find it."

JG: Any reason you wanted to play the trumpet?

JK: I always related to melodies, even as a little kid. I would pick up on melodies. My mom told me I was humming to myself in the crib.

BOTH: [Laughter].

JK: So I related to melodies, and the trumpet seemed like the ultimate melody instrument. In fourth grade when it was time to decide whether to join the school band or not, the teachers from my elementary school and junior high, who both became important figures in my early years, demonstrated all the different instruments between the two of them. I already liked the trumpet. But after that demonstration it just solidified my feeling. I liked that it just had three valves, knowing I wasn't the most coordinated kid. Little did I know, it is not as easy as it looks.

JG: Now, this was just outside of Detroit?

JK: Exactly. I grew up in a suburb of Detroit called Allen Park, just ten minutes outside of the city limits. When I picked up the trumpet I also started finding my parent's 78 rpm old swing era records. My dad was born in 1923, my mom 1927. My dad was more of a jazz guy, and his heroes were Harry James and Bunny Berigan. He'd played trumpet in high school, playing gigs around Detroit, doing swing and polka gigs.

We had a record player that would play these records and I couldn't believe it—I was enthralled!

These records got me really interested in swing music. I was listening to Benny Goodman and Harry James. My dad saw that and said, "Oh, well Harry James was my favorite. But if you like that, you might like Bunny Berigan." And he pulled out some Bunny Berigan 78s, and I liked those even more. He also had some Count Basie and Duke, and I was totally enthralled with that. I heard Cootie Williams and I was in love. I thought, "A trumpet could do that? Wow!"

Around the same time, I met one of my life-long friends, Mike Karoub. Not Mike Carubia who you might know from New York City, but Mike Karoub from Michigan. His father was the junior high band director. Mike played classical cello very young and picked up bass in fourth grade.

JG: It's great that you had family and friends that supported your love of music.

JK: I was very lucky. Anybody that was into jazz of any kind was thought of as weird in our generation, growing up in the '60s, '70s, and '80s. I was definitely considered weird for running around at age ten, eleven, twelve with my buddy Mike, riding our bikes around looking for antique stores with more 78s, because we had an insatiable appetite for hot music. Most of my dad's 78 collection disappeared when he went into World War II right out of high school. He was in the submarine service, which very few people survived. They didn't tell him that going into it, of course. He said two out of the one hundred that signed up when he did made it through the war. The Japanese were very good at sinking U.S. subs. He was very lucky, because they put him at Midway, repairing engines and submarines. He never went out on a mission on a submarine, though he kept asking to. But they told him, "No, you're too valuable to lose because you can repair the engines." My dad's mother sold or gave away his entire jazz collection of 78s during World War II because she didn't think he was going to come back. Not to mention his baseball cards. Ugh!

JG: Wow!

JK: Yeah, right?

JG: That's brutal!

JK : Yeah it was pretty brutal. And he was pretty pissed, because he had a great jazz collection. By the time I came around, there weren't many records in his collection, and it was stuff he'd picked up once he got back. He was forty when I was born.

JG: How old are you?

JK: I'm 49, born in '64. So, Karoub and I actually put together a big band when we were still in elementary school! We had ringers from junior high in the band because we didn't have enough kids from our elementary school that could play this music. We were playing improvised solos, or trying to anyway.

JG: Where'd you get the music!?

JK: Well, his dad, Carl Karoub, was (and still is) a fine French horn player along with being the band director at our junior high. He knew how to get arrangements. And our local music store actually had these books of arrangements. So, we got these two different books for big band with about 20–25 good arrangements in them!

JG: Wow!

JK: Yeah, we saved up our paper route money to do this.

JG: This is the most inspiring pre-junior high school jazz story I've ever heard!

BOTH: [Laughter]

JK: We were pretty weird, I gotta say. And we put this band together. This wasn't school band, this was outside of that. I remember going to the local music store, and finding these Octavo size arrangements. You know that small paper, smaller than 8X10. I remember finding King Porter Stomp, but an arrangement from the '20s that was more like the way the composer Jelly Roll Morton played the tune. It didn't sound anything like the version that we do now. Fletcher Henderson kind of re-wrote the song. Like that whole intro is not in the original tune. I still have some of these arrangements that I bought when I was in elementary school. So, we started getting way into swing music. We were playing "Song of India," "In the Mood," "7:20 in the Books," we had an arrangement of Bob Haggart's "South Rampart Street Parade."

JG: So you were a pro around the time you went to junior high school?

JK: I wouldn't say that. But I did have my first paying gig when I was in seventh grade.

JG: With that big band?

JK: It was a band within the band, eight pieces.

JG: That's incredible! So then, when you got to junior high, was there a music program there, or did they assimilate you into what they were doing, or... ?

JK: Yes, my buddy's father was the junior high band director. When I was in elementary school, he invited me to play with them. When I was in junior high I did some playing with the high school band. When I was in high school I played with the Henry Ford Community College summer jazz program, which was great, as well as the all-city Detroit honors band, and the Michigan Youth Symphony.

JG: Well, those experiences of getting to play with older guys are great.

JK: For sure. I also always had good private teachers thanks to my parents and Carl Karoub, who made great recommendations. I mean, he's a serious French horn player. He played some with the Detroit Symphony, was in the Windsor Symphony, among others. He'd been in the Korean War and played in the stage band during that time, doing '50s third stream big band stuff with French horns. Like Kenton and some of the John Lewis stuff. So, he had an appreciation for jazz as a classical guy.

JG: When did you get introduced to the jazz scene in Detroit?

JK: It kind of started to happen in junior high. This kid group that I talked about, once we got to junior high we decided to pare it down to the 6–8 piece combo.

Karoub amazingly created a steady summer gig for us during our junior high years, playing at Greenfield Village in Dearborn, part of the Henry Ford Museum. They have this back-in-time kind of outdoor park there. There was all this old Edison and Ford stuff, and a nice park with a gazebo. He just went there and said, "I think it would be great if you hired my Dixieland band to play on your gazebo during the summer months." They agreed, auditioned us, and gave us this six day a week, five hour a day gig! We actually had timecards, so we'd punch in in the morning and go to work. They made period costumes for us. Around that time we also started finding more ways to get out to hear the local jazz groups, of various styles, including trad jazz, and introduce ourselves, and sometimes sit in. That was very inspiring.

JG: So you've been a working jazz musician for almost forty years! That's incredible!

JK: That summer gig we had led to becoming part of the professional Detroit jazz scene. We'd need subs and would call the best guys we knew, not just kids in the school band. I needed subs sometimes because I was going off to summer music camp at Blue Lake and Interlochen. I loved both of those experiences, too, by the way.

JG: Who were some of the people there that helped you?

JK: I went to Blue Lake for classical music. The conductor there was Vaclav Nelhybel, a European composer. He was kicking our asses, in a most welcome way. I was in junior high but was doing the high school program.

JG: Were you ever a high note chops guy?

JK: Not really. I was studying classically, in addition to trying to learn jazz. When I went there I was playing in the symphonic band. It's a two-week thing. The first week you audition to see what your chair will be. The second week you get to challenge to move higher. I got nervous and didn't do well at the first audition and was seated next to last out of twenty trumpets. But I was also the youngest guy in the section. But when I challenged next, I did well and I ended up sitting second.

JG: Were there some teachers there that helped you?

JK: I can't remember the names of the trumpet teachers at Blue Lake, but they were terrific. During high school, I went to Interlochen All-State summer jazz camp. Barton Polat was, and is, a great jazz piano player, and a really good teacher and was really inspirational and generous with his time. I remember he gave me a transcription of Roy Eldridge's solo on "Body and Soul." Another guy named Greg Nielsen who's now in Florida, a trombone player, was really inspirational and a great teacher. They both were really cool with me, very encouraging as all my teachers were, fortunately. I studied privately in high school with Gordon Smith who was in the Detroit Symphony. So, I was trying to study classical as well as jazz.

JG: Did you do some classical gigs as well?

JK: Yeah. In junior high I played in the International Youth Symphony, with kids from Detroit and Windsor over the border in Canada, from elementary school to college age. The conductor of the Windsor Symphony, Matti Holli, was the conductor of this thing, and it was really great. We were playing some serious music. I got to play the "Firebird Suite" in the Michigan Youth Symphony which I joined in high school. That was a University of Michigan based thing.

I got myself into some challenging things. The way I got into the International Youth Symphony was funny. I had just tagged along to see my buddy Mike Karoub playing cello with them. His dad said, "Why don't you bring your trumpet, just in case." The second trumpet player didn't show up. Carl was playing in the Windsor Symphony, so he knew the conductor, and said, "My student has his trumpet, he could fill in…" I had never even heard of transposing before. There was a college kid on principal trumpet, I was in seventh grade. I'm seeing parts that say C trumpet, E♭ trumpet…

JG: Wow.

JK: And I only had a B♭ trumpet. I had never even heard of the others.

JG: How'd you do?

JK: Well, they had patience with me. The first trumpet player asked, "Do you know about intervals?" I said, "Yeah," So he said, "Well, play everything up a whole step." I asked him, "If it looks like it's in B♭, play it in C?" "Yeah." So, I guess I managed to get through the rehearsal without sucking too bad, because they asked me to join the group.

JG: Wow, that's amazing.

JK: I can't imagine that I did well enough, but I was bursting with enthusiasm. I was just getting to the level of studying that music. Then I started doing community orchestra gigs, brass quintets. Also, in high school I started meeting more of the great jazz guys in town. In the traditional scene it might be names that not too many folks would know. There was a trumpet player, Nate Panicacci. Tom Saunders had more of a national or international presence. He was a friend of Wild Bill Davison, a great traditional cornet player.

JG: You mentioned the other day that he was a big influence on you.

JK: Yeah, he became one of my favorites early on. Wild Bill played a lot with Eddie Condon and I found him on those records. He just played such a great, hot lead, a very distinct lead. I realized that was a great way to play the lead in an improvised multiple horn ensemble, because he would leave the right spaces. He would kind of be the traffic cop and play the lead but leave enough space so the other guys had room to do their thing too.

JG: Were there any contexts back then that you played with tuba instead of bass?

JK: Sure. What most people think of as "Dixieland," most people now prefer the term traditional jazz, especially if it's the more righteous stuff. In that style in the early days there were bands with guitar and bass, tuba and banjo, even bass sax, like what Vince Giordano does.

JG: I think I subbed on that band once twenty years ago.

JK: Was that at the Old Red Blazer Two?

JG: Yes.

JK: I think I was there and that was the first time we met actually.

JG: Wow! The reason I asked about the Detroit scene when you were coming up is that I played in Detroit a couple times in recent years, and I met a lot of people that still are very much about Detroit jazz history, and asked me, "Did you ever hear...?" Who were some of those people for you as you came up?

JK: Yes, Detroit had, and still has, a great scene. Marcus Belgrave was always one of my favorites and still is, and a big inspiration. He was always really cool with younger players that showed interest and was very encouraging. He ended up having me sit in with him way before I thought I was ready to. I just went to soak it up, which I did a lot. But I was also forward enough to introduce myself. He may have come and said hi, too. He probably saw me with this spark in my eye and adulation and this unbridled enthusiasm. And he always loved to encourage guys, and he still does. After a while, he said, "I want to hear you play."

JG: I love that about those guys and that generation.

JK: They were so welcoming, there was no pretense.

JG: The first guy that did that for me was Eddie Chamblee at Sweet Basil, at the Saturday brunch gig. Benny Powell, Percy France, Harold Ousley, and Don Light would often play as well. Don was a trumpet player and his son wrote the show *Sideman*. Speaking of the Detroit scene, another one of my musical fathers, Eddie Locke, when I interviewed him said, one of the most important things you can have to learn is to be in the right environment that nurtures whatever you're passionate about. And he certainly had that during his time in Detroit. And it sounds like you did too.

JK: I felt that, definitely, between the teachers, school bands and private teachers I had. And thankfully we had enough wherewithal with my buddies to get outside of school and find and make playing opportunities. All of that meant so much. And also, just having a passion for finding records, listening to stuff, reading about it. I wanted to learn this language and be able to speak it fluently.

Back in junior high school when we had that six day a week gig we had some arrangements, but not that many. But we bought more as we made money. We also figured what tunes we all knew and could blow on. So, we started learning and adding tunes and making tapes for each other, or lending each other the sheet music. We just didn't want to be bored with ourselves and play the same twelve, fifteen tunes over and over. So we learned a bunch of stuff that way. And then we'd go hear guys and take note of the tunes they played, like Tom Saunders, who had a great band, and he'd sometimes bring in guests like his friend Wild Bill Davison. They played at a nice club in a hotel, with dining and dancing. They had a steady six nights a week for years! We'd go and hear them and get inspired by that. We'd meet players, and introduce ourselves, make friends.

JG: You told me that by college you were driving all around the Detroit area working all kinds of gigs. Did you go to college in the area?

JK: I did, Wayne State in Detroit.

JG: Still doing all kinds of gigs, classical?

JK: All kinds. In a city like Detroit, to be a full-time professional musician you had to know more than one style, and the more the better. Some cities encourage that. New York tends to pigeonhole you into what you're best at because there are so many great musicians. You don't want to hire a traditional jazz guy who plays a little bebop to play the Vanguard band.

JG: So, who were the teachers at Wayne State that helped you?

JK: Matt Michaels was head of the program, a great guy, piano player, and arranger. Dennis Tini, also a pianist, Dave Van De Pitte, who had done a lot of the arranging for Motown. I went on and off for six years and eventually just decided to take the classes I wanted to take and play in the ensembles, rather than go for a degree. I had a music theory teacher that was cool, Szentkiralyi, an Eastern European guy. He knew one of the famous composers from that part of the world.

JG: Kodaly?

JK: Maybe Kodaly. Yeah, I think it was. 'Cause he wasn't old enough to know Bartok.

JG: Well, I thought of Kodaly, because he had this project with Bartok, where they studied, recorded and notated some of the local folk music that was happening out in the countryside in Eastern Europe in the early twentieth century.

JK: Where was Bartok from?

JG: Hungary, I think.

JK: Yeah, I think he was Hungarian. I'm going to Hungary next year for the first time in March. I'm gonna bring my own group to the Bohem Ragtime and Jazz Festival.

JG: Good for you! With who?

JK: My group, the Ear Regulars—Scott Robinson, Matt Munisteri, and Greg Cohen.

JG: Well, I love the stuff that you've posted with that group, with John Allred, Harry Allen, James Chirillo, and some of my favorite players.

JK: You gotta come down and play!

JG: I'd love to! Also, I love the stuff that Lincoln Center has been posting of you talking about and demonstrating the trumpet in traditional music.

JK: I was really honored to be asked by Jazz at Lincoln Center to do that. It was a surprise.

JG: Did you know the folks over there?

JK: I'm getting to know folks over there, including Wynton. They call that educational series the Jazz Academy. The first one I did was with Evan Christopher, a clarinetist buddy of mine who lives in New Orleans. He can really play the old traditional Creole style. But he'll play an Ornette tune, and then a Johnny Dodds tune, brings it all into the present tense. I think of New Orleans as a home away from home. I go there every year and have for twenty plus years. I love New Orleans and its music. I went for the first time when I was a senior in high school, instead of going to Florida for a senior trip. Me and some buddies drove down there from Michigan over the Christmas break.

JG: How long did that take?

JK: Twenty-something hours. [Laughter] We took turns driving a 1967 Buick Deuce and a Quarter (225), with the windows icing up on the inside of the windows—we had to scrape ice off the *inside* of the windshield while we were still up north. But that was our first trip down there, and we had a blast getting a taste for the city.

JG: Do you have friends or family down there, or regular gigs you do?

JK: Yeah, I'm always doing gigs when I go down there. Tom Saunders, the tuba and bass playing nephew of cornetist Tom Saunders, is one of the guys I'd visit. In 1989 he suggested to the Dukes of Dixieland that they give me a call. Their trumpet player, Frank Trapani, had died. They were busy six nights a week on Bourbon St. so they called me and asked me to audition with them. Oddly enough, that same month in 1989 I got a call to audition with Vince Giordano. Crazy timing. I'd never been called to go and audition with some band ever. I already loved New Orleans, and I'd also been to New York a couple of times, once when I was twelve visiting relatives, and once in college.

JG: Man, New York City in 1976. I remember that. It was a different thing. Just the vibe of the city. The trains, those giant cabs with the jump seats in the back.

JK : I was there for two weeks and fell in love, as I figured I would. So, I get a call to go play a week with the Dukes of Dixieland in New Orleans, and then I get a call from Vince Giordano to go play with the Nighthawks in New York City for a week, to basically audition for each other, to see if I liked it, if they liked me, and if it was a good fit.

JG: Were the auditions at the same time?

JK: Well, it was two separate weeks in August of '89. It was really crazy. They didn't overlap, thankfully. And I ended up getting offered both gigs. I had a tough choice to make. I loved both New York and New Orleans. I had been a fan of the Dukes of Dixieland and had their records. I'd heard of Vince, and had read about him in the New Yorker. I was fascinated, that here's this guy doing music from the '20s and '30s that I loved on a high level. I hadn't heard him but I'd read about him.

So I went to both places with an open mind and just tried to do my best and not suck. It was fun, I liked the guys, I had fun with both things. But I decided to go with Vince and the Nighthawks. The Dukes were going through a transition at the time. A lot of the guys had been in the band for a long time. They were all great players, but they were basically just going through the motions. We'd walk into the room at the club playing "A Closer Walk with Thee" every set, every night, same exact time. And then we'd walk out playing "When the Saints." It was like a real commercial kind of approach.

JG: So you were going to have to do the same thing sixteen or eighteen times a week.

JK: Yes. And also, you were locked into playing with that band every night. With the Nighthawks I realized I'd be getting into the New York scene, where I'd be playing one, two nights steady per week, and some private parties. And he was already introducing me to other bandleaders during that week I tried out. I realized that I was meeting all kinds of musicians, and the possibilities just seemed endless, which they still do. That's one of the things that I love about New York City. So that appealed to me and is why I decided to go with that. But I had these friends in New Orleans, like Tom Saunders the tuba player, and just decided to keep going back when I could to visit and play.

If it'd been a while since I'd been there I would call and say, "Hey, I'm looking to get away for a week or so," and he'd say, "Come on down! We can give you as many gigs as you want!" There was just a crapload of gigs there and there still are. Especially for a trumpet player that knows the repertoire. You'd think there'd be endless trumpet players in New Orleans that can do that. There are some, but they definitely have room for a guy like me, to have them throw me some gigs and not put anybody outta work.

JG: The first time I went to New Orleans was 1995, and the thing that struck me as I walked down Bourbon St. was, most of it was rock, blues, and zydeco.

JK: It's even worse now. I think there's one place on Bourbon St. that has trad jazz.

JG: In '99, 2000, and later I went back and played at a couple clubs that faced Armstrong Park, The Funky Butt and Donna's.

JK: Yeah! That's South Rampart St.

JG: Yeah, and getting to know New Orleans some from the mid '90s to the early 2000s was really cool. So along with your associations there, Ken Peplowski and others like the Ear Regulars, Vince is still a very important association for you after almost 25 years.

JK: Oh yeah. Coming up on 25 years. I joined the band and was very happy with my decision. I love the music, I always have. It was a great kick in the butt in the right way for me to delve further and deeper into the music of the '20s and '30s and this early classic jazz. But to play that gig you really have to dig your heels in and know it to do it as well as it needs to be.

JG: And you've been doing the music from *Boardwalk Empire* with Vince. It's at an interesting point now where it's dealing with some important issues around the beginnings of the music in the '20s, and I've been a big fan of the show. And you guys are the right band to deal with that music in a deep and sincere way.

JK: Well, I've always been very thankful for that gig. It's what got me into the New York scene. And I've met so many players from the band and subs and all that. And then this gig comes along, and it's really fun. They give us a lot of work, which is a godsend. I don't know what other band could do everything they're asking us to do as well as the Nighthawks. It may sound vain, but it's really true, 'cause there just aren't any other bands I know of that cover that era as specifically and in-depth as Vince does. Especially when you're talking about the library that Vince has to offer to dig into. When they call on two days' notice, and they want some obscure song from 1923, Vince has it and knows where it is. There aren't too many people who can pull that off. But he can do it and he knows who to call with his band or extra singers to do it.

JG: Who are the regular members?

JK: Mike Ponella on lead trumpet, and myself on second. Jim Fryer on trombone. Dan Block on lead alto, Dan Levinson plays alto, and Mark Lopeman plays tenor. They all double on clarinet, soprano, and baritone sax. Lopie's been in the band a long time. Peter Yarin is on piano, Ken Salvo plays banjo and guitar. It used to be Arnie Kinsella on drums for many years, but now it's Joe Saylor. And Andy Stein on violin.

JG: And Vince plays bass sax, tuba, and bass, right?

JK: Yes.

JG: That's a real trad thing that once you get into swing and bebop you don't see as much, those different doubles. I met a lot of guys in Scandinavia like that, that play trumpet, guitar, banjo, and bass, or with low instruments, like Vince. One other guy I know that does that is Howard Johnson, who plays baritone sax and tuba.

JK: He plays cornet, too.

JG: I didn't know that.

JK: He likes to play cornet and pennywhistle. In the '20s it was common for guys to double on bass and tuba. They'd start off on one and pick up the other depending on what gigs they got offered.

JG: I remember feeling two years ago that there was this rasp to your sound that reminded me of Roy Eldridge, and I mentioned it to you at one point. But then it occurred to me, you know the history of the trumpet as well we anyone I know. Do you attribute that to Roy, or maybe someone else?

JK: Oh, well, Roy is certainly one of my favorites, and I definitely associate that use of the growl or raspy tonal effect with him, along with guys like Wild Bill Davison and Hot Lips Page. Of course, that effect was used on other instruments, like clarinetist Edmond Hall, or tenor saxophonist Ben Webster.

JG: I was listening to that live "Stealin' Apples" performance that you played for me the other day. And I remember thinking, I don't remember hearing that much rasp and growl to Benny's sound. But Ken Peplowski said, "You hear it more on the live stuff."

JK: And also more on the earlier stuff, before he was a leader, in the '20s.

JG: Hmm. I remember when I was nineteen at an American Jazz Orchestra rehearsal, the guest conductor for an Ellington concert said, "Danny Bank is the continuation of the Harry Carney tradition. And Bill Easley is the continuation of the Jimmy Hamilton tradition." And you do hear that in those guys. When I think of your playing, I think of it as the continuation of Pops, Rex Stewart, Bix, Roy Eldridge, Ziggy Elman, all these different players. I love to hear history in people's playing. And I think that sometimes young players don't get this, it doesn't limit you, it just gives more depth to what you do.

JK: Well, thanks, those are some of my top favorites, for sure. And that's certainly another goal of mine. The reason I was going back and giving all this background to all this stuff, is that I always looked at this as learning a language.

JG: I love that analogy.

JK: And also learning different dialects. It seems to me that that's a great way to look at it. The best way to learn a language is to immerse yourself in it. I was lucky enough to find ways to do just that.

JG: So you're doing the Nighthawks, the Ear Inn…

JK: The two regulars on that gig are me and Matt Munisteri on guitar. And we just mix it up with all the great horn and bass players in New York and have a lot of fun with that. Scott Robinson and John Allred are two of our favorite horn players. On bass we'll often have Pat O'Leary, Neal Miner, Joel Forbes, Tal Ronen, Frank Tate, among others. I don't mean to slight anybody because we have a lot of favorites. We also sometimes put players in from out of town.

JG: That's the great thing about New York. All the different musicians that you meet and work with. The different things you learn and experience with all of them.

JK: I'm learning a lot as a leader, what combinations work well together. And with a drum-mer-less group, you want to be especially attentive to that. A lot of subtleties of chemistry you learn about with tempos. We like to explore and emphasize ensemble improvisation, which is something that's always been a love of mine. It comes from New Orleans music and all the things that came out of that. We don't just play New Orleans style music there. We mix it up and call standards, swing, mainstream, bebop, whatever. I just kind of go with the flow of what the personnel is that day. We have fun with that rather than boxing ourselves into a specific repertoire or style.

JG: I'm really glad that you mentioned that element of group improv. It's something I like to have in my music, and clearly that comes from the New Orleans tradition.

JK: It even goes further back, but in our context that's where it took shape. I'm sure Bach was a hell of an improviser, as was Mozart. And in Latin and Cuban music, there's tons of improvisation and ensemble call and response.

JG: Somehow along the way it's sad that improvisation got lost in classical music.

JK: I know! It's a shame, right?

JG: Yeah. But maybe we're finding a path back with it. The twentieth century in jazz is clearly a classic period in the history of all music, and it's not going anywhere. They're not playing it on the radio very much. But they're not playing Bach much either. That doesn't mean it's not great.

JK: Vince likes comparing early jazz to classical music, and says, "why not play it that way?" Meaning orchestrated. He takes that approach and takes it to a place that most bands don't, with transcriptions of not only the original arrangements but sometimes the solos, too. To present it as classical American music in a way.

JG: Certainly Wynton has done that to an extent.

JK: Wynton's brought a lot of attention to Pops and Duke and made it cool to like them in a way that I don't think it was before. When I went to jazz school, teachers and students were saying things like, 'Well, swing was pop music, not jazz." And they certainly wrote off traditional jazz and would say, "Oh Dixieland, that's some cornball stuff, that's not jazz." Until it was time where they needed a band to play a school function and then they'd ask you to put together a Dixieland band from the jazz band.

JG: I think another thing that may have helped bring appreciation for that period of the music was the swing dance resurgence. I remember playing the Cat Club in the late '80s. Now it's at Swing 46 and other places around the city.

JK: There's still a swing dance scene around.

JG: There's something lasting about the period in the music that we're talking about. Brilliant playing and writing that's going to be valid fifty years from now.

JK: It's something to be proud of as part of American history. Black American music, jazz, however you want to describe it. It's something to be proud of. And not just proud of, but aware of.

JG : It's been great talking, thanks for coming over.

JK: Thanks for inviting me.

JG: Here's to more hanging and playing in the future.

JK -Yes, please!

Eddie Chamblee on Paul Gonsalves

Sweet Basil, New York City – 1985

One day when I was at Sweet Basil sitting in with Eddie Chamblee, I said to him on a break, "Hey Eddie! I've been listening to Paul Gonsalves lately. Wow, he's amazing! So free! Like Lockjaw (Eddie's favorite tenor player, Eddie Lockjaw Davis), but different."

Eddie raised his right index finger and slowly said, "One word… CON–CEP–TION!" Man, did that one word ever nail it! Both those guys had such a *personal concept*. A totally original approach to the horn and lines that they played!

Jimmy Lewis on Eddie Lockjaw Davis

Sweet Basil, New York City – 1986

The regular bassist on Eddie Chamblee's band at Sweet Basil in the '80s into the '90s was Jimmy Lewis. Jimmy was a brilliant player, had an amazing quarter note, was a great soloist, and was dubbed by Phil Schaap (a New York City DJ and jazz historian), as "The Dorian Gray of Jazz." At 75 he could have easily passed for 35 or 40! He'd played with lots of great people, including Alberta Hunter, King Curtis, The Modern Jazz Quartet, and Galt MacDermot among others, and played a good bit with Count Basie in the 1950s. Jimmy was very kind to me and would often talk to me about different musicians he'd played with.

I remember one time he said, "Man… when Lockjaw came on Basie's band with us… we didn't know *what* in the *world* that man was playin'!… but over time, we came to see how great and special he was!"

Chuck Redd
Japan - 2013

JG: So, Chuck Redd, a great drummer and vibraphonist that I've worked with over the years with Ken Peplowski, Loren Schoenberg, The Smithsonian Jazz Orchestra and others... man, it's funny... I saw you in New York so many times that I thought you lived there. But you were just telling me that you're from Silver Spring, Maryland and have always kept a place in the DC area.

CR: I've had an interesting relationship with New York. Other musicians thought I was living there because I played and hung out there so much. I've always been willing to be there quite a bit for gigs over the years. One of the reasons we go to a place like that is to try to get a steady gig with somebody. But I'd already landed the gig with Charlie Byrd when I was 21 in the early '80s, from knowing him and getting to play in DC with him some. I began spending time in New York because so many of my heroes were there and I wanted to be around the music being played there.

JG: And like so many people that I've known over the years, if you can let your gigs take you to New York and live elsewhere, you can generally have a higher standard of living for a lot less money. Red Holloway told me, "Man, all the years I lived in New York I never had any money! As soon as I moved I was able to get ahead more, 'cause it was so damn expensive to live there!"

CR: That was definitely part of the decision for me. And one great thing about my gig with the Charlie Byrd Trio was that I played most of the major venues in New York with him—the Vanguard, the Blue Note, the Village Gate, Fat Tuesday's, and Carnegie Hall a few times.

JG: Well, we're on tour in Japan, and you were starting to tell me some great stories at breakfast this morning.

CR: Man, let me tell you about the first time I met Dizzy and Mickey Roker. Both of those guys went on to become really important to me and were so good to me, such great people and teachers. I went to hear Dizzy at the Showboat which was five minutes from our home in Silver Spring! This reincarnation of this club was only there in the DC area for two years, but it was so great. I heard so much great music there, including Count Basie, Joe Williams, Buddy Rich, Al and Zoot, Milt Jackson, Monty Alexander, Yusef Lateef, and Joao Gilberto. I was just starting to go out and hear live jazz. I'd been naturally checking out the drummers. In the weeks before hearing Dizzy, I'd heard Eddie Gladden with Dexter, Freddie Waits with Billy Taylor, and Bill Goodwin with Phil Woods.

JG: Oh man! That must have been when they made that live record at the Showboat! That's one of the greatest Phil records!

CR: Man, I was there every night for that, and it was incredible to hear it live! My brother Robert is a wonderful piano player. He and I had gotten to be friendly with the owner of the club, and he'd always have a table for us right down front and he'd set up a couple of orange juices for us. We were just teenagers and couldn't really drink. But we just wanted to hear the music, and it was so great that they embraced us like that. Well, I was hearing different drummers and how they played. But I noticed that Mickey was, for the most part, just playing time—*burning* time! But not reacting to the soloists as much as Bill Goodwin or Eddie Gladden had.

So I walked up to Dizzy and Mickey one night after a set and said, "Hi Mr. Roker, I'm a drummer and I have a question. I've been listening to different drummers here in the past few weeks. It seems like some of them do a lot of reacting to the soloists. I noticed you didn't do as much of that and I was just wondering why?" Mickey, still standing right next to Dizzy said, loud enough for him to hear, "Well, maybe they're not playing anything worth responding to!" And both he and Dizzy just fell out and laughed their asses off! I was laughing too but was also a bit confused by the comment at first. But over time I learned that this was like Mickey, to bring out the humor in the situation and rib even Dizzy.

JG: And Mickey's from Philly, right? So he wasn't that far away from you.

CR: Oh yeah, I got to hear him and hang with him a lot, and he was a great guy and a big influence. I'd drive to Philly and hear Mickey at Ortlieb's, the wonderful little club there. He would always ask me to sit in. Well, a few years after that first time meeting those guys, when I was 22, I was on the road with Charlie Byrd, Barney Kessel, and Herb Ellis and we were in a hotel in Geneva. Herb introduced me to Dizzy and said, "Hey Dizzy, this is our drummer, Chuck Redd. And he's a *real* drummer!" Man, that meant the world to me!

And Dizzy was so nice to me, he said, "Oh yeah? Man, why don't you come up to my room and hang out?" He just loved drummers, rhythms, and teaching. So, we spent hours talking, listening to music. And he showed me his unique, percussive hand clapping thing… I started with my hands too far apart so he told me, "No, keep them close." He also showed me the right way to play Salt Peanuts—snare, snare bass, snare snare, bass—and he started teaching me to sing the rhythm of "The Shim Sham Shimmy," a dance rhythm. We were up until after 2 a.m. talking and hanging out and it was one of those hotels with very thin walls. The next day, the musicians in his band were mad at us, because Dizzy would get so loud and happy when I got one of the things he was teaching me, shouting, "Yeah man! That's it!" The next day we started up again and he kept showing me all this stuff. He just *loved* to teach!

A few months later, he was playing at the Blues Alley in DC, and when I said hi to Dizzy after the gig he recognized me right away and gave me a big hug. Then the club owner mentioned to Dizzy, "You know, Chuck's mom is an amazing cook!" Dizzy said, "Really? Let's go over for dinner!" I just started to laugh thinking he was joking. But Dizzy just kept looking at me with this questioning look, so I finally said, "Uh, sure Dizzy! I'll call my mom." Can you imagine that phone call? "Hey Mom, can Dizzy Gillespie and his drummer Bernard Purdie come over for dinner tomorrow night?"

So, the next day they came for dinner and we had a ball. And every year that he played in DC after that he'd come to our house for dinner, usually Thanksgiving. One time he brought a lady that he'd known from his childhood. She was a very dignified, beautiful, elegant woman, and would only refer to Dizzy as John. You could see that they'd been friends for life. But she had no interest in Dizzy as this iconic jazz musician—she was more interested in "John" having proper manners, which he didn't of course—so that was pretty funny.

In 1990, Dizzy actually called me for a gig one time to go with him and his band to Namibia, for their independence celebration. What a thrill that was! His quintet was playing a lot of straight eighth things in those days, so I wasn't sure if I was the right guy for the gig. But Dizzy had heard me play and just the fact that Dizzy believed in me enough to call me gave me the confidence to know to be myself there, and I had a blast. Ed Cherry, John Lee, and the other guys were very kind to me and we're still friends.

When I arrived in Namibia after flying for the better part of two days, I got to my room and went into that deep sleep that can hit you after that kind of traveling. The next morning, I was dreaming about a Cuban rhythm, only to realize when I woke up that it was being banged out on my door. I jumped up, opened the door and there stood Dizzy! He was in red plaid pants, with a cigar in his mouth. He gave me a big hug, welcomed me to Africa. He then told me he'd seen my drums in the corner of the lobby the night before and thought they may not be safe there, so he'd brought them to his room and now had brought them down on the elevator to me. What a beautiful person he was.

JG: Tell me about your association with Charlie Byrd. It seems like he was clearly a really important guy for you in your formative years.

CR: Oh yeah, absolutely. Charlie was my steady gig for years. He introduced me to the scene, recording and touring, and was so important to me on every level. He was really almost like a second father to me. Gail and I even named our son Charlie in honor of him. He'd been one of just a couple guys in his platoon to survive a battle in a foxhole in World War II. So, he didn't sweat the small stuff you know? He had a great perspective on life.

At some point, pretty early on in my association with Charlie Byrd, he introduced me to Barney Kessel and Herb Ellis, who I eventually did a lot of playing with in various contexts. Those three guys also had a group together called the Great Guitars that I worked with for years.

JG: Man, I got to meet and play some with Barney Kessel at the Oslo Jazz Fest when I was 22. He was incredible! The people he'd played with! Pops, Bird, Pres, Lady Day… but he talked a lot to me about staying modern and stretching, and told me he was very into Bill Evans too. But the thing about him that blew me away was the kind of blues player he was! Damn! Joe Williams came and sat in with us a couple nights, and you know Joe was gonna call a blues! Barney just transformed…

CR: Yeah, it was like he was possessed!

JG: Yeah! That's just what I thought!

CR: He would even drool sometimes when he played the blues…

JG: The eyelids would flutter. And he went from being this sophisticated all-time great jazz guitarist, to like, this down-home country boy that played the *shit* out of the blues!

CR: Oh man, he was incredible. I got very close with him and we played together so much. Early on, at one point, after playing with him for a few months I got the feeling that he wasn't happy with something. I had the sense that he wanted to say something to me. Finally, he came out and said, "You know, you sound like a guy that's very comfortable. You sound very comfortable with how you're playing and what you're doing, and the work you're getting. You've got a girlfriend now, a steady gig with Charlie, enough money… and it all sounds very safe and comfortable, like you have no worries. But I want to you to always play like you need the gig to eat!"

I really thought about was he saying to me, and took it to heart, and really put a lot more urgency in my playing. And the next time I played with him, a month or so later, at one point he turned to me on the bandstand and said, "This is the best the time has ever felt." A lot of the musicians I was playing with at the time in the DC area made similar comments around that time. My playing and professional life got a lot better from that one talk with Barney. I'll never forget going to see him after he had his stroke in 1992. He was living in a modest house out in San Diego, and I went out to visit him and his wife Phyllis. I was sitting in his living room. He walked into the room with a cane, making sure to show me that he could walk in on his power. And the first thing he said was, "I'm *still* right here," as he pointed to his chest.

JG: Wow.

CR: I actually broke down at one point, because it was so hard to see him like that. And of course, after all the work he'd done, all the years in the studios, he'd lost a lot to his previous marriages. But Phyllis was great and took great care of him. And you know, he'd said something to me at one point before the stroke that was quite prophetic, "It's important to think about what you would do if you couldn't play—how you'd deal with it." And I've thought about that many times since. How would you make a contribution, and still express yourself, if you were still here, as he'd said to me, but that was taken from you?

I had a grand mal seizure in 1999 and that definitely made me think about that. It made me much more health conscious, and I really got into running. I think that's really helped me a lot in terms of my overall health in the years since. At one point, back in the '80s, a few years into playing with Charlie, I got a call from Monty Alexander about a gig. I had gotten to know him from seeing him on the road with Charlie Byrd, Herb Ellis, and Barney Kessel. Monty called me for a couple of concerts in Florida. The band was Monty, Herb Ellis, and Ray Brown, with special guests Joe Wilder and John Frigo.

JG: Wow!

CR: But it was at the same time that I had a week booked with Charlie. So I called Charlie and asked him if I could get out of a couple nights, and he said, "No." Charlie was so important to me and had been like a father to me and given me so much work. I think he felt a little bit like he wanted me to be loyal to him and I could understand that of course. But I also knew in my heart that I had to take this opportunity to play with Ray Brown. So, I called Charlie again and expressed how important this was to me, and he finally said OK. I didn't want to lose my gig with him, or have him feel disrespected. But this was such an important thing for me.

When I got down to Florida, Monty called a rehearsal. He started playing "I'll Remember April." Now, Ray is known for playing very on top of the beat—that whole thing with the Oscar Peterson trio. You know, really going for it, with that driving feel to the time. And I made sure I listened to every quarter note and was right with him. But by doing that it got faster every chorus. And by the end it had gotten really fast, so fast that we were struggling to keep it together. But Herb looked to me after we finished and said, "Don't get up there with him, just play the way you play." So, when I really laid it down and played with more conviction when we played some more, Herb leaned back and says, "That's it *baby, fuck* him!" I realized Herb knew from years of playing with him and being such a great time player himself, that what he was telling me is that the way to make it feel good and not take off was to rein him in a bit and balance that forward drive and motion. So, I knew I couldn't play with him that way I just had, and that I had to play my feel against his to make it work. That next tune we played was some of the best feeling music I've ever played. Of course, Ray was unphased by what Herb had said because they were like brothers.

JG: How do you get into playing the vibes?

CR: Well, a teacher named Debrah Lowery played me a Milt Jackson record in high school and I just had to go find a set of vibes and make those sounds! My father bought me a set of vibes around that time that are still my practice set at my house today. I felt I had a natural feeling for the vibes when I first started playing the instrument in high school, and I immediately got good feedback about my vibes playing.

Later, over a period of years, I felt like maybe I was overthinking it too much and felt like I'd lost some of that natural feel and ability for the instrument that I had when I first began. But eventually, I think I came to a good healthy place mentally with it, where I wasn't judging myself as much as I'd been for some years, and think I got back to the natural thing that led me to the instrument. I got the Kenny Werner book *Effortless Mastery* and a few others that really helped me.

JG: Have you made any records as a leader?

CR: Yes, I've made six as a leader. I've really enjoyed those experiences and I'm pretty happy with all of my records. Thanks to Arbors Records and others, I've been able to hire some of my favorite musicians to record with me (on vibes), including some of the greatest drummers! Jeff Hamilton, Mickey Roker, Victor Lewis, and Lewis Nash have been on my recordings. I feel like I could write a book about what it's like to be a drummer and play with other drummers, especially these heavy cats—I learn so much.

In the mid 2000s, a very nice teaching gig fell in my lap at the University of Maryland, which is near my house. Last year, I stepped down from teaching there because touring has gotten so busy. I'm currently the music director for The Oregon Festival of America Music, a position that Ken Peplowski held for ten years. It's thanks to Ken that I'm involved there. It's a demanding position but I really love it. So, between that, my sideman work and gigs I do as a leader I stay very busy.

JG: That's great. Yeah, teaching has become very important for me too in recent years and a big part of what I do. Well, thanks for sharing some of your stories! I look forward to seeing you on a gig again soon and getting to hang some more!

CR: My pleasure.

Coda

One really cool thing happened right after we had this talk, at the end of this Japan tour. Chuck and I got a lift from a friend of mine from the airport to the neighborhood around Stuyvesant Town, near 14th St. and 1st Ave. His son and my two sons lived within a couple blocks of each other in that neighborhood. It was a few days before Christmas of 2013. As we got to talking, I learned that Chuck's son, Charlie, happened to live in the same building complex as my ex-sister-in-law, Elizabeth. She was, and is, a big time TV producer. Charlie, after four years at NYU film school, was looking to get into that business. I asked Elizabeth if my friend's son might be able to take her out for coffee to learn about the business, and she was kind enough to say yes. She met with him about a month later, loved him, and to our shock and joy, hired him to be a part of the John Oliver show on HBO! And now, six-plus years and several Emmys later, I'm just so happy for Charlie, and thankful that Elizabeth agreed to meet him and that he got that break!

Bill Charlap

Summit, NJ – July 2006

We start out with Bill saying, "OK, you're not recording yet right?" "Right," I say. He's putting things away after a rehearsal we've just finished, and we're talking for a few minutes, just joking around. Then he says, "You're still not recording right?" I respond, "So, I actually lied and have been recording all along." And I press the record button at that moment...

BC: [Laughter]

JG: So I'm here with Bill Charlap at his house in Summit, New Jersey.

BC: A half a house... [It was one of those split houses, one door on each side.]

JG: But a helluva half a house, I might say. We just had a rehearsal for this Harold Arlen concert we're doing next month. And I've done these interviews, and I really enjoy them and I'm very thankful for all the great people I have in my life as friends and musicians. But I have no idea where to begin with you.

BOTH: [Laughter]

JG: Because, we could go so many different directions, and talk about so much shared history.

BOTH: [Laughter]

JG: Or you could just throw me out in the next few minutes.

BC: You've got thirty more seconds.

JG: OK, tell me everything in thirty seconds.

BC: Well, I kinda separate my life into before meeting you...

JG: Right...

BC: And knowing you...

JG: Right... when it got really good to be alive.

BOTH: [Laughter]

JG: Once you got to know me, that's when life was gettin' good to you Jack!

BC: Oh, this is too silly. This is like an interview we're making for each other to listen to.

JG: Well, maybe that'll be it.

BC: That's what it might be!

JG: Yeah. [Long, silent pause]

BC: How's it going so far?

JG: It's going smashingly...

BOTH: [Laughter]

JG: So I think what I'd like to ask you about is, how when we first met in high school at

Performing Arts at thirteen years old, you were playing a lot of Keith Emerson from ELP and Rick Wakeman from YES. But you always had this magic to how you played. It always seemed like you could tell a story in what you were doing, right from the very beginning, that immediately conveyed this amazing talent and gift, to everyone—except for maybe some of the teachers. The students all knew it.

I sometimes feel that your talents were not at all properly recognized there. Similar to other students who weren't primarily classical players—Steven Scott, Justin Robinson, and Jay Rodriguez come to mind. But your evolution in your playing is fascinating to me in that way, where you came from. And also, I learned so much from you playing me these recordings that you had and knew about. One of the things I learned, along with the music itself, was that when someone plays you music they really know, you sometimes hear it differently than if you just discovered it yourself. It's almost like you can sometimes hear it through their ears…

BC: I think the interview's going great…

BOTH: [Laughter]

JG: Was that too long a question?

BC: Was that a question!?

JG: Oh, it was so many things…

BOTH [Laughter]

BC: No listen, here's the thing. It's funny sitting here talking to you, because it's not just an interview, it's sitting here talking to one of my oldest, closest friends. We have so much history, and we can just look at each other and laugh about things. I remember reading about these comedians, and they'd get together at the Edison Hotel. And they had so many jokes that they knew that they'd just say, "Number 57!" and they'd all fall out. And it's like that with you, and Sean Smith, and well, not too many other people that I really grew up with, like you, who I've known since I was thirteen years old in high school. As far as musical evolution and being into progressive rock bands and keyboardists, that's most certainly true. It kinda goes like this. I grew up with my mom and dad… ah, this is gonna sound silly, they were in the house. It's a good thing they were there.

JG: You were on the roof! They couldn't find you.

BC: Well, you know, I still gotta get back to the roof… Number 54!

BOTH: [Laughter]

BC: But the first music I heard was my father, Moose Charlap, sitting at the piano, playing the piano and writing his songs. And he wasn't really a piano player, per se. But he had an energy when he sang and played that, you know, that people really responded to. Where he could sell you the song and sell you the show. Even other composers would sometimes ask him to do their backer's auditions.

In high school I was involved in this thing, sort of a competition, for the National Foundation for the Advancement of the Arts, and they recognized some students. You know about all this. But I played an event for them at the Vivian Beaumont Theater. And the person that spoke about all the different young people who were playing, acting, or dancing that day was Stephen Sondheim. He came up to me at one point and said, "There's a record of a composer singing and playing his own songs. I always play it for people when they want to know what musical theater is all about—that's your dad."

JG: Wow...

BC: Singing his songs from *Kelly*. And this record is just an LP that was put out by my father's partner on that show, Eddie Lawrence, who was also Eisler, a painter, who was a student of Léger. He was also The Old Philosopher, if anyone recognizes that old comedic bit. You would probably recognize some of the comedy routines and things. But he was the playwright and lyricist on that show. I'm talking way too much about this.

JG: No, not at all.

BC: But that's what that LP was, it was something I had after my father's death. It was basically a backer's audition on tape, probably from a reel to reel tape. It's not very good fidelity.

JG: Is that the one you played for me, "I'm out to steal you from the guy who brought you!?"

BC: No, that's something else.

JG: That's the one I always remember of your dad.

BC: Yeah, I have a lot of acetates... before there were CDs and DVDs, and even cassettes, if you had a demo for a show or a song, it was done on an acetate record. You could go into a studio and actually make an LP of these things. They're very thick and heavy. Anyhow, this particular record was put out after my father's death. It was just basically a boutique album. Not many were printed. But people who are in musical theater are aware of it. It's just him kind of playing the piano and screaming the songs.

JG: [Laughter] Yeah.

BC: And it's wonderful to listen to. It's very affecting. Anyhow, that's what I grew up listening to. His energy. My mother, Sandy Stewart, singing his songs. Because at the time she was no longer an active part of the music scene except for working on my father's demos. But she had had a very strong career before that. She'd been a TV personality. She was on *The Perry Como Show*, *The Mitch Miller Show*... she'd been on the road with Benny Goodman, she'd recorded pop albums, and she had a hit recording with song called "My Coloring Book," which was Kander and Ebb's first big hit.

JG: And she was nominated for a Grammy around '57, right?

BC: I think it was later than that, I think it was '59. Ella took the Grammy that year.

JG: Did I ever tell you that my mother sang on the King Sisters TV show?

BC: Yeah, you did.

JG: Yeah, I learned more about this after she passed from Jack Montrose, the west coast tenor player. I didn't know much about her career, but he told me she was a great singer. She never sang a note during my life. But, it's just an odd coincidence that both our mothers were singers.

BC: As you know I used to talk to your mom. I'd call to talk to you in high school and we'd just get to talking. You'd be practicing in the background. It was really nice. She was a great person.

JG: Well, it was great because you were one of the few people that knew me in those years that got to know her.

BC: Well, she was great. She'd take the phone and say, "Listen to him!" She was very proud of you. That happened all the time and you did sound great. You talked about me having a quality that came through, but you had that quality too. It was always very visceral and vital, and you always had that fluidity on your instrument.

JG: Well, that's nice of you to say. I don't know what you auditioned on to get into the school.

I auditioned by playing the concert band alto part of selections from *Rocky*. So, I was not on a high level!

BC: Yeah, but you played it with soul.

JG: But when I got there and I heard you, Chunga Song, and Eleonor Bindman, and a few other people like that, you inspired me so much. And I know I grew a lot from being around players like you who were all on a really high level.

BC: Well, I was not taken under the wing of the establishment there, at least not until a couple years later, by a couple of the teachers like Jerry Trevor. Basically, because it was a classical school. It was setting kids up to go to classical conservatories, and that's not what I was doing. I was not playing classical piano. I'd not really studied classical piano. Everything I did, I did by ear. And everything I did, I did my own way. It was kind of my interpretation of someone else's interpretation.

JG: Were you reading at all when you started high school?

BC: No, I couldn't read a note.

JG: That's what I thought.

BC: No, I couldn't read anything. It was painful. I mean, I knew what the notes were, and how it worked mathematically.

JG: I remember you used to play cello in the orchestra.

BS: Yeah but that was only because it was handed out to me and all the pianists had to play a second instrument in the orchestra.

JG: Yeah, but I just remember the seriousness of your intention, even with the cello. You would have a laugh about it at your own expense at times. But I remember seeing you in the orchestra and I could see your love of music came through. It's like our friend Tyrone. He never practiced much.

BC: Oh, but he was a total natural.

JG: And he would get a great sound out of the tuba, and he really played beautifully.

BC: I remember.

JG: But I remember seeing you in the orchestra and I could see the same kind of thing, your musicianship and your love of music came through.

BC: Well, I was a terrible cello player. But get me to an open D string on a stretto section and I was gonna lay into it!

JG: [Laughter] Yeah, right!

BC: Well, I digressed earlier when I mentioned the album of my father singing his music. I just wanted to say about the development of getting into progressive rock groups and things like that. My first experience at the piano was imitating my father. Then listening to, primarily, theater music and Broadway shows, and hearing the music my father was listening to. A lot of it was theater music. But also, as a composer of course, he was listening to Ravel, Respighi, and all the guys who were masters of orchestration and development and wrote all that incredible music, so that music was on too. He was of course theatrically minded because that's what he came from. I talked about my mom. My dad was a composer named Moose Charlap, and he was most famous for most of the music from the Mary Martin version of *Peter Pan*.

JG: Your brother Tom is a bass player.

BC: Yeah, my brother Tom is a bass player from my father's first marriage. But that was my first musical experience, listening to that music of my father. One of my first records that I got into was called *Sparky and His Magic Piano*.

JG: [Laughter] OK.

BC: It was a children's record. It's about this kid that plays the piano. And it's all with music in the background and a talking piano which came through what must have been an early day vocoder of sorts. It was very freaky sounding. But it turns out that the music was written by Billy May.

JG: Oh, OK.

BC: The great arranger and orchestrator. And it was very good. Now when I listen to it, I think, that was very good radio! Like when you listen to cartoons of Tom and Jerry, you hear how good those guys were that were playing that music. It was something like that. But there were a couple pieces on there, like the Rachmaninoff prelude in C♯ minor, some Chopin, I think the E minor posthumous waltz. And that kind of whet my appetite for classical music. 'Cause even though I wasn't playing the music I was a big fan. And I was listening to every-thing, you know? My father had albums so I listened to all the records. And, it was funny, even in high school I didn't play any of the music, but I knew the repertoire. I got to know it very well, not from playing it but the recordings. I got to know all of Prokofiev's music, Stravinsky, Schoenberg…

JG: Well, your record collection even when we were fourteen years old… I mean, we're sitting here next to an entire wall taken up of just records.

BC: And we do mean LPs. There's a lot here. I don't rival Kenny Washington by any means.

JG: No, but you basically had this many records when I met you. Plus, now you've got tons of other things on CD, and I remember you having boxes and boxes of tapes. And you didn't just have it, you knew it. You were always such an incredible listener. You played me so much music that I was hearing for the first time. I remember when you played me Chick Corea's *Three Quartets*, Weather Report, late Miles. The first time I heard "A Love Supreme" you played that for me. Jaco—*Word of Mouth*—man, that was a revelation for me. You played me the Stravinsky conducting Stravinsky that we love so much with *Petrouchka* and *The Rite of Spring*. That's always been my favorite version of both those pieces.

BC: The tempos are so great.

JG: And the time. Not only the tempos but the way the time is felt.

BC: Yeah, it's groovin'.

JG: It just seems like he understands time in a deeper way than some classical musicians.

BC: Listen, he'll even have sections in there where it starts to gets funky for a minute.

JG: That's the *thing*!

BC: You know that moment in *The Rite of Spring*. [Bill sings] Stravinsky writing a back beat for a couple of bars!

JG: I know, yeah!

BC: It's kind of incredible! If he'd kept that up for a little while he might have had a hit!

JG: Yeah…. as opposed to a riot.

BC: [Laughter] Somebody barred *The Rite of Spring* in 4, kind of halfway as a joke. The kind of thing Slonimsky would do. So, just to continue—listening to my father, listening to classical music. Learning some classical pieces, but by ear, not from the music.

JG: Right, I remember you playing me some Debussy back in high school.

BC: Right. I would learn it by ear. In a way it made it hard for me to read music, but easy to hear music. So that's kind of a good thing. It's like Dizzy said, "If you can hear it, you can have it." And then I started hearing a couple of other things. Like I met Barbara Carroll, she gave me one of her records. This was after my father passed away. I was about nine years old or so.

But by that time I'd become aware of other records in my mother's collection, such as Sarah Vaughan and Count Basie, Bill Evans, Oscar Peterson, Bob Brookmeyer and Clark Terry, and other things she had. And another thing that turned my ear to jazz more… I was aware of those records and things even freshman year in high school. But I was also listening to all of the rock music of the time. And the stuff that turned me on the most was ELP and YES. And even though they weren't the most groovin', soulful sounds, those guys could really play their instruments, especially the piano players. They were composing and they were writing things that I could relate to because of their sectional nature. Most rock and roll was guitar oriented, but here was something that was keyboard oriented. And also, there was a relationship to classical music, almost like classical music for the people. There were other things I was listening to—pop music, whatever was on the radio. I used to collect 45s. This predates getting into full albums of these groups.

JG: One of the other things that people might not know about you is that you just have incredible energy. When we were kids it was unbelievable! I remember sleeping over at your house on a weeknight at times during that period. The alarm would go off in the morning, maybe around 7 a.m. or so, for us to get to school a little after 8:00. And you would literally start jumping from the bed up to the ceiling, which you would smack, and shout, "Time to get UP!!"

BC: I was crackin' the whip pretty hard.

JG: Ha, yeah, it was just part of your nature. But even back in those days it was always still really clear that there was this good, caring person there. At first, we saw the talent and the energy. But shortly after that we'd start to see the other stuff. I remember one time that I saw that, it was maybe sophomore year, you said, "Jon, I've got to play this for you! It's absolutely incredible!" And you played, and to my surprise, sang, "Lush Life" for me. I was blown away! I just said, what is that!?

BC: Well, I was starting to get really turned around about then. What year was that?

JG: I don't know for sure. I wanna say early part of sophomore year.

BC: Well, one of the first gigs I had was playing at an acting company called First Amendment, at 2 Bond St.

JG: Yeah, I remember that.

BC: And that was sort like an Actor's Studio approach to actor's improvisation. Like the show Who's Line is it Anyway? They'd take suggestions from the audience and they'd make a skit out of it. And my job was, I was kind of like a silent movie pianist. So, I'd have to underscore any kind of scene, or make up impromptu songs with them. I would get a good twenty minutes to play anything I wanted as the people filed in. I was, I don't know, fifteen or sixteen at the time, doing that gig. And, at that time I was discovering more of my mom's records. I remember a particular one of Sarah Vaughan singing "Lush Life" with the full orchestra. And then I found the 45 of Nat Cole doing "Lush Life."

JG: The Pete Rugolo arrangement?

BC: The Pete Rugolo, that great arrangement, all those amazing things going on in there. And of course, that song really turned me on and the way that Sarah sang it as well was very moving to me. There was an actor at that place, I remember his name was Ash Harland. I don't know what happened to him afterwards, but he was an improviser as an actor. He was a great jazz lover and he played some piano too. I remember him playing Gigi Gryce's "Minority," with the 5th raising up to the flat 6th to the 6th. [He sings the third and fourth bar of the tune.] He showed me that voicing, and that really turned me on, so I started moving it around. And he made me cassettes. Those cassettes were really important for me. They had everything from Miles *Birth of The Cool*, to Lou Donaldson, to MJQ, to Gerry Mulligan, the piano-less quartets with Chet Baker, Art Farmer with Jimmy Heath and Cedar Walton. But one track each of all these things. And he'd put them in chronological order. So, you'd get Bud playing "Woody'n'You," then you'd get Bill Evans playing it. It wasn't always the same tune like that, but sometimes you'd get those little things next to each other.

Another real important one for me was Horace Silver and the Messengers doing "Room 608." That's the first solo I ever took down—or at least some of it. It's essentially a rhythm changes type of tune with a different bridge. That was really important for me. I remember, I used to play... [he sings some of Horace's solo]. And that was one of the first things I heard going into the IV chord, was Horace. Horace's music is so direct. He takes the bop language, even when he solos, in a way, it's like, "Everyone sing along with Horace!" in a way. It's just so direct. He's figured out a way to make it so super clear cut, you know, some of these solos. And of course, the energy, if you listen to his left hand. He and Blakey and Doug Watkins were made for each other. I mean, what's going on in the rhythm section... his left hand is kinda going like [he vocalizes the hits]. It's not even about the notes, it has nothing to do with the notes he's playing, it's like he's being another snare drum and just being rhythmic. And to hear the accuracy and the beauty of his right hand, you know, and the articulation. And then that left hand which was just like all about... like a boxer.

JG: Yeah, yeah.

BC: Like jabs in your gut. And I said, oh, this is *really* a different kind of piano playing. This is *not* like playing a Mozart concerto. This is being a drummer and being vocal at the piano. It's not about the piano anymore. It's about saying something about music with the piano, like Monk, the architect, and all of those great things. And at the same time, each time I'd get one of those cassettes, if I had one track of *Birth of the Cool*, I'd go get the whole record. Or if I had a track with the Gerry Mulligan Quartet I'd do the same with that. I saw Sonny Clark was in the rhythm section of one album. I liked the way he sounded, so I'd look for anything with Sonny Clark. Same with Blakey. I didn't know who any of those names were, or who they were historically.

It was the same with discovering classical music. You could kind of see the pieces of the family tree fall into place. I started to learn about the history. I learned that "The Sting" ("The Entertainer") wasn't necessarily written for a movie with Paul Newman and Robert Redford. Even though it was great that it got Scott Joplin's music out to a lot of people in the '70s, because of Marvin Hamlisch's arrangements. Of course, there was also a resurgence of Joplin with those records Joshua Rikfin made for Nonesuch of the piano rags. Between those two things it brought a resurgence of Joplin's music. But I'm just saying, I got drawn to all the different tentacles of both my instrument and all the instruments this way. 'Cause I'd hear Charlie Parker and say, "How did that happen?" I think that one of the best ways to learn about a style that you love, is to try to imagine putting yourself in the shoes of those musicians and think about what they were hearing at the time. You know, it's a very obvious thing to see how something can develop. If you listen to Bud Powell you can see to hear his relationship with Teddy Wilson. And how the linear style of playing happened that way. Or Bird's relationship to Lester Young, or Herbie's relationship to Bill Evans and Wynton Kelly. You start to hear all those things and they start to come together. If you're a fan of anything you start to figure it out. Go to a whole bunch of museums, look at a retrospective of any of the major artists. So, you can see a lot of the guys and who's influencing who, and who are the ones that really have such a strong imprint, you know? There are major innovators like McCoy Tyner, but there are also players who weren't perhaps so uniquely original but were also great contributors.

JG: One of the things I wanted to get to was when I became aware of your full commitment to be a jazz musician. I was watching it develop. It was certainly there by beginning of senior year.

BC: I think I got bored of the other stuff. You know? It just didn't balance on every level.

JG: Right.

BC: You had to balance on the technical level, on the human level...

JG: I know what you mean.

BC: You know exactly what I'm talking about. It was almost like the blueprint had to all be there. It's like, I think a truly great composer can compose out of anything. It's not necessarily just about texture, or drama, it's sort of everything. The development of small ideas perhaps. I can be just as moved by a great drummer playing a snare drum, a hi-hat, and a cymbal, a guy playing melodica, and a bass player playing a wash tub if it's something with a kind of meaning. You know, jazz has such an incredible history. People who really just had no commercial end to playing this music, the way it is today. And of course, it speaks to so much about our nation. Some of it incredibly ugly and some of it incredibly great.

You know, there were a few other things that happened for me in putting some of the pieces together as I grew. You know, my brother is a bass player. And he's about ten years older than me. So, he was playing gigs around and I'd hear him playing, walking a blues, playing a standard, you know.

JG: And I remember you really looked up to him and you talked to me about him a lot at that time.

BC: Well, I could hear him just in a restaurant playing tunes and I'd think, wow! How do they do that? Or he and his friends would get together and play. He had a friend named Barry Olsen who plays trombone, great trombone player. He's out there working these days. And he played some piano too. I remember they played "Blues for Alice." This is right in our time and I think I played that for you. And I learned it from a tape of Tom and Barry playing it, not from Bird originally. But my brother hipped me to a few things. He bought me the Weather Report record, *Heavy Weather*, because he knew I liked synthesizers. And he knew I liked listening to guys who played a lot of keyboards.

Now at the time I heard some of those melodies [sings "Birdland"] and to my ear at the time I wanted to hear something more angular and tough. Something closer to Bernstein or Ginastera. So, I dismissed it at first. Except for "Teen Town," which was rough enough for me I thought. But then of course I started to hear it more, and hear the melodies, and hear how beautiful Wayne Shorter was of course.

JG: Well you played me some of that around that time.

BC: I started to hear it. It took a minute. He also bought me a George Shearing duo album. And that was really important too. To hear someone with a touch like that, and such great harmony. And play with such love of the melody, the way Shearing did and does. His contribution is immense. Shearing is certainly someone who was influential to Bill Evans, and Herbie Hancock and others. So, I think Tommy buying me those records was important. After hearing Wayne Shorter and Joe Zawinul, I then went out and accidentally bought Ben Webster with Joe Zawinul, and that was a very happy accident! Because I heard Joe the piano player who played great! He had a beautiful touch like Hank Jones. And on that record was also Jimmy Rowles.

JG: Which record is it?

BC: Well it was a record they made together…

JG: It might have been a compilation with the two piano players…

BC: It was a compilation. It was two dates. But with the famous record they made together, called *Soulmates*.

JG: Not *See You at the Fair*?

BC: No that's Ben with Roger Kellaway. In any event, hearing that, and hearing "Frogs Legs."

JG: Yeah.

BC: That's one of the tunes on there, it's a blues. And it's Zawinul. And I could hear the genesis of some of that Weather Report writing coming because of those little statements. [He sings it]

JG: Yeah.

BC: It's like you could almost hear where…

JG: You could almost hear Jaco under that.

BC: [Sings it again] But that's swingin' bebop. But you know, it's so related. It's almost like, the tentacles are so strong in a band like Weather Report. It's *not* fusion music. It's their music. And, of course, their personalities.

JG: And then when you hear Zawinul play with Cannonball, that's another step along the way to the realization of Weather Report. I love that music. It drives me crazy when people say there hasn't been anything great in the last forty years.

BC: I've got a music history book here someplace with a quote like, "Everything that can be done has been done. Now it's just about putting all the information together in an original way. But everything has been covered harmonically and rhythmically that's possible." Palestrina in the 1500s. So, you know, that's always the party line. That's human nature, that we can't discover something new. Well…

JG: Maybe it's safer to think we've got it all covered.

BC: It might be. I don't know why it's human nature to think that way. And I'm not saying it's not valid if it's not new. That's not true either. It's just valid if it's honest.

JG: So, to pick up on your growth, we got outta high school, you went to Purchase…

BC: Yeah… and by that time, even by sophomore year in high school, I was less and less interested in anything but... it had to happen at the piano. I kind of grew out of anything electronic. It just didn't speak to me anymore. It needed to be more human. It's still kinda that way. I can easily, personally, get bored playing something electronic. Doesn't mean there isn't great stuff out there.

JG: I've never done much of that though I have enjoyed experimenting with it some. I've did some tracks recently for a friend and played through some effects. I'd like to learn more about it at some point. It's another possibility, another color.

BC: But you know, with Zawinul, he grew up playing the accordion. So, he had that.

JG: Yes, he was hearing something else.

BC: It's like the wind behind the sound. So he wants to put that in it. And if it's in your inner ear...

JG: You'll feel it differently.

BC: And you'll figure out how to get it out there.

JG: Right.

BC: You know, it's like, look, I'm not singing the lyrics of the song. But by knowing the lyrics, something behind the note comes out, you know? A great lyric drips off the notes. Something behind it, something extra, that's musical. You said it before. What happens when you listen with somebody else? Well, sometimes if you're actually experiencing music with someone else, something you've heard before, whether it's something you know and love that you're bringing to them, or something you're both listening to together for the first time, you hear differently.

JG: Absolutely.

BC: I'm certain there's a collective experience that can happen. There's a universal mind that Bill Evans talked about.

JG: There's that famous scientific theory of how the observer affects the experiment being observed by observing it, which kind of speaks to that.

BC: We're always trying to get out of ourselves. You know what helps me? I remember seeing this in a Chick Corea interview. It might have been something Ted Rosenthal did with Chick and Ted told me about. I think it was one of the piano magazines and Ted was interviewing a lot of the major cats at the time. And Chick said something like, "Sometimes I just pick my head up from the keyboard and look at the people I'm playing with." It was simple. "I'm not sticking my head in my own stuff. I'm looking out there," and so you're letting them in, and communicating, and now it's easier.

JG: So, when did you start to play with Gerry Mulligan? Was that soon after college?

BC: Well, yes, shortly after that. I left Purchase after two years, because I needed to study. I couldn't be in college in a classical conservatory and studying music the way I needed to. I needed to be studying jazz and jazz piano. As great as it might have been to play chamber music and study classical accompanying and all that, it just took too much time to do it well. I was lucky, I had a benefactor. I had an uncle who gave me some money every month.

JG: Paul?

BC: Paul.

JG: What a blessing.

BC: It wasn't a ton of money, but it was enough for me to rent an apartment on 200th St. and rent a piano. You remember this.

JG: Sure.

BC: I built a wooden platform and put the piano on that. I rented it from Steinway.

JG: And you played that piano at all hours of the night! Your neighbors never seemed to mind!

BC: Well, I also filled the platform the piano was on with acoustical foam. And I put the foam on the walls, and I built a second door.

JG: Yeah, you took care of business.

BC: There was a lot of stuff I did to soundproof. But there was one wall that really wasn't soundproofed that was next to the neighbors. But luckily on 200th Street, there was also a lot of loud salsa music that was being played in the middle of the night.

JG: You know, this brings up an interesting point. A lot of times I have students that say to me, "I want to go to some college that's $50–60,000, what do you think?" When I started at MSM in 1984 it was $4,000, and it was all I could do to deal with the few hundred bucks I owed per semester, even with the TAP and PELL grants I got, which covered most of it. If I had to come up with that kind of money now, I'd never be able to do it.

I sometimes tell students that if you just come to a place like New York where you can listen to music live on a regular basis, play with people who are at a high level, and study with people you admire and make enough money to get by, that's another way to go. Let's say you're a sax player, and your day is two, three hours a day at the saxophone, an hour-plus on your doubles, an hour or so at the piano, and some composition. And you'd say, OK, I'm gonna take two sax lessons this month, a piano lesson, a flute lesson, a composition lesson, you know? As opposed to being forced into a very expensive program that's going to put you deeply in debt.

BC: Well look, I was really lucky in those years. I remember telling my uncle, who was a successful businessman and not musically minded at all (even though he was my father's brother he did NOT get the music gene), that I was going to leave school to study. And he was livid! He said, "You can't leave school, what do you think you're doing?" The same as a lot of people experience. And he wouldn't even talk to me. He made me talk to his friend Vic, this business partner of his. And I had to explain it to him, what I was doing and why I was doing it. The whole thing was so funny, 'cause, Paul wouldn't talk to me. Vic would say, "Billy, what your uncle is saying…"

JG: [Laughter]

BC: It was one of the most surreal conversations, but I can be convincing I suppose. I did finally convince him it was the right thing, and luckily it was. You know, like I say, all I did was I practiced all day. I practiced, I studied. It's all I did. I woke up in the morning, I fell out of bed and I got to the piano. I ate when I was hungry. That's what I did all day. I had my lessons. I'd go to my lessons. I'd come back and practice. At night I'd get on the train and I'd go downtown, and I'd hear Kenny Barron, or Roger Kellaway, or Steve Kuhn, or Tommy Flanagan, or Red Mitchell, or Ray Drummond. You know, I'm thinking about Bradley's. All those cats, playin' all the great tunes.

JG: Well, you probably worked harder and spent more time at your instrument than anyone I've ever known.

BC: I need to work harder now.

JG: Well, don't we all? I think that's one of the great blessings of that energy that you have. I had a period of about ten days that I stayed at our friend Bill Mays' cabin in Pennsylvania, watching his dog, and I worked on music twelve to fourteen hours a day. And I used to try to get in the practice rooms at MSM right when school opened at 7 a.m. as often as I could to work straight through until noon when I had classes.

BC: Well, you need to do it when you're young, before you have kids.

JG: Absolutely. You can't say I'm 35 now and going to start a ten-hour-a-day practice regimen.

BC: It's hard. I still make the time to work hard. I was in that apartment for about a year and a half. And all this time, I was influenced by our elders and the people we went and listened to. But we're also influenced by our peers.

JG: Oh yeah.

BC: Just as important, if not more so, are the people you're playing with. You, Sean Smith, Dan Rochlis on guitar, Justin Page on drums, we had a band together.

JG: We also had Kevin Hays, Pat Zimmerli, Justin Robinson, and some other young musicians around us as well in those days.

BC: And we learned from each other too. Eddie Locke was very important to us too. He took a lot of younger musicians under his wing. He tried to keep us in the right place in terms of the feeling of the music. We were all working on the technical side of things, but he always pulled our coats and reminded us it's feeling first.

JG: Well, since we were talking about college years and Eddie, I just have to tell this story. You know it very well—when I went to Eddie to tell him I'd run out of money to finish college.

BC: Oh, this is a great story! [Laughter]

JG: I'd done three semesters as a classical major because there was no jazz major at MSM at the time. I'd taken a semester off. And then they started a jazz undergrad program. And I did five semesters of that, not realizing that my TAP and PELL grant money would only cover eight semesters, and that if it took longer to finish the undergrad degree I was on my own. I'd just borrowed money to buy instruments that year and had no way to borrow any more. And Eddie was the one guy I felt I had to tell this to.

BC: By the way, this is joke Number 51.

JG: Yeah, this is right up there in the repertoire. Because Eddie had gotten me my first apartment in New York housesitting for his neighbor across the hall, and that was a huge blessing for me for part of two years while I was in college. I just thought, I gotta tell Eddie, but it's gonna be really hard. So, I call him and say I gotta come up and see you. He says, come on up. So, as I come in the apartment, he's on the phone with another young musician he knows and is finishing up the call. As he hangs up, and I'm walking in, he says, "Man! See, that's a guy that left school when I told him he should *never* do that! And he thinks he so high and mighty and all that. And see!? That's the thing I always *loved* about you! You stayed in school! You didn't get all arrogant and think you knew *so much*! And some people do that, and I hate that. And lemme just tell you, if you *ever* leave that school without a degree I'LL KILL YOU!"

BC: [Laughter] I already know the punch line…

JG: "Now what did you want to talk about?"

BC: [Laughter]

JG: So I started slowly and said, "Well, Eddie, um, you know, I, um, did three semesters as a classical major, you know? And then I became a jazz major when they started that, but I didn't know that it would take me longer than eight semesters to finish the program, and the lady in the business office told me last week that they needed several thousands of dollars from me this week to continue to go, and, um, but I just borrowed money to buy horns, and…. well… um… I have to leave school."

BC: [Laughter]

JG: But without missing a beat he quickly said, "Oh, well you can always go back! What else is shakin' Jim?"

BC: [Laughter] That's just how much he loves you! Sometimes we'll call each other and end the call by saying, "You can always go back!"

JG: I used to joke that I heard every phone call he had when I lived in the building.

BC: Well, you don't hear Eddie much south of 58th Street.

JG: [Laughter] That's right!

BC: His place is on 106th.

JG: So, in the time remaining, you just played me this duo of you and Tony Bennett singing "I Left My Heart in San Francisco"—probably his biggest hit, and one of the of the great singers ever. I remember meeting him at a club called Jay's, maybe fifteen years ago, where he was doing sketches of you as you played. And he's known you since you were a kid. You showed me that photo earlier of you, your mom, and Kaye Ballard. Dick Hyman is a relative of yours and has been a big part of your life and growth as a musician for sure. And I love the story you told me about Yip Harburg coming over to the house, who wrote all the lyrics in the *Wizard of Oz*.

I think it's amazing how your career at this point encompasses your love for jazz, and also where you come from in your family, your parents and those associations and others. And people like Gerry Mulligan and Phil Woods who you've had long working associations with. Also, Wynton Marsalis who's really been in your corner. You've been able to connect where you come from, with your love of jazz, and bring them together in a great, organic way, and create popular success and an amazing career. But more importantly, you've succeeded artistically and have one of the truly great piano trios in the world. I think it speaks to all the hard work you've done, all the music that you know and love and have synthesized in a brilliant way. You're making a great contribution in what you're doing.

BC: Well look, you're very sweet in what you're saying. You've always been very important as support to me as a friend. We need the people that care about us and believe in us. It means a lot. But you know, I never set out and said 'I'm going to do the American Popular Song. I didn't write that story. I know that for a lot of people that's what I'm associated with now, because it's a very big part of what I do. It's a primary part of the repertoire I play. There's nothing calculated about it. I just do what I love. I was very lucky. I grew up around some of the last of the great American theater writers. Charles Strouse used to come over to my house. Yip Harburg, Marilyn and Alan Bergman, who are good friends of mine today. Knowing and being a friend to such an important interpreter of American popular song as Tony Bennett. It's a very great blessing.

I mean, I've been really lucky! I've been around some of these seminal forces in American popular music, in terms of the composers and the lyricists, and the energy of the American musical theater. So, it kind of comes naturally. I love the songs and the writers. I love knowing what makes Kern so special, or Berlin, or Harold Arlen. Again, it's like being a fan. It's the same thing as how I went to get the records. When they told me Stravinsky was good I wanted to listen to everything he ever wrote. Well, it's the same thing. I wanna know the difference between a Kern song and an Arlen song. Just as a fan, it happened naturally. And when I would learn those tunes, I'd learn the whole thing, the words and music, how it was originally. And I'd think, how can we put it through our own experience? What is it about a Coleman Hawkins performance of "Climb Every Mountain" that makes it different from the film or the show of a *Sound of Music*?

JG: But it just makes so much sense that you have something to say on these kinds of tunes, because you were around those folks, and your parents were in these worlds.

BC: Well, I'm a jazz musician first and foremost. That's what I'm gonna sit down and listen to. I'm gonna put on Bud Powell records. Or I'm gonna put on Armstrong, or Miles Davis. But I also love theater music, popular music, classical music. There's so much music out there. And it all makes a complete musical package finally. If anything makes the music fly for me, it's that I'm not myopic in my feelings about music. And I don't really discriminate stylistically. Whether or not I play certain things or strive for certain things doesn't mean I'd dismiss other things from anyone else. In fact, it may be there but in a more subtle way sometimes. And I think I've just been really lucky. Master musicians who've just been supportive. Also, Kenny Washington and Peter Washington, who've been my partners for eight and a half years in my band. It's really our band. The way that they play, it's the perfect combination for me to express all the things I care about. You're not just getting me, you're getting all of Peter's love for the history of his instrument and all the music he loves. And Kenny is encyclopedic as people know. But it's also passion. I mean, the passion to play is there. The lust for music. You must have the lust for music.

You know, Tony Bennett is eighty years old. I've had many conversations with him where he says, "You know the whole day for me is waiting to get to the bandstand. You know, I just can't wait to get out there." He's played thousands of concerts. He's eighty, he sounds great. He's still out there and connecting to everyone. You know, this is the thing with a great artist. There's an illusion that a great artist makes you feel, that only you have that particular personal relationship to their music. Like, it was made for you. It's so direct that Bill Evans is having a conversation directly with you. Or, Billie Holiday is singing right to you. And nobody's ever felt that music so directly, and so one to one, as you have.

JG: There's a kind of an intimacy that they create

BC: They're able to do it. It's just an incredible thing.

JG: Well, you said you're lucky. I suppose we're all lucky to be playing music. And the things that you talked about that you're thankful for I'm thankful for too; the great people that have been around us and helped and inspired us. But you've worked damned hard too. You've earned the great things that have happened to you. It's been your love of the music, and your hard work. If you're not playing, you're listening, or you're playing music for somebody else to listen to. So, your energy and commitment to music has been a major inspiration to me. And I'm very thankful for you in my life.

BC: Well, you've been an inspiration to me too. Thank God for music. Thank God for friends like you.

JG: Thanks for doing this Bub.

McCoy Tyner
Jazz Baltica, Germany – 2001

In the summer of 2001, Martin Wind put a band together that I was a part of to play the Jazz Baltica Festival. It was a really fun group with Joel Frahm, Bill Charlap, and Billy Drummond. After we performed our set at the festival, Joel and I went backstage and happened to meet McCoy Tyner, who was going to be playing the following set about an hour after ours. We talked to McCoy for about 30–40 minutes backstage after our gig, and before his, and he was truly amazing! He just couldn't have been nicer, more positive, or supportive.

At one point, as he was saying something very humble and self-effacing, I said something like, "Wow. That's so amazing coming from you, who's such an important contributor in the history of the music."

He said, "But I don't feel that way. I just feel like we're all in it together. I stand on the shoulders of so many people that helped me, taught me, took care of me, and inspired me… folks you'll never hear of or know about. But they're a part of everything I do, and I'm only here because of them."

I was very moved by that. I was very impressed and touched by how genuine his humility was, and the feeling it left with me. As I thought about what he'd said, and the people whose shoulders he stood on that most folks would never know, I also knew for sure that the same thing was true for me, and most likely all of us.

Melissa Aldana
Winnipeg, Canada – August 2019

JG: So, Melissa Aldana, really good to get a chance to talk with you, thanks for doing this. We met each other on a gig last year with Bill Charlap.

MA: Yes!

JG: And you were kind enough to send me your recipe for gluten-free corn bread!

MA, Yes, I did.

JG: Thanks for that! I look forward to trying it. So, I just today learned a lot about you at your masterclass that you gave at our school's jazz camp, and your father and grandfather being saxophonists. You were born in Santiago, Chile?

MA: Yes. I grew up seeing my father teaching at home. He used to do group lessons all the time. My grandfather died when I was around five so I don't have many memories of him. But apparently, I was always following him around asking to hold his horn for him to show me how to play a few notes. One day my dad was doing a group lesson and they were playing a tune called "Brazil." They were doing a sax quartet and they needed another person to fill out the harmony. So my dad gave me the alto for the first time and showed me how to play two notes. I was like six, and I fell in love with the instrument. So, I was very excited for him to teach me. I was following him around the house asking him and he said one day, "OK, we will do it." He showed me mostly how to play the notes and scales. But after a few months he got me into transcriptions. We used to do that on cassettes. That's why I noticed you had one on your desk here, it reminds me of how we used to do it.

JG: You mentioned today that you did everything by ear, and you didn't learn to read right away.

MA: Yes, that's how my father wanted me to learn. We did a lot of ear training. We did a lot of scales. At first me he taught me all the major scales. But then he made me analyze them and have me make my own conclusions about what modes were on the minor scales, you know, melodic minor, harmonic minor. So, we did everything by thinking and analyzing all the time. Instead of him telling me what things were, he encouraged me to think. So, he went through the whole process with me.

JG: To find your own way.

MA: Yeah, just to name the scales. For example, he taught me the Lydian scale. And then when we were analyzing the modes, with the melodic minor, the 4th mode is dominant but Lydian dominant. So instead of him telling me that, he made me by conclusion say, OK, this is dominant but also has a sharp 11 so what is this? I think that by doing it that way it really stayed with me. He always encouraged me to think to hear and learn everything by heart. So, it was quite tricky when I came to Boston and I had to learn to read for the first time.

JG: And you were eighteen or nineteen when you came to Boston for Berklee?

MA: Yes.

JG: Well, and to backtrack a bit, you said you met Danilo Perez when you were fifteen and he heard you and invited you to the Panama Jazz Festival.

MA: Yes, he heard me playing in Santiago with my band. It was near a venue he was playing. I was playing with some local musicians. Now I play with a bass player from Chile. I don't remember who was on the gig then. But I remember that Danilo came to the club and stayed and sat in and played the rest of the gig and it became a jam session.

JG: Wow.

MA: His wife was super-close to my dad. She's a saxophone player and she used to study with my dad in her late teens before she moved to Boston. That's the connection I have with him.

JG: So then at eighteen you moved to Boston and learned to read.

MA: Yes. I did this audition and they do these ratings, and I got good marks. But for reading I got marked like a one. My teacher was Dino Giovanno for one year. He gave me all this sight reading and etudes for one year. I'm still not super-fast at reading. I've never been part of a big band and forced to do it. But I can do it pretty well now. Dino was my teacher for the first year and then I took lessons with George Garzone.

JG: Great, how long did you study with him?

MA: For a good two and a half years, every week. I had him for ensembles as well. I didn't understand a lot that he was saying at first. But all the info he's given me has made sense as the years have gone on. He'd sit at the piano and we'd play a lot. We did hang a lot, we talked a lot about music and practicing. He was one of the teachers that was at the school practicing at 6 a.m. doing long tones every day. So, he really inspired me in that sense. Just seeing the process and the love he has for music.

JG: And you mentioned earlier today at the masterclass that your father also imparted that love of practicing as well. I think you said he was that kind of practicer as well?

MA: I don't remember my father being strict, but apparently he was. Danilo knows the whole story because his wife was there when I started playing saxophone. So, she said my dad was like, "7 a.m., before school, play your long tones."

JG: [Laughter]

MA: And we had an outside area with squares on the ground. So, we would learn a solo. It would take a long time, but we'd learn each phrase on one square and eventually go through the whole house, and then back. And that way I memorized so much music. I was very lucky to have him next to him telling me, play like this. It was very helpful

JG: My youngest son played saxophone, and he was talented. I tried to show him a few things. But I just wanted him to have fun with it. But you were hungry for it.

MA: Yeah, I always loved it for some reason. My sister, he tried to do the same thing with her. But she never did it. She hated him and the saxophone.

BOTH: [Laughter]

MA: But I was always very passionate about it. To the point where, when I was 18 and I went to Boston, I didn't go back for a few years and I didn't miss it. It always felt very natural to leave for Boston and then New York.

JG: Who else did you study with after Garzone?

MA: Lovano was my ensemble teacher.

JG: One of my big inspirations for sure.

MA: Yeah, I grew up listening to him. So, he was there in my first class my first day. I was so scared. I didn't really speak English, and, there he was, like a god for me.

JG: What were some of the recordings of his that really impacted you?

MA: *Live at the Vanguard*. One of my favorites!

JG: Oh yeah! "Lonnie's Lament!"

MA: Yes! Or "Reflections." There are a lot of recordings over the years. There's one with Scofield.

JG: *Meant to Be?*

MA: I can't remember the name. But back then we were playing one of the tunes from that album, it'll come back to me. The one with Greg Osby is really beautiful too.

JG: I loved the Paul Motian trio. And some of the stuff with Mel and the Vanguard Orchestra.

MA: Yeah, but that *Live at the Vanguard* is definitely one of my favorites.

JG: I remember driving home from a Monday with Maria at Visiones and heard that "Lonnie's Lament" on the radio. I was close to home, but I had to pull over to listen, it was just amazing.

MA: Yes, I always loved his playing so much. He was a great teacher too. He didn't say much, but he said like a few little things here and there that made me think a lot.

JG: I had one lesson with Joe when I was twenty at his old place on 23rd near 7th Ave. It was incredible! He's consistently inspired and inspiring.

MA: Yes. And you know, now that you mentioned it, me and my father used to transcribe a lot of Phil Woods.

JG: What Phil did you transcribe?

MA: You know that version of "Cheek to Cheek?"

JG: *Live at the Showboat!*

MA: That was the first one of his we did.

JG: Well I asked you today if you worked on much classical, and he starts that by quoting the Ibert Concertino.

MA: Yes! Yeah, we did that with my father and I remember being so into it. And to this day I still kind of remember it on the alto. Because we played over it so much. And it was one of my favorite solos back then.

JG: Well, that record is just incredible. So, along with Garzone and Lovano, what were some of the other things that were happening and inspiring your growth in Boston?

MA: Well, I think the main difference for me was that I was around young musicians that wanted to do the same thing as me. In Chile, I mostly practiced a lot. I went to a normal high school. And there weren't that many musicians that were playing, it was mostly elders. So, I didn't have that kind of experience just playing with people and being around people who were better than me. So, going to Berklee and seeing kids younger than me or my same age playing so much horn really inspired me! So, we used to play jam sessions every night. I went to Wally's, which is one of the most vibey jam sessions I ever went to in my life.

JG: Ha! Why is it a vibey jam session?

MA: It's kind of like very old school in a sense. Because if you don't have your shit together they'll let you know it. It doesn't matter who you are. But also, it was helpful for me because I went there when I was nineteen. And they started playing "My Shining Hour" and then they went through all the keys *super-fast*! And I just left feeling very vulnerable. You know, I was kind of crying, wondering why am I feeling like this. And you know that's the feeling of a lot of kids when they go to jam sessions. Wally's is a scary place for jam sessions in general. But I promised myself that I would just learn the music and keep going, going, going. So that was an important education for me. Just forget about trying to sound killing. Just go and play, be yourself. So, I went there three times a week until I got the actual gig.

JG: Oh, great!

MA: So that was the last year I was there.

JG: What years were you there?

MA: 2008 to 2010.

JG: I remember hearing about jam sessions up there, but I also heard that students who were there when I was school in the '80s would sometimes drive a long way to find other sessions. I just remember hearing there weren't a lot of places to play.

MA: Yeah, I think it's still kind of the same there, or it was when I was there. It was like Wally's and maybe one other place.

JG: It's a little hard if you've got a big jazz program and lots of horn players and say let's jam.

MA: And people were going there, but sometimes they wouldn't come back. And back then Jason Palmer was running the jam session and he was playing a lot of Kurt Rosenwinkel tunes. I remember they were playing a tune by Mark Turner called "Jackie's Place," and I just realized I had to learn that music.

JG: Yeah, I interviewed Mark for my site and this book. I've played with him a lot and he's one of my all-time favorites. But when I interviewed him it bothered me that the media didn't seem to appreciate what he and Kurt were doing. You and I have a similar feeling about that music.

MA: Yeah, I have the feeling that it was never recognized as much as it should have been. It really changed the direction of the music. And really influenced a lot of young players. My generation of tenor players, everyone went through Mark. He defined a new way of playing the saxophone.

JG: Well, you mentioned three tenor players today who were important influences for you were Don Byas, Sonny Rollins, and Mark. I didn't get to know and hear Mark until '94, and he was Mark by then to me. People told me that they heard him in the earlier Boston days when he was going through Trane, Joe Henderson, Lennie Tristano, and Warne Marsh. His voice was so important on Kurt's records, Ed Simon, his own projects. I talked with him about that and I certainly have been very inspired by him.

MA: Yeah. You know, when I got to practice with him…

JG: So you did take some lessons with him?

MA: Well, I took one with him when I was fifteen in Panama at the jazz festival when he gave me a free lesson. I didn't know much of him. I just heard him play and said—*wow*! What is this? I went and asked him, "What did you play on that augmented chord?" He took the time to talk to me, he was super-nice. And then back at Berklee he did a masterclass there and I got a chance to play with him. Then recently I took a lesson with him in New York. When I had the Monk Scholarship I just wanted to take lessons and talk about the process of all these musicians that I admired.

JG: When was that?

MA: About three years ago.

JG: And who are some other musicians that you took some lessons with in recent years?

MA: I took some lessons with Chris Potter.

JG: How was that?

MA: That was cool. I thought that he'd say that he was very specific when it comes to practicing. But he said he mostly plays. He was never a player that practiced on specific things so much as just playing a lot.

JG: A student here asked me to introduce him at the jazz festival here a few years ago, and he asked him what he did to grow and he said he played with his favorite records.

MA: Yeah, which is amazing. And just understanding what he was talking about, how he took all the Charlie Parker influence and started changing it. You know, I was just very curious about the process and how he's achieved what he has and how he plays now.

JG: Yeah, there's a YouTube clip of Chris and Mark in a band led by Johnathan Blake. And there's some great videos of Chris and Lovano together.

MA: Yeah, I did transcribe that. "Four" and "Bye Bye Blackbird."

JG: Yeah, some beautiful playing on that. Any other lessons?

MA: I took some lessons with Chris Cheek.

JG: Yeah! Chris is great.

MA: I always loved his playing.

JG: Very personal sound and approach.

MA: Yes, very melodic too. I took one with Seamus.

JG: Oh, Seamus is one of my favorites.

MA: But one thing that everyone has in common is that everyone went through the transcription, imitation process. Absorbing the information and making it their own. So, nobody talked about something really new to me. But it was just really inspiring to see that they're in this place because of this work. And I still have more people that I want to study with. I took some lessons with George Coleman.

JG: Great!

MA: And it wasn't through the Monk Competition. It was through Emilio Lyons, the saxophone repairman in Boston. He's like a second father to me. When I moved to New York he told me you need to meet George Coleman. So, he called George when I was at his place and made me play a tune for George. George liked it and he invited me to his house, and I had a few lessons with him and I had the chance to sit in with him. Those were some of the best lessons that I had, just talking about harmony and how to get around your horn in all keys easily. And then I took some composition lessons with Miguel Zenon. I still have some saxophone players I want to take lessons with.

JG: What are some of the things that Miguel talked with you about in terms of composition?

MA: A lot of things. But the thing that stood out to me was, he approached composition the way he approached practicing. So, it's something he does every day. He said, even if you don't write a whole tune just practice getting your ideas out. He had a book where he'd write, like make a road map of what the tune would be like. And that really stood out to me because I found a lot of things that I liked, or worked or didn't work, just by doing that every day, through that consistency. So that's the thing that really resonated with me.

JG: That's something that Phil Woods told me when I studied with him. I don't do that every day in the same way as I have at certain times. But composition and arranging is a really important part of what we do. Because we have this in-the-moment creative process of improvisers, which very few other art forms have. And if you also have the compositional process which takes place over time, like a sculptor, or a playwright, it's an incredible mix and balance.

MA: Yeah, and I think for me it's very important. I wish I could spend more time. It's hard to do it every day with all the traveling and everything. But it's very useful to find your own thing.

JG: Yes.

MA: Finding out what you like or don't like. Instead of playing standards or other people's music, I find it's been a good way for me to understand myself a little bit better.

JG: I think that's very well put. Because we've all that moment where you write something, you go to play on it, and it really kicks your butt. So, what do I play on this and what do I need to learn to do that? Have you had that experience too?

MA: Oh sure. Most of my tunes are built that way. I write something where the melody speaks to me but is also a little bit challenging. And also, I'm putting myself in a situation where I have to work on certain things, so I'm trying to find a balance that way.

JG: So, after Berklee from 2008–2010, you were in the Monk Competition in 2013. A couple of my former students were in the semi-finals that year, Sam Dillon and Andrew Gould.

MA: Oh yeah, they sounded great.

JG: I'd worked with Andrew quite a bit at Purchase, and some with Sam as well, and I was very happy for and proud of those guys. And your dad was in the semi-finals in 1991, the year that Joshua Redman won, right?

MA: Yes.

JG: What did he tell you about that experience?

MA: He said it was pretty scary for him. Back then he was just a guy from Chile who didn't speak much English. And Chris Potter was there, and Joshua Redman, and Eric Alexander. He told me the first day he arrived he and Joshua were asked to do an interview for TV, and he said Joshua took out his horn and just killed it! So, he told me it was a beautiful experience, but very scary, being around those kinds of players.

JG: And what was your experience like there?

MA: My experience was a little overwhelming. But I did a lot of psychological preparation, you know? Like, I didn't go there trying to win or thinking anything like that. I just went and tried to do my best, and be myself, as much as I could. I was the last one to play at rehearsal. So, I got there a little early, and I heard people playing some ridiculous things on the saxophone! Everyone could really play the horn. So, I was really thinking about, what do I have to say?

JG: Right. What do you have to offer?

MA: Yeah.

JG: I remember, I had a great lesson with Dick Oatts when I was nineteen, and he said, "You sound good. But I want to hear you play less saxophone and more music." And I got it. I really heard him. I hear that kind of thinking in your playing. You understand that. You play the saxophone great and you work very hard on it. Being around you a couple days I see that dedication to craft, and that's great. But ultimately it has to be a means to an end.

MA: Yeah.

JG: Not an end in itself. It's got to take us on some kind of deeper emotional, spiritual journey.

MA: I think that's the whole point.

JG: Yes.

MA: I do spend a lot of hours practicing and trying to achieve technique, learn standards, and the language really well. But then at the moment of playing I just want to play, and I don't want to think about that. So that was the way I was trying to play there. I practiced as much as I could. I did my best. I just wanna go and play. Plus, if I played something that wasn't me, it wouldn't come out natural, you know? I just knew it. Plus, I was lucky to have experience as a band leader. So, when I was there, I was playing with the band. I was really trying to be musical and interact with the band and do it as though I was doing my own concert. My set of music wasn't the most perfect. The band got lost on the last tune.

JG: At the semi-finals?

MA: Yeah, and my knees were shaking. But I think that was good because that brought me back to the moment and I thought, "OK, we need to deal with this, how are we gonna finish the tune?" But I learned so much. Everyone is different and has different skills. The only thing you can do is try to do your best. And that counts for anything in life. There's always going to be someone better than me, in different ways. And that's something I keep in mind about New York. So, if I start thinking about, who can play more horn than me, or faster, you just get depressed. I just try and do my best, that's the best thing you can go for.

JG: That's it.

MA: Yeah. And I think maybe there's a generational thing, but it feels like, at least my genera-tion, where you have to be killing all the time. And it's something you feel as a young musician when you move to New York. Which is, kind of like, it's not the point.

JG: Thank you.

MA: So a lot of people get scared with that, and you go to Smalls and everyone is just like trying to play the right changes, and actually, that's not the point. Maybe it's a generational thing, I'm not sure.

JG: Even that language... killing?... I don't know.

MA: Yeah.

JG: You know? Like, on a subconscious level with that language, where are we going with that? I wanna move people. I wanna to be inspired, and I hope to inspire. The year I was there I heard a lot of people that really impressed me. One of them was John Ellis, one of my favorites since then. He was 21. I thought he played beautifully. He didn't play a whole lot of fast, impressive stuff. But beautiful sound, time, and language. At dinner one night there Jackie McLean said, "Man, that cat John Ellis really impressed me," and I went over and got John and brought him to hear that from Jackie to know that he really dug him. When I went there I had a very similar outlook to what you described. I just hoped everybody played good and had fun. And anything that gets the music out there… like with people that get grants, God bless them. You know? But just go and enjoy the process. And that first day I really felt that. Joel Frahm, Jimmy Greene, John Ellis, I love the way these guys play! Ralph Bowen… you can't play the saxophone any better than Ralph Bowen! I think Mark Turner sent a tape but he didn't make it. I called his house not long after and Helena picked up and I told her if it were up to me, I would've just given it to Mark. But it's all so arbitrary, there's so much luck involved. But I was fortunate that night. And you had a great night.

MA: Yeah, it was cool. I was pretty scared. But after the semi-finals I knew I got some money. So, whatever, I don't care what happens.

JG: [Laughter]

MA: And back then I needed it so much. I was doing like three gigs a day for $40. Barely making it… but making it somehow. A brunch gig, Café Vivaldi, The Bar Next Door the early set, and the Smalls jam session. So, this really helped a lot. For the finals I played one of my tunes and "I Thought About You." By then I had a really good vibe with the other musicians, Rodney Whitaker and Carl Allen, and I wound up working with them afterwards. They really made me feel relaxed and have a good time. And then Godwin Louis and Tivon Pennicott, who were also in the finals, are good friends of mine.

JG: And they're both great players.

MA: They are. And we were hanging from day one of when we arrived. A lot of people had a pretty intense vibe. But between the three of us we were just like cool you know. So, it felt like family. I was relaxed.

JG: Yeah, it's nice when you can just have fun, including if you go to any of the other ones. I mean, how many times are you going to get to meet and hang around Stevie Wonder?

MA: You know, I went back a few years later when Marquis Hill won. At some point they were giving a lifetime achievement award to Bill Clinton. I was backstage and Wayne Shorter comes by me. Then Jimmy Heath and Joshua Redman comes. And then Bill Clinton comes over to us.

JG: Wow.

MA: So I'm sitting there hanging with all those people, and Bill Clinton says, "I know that saxophone you're playing was your grandfather's horn."

JG: Wow! So, he knew that much about you? And you're playing the same horn your grandfather played?

MA: I used to, I'll show you a picture. Jimmy said we need a picture!

JG: And President Clinton knew enough about you to know you were playing your grandfather's horn!

MA: Yes.

JG: Well, it's often been said about him, he knows a lot about a lot of things. I know people that have met him and he knows more about the saxophone than we might expect.

MA: He took my saxophone, and he kind of took it in a weird way where I was almost worried about how he was holding the horn, so I was almost like, wait, give me the saxophone back. Here's the picture. [She shows me the picture.]

JG: Oh wow! That's a great photo with you, Jimmy Heath, and Bill Clinton. That's great!

MA: But back then I didn't really realize. I kind of knew. But I wasn't nervous. I was around these people, but it just felt natural. But he was taking my horn in a weird way.

JG: Yeah, you may be a very famous and important person but don't break my horn!

MA: Yeah! And he talked to Wayne and Jimmy and the rest of the people there in such a respectful way. You know, the Masters! And he's talking about the history and the recordings.

JG: He's a fan!

MA: I never felt like I was sitting with a President. He just felt like a normal guy.

JG: So, tell us about the last five to six years or so and how things are moving forward.

MA: Well, I think the best part of the Monk thing, beside the money which was very helpful, is that it opened a lot of doors for me faster, and it kind of put me on the map. But also, it hasn't been easy. I'm lucky to have management and a booking agent. But I've done a lot of touring for no money as a band leader.

JG: Yeah.

MA: So you tour, and then you do things on the side so you can keep your touring going. But things have been getting better slowly. But it's taken years to build up and get better fees for my own band. But the fact that I was the first female and the first South American to win, that kind of put me in a certain place. I think it opened up a lot more doors and made people aware. Even though I don't really care about this gender thing. It's not something that I mention or that I want to be a part of. Even though I acknowledge that there's been disadvantage and imbalance throughout history. But my generation, we haven't really suffered from it, to be honest. So, I'm happy that this has been helpful for my career, to be a female, because I'm the first one. But I don't like to think about it this way. I just think of it as a good opportunity. And as a result, I was able to record my second album with a big label.

JG: Which one?

MA: Concord.

JG: Great.

MA: So, it's just been mostly a lot of exposure. But you know, it's been six years. And the thing of the Monk Competition winner washes away, and now I'm just trying to figure out what I want to do and who I am as a musician. Rather than the winner of the 2013… you know what I mean?

JG: Oh, yeah, of course. But when you get things like that hopefully it can be a jumping-off point and help create opportunities for you. In the time we have left, we talked earlier today about Isabel Allende, the great Chilean writer who we're both fans of. Is there any Chilean music that was impactful to you, or that was a part of the culture that you have an affinity for?

MA: Actually no. I have a little bit of a different situation. And also, it's because of the country and the time when I was born. I'm from the generation of the late '80s and early '90s after Pinochet, the dictator of Chile was taken away. So, there was a good amount of ten years where culturally you didn't embrace the culture and folklore of Chile. I've been to Cuba, Argentina, and Peru, where these kids, they really know their heritage. It's very important, and like the first thing they learn. For some reason Chile is not like that. I see this to this day. It's like a kind of lack of identity. For example, I don't know if you know Ernesto Jodos or Guillermo Klein, for them being Argentinian is a big part of their music and who they are.

JG: I was thinking there might be a Chilean composer like Piazzolla or Ginastera.

MA: There's not really, actually. For musicians, my grandfather was one of the first jazz musicians. But in the jazz scene, and this is something I can see now if you go to Argentina, everyone is starting to make a mix of their folk music. But if you go to Chile, they're still playing standards. They're still trying to sound like Americans. There's a lack of identity and culture. And growing up in school we didn't talk a lot about the history of Chile. A lot of important singer songwriters like Violeta Parra were pushed aside because they were not politically involved in the Pinochet area. So, I hardly grew up listening to cueca or knowing about Parra which is like the history of my country. I had a father who was like, Charlie Parker is like the hippest musician in the world. Parker, Cannonball, and Phil Woods were his guys. Those were my strongest guys.

JG: Was your dad mainly an alto player?

MA: Yeah, he was mostly an alto player. And he was so in love with Cannonball and Phil Woods. So, I grew up with that. He also was crazy about Michael Brecker. I grew up with all that era of the Brecker Brothers, Steps Ahead, Return to Forever.

JG: And you were playing the Dave Guardala Brecker mouthpiece, then some time after you met Mark you switched to the hard rubber and changed sound concept?

MA: Yeah, but I was playing alto until I was twelve, but then I heard Sonny for the first time…

JG: Ah!

MA: And I told my father I wanted the tenor. So, that's when I started playing tenor, and I didn't pick up the alto for many years after that.

JG: As you said earlier, Don Byas, Sonny Rollins, and Mark Turner were the three tenor players that you studied the most and tried to emulate, transcribe, and assimilate the most.

MA: Yeah, well I've always been a huge transcriber. So, for me it's like, every two weeks a new solo. It keeps me inspired a lot, you know, and it helps me to come up with new ideas. I don't know if you're like this too, but sometimes I'm not super-inspired to practice or get into something new. But then a lot of the practice is just discipline and consistency, trying to keep it going, and then when I'm inspired and feeling it, it's great.

JG: Yeah, it's great when you find something new like that to work on that really inspires you. I never knew the Stan Getz with Oscar Peterson Trio record, and then I heard it a few years ago. Such great playing! Such an amazing time feel without the drummer. It was so fun to find that and play along with it. We talked about that today when we played duo.

MA: Yeah, I love Stan too. You know, at some point I started transcribing with Coleman Hawkins. And I really started checking out a lot of people—Lucky Thompson, Gene Ammons, Jimmy Forrest. I just started studying the instrument, you know? The people I mentioned that spoke the most to me were Don Byas, Rollins, and Mark. But I did a lot of Joe Lovano as well… Lucky Thompson quite a bit. And even… I love Don Byas and Mark, but there's something about Sonny that I gravitate to. Like, it never gets old to me.

JG: You mentioned something earlier today about Sonny Rollins, about his humor.

MA: He's so funny, yeah.

JG: Yeah, well, sometimes we want to be deep and serious, and Sonny of course has that. But he also has a kind of lightness and humor, and that in-the-moment thing where he can turn on a dime and go any direction, idea-wise, conceptually.

MA: Yeah, I love that about him. To this day, every time I hear him play a ballad, it just gets me so much.

JG: Did you ever meet him?

MA: Yeah.

JG: What was that like?

MA: Well I actually recorded an album called *Back Home*. It's kind of a tribute to Sonny, but it's not playing like him or anything. The title refers to the first time I heard Sonny playing tenor, back home in Chile. So somehow, because of that, his manager heard about this and somebody asked me to do an interview with Sonny. So, I interviewed him for his latest album, *On the Road*.

JG: Did you go up to his house in Upstate New York?

MA: No, I was in Slovenia, so I called him.

JG: So this was a few years ago?

MA: Yeah, it's on the internet actually. I was supposed to ask him about the album. I was really nervous, I had written down all these questions, you know. So, I finished asking him about the album. He knew about me because he's very close to Emilio Lyons, and Emilio had talked to him about me. He knew that I loved Don Byas, and that my father and grandfather played the saxophone. He took the time to talk to me, and we ended up talking for over an hour. I started asking him about his process, and why he played long solos, and how his practicing has changed through the years. He was so kind to talk to me. One of the things that he said was, "Never trust the audience, the other musicians, promoters, or managers. Always do what you believe that you should be doing. And that's the most important thing."

JG: Well, that's pretty great advice to end on. I really appreciate your time.

MA: Of course, thanks.

JG: It's great talking and getting to know you and hear you. I look forward to hanging more in the coming years.

MA: Thank you Jon.

JG: Thank you.

The T.S. Monk Sextet and Tentet & Ronnie Mathews
1995-97

From the mid '90s on I used to sub quite a bit in the T.S. Monk Sextet. I played on a recording the band did during that period. We also did some gigs as a tentet, featuring the arrangements of Hall Overton that Monk had recorded on the *Live at Town Hall* recording. There were a number of tours in the U.S., Europe, and Canada. Nellie Monk, Thelonious' wife and T.S.'s mom, would sometimes come to gigs in the New York City or New Jersey area, and that was really a thrill. The sextet was Don Sickler, Willie Williams, Ronnie Mathews, Gary Wang, and T.S. or Toot, on drums. I really enjoyed the band and getting to know a lot more of Monk's music.

The first rehearsal I played, I sight-read Monk's solo on "Little Rootie Tootie" from the Hall Overton arrangement. I hung on for dear life but got through it. So, I think that's why they thought to call me sometimes when their regular alto player, the great Bobby Porcelli, couldn't make it.

I think the first gig I did was in LA or San Diego, in the late summer of 1995. We played a couple tunes I'd seen before. Then Ronnie Mathews called out on the bandstand, "Hey Jon! Do you know "Skippy?"" I thought a moment and said, "No, I don' think I've played that one." He said, "Oh, OK. Hey Don, Toot, let's play that. Jon, you take the first solo." I said, "OK," having no idea what I was in store for.

Toot counted it off, medium up, not super-fast, but it was a challenging melody for sure! I got through it OK, I thought, and then went right to the solo.

First of all, the changes moved in a way I was totally unaccustomed to. It was moving dominant chords every two beats, which didn't at all imply the kind of dominant to tonic, or V-I, or ii-V-I harmony that we often deal with in bebop. I was doing my best to again hang on as best as I could. But when we got to the last eight bars of the form I saw the chords literally moved one chord per beat! I just did a double take, took the horn out of mouth, looked at the page real hard and mouthed—*What the fuck*!?

I wanna tell you, out of the corner of my eye at that moment, I saw Ronnie Mathews almost fall off of the piano bench from laughter! I grabbed what I could, played another chorus, bullshitted my way through most of it, especially that last eight bars, and looked over at Ronnie, both embarrassed but laughing at the same time. Ronnie was smiling from ear to ear and still giggling some at my struggles. Damn! Did that tune ever kick my ass! I mean, when I got to that one spot where the chords moved so fast, I'd just never seen anything like that and had no idea what to do! But sometimes guys of that generation liked to show you early to stay humble, and boy did that ever work on me! I frankly always felt like I was scuffling on much of that music, but my appreciation for the genius of it certainly grew as I tried to learn how to play it.

Ronnie was, to me, the greatest interpreter of Monk's music that I ever heard live or played with. Sometimes people play clusters on the piano in some kind of cutesy way and think they're getting Monk. That ain't it. The feel, the accents, the voicings—Ronnie was a master with that, and made the rhythm section feel great. I told him I'd never heard anyone play Thelonious' music as well as he did. He said, "Well, I appreciate that man. But you know,

Nellie gave me the compliment of a lifetime a couple years ago and told me the same thing!" Can you imagine a compliment like that? Ronnie was also close to Hall Overton and knew those arrangements too.

I remember in late November or early December of 1996 we had a gig at Syracuse College in Upstate New York. It was the week after I'd won the Monk Competition, and I'd seen Don and Toot there and gotten to talk with them about it some, though not the other guys. I was living in Nyack, about 40 minutes north of New York City, on the way to the gig, and the other guys were in a small bus coming up from the city. They met me at a gas station and store near the highway, not far from my place. They pulled up, and Ronnie was the first person to get off the bus. I gave him a big smile and wave as he stepped down the stairs of the small bus, sort of expecting some words of congratulations. But instead he walked right up to me and loudly said, "I need a loan, motherfucker!" And then quickly walked past me towards the store, with what I used to think of as "the George Jefferson walk" where one arm after the other swung behind you as you walked, quickly and with attitude! I just cracked up! When he got back on the bus we had a laugh about it. I threw on a video cassette of George Carlin, *40 years of Comedy* (one of my heroes!) and we laughed our asses off on the way to the gig.

In June of 1997, we had about a ten-day tour across Canada, playing the jazz festivals, as they moved from east to west across the country over 2–3 weeks or so in the summer. At one point, when we were flying from Calgary to Edmonton, the flight had been oversold by one ticket. Somehow, seeming to personally embody Murphy's Law, the airline decided that I, of all people, should again be the one person not to get on the flight. You can't make it up. So, we explained the situation to the airline staff and crew. It's a sextet—none of the music we played was gonna work without all three horns. I asked, "Is there any way we can make this work?" It's a forty minute flight. I'll sit on the floor, I don't care." Again, this would *never* happen post-9/11, but they said, "Well, there is one option if you don't mind being a bit cramped. There's a jumpseat in the cockpit between the two pilots. If we do this, we'd just ask that you stay there in your seat for the whole flight and don't talk to the pilots." "Sure," I said, "Sounds great!" So I get up there, which first of all I gotta say, was pretty cool! But then we get up in the air, and the view of the Rockies to my left was amazing! For most of the flight I was just stunned at how beautiful it was looking at the mountains. We were heading pretty due north, and over time the mountains veered off more to the west so there wasn't as much of a view as we approached Edmonton. But still, having made it on the flight, and getting that view as well? I counted myself as pretty lucky!

Kevin Hays

Harlem, New York City – Spring 2014

JG: So, Kevin Hays! How long have we known each other? When did we first meet?

KH: Well, that was when you were playing with the Manhattan Jazz Quintet.

JG: At Augie's?

KH: Well, I meet you through Sean Smith for sure, who was in that group.

JG: '84 or '85?

KH: That sounds about right.

JG: And I remember you sitting in with us really early at Augie's, like 1984.

KH: Augie's! Really? I sat in?

JG: Yeah, a couple times… on that horrific piano.

KH: [Laughter]

JG: And I remember playing with you at Mikell's in '86–87, and your playing went on this incredible trajectory! It was just amazing what was happening with you and your growth! You were playing so great. So, what was your start in music?

KH: Probably my father playing the piano.

JG: I didn't know your dad played the piano!

KH: You don't remember that?

JG: No. I remember he was really enthusiastic about music.

KH: Yeah, he played. I'd hear him play in the living room. He played a kind of stride type of thing. He'd play some standards, not professionally or anything. My first teacher was his first teacher, Lou Stein. He played on *Bird with Strings*.

JG: Wow, I didn't realize that.

KH: He was kind of a session guy. Straight forward, good jazz player. I learned a lot from him.

JG: He was near you in Connecticut?

KH: He was over the border in Pound Ridge.

JG: I think that's pretty close to where the great trombonist Eddie Bert lived.

KH: That would make sense.

JG: They were of a similar generation.

KH: Yeah.

JG: So, in those years, you went on this incredible growth spurt, and by the late '80s you were working a lot as a sideman, including Joe Henderson I think?

KH: Well, I wasn't playing with Joe by the late '80s. I made my first record in '91 with Scott Colley, Bill Stewart, Steve Wilson, and Joe did it. It was for a Japanese label, Jazz City.

JG: So, had you played with Joe before that?

KH: No.

JG: But then he called you after that date?

KH: Yeah. I got his number from Don Sickler.

JG: Wow.

KH: I called up Don and said, "I've got this record date. Do you think Joe would play on it?" So, I called him up. I'm pretty sure I sent him a cassette of the music. I don't know if he knew if I could play. Maybe he called Don, or maybe I sent him a demo. Or maybe he was just down to do a recording with anyone who would pay back then. [Laughter]

JG: If the money was green…

KH: He did some record dates around then.

JG: Well, even though he was a big star in '91, I know he played with Blood, Sweat & Tears in the '70s. Ronnie Mathews told me that the '70s were rough for a lot of people. He worked at Sears and told me it was tough for lots of guys to make a living.

KH: I have a funny story about Joe, speaking of surviving. We had a gig in Spain, with this drummer who couldn't get it together. He didn't know any of Joe's tunes. He just called him. Dwayne Burno was on the gig. The late Dwayne Burno…

JG: I know, unbelievable…

KH: Anyway, so, Joe arrives, we'd already played a week with Vincent Herring, and the drummer wasn't great. Joe gets there, we're talking at the bar, and he says, "So, how is he?" We were trying to be nice about it. "Well, he's a good guy," stuff like that. Then he says, "C'mon fellas! This is Joe! How is he?!"

BOTH: [Laughter]

KH: So we told him. But then the conversation changed and he started talking about "walkin' the bar" back in the day. I said, "You walked the bar!?" He said, "Of course, what are you talking about?"

JG: Trane walked the bar.

KH: He said that, "Trane walked the bar, we all did." That must've been some bar…

JG: So how much did you work with him in the '90s?

KH: I did a few gigs, Boston, San Diego, my first gig was there. I was super nervous.

JG: But he kept calling you, so…

KH: Yeah! For a little bit.

JG: And you did some gigs with Rollins around then too, right?

KH: Yeah, after that. Mid-'90s… '95, '97. You know, I did Josh's first record. I was just looking at it, it was around then. Before that I was working with Benny Golson.

JG: Right.

KH: I worked with Benny for a number of years.

JG: Wow. How long did you work with Rollins?

KH: About two years or so.

JG: That must have been incredible, playing with that energy and presence on the bandstand.

KH: Yeah! Serious presence, pretty amazing. It's interesting too, because I remember, you were the one that basically hipped me to Joe. I was really into Sonny.

JG: How could you not be?

KH: I was so into Sonny! I even borrowed your tenor at one point.

JG: Oh yeah! I remember that!

KH: That was a disaster!

JG: [Laughter]

KH: Somewhere there's a tape of me trying to play "St. Thomas."

BOTH: [Laughter]

KH: But I remember you telling me about Joe live at the Vanguard. And I was getting into Sonny at the Vanguard and I thought, "Hey, this guy is ripping off Sonny!" And you said, "Well, check it out." And I finally did realize that it was really happening too!

JG: Well, I've found that some recordings that I heard when I was first coming up, I might not have gotten right away. But once I heard those people live, I went back and understood the recordings more deeply. He was like that for me. I really liked the recordings, but once I heard him live! Then, and now, I think he's one of the greatest improvisers I ever heard. He really blew my mind. When did you start to realize how great he was?

KH: I don't know. I think I had some strong opinions back then. You probably remember.

JG: Well, a lot of us were like that. But we didn't know what we didn't know.

KH: Yeah.

JG: And that's always the case. I see that in some of my students sometimes. They think they've got things figured out that they don't. But I remember one time in Eddie Locke's building, that apartment I watched… you played me Miles *Live at the Blackhawk*.

KH: Yeah.

JG: I'd never heard it. And you said, if I listen to this before I play a gig, I feel like I play better. And we listened to Hank Mobley's solo on "Bye Bye Blackbird."

KH: Right.

JG: And right before that, Mobley was at Sickler's and I met him briefly. Maybe you met him too, because you were involved in the Young Sounds group Don had.

KH: Yeah, I did meet him there. He showed me the right turnaround to "Tune Up."

JG: You're kidding! What's the right turnaround?

KH: The one you know, it was just I didn't know it then.

JG: Wow. Did he play?

KH: He didn't play, but he did show me that.

JG: Well I was there at Don's in late '85 and he said, "I wanna introduce you to Mobley. You know who he is?" I said I did but that I didn't know his playing well. I was eighteen, you know.

So, Hank comes out, he couldn't have been nicer! Don said, "Man, you don't know this record with Trane, Hank, and Griffin? I wanna play you this record."

KH: It's not the Zoot, Al record?

JG: No, I think that's *Tenor Conclave* with Trane.

KH: That's great!

JG: Yeah, I heard that one around then or soon after, but I didn't know about this one at all. And Don said, I'm gonna play you this." If you remember, Don's office was surrounded by records on the walls. And Hank fell back into one of the walls of records and put his hands up and said, "Oh man! Please don't play that record! Those guys kicked my ass so bad!"

BOTH: [Laughter]

JG: But Don said, "Those guys played great, but you did too! Mobley's a melody player man! He's a melody player!" And I said, yeah, but I didn't really get it in that moment. But then you played me Miles *Live at the Blackhawk*...

KH: That line...

JG: That *line*! And you sang it when we got there, at the top of one of Hank's choruses on "Bye Bye Blackbird."

BOTH: [Singing]

JG: And a light went on, and I got it! And you know, every time I play that tune since then I quote that.

KH: You know man, we should do a video.

JG: I'd like to. I don't have the equipment.

KH: You should set it up.

JG: Yeah, we could do a barbershop duo of us singing Hank Mobley solos badly.

KH: It's interesting because...

JG: That was the spring of '86.

KH: I think I always have had a penchant for melody. I don't know why. I try to be modern, you know... [Laughter]

JG: What's more modern than melody?

KH: I'm just kidding. Honestly, this just popped up, but I haven't been listening to jazz as much lately.

JG: What are you listening to?

KH: A lot of classical music. When I put on the iTunes radio thing I listened to Monk, and some Hank came up too.

JG: What iTunes radio thing?

KH: It's a way to sell you stuff. They have channels. You put in an artist and they make you a play list. I just put in Monk the other day, which was great. And I just heard Hank on "Remember" the other night on there. It's so great, so melodic, so beautiful.

JG: Yeah. I just remembered a great tune that you hipped me to that I ended up recording—"Gaslight" by Duke Pearson.

KH: Yeah! That's a great tune.

JG: All those half-step approaches. Man! It's one thing if you do it on a major chord, but he also does it on an augmented chord, so you end up getting that polytonal, hexatonic sound. Two augmented triads a half-step away.

KH: Yeah, Dwayne Burno hipped me to Duke Pearson.

JG: Yeah. I didn't know Dwayne all that well, but we just lost him about a month ago. Were you at the memorial for him?

KH: I couldn't go. David Weiss asked me to go, 'cause Dwayne had a band with me, Dion Parson, Myron Walden, Monte Croft. Dwayne and I played a lot together. With Vincent Herring, Benny Golson, Joe Chambers, Roy Haynes…

JG: I didn't know you played with Roy Haynes' band. When did you do that?

KH: Oh, around that same time, mid '90s.

JG: It's incredible how many people you played with man. There are very few people who have been as prolific a sideman and played with all the history you have.

KH: Yeah, well, I was pinching myself in the moment when it was happening. Some really great experiences, with a lot of great drummers, saxophone players, and bass players.

JG: The other thing I just remembered was that period when you, Bill Stewart, and Hagans got signed to Blue Note. I actually did a concert with my band and your three bands at Damrosch Park around then that Joanne Jimenez got me on. Was it two records you made for them?

KH: Three.

JG: Three… what was the first one?

KH: *Seventh Sense.*

JG: That's right, I remember that one.

KH: Seamus Blake, Brian Blade, Doug Weiss, and Steve Nelson. Then I did a two-tenor record with Steve Hall, Seamus, Billy Hart, and Doug, called *Go Round.*

JG: I think I heard some of that. What was the third one?

KH: The trio album with Ron and Jack.

JG: I don't think I ever heard that.

KH: You may never. [Laughter]

JG: Well, you still have copies don't you?

KH: No, I don't have any copies of that.

JG: Yeah, Belden mentioned to me that they kind of squashed those projects unfortunately. No idea why they'd do that, they were great!

KH: Belden produced that last trio CD.

JG: Well, I think you know him better than I do, but he told me about that. Did he produce any of the others?

KH: No, Scofield produced the first one. The second one I think I produced.

JG: Scofield is another great musician you had a long-time association with, right?

KH: Well, I worked with him for about a year and a half or two.

JG: Was that around the time we did that record of mine that John was kind enough to do?

KH: I think it was before that. I was playing with Sonny and John in that period. Whenever his *Quiet* record came out.

JG: I remember thinking that you and Bill Stewart had an association with him at that time, going into that recording.

KH: Well, you know we were roommates when we made my first record.

JG: Yeah. Do you see Bill much these days?

KH: Yeah, we get together. We've been playing duo lately.

JG: Did I ever tell you this story? In '98 I made a record and Bill was on it. He called me a few months later and asked me for the contact of the producer. He said he had this project with you and Larry Goldings and I thought, great! So, I gave it to him, and called the producer and said, "Man, you should really go with this!" But he said, "A drummer and two piano players? Nobody's ever done that. Why would I want to produce something like that?" And I just thought, well, I think … [Laughter]

KH: Well that's one reason to try it at least!

JG: [Laughter] Yeah! Was it one or two records you guys made?

KH: Two.

JG: That's a great group.

KH: Yeah, a fun record. We did some nice touring.

JG: Yeah.

KH: So it's interesting, I've also done some duos with Larry which we need to get released. We did some nice touring. We played in this big organ cathedral in Amsterdam and we got a pretty nice recording from it. We tried to sell it and it was sort of the same thing, why would you want to do that? The recording had some issues, but it was a nice concert!

JG: Great!

KH: Larry's up in the pipe organ loft…

JG: Wow!

KH: He's playing a huge pipe organ, and a really nice grand piano. Then they had these mini-organs, so we were just kind of bouncing around. It's fantastic.

JG: Great.

KH: And so I'm doing some duo with him, and some duo with Bill.

JG: And in recent years you've been doing some duo stuff with Brad Mehldau too, right?

KH: Yeah.

JG: Tell me about that project.

KH: When I was living in New Mexico I contacted Brad. We knew each other a little bit from being in New York and hanging at the Village Gate or wherever together. I loved his playing and just asked if he'd been interested in doing something together. I had this idea to improvise on some twentieth century classical pieces. Pat Zimmerli got involved and Brad said yeah, he'd love to do it. I mentioned this Strauss piece *Metamorphosen*, that he said he'd been checking out too. We just sort of reconnected after a number of years.

JG: Well you guys were both from Connecticut.

KH: But I didn't know him there. Brad and Pat went to West Hartford High School together.

JG: Joel Frahm was maybe there too?

KH: Yeah, he was. But I didn't know Brad then. So, it took several years to happen. We rehearsed a lot, whenever he was in town, we'd just get together. I was living Upstate, I'd moved back to New York. I brought my keyboard over to his place. And we just played some two-piano things. Pat got involved and wrote and arranged some material. It took a few years and we finally recorded it in, maybe 2011? We didn't tour immediately, but we did tour like a year ago.

JG: Just the two of you?

KH: Yeah, he's incredible. We're going to do a little bit of playing this year.

JG: What's that?

KH: We have a concert in Brazil in August.

JG: Is that your most recent recording?

KH: No, I did a solo record, and Pat Zimmerli helped produce it.

JG: When was that?

KH: It came out a couple years ago.

JG: So Pat produced it?

KH: Well, Jason Seitzer was the producer, but I brought Pat in as an associate producer to help me organize the material, like as a…

JG: Consultant…

KH: Yeah. To help me develop it. It was mainly improvised. I had some sketches and some ideas, but it was mainly improvised.

JG: I knew Pat from when we were teenagers, and even then he was talking about Elliot Carter and modern through composed classical music. I know you've done some projects with him of his writing.

KH: Yeah, his stuff is a lot less out there than Elliot Carter and is much more tonal. He's been writing chamber and orchestral music for a while. He's writing some beautiful music.

JG: Great, I'd love to hear it. So what's coming up for you?

KH: I've got this New Day Trio. We've been touring and getting ready to record. That's going to come out on Sunnyside. Just getting that going, playing, writing, teaching…

JG: Well, we know each other a long time. And in certain ways we know each other very well, and then in other ways we might go five years and only talk two or three times. But you're one of my friends that I'm most proud of. To make the kind of contribution that you've made out here for a long time. It's odd, because I still think of us as seventeen… eighteen, trying to get our shit together.

KH: [Laughter] Right.

JG: Now we're 46… 47, trying to get our shit together. But I'm glad we had a chance to talk. I sometimes talk about people's history with one or two people. With you we could talk about Rollins, Joe Hen, Sco, Benny Golson… you've made an incredible contribution. Players and students know, around the world, when your name comes up, they know. But I also think that you're one of the more underrated guys from a business perspective. Like, I'd love to see you have a week at the Vanguard. Did you ever have one?

KH: Not on my own… working on it.

JG: Well, I certainly think you're deserving of that. To me, over the last 25 years you're one of a handful of the most important jazz piano players in the world. So, thanks Kevin.

KH: Thank you.

Jim McNeely

JG: I'm sitting here in Puerto Rico with Jim McNeely. We played last night here at a jazz festival with Phil Woods. He played amazing as always. And Jim is a guy that I feel is one of the most important jazz pianists, composers, and arrangers in the world. I still can't believe that *Lickety Split* didn't win a Grammy, one of the really great big band recordings in recent years, in my opinion.

JM: Well, thanks. There are plenty of great records that don't win Grammys. They're more of a music industry award than a musician's award, so there's a different parameter at work there.

JG: So how did you get started in music, Jim?

JM: My dad bought a piano, he played... picked up tunes by ear. Played everything in the key of G♭. He decided as a kid that there's only five black keys to the octave so it would be easier to learn than the seven white keys. So, he'd hammer out a tune and if the bridge went somewhere else there'd be a bar or two of confusion and he'd still be in G♭.

BOTH: [Laughter]

JM: Everything was in that vice. So, he bought this little Betsy Ross spinet piano, though it was terrible. My aunt taught me "Chopsticks." I was about five years old at the time. I remember my mother saying, "Well we should sign you up for piano lessons at school." And then she did and I thought, "Well, I already know "Chopsticks," what else is there?"

BOTH: [Laughter]

JM: So I began in first grade with a nun at my school. After about a year and a half she got sick, and my mother arranged to have a teacher come to the house. Bruno Michelotti was his name. And I'll never forget it, before I played a note, he wrote the word "Theory" on the top of a piece of music paper. I asked, "What's theory?" He told me, "Well, theory is what you have to learn to be able to make music."

He wasn't a jazz guy by any stretch of the imagination. But I was with him all through my grammar school years, and he taught me how to read chord symbols and a basic lead sheet, and standard piano stuff. He also taught clarinet and sax, so I took some clarinet lessons for a couple of years and a year of sax lessons. I was building this foundation. My school had no band to play in, though I was playing clarinet and piano. But I had this feeling that there must be some kind of music out there where I could use some of this knowledge.

JG: [Laughter]

JM: My dad listened to two kinds of music, big band and polka music. And the high school I went to had a jazz band. I remember, even before then, seeing Duke Ellington on TV and being knocked out by the music. The way these guys carried themselves was so suave and hip and the music was great. The high school I ended up going to was Notre Dame High School just north of Chicago. I'd heard their big band on a local TV show and thought, "This is where I want to go!" So, I started to find out about jazz. My father was helpful and got me *DownBeat* magazine and the Leonard Feather *Encyclopedia of Jazz*. I started reading about these guys and buying records.

So, I put together a little band at school, and played in the school jazz band and that's where I started to write arrangements. I had a great band director, a Holy Cross priest, George Whisker. He encouraged me to write. This was in the mid '60s. At that time all the local school big bands were into Maynard or Kenton. But George was into Basie and he had gotten to know Frank Wess. If Basie was in town for a week he'd go to the gig and say to Frank, "Man, I really dug that chart you played. Do you think I could borrow it?" Frank would say, "Yeah, but you have to have it back tomorrow night!" Then he'd take them home, hand-copy them all night and get them back to the band the next night.

JG: Wow!

JM: So, we were playing that kind of music at school. It was great! Also, my senior year I was writing for the marching band. He'd farm out to me and another guy the writing for the band. Using a six-staff system, where you'd fill in the melody and a harmony part and the oompah, etc. And that way he'd have the flexibility to say, "OK, for this formation here I want sixteen bars of "She's Only a Bird in a Gilded Cage," then go into Trane's version of "My Favorite Things," and you'll play soprano sax out in the field."

JG: Wow!

JM: And I'd say, "OK!" And that was my first experience of writing to a deadline. We had to get the stuff done by Friday so he could copy the parts and get them to us by Monday morning. Then I went to the University of Illinois as a composition major. They had a great big band there at the time. I met a lot of guys that were older and more experienced and played better than me. In general, that's how you learn—you get yourself in positions with guys that are older and more experienced and knowledgeable than you and learn from those guys that are better than you. So, I had a bunch of folks that were very helpful to me. We'd play jam sessions. They'd call a tune, and if I didn't know the tune they'd say, "OK, it's in F, and the bridge goes to the four. One two three…" And we'd start to play and you had to learn it. I wrote some for the big band there at the University. And in late high school I started to work some gigs.

I begin to realize all the sudden I was financially a little more independent. Finally, in '75, after eight years, I got out of University. I got my degree and moved to New York. It's a long story of why it took so long. I'd been thinking about moving back to Chicago. There were some great musicians there, but not so much of a club scene. New York was the mecca for jazz musicians. I was single and naive enough to have a dream of going there, so I came out.

JG: I think the first time I saw you was in a video with was Stan Getz. When did you start working with him?

JM: That was '81. That was probably with Victor Lewis and Marc Johnson.

JG: How did that come about?

JM: Well, as it was in those days, and I think it still is to some extent, you get recommended to band leaders because you've gotten to know some of the other people in the band. So rather than trying to getting to know Stan Getz, I got to know, by happenstance, Joanne Brackeen, Billy Hart, Clint Houston, Andy Laverne, Mike Richmond, and others. So, I always knew the musicians playing with Stan. And, this is typical, Stan needed a piano player and asked the rhythm section, "Who's around? Who would you recommend?" So, he called me. But the first time he called I couldn't make it. I was working with Mel Lewis' band, for one of the rare two-week tours we did.

JG: Aren't you on the first record that Mel made after Thad left, the one with all the Brook-meyer arrangements, with Clark Terry and "Skylark?"

JM: Yeah.

JG: Oh, I love that record! Phil played me that record to hear Oatts on "Skylark!" You play great on that record.

JM: Yeah, and Bob wrote a couple things for me to play on—"First Love Song" and "Ding Dong Ding." Those were both where the band played things and just stopped and I could just do whatever I wanted. And that was a real challenge for me. Especially when we'd go on the road for a three-week tour. I'd be playing those things every night and I'd be thinking, "What am I gonna play tonight?" I quickly realized that I couldn't prepare anything—the hole opened up and you just kinda jumped in. I'd get my hands on the keys and see where everything went. So, it was an interesting place for me to develop, Mel's band.

We'd do a couple of tours like that a year. And one time was when Stan asked me to work with him. But then he called me again about six months later. He was looking for a permanent replacement by this time. He'd moved back out to the West Coast, the San Francisco area. He was playing with his old buddy Lou Levy on piano. I think Victor was playing, and I think Marc was on the band. And Lou didn't wanna travel. He was busy doing a lot of work in LA. So, Stan called me again and we got together and played duo one day. It worked and he offered me the job, so that was '81.

JG: Man, that's great. So, you were working with Mel's band and Stan. How long did you work with Stan?

JM: I worked with him full time from '81 to sometime in '85. And then, after that kind of on and off. There was a period there I would work with him, Kenny Barron would, a couple of other people occasionally. I started to get into other things and Stan started to get into a really great rapport with Kenny. So, they ended up working together.

JG: Did you ever write much for Stan?

JM: I wrote some tunes for him. At first he said, I hear you write tunes so bring in some in. But they were all these slash chord kinda tunes, this over that kind of harmonies, which he could deal with. But he wasn't quite as comfortable with that stuff. So, I began to write some tunes that I felt he could deal with more, and really write for him. But the other thing was, to have his sound in mind, meant that you could write a very simple melody, and he would do all these kind of "Stan" things to the melody—little embellishments and so forth. And so, it was great to write for him. To hear him play your tune, he'd make it sound beautiful. I regret that I didn't start to develop as a big band writer until near the time that he passed. I would have loved to have written a project for him with one of the radio bands in Europe and just never did.

JG: When did you start working with Phil?

JM: Officially the end of 1990. Hal Galper was playing with the band at the time. There was a gig he couldn't make. I knew Steve Gilmore and Bill Goodwin for some years. I'd met Phil at some festivals. We'd hung out. Phil knew me and I knew the guys. So, Galper couldn't make the gig and they called me and it worked out pretty well. And then a couple months later Phil had a six-week tour of Europe and Hal could only make the first three weeks. So, they called me and I said, yeah. I met them in Barcelona. I remember I got off the plane. Somebody picked me up and brought me to the hotel. I called Phil and he said, "Alright! I'll come down and we'll talk about the music!" He brings down that big folder of music, and he proceeds to pull out about thirty different tunes and says, "OK, we might do this one! And we'll probably do this one!" We're drinking coffee. "And maybe, we might do this one. Alright baby! This'll be great!" And he goes back to his room.

JG: [Laughter]

JM: And I'm thinking, I've got two choices—I can either look at this stuff, or go take a real nice nap so I'm up for the gig. So, I thought, I'm gonna go to sleep. 'Cause I figured I could read the music well enough for the first time, even if I made a few mistakes. The important thing was to be mentally ready. So, I had a nice long sleep, and the gig went pretty well. I finished the tour, and at the end of the tour they asked me to join the band. By then Hal had been there for some years and was looking to do other things.

JG: Was Tom Harrell still playing then?

JM: No, that was Hal Crook by that time, and then a few years later Brian Lynch came in on trumpet on the band. Hal's a great musician, writer, and player. And an interesting wig, as we used to say.

JG: Well, man, you've had some incredible associations. Not only Mel, Stan, and Phil, but also being the main writer for the Vanguard Jazz Orchestra the past decade plus.

JM: Well, when I joined the band it was Thad and Mel. When I was in high school and Thad and Mel started to release recordings there was something about Thad's writing that killed me. Something about the harmonies, coupled with the fact it swung so hard and the band sounded so good with Mel. Plus, I loved Roland Hanna especially. I really dug the way he played with the band.

But when I came to New York I really had no aspirations to be a writer. I really came to have a career as a piano player. And again, I got to know Harold Danko who was the piano player with Thad and Mel at that time. And the same pattern—he couldn't make the gig, they called me, I subbed. So, when Harold finally left, Mel called me and I joined the band. Thad was still there. Just to play with him was such a great experience. Six months into that is when Thad left. And I was lucky then to be there when Bob Brookmeyer came in as musical director. And that's when I wrote a chart, and it went OK. I wrote another chart and it went a little better. But it wasn't until I left Mel's band in '84 that I really started to write. And by '87 I was writing projects once a year, sometimes twice a year for the West German Radio Big Band. So, there was a number of years there, including '90–'94 when I was with Phil, that I was doing more and more big band writing.

So, when I left Phil's group in '94, Mel had passed and it was now the Vanguard Jazz Orchestra, and they wanted someone to write a CD for them. And I had history with the band, and I was starting to get a rep as an arranger and composer. So, they asked me to do it, and that was the *Lickety Split* album. And as I was writing the music, I'd come in from time to time to hear the band play it, and there was a lot of little things in the piano part as cues for setting up things in the band. And once in a while I'd sub. Kenny Werner was the official piano player. But he was hardly there because he was so busy. So that was part of the problem, there were often different guys reading the chart. And once in a while I'd sub, and I kind of realized the band was playing my new stuff better when I was there to oversee it. By then the band asked me to come back in the band, and that was '95. We recorded the album in '97.

My official title is composer in residence, which means if I write something I can get them together to read it without them laughing me out of the room. So yeah, we just released a second CD of my material, *Up from the Skies*. I feel like I've grown with the band, and they've grown with me and it's been a good relationship.

JG: And the other thing you do, that many of the great big band writers do, is that you know the band so well, and you're writing with their sound and vibe in mind.

JM: Oh yeah, definitely. Every player has a certain kind of energy, sound, and harmonic language they're really comfortable with. One of the things I like to do is to take a player I respect and throw him into a harmonic area he's not so familiar with. Because a really good player is gonna respond with something. I did that with Phil a number of years ago, in '90 or '91, for the West German Radio Band. Here's a guy that a lot of his language is bebop, functional harmony, ii-V-I kind of stuff. But I knew that there's another side of him, that if you prod him, he'll go there.

JG: Yep, and I love that side of him.

JM: I know, yeah. But left to his own devices he stays in the kind of stuff he's comfortable with. So, I write this thing, and there wasn't one ii-V in the whole piece. Some of it was just intervallic. I'd say, play 5ths and I'll play 4ths. Or play 3rds. And it was interesting. We did a live broadcast on the air in Germany. And just to hear how he responded to it and the way he dealt with it… he's such a great player.

JG: Yeah, he's such a master. Yesterday at the gig, all the cats in the next band off stage—Mike Rodriguez, Yosvany Terry, Dafnis Prieto— they were saying, "*Oh my god*! He sounds amazing! How old is he?" I told them, "He's turning 75." They were like, "Holy shit, his sound!" But I love the side of Phil that you're talking about. I mean you can't play changes or the alto any better than Phil. So, it forces me to try to find something else I can go to. And when he goes those directions it's amazing! I know about that side of him because he'd have us play Bartok violin duets, or play me Ives at lessons. When he uses that side of him it's incredible. Getz was a little like that too. Hearing him in that orchestral setting was amazing.

JM: I think he did that on purpose. I think he knew if he left himself to his own comfort zone he'd still be playing with Jack Teagarden and Benny Goodman—which was great, of course, and that put him on the map. But he put himself in more challenging situations, like the rhythm section with Chick Corea. And in all the years I knew Stan, if anyone ever asked him "What's your favorite album of your own?" Without hesitation, he'd always say *Focus*, that record he did with Eddie Sauter with a small string orchestra.

JG: Yes!

JM: Especially because his mother had died, and he couldn't be at the session. But he came in later and overdubbed all of his parts, with no music. Especially the first track, "I'm Late." They took the track and pasted it together so it's twice through the whole thing. And he just kinda blows over it. So, in that way, he loved to put himself in a challenge. Especially one that wasn't way beyond his abilities. I think we're all like this. You don't want to be thrown in where you're so in over your head you're gonna drown. But on the other hand, where you've gotta find some energy, and dig into yourself to get yourself up to that next level. Unless we do that, we don't grow. And Stan, with his own rhythm sections, he would get guys that would write tunes that would challenge him.

JG: You know, I loved some of the small group writing you did for Phil in the '90s that I got to play when I'd sub for Brian Lynch. That tune in G, in 6?

JM: Oh, "A Perfect Six."

JG: That was great!

JM: Yeah, thanks. To write for Phil's group was really great. Again, I tried to get a little beyond the normal play a head to solos. And in Phil's writing there was all these little shout choruses, interludes, and send offs. There were always arranged features to the tunes, though it was only a quintet. So, I figured I'll take that a step or two farther. That was the album we did when I left the band, *The Phil Woods Quintet Plays the Music of Jim McNeely*. To me, it was the equivalent of, if I was a classical composer, and the Juilliard or Emerson String Quartet did a whole CD of my string quartet writing. I mean, here's one of the premiere groups in jazz, especially in terms of longevity, playing this whole CD of my tunes. And I was really happy with that CD, the way it came out. I enjoyed writing for Phil. The first album I did for Phil after I joined the band was *Real Life*, the little big band album. I'd just joined the band and he said, "We're gonna do this CD and I want you to write something for me… and stretch me!" So that's the first thing I wrote for him, and it's got some pedals that he plays over, and he played great on it.

JG: Well, just to wrap up, I wanted to thank you so much for everything you taught me at the BMI Composer's Workshop, and then when I studied with you privately. I think the three big band charts I wrote didn't change western music. I had the parts all fouled up on the first one, and I thought Manny Albam was gonna kill me!

JM: [Laughter] I remember that!

JG: But I got it a little more together after that. Enough to get another piece played. It wasn't that strong, but at least somewhat presentable. But mostly what I was hearing up until then was more small-group stuff. But a lot of the principles that we talked about, like around pitch-cells, I was sort of doing a bit already instinctively without fully realizing it, like building a piece around a 2nd. And I eventually wrote and recorded three pieces on the pitch-cell you gave me at a lesson.

JM: Yeah, I remember that.

JG: So I just wanted to thank you for showing me that stuff. I just think it's fascinating. It reminded me a little bit of the Bartok Golden Mean theory.

JM: Yeah.

JG: When I first heard that I thought, how can this guy write such amazing, passionate music based on a mathematical theory?

JM: Yeah.

JG: And the pitch-cell concept is certainly not nearly that figured out, but you have this intervallic motive you can always refer back to.

JM: Yeah. Look, I'm convinced that if the passion is there you can write a great piece based on names pulled out of the phone book. A lot of times when people talk about 12-tone theory, or pitch-cells, they object to it and think it's just a lot of numbers and think, "Oh, I'm gonna lose my personal thing." And I really disagree with that. You listen to Schoenberg as opposed to Webern, their music sounds so different, because each person was so different. Their rhythmic ideas, their orchestration ideas, all that was their own. You bring a lot more to the plate than just the pitches, number one. And number two, if the passion is there, you can use anything to make the music, and that's gonna come through.

One thing I've learned from playing with Stan, and Phil, and a lot of other great musicians is the three most important things that people respond to are your sound, your time, and most importantly, the degree to which you absolutely believe what you're doing in the moment.

JG: Yeah.

JM: What the notes are, that's really way down on the list.

JG: Jim, thanks so much man.

JM: You're welcome, alright.

Steve Wilson
New York City – 2007

JG: Well, I'm here at a little café on the Lower East Side, with my friend Steve Wilson, one of my favorite people, musicians, and alto and soprano saxophone players who was nice enough to come and do this interview with me. So, where are you from and how did you get into music?

SW: I'm from Hampton, Virginia. It's part of what they call the Tidewater area, which is basically on the Chesapeake Bay across the water from Norfolk and Virginia Beach. I grew up there in the '60s and '70s, and had pretty much a normal upbringing. Not a big city, not really country. Lots of friends in the neighborhood that played music. As a matter of fact, all we did was play music and sports. All year, all summer, so that's really what my roots are.

JG: That sounds like an ideal childhood.

SW: It was fun, you know. No big events or anything like that. With one exception, the Hampton Jazz Festival which happened every summer. It started on the campus of what was then the Hampton Institute, it's now Hampton University. It was actually one of the major festivals that George Wein produced on the East Coast in the '60s and '70s. And that's where I saw my first live jazz music, people like Eddie Harris, Rahsaan Roland Kirk, Cannonball Adderley…

JG: You saw Cannonball live? Wow!

SW: Yeah. The record *Country Preacher* was a big record for him at the time. He came through with that band with Joe Zawinul and Nat Adderley, Roy McCurdy and Walter Booker…

JG: Oh man, what I would have given to see that.

SW: And that was a life-changing experience. I think I was about nine or ten when that record came out, it totally changed my life.

JG: Wow!

SW: Yeah.

JG: Didn't you mention to me recently that you came up with some of the guys that play in the Dave Mathews Band?

SW: Well that happened later on in the mid '80s. The drummer Carter Beauford and I were in a band together, like a fusion/funk/R&B cover and originals band for about three years. And we had a steady house gig in Richmond, Virginia. He was Billy Drummond's roommate at Shenandoah Conservatory. So they go way back.

JG: Who were some of the other Virginia guys you knew?

SW: Well, I knew Billy, because he lived in the neighboring town of Newport News. And his neighbors who lived right on the corner were the Wooten Brothers. And people may be familiar with some of them from their work with Bela Fleck, that would be Victor and Roy. Roy's been known as future-man for his work with synthesized drums. But there were five brothers all together. And there were times that we'd all hang at their place and play and talk about music. They were all very multi-talented. I've known Billy since I was about sixteen or seventeen, and we used to play a lot actually, in Norfolk and Virginia Beach and Richmond. And I learned so much from him. I credit him for me knowing anything I know about this music. He taught me so much. He had a lot of recordings. His father was a drummer also. And when I would go to his house he'd always keep a cymbal set up in his bedroom. He would play different records, like Tony Williams, Philly Jo Jones, Pappa Jo Jones, all the great drummers. And he would always try to cop their ride pattern.

JG: Well it's funny that you should say that. Because if I had to pick one drummer that I've played with whose ride cymbal just consistently kills me, it's Billy.

SW: Yeah.

JG: I mean, his ride cymbal… I remember, I did this record when I was 27, my first date for Criss Cross. And I was really sick. I hadn't played for some days. And Gerry Teekens, who I'd been trying to get a date from for five years, called me right then and said, "Hey man, I got a last-minute opening, let's do a date."

SW: [Laughter]

JG: And I said, well I can't say no, I been hitting on him for five years! I was sick as a dog. But when we put the band together it was Tim Hagans, Charlap, Larry Grenadier, and Billy. And we played this great Duke Pearson tune at the rehearsal, "Gaslight." We hit the second chorus of the melody, and Larry started playing quarter notes, and Billy's ride cymbal, and the time feel those guys laid down… *man*, that was amazing! I actually met both you and him at Augie's. I was playing there with him, and one night you came in and that's when I met you.

SW: Yeah, I recall that. 'Cause Billy moved to town about six months after I did. I moved in '87. He came in the winter of '88, so maybe it was some time in '88 or '89.

JG: Yeah, I used to play there with a few different people. I'd had a steady night there a few years earlier, which was great. But that's the first place I met you.

SW: I think I might recall that night. I think you were playing something in G. I walked in and you were playing and I was like, *wow*. First of all, it was your sound, and your command, and you were playing in G Concert. Oh man, this is… I don't remember the tune but it was killing.

JG: Well, thanks.

SW: And I just remember thinking I gotta go home and get my shit together, 'cause you sounded so great.

JG: Oh, man, well thanks for the compliment. You know, I should mention, I've been subbing for you, teaching at Purchase, and getting to know and work with some of your students up there. And the thing I always tell them, and other young players… to me, you're the most complete alto player I know of. I've never played with anybody in a section, or heard anybody in person, who I thought played lead alto any better than you. You're basically my favorite lead alto player.

SW: Oh man.

JG: I've never heard anybody do the Johnny Hodges concept like you can, other than some-one like Norris Turney who played in Duke's band.

SW: Oh well, Norris is a master.

JG: And you've also got your own personal sound and concept, in so many great contexts. And I think that comes across very clearly. Like, for example, this recording you did with Leon

Parker comes back to me. It was a tune with just you and Leon and a vocalist. It was a very simple little thing. But your time, your phrasing was so great. And I tell students, "Steve is the most in-demand sideman on the alto in the world."

SW: I wouldn't say that! [Laughter]

JG: Well, you really are. You do all these things so well. And you're also one of the nicest people in the music. Anybody in the scene knows that. I mean, you're nice enough to come and do this interview with me…

SW: No, it's an honor!

JG: And then said, "Hey, let me buy you lunch," and I said, "Hey wait a minute! You're coming and doing this for me, how you gonna buy me lunch too?"

BOTH: [Laughter]

SW: [Laughter] No, it's an honor. First of all, thanks for all that Jon. That's very kind and humbling, truly. From the first time I heard you, I think that night at Augie's, the first thing that grabbed me was that sound. Because at that time I was really struggling with sound. I had no sound on alto. I had another instrument and setup, the whole deal. So, when I got here to New York I had to start all over again, in terms of dealing with sound, and just learning to play the alto saxophone. Obviously, it's something we've talked about a lot.

JG: Yeah.

SW: But I recall that night, I think Freddie Bryant might have been there.

JG: Yeah, could've been.

SW: But that was the first time I heard you and that sound hit me, and it was so clear. First of all, I thought, who is this cat? And he's playing something in G that was killing. And honestly, I didn't have anything together other than some funk riffs.

JG: I've never heard you not sound great. And I can't imagine what you're talking about with sound. That's something that's so consistent about you. I've felt very inconsistent at times and had my struggles with some things. And you've always had this great sound and control. We've talked a lot about it as alto players.

SW: Hm mmm…

JG: And let's face it, we're prejudiced, OK?

SW: Right! [Laughter]

JG: But we've come to the conclusion that the alto is the hardest saxophone to play.

SW: No *question*.

JG: Any alto player will tell you that. [Laughter]

SW: No question.

JG: You put it best and said this to me one time. I tell people this a lot. I can go three weeks and not touch the soprano and pick it up and bang, there's a sound.

SW: Yep, I'm the same way.

JG: I can practice the alto for three hours, and the next day I feel like I'm starting from scratch.

SW: Yeah, yeah.

JG: I know brass players that can buy a horn and play it on the gig that night. I'm like, I would need eight months… ten kinds of reeds…

SW: [Laughter]

JG: Five or six mouthpieces, I'd have to get the key heights changed… Charles McPherson told me, "I played trumpet, and I played alto. And the alto is so much tougher, because the resistance from note to note is so inconsistent."

SW: That's right.

JG: I tell my students… to try to get a big sound, to play soft, and loud, play consistent, to play the bottom of the horn, the altissimo, to get the lower partials, the upper partials, to play in tune, project and blend… to do all that, is a lot!

SW: It's a lifetime study man. You're absolutely right. I was out at the U of Michigan, adjudicating a high school festival. Unfortunately I didn't think ahead enough to get a lesson with Donald Sinta, of course, you know, who's been out there many years and I've heard a lot about his work. We know people who've studied with him. But I did get together with a couple of his students. And they talked about his approach and the things he can do, and his main thing, is like, his command of pitch is unbelievable. They told me, and I heard this from Tim Ries as well, he'll set up a strobe, turn his back to it, and every note is perfectly in tune.

JG: Wow.

SW: Which, I mean, I can't even fathom that. I'd hate to see what the strobe would look like when I did that! But yeah, it's a constant struggle with sound. But really literally the first time I heard you, and I'd heard a few people live in New York, but when I heard your sound it was just so clear. And it gave me a real lesson as to the direction I needed to go. You had a sound that projected, was even, but was strident enough that it carried, you know. And it was lyrical. So it really set me on the path. So, I know I have to get another instrument, 'cause the one I had wasn't gonna make it.

JG: Now, you were playing with Out of the Blue, right?

SW: Yeah.

JG: Which Kenny Garrett had been in.

SW: Right.

JG: And you came in, and that was a great, high-profile opportunity, deservedly so. And that was the first time I heard about you.

SW: Well, I gotta tell you, when I got to New York, and I heard other people like yourself and a few others, I realized how lucky I was to have that gig. As it would have it, the band lasted another two years before it folded. There were various other things going on within and without the band. I knew how lucky I was. I heard you, Vincent Herring, Donald Harrison, and not to mention Dick Oatts, who I got a chance to hear and meet when I first got to town. And, you know, you just hear all these great players and think, "Oh my god! Man, I've gotta lot of work to do."

JG: Well, there might have been some cats that could play out here Steve, but it wasn't luck!

SW: [Laughter]

JG: It was the fact that you always played great.

SW: Well, I considered that I was in the right place in the right time. I had met Kenny a few years before and we had a chance to hang. And of course, that was a revelation, because he'd always had his own sound and approach. Long before he became famous.

JG: I met him in the last year. I see him sometimes at La Lanterna.

SW: Whenever he's around he always hangs out. He really likes to go out and hear music.

JG: Yeah, and he was really nice. I'd never met him. I think without a doubt he's the most influential voice on the alto in the last twenty years.

SW: Absolutely.

JG: There are certain guys that come to mind on various instruments. When I was in college there were a lot of guys trying to sound like Michael Brecker on the tenor, and Phil Woods on the alto.

SW: Right.

JG: But more recently everybody's trying to sound like Kenny. Which, it's a great sound concept, but like anything else, you have try to find your own thing.

SW: Absolutely.

JG: You get these guys that are like seventeen… eighteen, and they sound amazing. But it's like, OK, use that influence as a reference, but then say I'm not gonna stay here, 'cause this is not mine.

SW: That's right, absolutely.

JG: This is gonna be like a template, that I'm gonna use to get some stuff in my head and under my fingers, that I'm gonna use to go on and find my own thing.

SW: Yeah, that's a good point. Because, what I've told a lot of my students in the past, and now, and younger players, particularly that are into Kenny, is that, that's great for obvious reasons. And talk about complete musicians! He's been one of my role models, and there have been many. But when I met Kenny, he was traveling with the pit band doing *Sophisticated Ladies*.

I got called as a local in Virginia to play bari and tenor in the section and he was playing lead alto. And he said, "Man is there a jam session around we could go play?" I said, yeah, there's a place. He said, "Why don't you come by, here's where I'm staying." So, I went by his hotel room, and he had his music stand set up and he was playing clarinet etudes. I think he was studying with Leon Russianoff at the time, and he had his flute out. And we went out to jam. The next day we're in the pit, and in between shows he asked, "Hey man, do you play piano?" I said, very little. And he said, "Well, man, I'm trying to get work on this thing on the piano. Let's go down and play a little bit." I could kind of get through a blues on piano. And then he started playing piano, and man, he's a real piano player!

JG: Wow!

SW: So, all this stuff goes back, and comes forward. Because, this is in the tradition of all the guys that you and I talk about and look up to. Phil Woods, Charles McPherson, you know. These guys are complete musicians. Because they came up in an era, where if you weren't playing in a show, if you weren't playing in the studio, you knew people that were. And there wasn't the kind of media hype that's distracting about, "It's about this guy or that guy." These guys were all in it together. I just put this quote up on the door at school, at Purchase. I can't remember the philosophers' name, he's Japanese. I first saw it in a Keith Jarret interview, years ago, "Seek not to follow the wise, but seek what they sought."

JG: Yeah.

SW: That's what it gets down to. Finding your voice and then going to the source that they drew from. So, when you look at the Kenny Garrets, the Phil Woods, Dick Oatts, Jerry Dodgion, the lineage, the great lineage that they came from. And talking about Hodges, it goes all the way back to come all the way forward.

JG: There's so much in what you said that sparks so many thoughts in my mind. But, yeah, following that path, rather than trying to be somebody else. There are so many people that are so deeply affected by some of these great musicians like a Kenny, and they just get stuck in there. But you have to follow that path. And realize that it's not gonna happen when you're seventeen or eighteen.

SW: That's right. And also, to have the awareness to put themselves around the people who are going to encourage them and nurture an original sound.

JG: Exactly.

SW: It's like when Jackie McLean said that Mingus told him, "You gotta stop sounding like Bird. You gotta find you own sound!" And that's pretty deep when you think about Jackie's roots and the influence of Charlie Parker, which was still very prevalent, years after he passed on. So, I look at those situations and what those guys were doing. That's how they found their sound, they had to!

JG: Yeah, and when you said you've got to be around those people, that's something I think about a lot, those mentors. We've been lucky to be around some great ones. And that's amazing about Kenny's doubling and piano playing, I didn't know about that. He does all that work and still has this amazing and original sound and concept as an alto player.

SW: Yeah.

JG: It shows too, that he's a guy that obviously has worked very hard and has a lot of appreciation of the tradition, and comes from a place of humility.

SW: Yep.

JG: Whatever you're doing, you know? There's a student that you have up at Purchase that I've worked with a bit when I've subbed for you that I really like…

SW: Oh yeah, Andrew Gould…

JG: Yeah, because he's very talented. But I just think that the kind of person you are really helps a lot and means a lot.

SW: That's right. Absolutely.

JG: Yeah, and I really think that humility is what brings you to your highest place.

SW: I totally agree. I remember, at Clifford Jordan's memorial service at Saint Peter's… this was right after Barry Harris had his stroke. He got up to play, and played primarily with his right hand. Maybe at that time only with his right hand. I recall him giving a little speech before talking about Clifford, and he said something like, "You have to be ready to receive."

JG: Yeah.

SW: And that always stayed with me. Because man, the gifts come. The gifts are there. But if you're not open to it… if you're not ready, it'll pass you right by and you won't even know it.

JG: Yeah.

SW: As a matter of fact, I had a gig last weekend. And somebody reminded about a story I told them about one of the first people who influenced me, our postman when I was growing, the guy who delivered our mail. I was fifteen, sixteen, I'd be practicing, you know, and at 11:30 he'd deliver our mail. And day after day he'd come by and he'd say, "Yeah, sounds good man, sounds good." And then one day he came in and said, "Man, you ever heard of the whole tone scale?" I said, *what*!?

JG: Wow! [Laughter]

SW: He said, give me your horn. And he started playing the whole tone scale. I didn't even know he was a saxophonist! And he told me basically, there are two whole tone scales, and here they are, boom boom boom. And it had a big impact on me, because I wasn't dealing with any harmony at that point, and that set me on the way. He told me "You gotta check out Bird and Trane and these guys." And there it was, that was one of my biggest gifts. I learned a lot from that one instance, because you never know where it'll come from.

JG: Yeah, it's true. And being open to receive, you have to know that there's more to be learned. You have to be in a posture, psychologically, emotionally, and spiritually, of like, "I still have plenty to learn." And great musicians that we admire are that way because of that.

SW: Absolutely. And they also know that the gifts, many times, come from contexts other than music. They come from other sources.

JG: Well, I could talk with you like this for another nineteen hours.

SW: Me too.

JG: But I just want to wrap up with something that Charles McPherson told me. Man, I'm so lucky. I got to hang out with Charles when he stayed at my apartment twice for two weeks when I was nineteen and twenty.

SW: Wow. That's amazing

JG: That cat is so deep. But he said, "At one point, I got it, sitting in the Vanguard, that it wasn't just about Sonny Rollins and the trio… that something else was happening," and pointed to the sky.

SW: Mmm.

JG: And it's difficult to put these kinds of thoughts into words. But I really think that's what you're getting at. It's essentially a spiritual experience.

SW: Yeah.

JG: And I've always sensed with you, as a person, just an incredibly high quality of integrity, humility, and openness, and I can't thank you enough for doing this.

SW: Well, thank you Jon. But I gotta give credit to my elders, the generation that both you and I grew up around and respect. That's the foundation. Just two quick things—the best definition I've heard of this music comes from Billy Higgins, "Sanctified Intelligence." And number two, the music is bigger than all of us. We're a part of something bigger.

JG: Yeah, that's right. Thanks man.

SW: Thanks Jon.

Red Holloway, Barney Kessel, & Joe Williams

Oslo, Norway - 1989

In 1989 I was in Oslo during their annual jazz festival in August. The two previous years I was hired to play the festival. I played the festival again in '91, doing a couple of two-alto gigs with Phil Woods, and played it several times after that. But in '89 I went to hang with my friends, Bjorn and Mona Pedersen who helped run the festival, catch some of the music, do some promotion for a CD I'd done, record as a sideman for a local musician, and then do some touring around Norway that Bjorn and Mona hooked up for me. The recording was with a trumpet player, Atle Hammer, and the great Red Holloway on tenor! Whoo, man! Red was one of the great blues tenor players ever! I had a great time hanging with Red and talking for hours at breakfast every morning in the Grand Hotel and was very inspired by getting to play with him. What a learning experience, he was amazing!

The other person who really took me under their wing that year was Barney Kessel. I knew who he was, and I had him on some Jazz at the Philharmonic records with Bird and others, and knew he was an all-time great guitar player. He was doing a gig with a very good Norwegian tenor player named Bjarne Nerem. Barney invited me to come and play some with them, and I was thrilled to do so. We talked quite a bit more after the gig. He mentioned that while he came up in an era where he got to play with Louis Armstrong, Pres, and Bird, he was very into Bill Evans and the music that came in the generations afterwards. He also told me something he thought was a key to being a great player. He said, "There are certain things that I want my music to have and be. I want the music to be an event, something fresh. And to me, one of the biggest keys to being a player is, stay hot! Keep your practicing up all the time! Keep working on your ideas and language. So that if a last-minute gig comes in, you're ready, rather than trying to figure out how to get ready."

The highlight of the week for me was a couple of nights in the lobby restaurant at the Grand Hotel where Barney's trio was playing, and he invited me to play with him both nights. On the last set of both nights, the great Joe Williams came and sat in with us for several tunes. I'd met Joe there the previous year, and he was very nice, but I hadn't had a chance to play with him. And man, what a presence he was, standing next to him on the bandstand! He sang some of his famous blues hits with Basie, like "Every Day," "Smack Dab in the Middle," "Alright, OK, You Win," that he was very well known for. Joe was one of the all-time great blues singers, but he was also an incredible ballad singer! Just one of the greatest vocalists in the history of the music. But the revelation for me was what kind of blues player Barney Kessel was. I knew that Barney was a great player and had made an incredible contribution over his career. But I just didn't realize he had this other gear as a blues player! He started to sing his lines a little more. His head would shake some. His eyes would kinda roll back in his head. He just went somewhere else and really got taken by spirit. So, getting to play with both those legends was amazing! Seeing and feeling the depth and complexity of the kinds of musicians they were on the bandstand, beyond just the hits and contributions they were known for, really blew me away.

Quincy Davis

Phone call, Winnipeg/NYC – December 2019

JG: Hey Quincy! So, what are you up to in New York?

QD: I'm hosting some friends from Japan, taking them to lots of jazz clubs.

JG: Great.

QD: Yeah, it's been cool.

JG: You studied Japanese in recent years, right?

QD: Yeah, I speak it fluently and they don't speak English so they need some help getting around. It's been fun. This is actually my fifth time doing it. They bring me here, put me up, and then I take them out to jazz clubs every night.

JG: Great! What are you going to hear?

QD: Today we're going to Smoke to see Allan Harris. It's like a Christmas thing. And then Linda Oh is playing tomorrow at the Jazz Gallery. We were supposed to go see Maria Schneider tomorrow, but I have to leave early because there's a snowstorm coming in tomorrow, so I changed my ticket to leave before that. I was gonna leave Monday.

JG: Gotcha. Yeah, I know Maria always has a run at the Jazz Standard around Thanksgiving. So, I thought you'd be a perfect candidate for this because I always start by asking people how they got into music, and I know you have a very musical family, so tell me about your upbringing and how you got into music.

QD: Yeah! Well, my father Duane is in the choral and the vocal jazz world. He's a former choral and vocal jazz professor at Grand Rapids Community College, Western Michigan University, and Indiana University. He's retired now. My mother Karetha is a piano player, clarinet player, and flautist. She majored in clarinet in school, plays classical and gospel piano, conducts, and plays piano for her church's children's choir. My brother Xavier is a jazz piano player as you know, though he started on trombone, that was his major for a long time. He currently teaches jazz piano at Michigan State University.

JG: Really! Xavier started on trombone, wow!

QD: Yeah, and my sister, Erica, never studied music at a school but she plays piano and is a wonderful visual artist.

JG: So your dad is very well known in the choral and vocal jazz world.

QD: Yes! He's done a lot of work with a lot of different choirs, all-state things, vocal jazz. He's quite a great educator actually. He's taught for over thirty years and has had a lot of very successful students. He's highly respected throughout the world in that choir world.

JG: Well, having gotten to know you so well over the last eight to ten years, I can see that correlation for sure. And your sister I think you said is a principal now?

QD: Yes, she just started as a principal at a school in Brooklyn this year.

JG: Remind me of where you grew up in Michigan?

QD: Grand Rapids.

JG: When you were a kid was there some kind of music program that you got involved with in school? And were either of your parents teachers for you?

QD: Well, I took piano lessons very early, when I was young. I kinda lost interest in it. But then they saw that I took a liking to hitting things. So, they bought me a drum and I started taking lessons at the music store. And when I got good enough me and my brother started jamming together. He was playing a DX7 and other synths. We jammed a lot and we listened a lot. And in elementary school I took up the trumpet for whatever reason. I don't know why I didn't play the drums. And later I switched to the tuba halfway through middle school. So, I didn't play drums or percussion in elementary or middle school. I was quite a good trumpet player. But I always played drums at home.

JG: Interesting.

QD: Yeah, and even in high school, the first two years I was in the marching band but I wasn't in the percussion line.

JG: Oh man, you did a marching band in Michigan?!

QD: Yeah!

JG: Oh my goodness. Were you there for football games in the fall and winter?

QD: It was rough! And I played tuba, actually I played the sousaphone.

BOTH: [Laughter]

JG: Oh! You met my friend Tyrone at the Kitano?

QD: Yeah.

JG: He played sousaphone in a marching band we were in, called the Big Apple Marching Band, led by our junior high band director, Larry Laurenzano. And poor Tyrone! I've never seen anyone sweat as much as he did at the end of those summer marches playing sousaphone. We'd finish and sweat poured off of him in puddles. It was brutal for me, but he looked like he could barely stand at the end.

QD: Oh yeah man, it was no joke.

JG: So, who's older, you or Xavier?

QD: Xavier is six years older.

JG: Obviously you got more serious about music in high school?

QD: Yeah, so high school I was playing tuba and trumpet, but also playing drums at home. But then one day my mother, she went up to my school, it was a public school. I was really into sports. I was playing sports every day, basketball and tennis, and I had hopes of being a professional in those areas. But my mother went up to the school one day. And I think she was trying to find me. She was asking where I was, what class I was in. And nobody could help her in the office. That was a kind of tipping point for her, and she asked if I wanted to go to the same school that my brother and sister went to, which was a private arts school up north in Michigan, called Interlochen Arts Academy, where I would major in percussion. And I said, "You know, I don't see me becoming a pro in these sports, so uh, sure." So, I started my junior year at Interlochen. And that's when I got very serious about percussion, and learning how to read and all those kinds of things. I studied classical percussion actually, I didn't even take drum set.

JG: That sounds like you had to move away from home for that?

QD: Yeah, it was about two and a half hours away, near Travers City.

JG: That friend of yours we met in Kelowna, is that where you knew him from?

QD: James Danderfer. Yeah, that's where we went to school together.

JG: When did you start to focus on jazz?

QD: I'd say my senior year at Interlochen. I was playing in a combo at a weekly gig with my friend James. That got me playing regularly. And I got very serious over that summer. I was practicing a lot. I decided to go into music, percussion, for my major in college. I went to Western Michigan University in Kalamazoo.

JG: So, was there someone you studied with there that really inspired you?

QD: Yeah, I got to study with the great Billy Hart there.

JG: Oh yeah!

QD: So, he would come in a couple times a semester, and kinda fill the cup up with a lot of stuff for me to investigate and learn about. And we'd have great philosophical, deep thought kind of lessons, that got me really thinking about the why, the where, the when, the how, the who… instead of just thinking about the immediate things I was into. My studies with him were much more cerebral than technical.

JG: Yeah, that's interesting. You know, for students, you want to talk to people that know a lot about your instrument, the music, and are a part of that history and lineage, the way Billy Hart is. But I think what you don't expect sometimes is what you just talked about. Because, it's not just about the technical things on the instrument. What's the goal? Where are we going with those things?

QD: That's right. Yeah, it was really kind of eye-opening and it helped give me a perspective on everything that I was doing. And that's definitely informed me in how I play and teach today.

JG: So, did you come immediately to New York after college?

QD: I took a year and I was actually a substitute teacher in the Grand Rapids public school system. I got a chance to work with mostly middle school and elementary school music students. And that was the first time really that I taught. I didn't even know if I could do it. [Laughter] And it was fine, it was OK. The idea was I was going to spend a year and save money and move to New York. So, the first semester I did that, I substitute taught. But then I got called in the second semester to go into a middle school and take over for a teacher who kinda had a nervous breakdown and quit his job, basically. And I was pretty much the only music substitute teacher, I think. So, they thought of me and gave me a call, and I said yes. But I didn't know what I was getting into. I had no idea if I could even do it. I was thrown into a full-time gig suddenly. And I didn't go to school for teaching. So, I started that in January of 2000. And it was literally like the movie *Lean On Me* with Morgan Freeman, like Cooley High. You go into the class, and kids are cursing, throwing paper, you know, doing all kinds of adolescent things, being loud, all the things you see in movie scenes with a substitute teacher. And I thought, "Oh my Lord! What am I going to do with these kids!"

JG: [Laughter] Right!

QD: I had a full load. I had beginner, intermediate, and advanced bands, intermediate and advanced strings. You know, I knew nothing about these instruments! But you know, I found myself up there, and this is where I called upon all these nuggets of advice and wisdom that I learned from my parents and all my teachers. And I just found myself saying all the things they said to me. And just kind of tried to relate to the students, to get them to buy in to what I was saying, and trying to be as productive as possible while having fun too. And it actually ended up being a really great semester.

JG: Hmm!

QD: And we gave a concert, our annual spring concert. It was really great! I learned so much about teaching that I didn't even know was in me. They actually wanted me to come back full time in the fall. But I had already made plans to move to New York. And I had no interest in going back and teaching full-time there. [Laughter] But it was actually an invaluable experience that I believe helped shape the way I teach now. I got here to New York and a good friend of mine, Randy Napoleon, had been living here. He's a great guitarist who now teaches at Michigan State, but is the long-time guitarist for Freddy Cole. We'd been friends for a long time, and we were roommates. And he was here a year before me and he kind of spread the word about me coming, which was nice of him. So, when I got here some people knew about me. Like, Julius Tolentino. Do you know Julius?

JG: Yeah! Julius and Jimmy Greene were roommates back in the day at Hartt.

QD: That's right! So, I met Julius right away. I became the house drummer for him at Cleopatra's Needle. And shortly after that I met Jeremy Pelt and started working with him at his weekly gig at Cleo's. And that was a great place where I met so many musicians. I lived right near there. I made a lot of important associations right there. I guess the first major thing I did was I started working with Tom Harrell in his quintet. In the band was Jimmy Greene, my brother Xavier and Ugonna Okegwo.

JG: And what year was that?

QD: I wanna say 2001. So, I was in his band for about three and a half years. I was also working with Benny Green's trio with Barak Mori on bass. I worked with Eric Reed a bit, Cyrus Chestnut a bit. So, those were some of the things I was doing at that time.

JG: I remember we played at La Lanterna a couple times. And then we played at Smalls, with a tenor player from Adelaide, Australia, that's since passed named Mike Stewart. And there's a wonderful video of you playing with Frank Wess at the Vanguard with a two-tenor group with Frank and Scott Robinson.

QD: Oh yeah! That was in 2009 I think.

JG: Were you teaching much in New York when you were there?

QD: I wasn't really. A few lessons here and there.

JG: And I guess you got the call to come up and interview for the position at the University of Manitoba in 2010?

QD: Yeah. I was playing with Jimmy Greene somewhere in Midtown. He told me he was teaching in Winnipeg, Manitoba… which I thought was a lot closer to New York than it was…

JG: [Laughter] Little did you know…

QD: But he said they were doing a search and I should apply. So, I did, and they offered me the gig. And it was a really hard decision, because I'd been in New York for ten years. New

York, as you know, becomes a big part of you. But I came to the decision that I should take the opportunity, because it's a rare one. And if I didn't like it, I'd move back. So that was the plan. So, when I got there it was George Colligan, Jimmy Greene, Steve Kirby, Larry Roy, who'd been there a long time, and Anna Lisa Kirby was teaching voice. I knew everyone from New York so it made the transition a little easier, though it still was hard.

JG: Derrick Gardner came in the year after you, then Will Bonness. Craig Bailey did an interim year after Jimmy. I came up in 2013, I think that was your fourth year.

QD: Oh yeah, OK.

JG: I was telling someone recently in New York, "Hey, it's sunny and 25 degrees here in Winnipeg, it's really not bad!" And people that aren't from Winnipeg are like, "Oh, so you realize this is some kind of coping mechanism, right?"

BOTH: [Laughter]

JG: And I remember, the first person I saw when I came up here to interview was you. It was late April, thirty degrees and cloudy, and I ran into you outside the school and I said, "It's not really a nice weather day." You said, "What? This... is nice!" And I just thought, "Oh Quincy, what have they done to you?"

QD: [Laughter]

JG: And so now you're down there in Denton and you'll post a pic of folks walking around in shorts in December on a 75 degree day...

QD: [Laughter] Yeah, I can't get enough of that.

JG: I know... and everything has its pluses and minuses.

QD: That's right.

JG: On the other hand it's beautiful up here in the summer, though I'm not here too much then. But down there July and August...

QD: Oh it's rough... people leave to go north in the summer.

JG: But that's where we got to know each other. I knew you as a great drummer in New York. And as a person, you're someone that everybody likes. But one of the first school jam sessions we did, I heard you sing! I know you're not super serious about it, but you could do it. And then I heard you sit at the piano and comp, and quickly saw that you're a very complete musician! Then I got to learn about your writing, which is great. And you know, some of my favorite small group band leaders and composers are drummers.

QD: Wow.

JG: No, it's true. You think about Blakey, Arthur Taylor's Wailers, Brian Blade, the records that Bill Stewart made on Blue Note...

QD: Tony...

JG: Tony Williams for sure!

QD: Victor Lewis...

JG: Yeah! You just posted a photo of you and Victor on Facebook today.

QD: Yes! Pretty amazing!

JG: So tell me about how your music and writing developed over the years.

QD: Yeah, so, moving to Winnipeg and taking that gig, it just kind of gave me time, space, and resources to explore other parts of my musicianship that I never felt I could tap into as deeply here in New York. So, I think that was a really great thing that came out of that. It gave me a chance to write for students. I created the student group Promise for that reason, to have a vehicle to write for. And, I enjoy all kinds of music. I listen to classical music a lot. I listen to R&B, gospel, obviously jazz. And I think that my writing kind of incorporates all of that in some way that's more of a jazz aesthetic. But it's definitely influenced by many different styles.

I think that, because of growing up listening to my brother practice the piano, we'd sit and listen to music together and he'd point out things in the harmony. I'd sit and listen to symphonies with my dad. So that kinda got my ears more attuned to harmony. And I'd definitely say that since I'm a drummer and we don't get a chance to play harmony or melody on the drums in a tonal sense, I gravitate towards more melodic and harmonic writing, rather than rhythmic writing. I ironically feel more at home with harmony than rhythm.

JG: Well, I've really loved getting to know your music. I remember hearing Promise play a great arrangement of yours on "Tune Up." There's a tune of yours that we've played on some of your gigs and mine in recent years called "Ponder This" that I love. And I think your music has a very personal thing. And I think all those influences do come through and you that you put it together in a great way.

QD: I appreciate that.

JG: Yeah, for real. And the other thing is… other than my first year up here I haven't had a car. So…

BOTH: [Laughter]

JG: And at one point we were living across the street from each other, and I got a lot of lifts from you. And the cool thing was, "Hey I got a lift rather than waiting for a bus in minus twenty!" But the other thing was, "What's Quincy listening to today?"

QD: [Laughter]

JG: And it was great to hear music that was inspiring you. And one of the things that really had a big impact on me that you played for me, are those recordings of the outtakes and talking between takes on the *Nefertiti* sessions.

QD: Oh yeah!

JG: That was amazing! Listening to what Miles and the band were saying to each other, and Teo… the realization that they didn't record the first take of "Nefertiti"…

QD: Yeah.

JG: And different things on "Freedom Jazz Dance." Miles at one point just kind of laughing and saying, "You realize I can't play this shit, right?"

BOTH: [Laughter]

JG: It's so funny… He wanted Herbie to play that voicing. He wanted Tony to play something specific, he was coming in and out with that melody. And just listening to that discussion… because we just hear the end result.

QD: Yeah.

JG: And the one take of "Nefertiti" that we know is magic! It would never occur to me that that was the fourth take because it feels so fresh!

QD: That's right.

JG: So it was nice to hang up here and check out what you were listening to. So now, you're currently in your third year at the University of North Texas.

QD: Yeah, third year. And I should also mention that I recently finished my master's. I started pursuing a master's in composition at the Vermont College of Fine Arts in my first year here, in composition. It's a very liberal low-resident program that makes it possible for working professionals to pursue a masters while keeping up a regular job. It was really great. I got the chance to work with some great composers, really work on studying scores, understanding forms better. So, I finished that in August. And yeah, this is my third year here, and it's almost the exact opposite of the U of Manitoba… in that, its huge…

BOTH: [Laughter]

QD: First thing… so just trying to deal with the numbers… I'm the head of the drum set department. So, all questions, all emails, everything comes to me. Which I was used to before, but it was just on a smaller scale. So, the admin portion of the job is like a job in and of itself. But I'm used to it now, so it's not as big a deal. But it's been great. I've learned a lot and the students are very dedicated, serious, and nice. No vibe… they're very easy to work with. There's about thirty-plus drummers. But I don't want it to feel as large as it is. I try to create a close family vibe, like before when I was working at the University of Manitoba.

JG: I should tell you, Anna Blackmore has put together a group of graduating students and recent grads. And they did a midday concert on Monday. The played mostly originals, and they call themselves Promise. So, your work lives on here!

QD: Alright!

JG: Yeah, I remember when you first got down there you sounded pretty tired!

BOTH: [Laughter]

JG: You said, "I never worked like this before!"

QD: Yeah!

JG: But once you're there you learn how to be present in that, and there are a lot of rewards from working with great students. It's great to still tour and play, which you're doing. And we're going to be in New York City next week.

QD: That's right!

JG: Yeah. We just called each other for the same weekend's worth of gigs that neither one of us could make with each other!

QD: [Laughter] That's right.

JG: But I'm glad that you're gonna be at Smalls next weekend. And you're working some with Cécile McLorin Salvant, Aaron Diehl, and others, along with your own projects. And I'm glad we've been able to work together with my group, and your group at the Winnipeg Jazz Festival. So, thanks so much for taking the time to do this. And here's to many more years of playing and hanging together.

QD: Absolutely!

Bob Mintzer

Phone call San Francisco to Los Angeles – February 2020

JG: So, Bob, I met you at Manhattan School of Music in 1986 when I was nineteen.

BM: Wow!

JG: And I had such a great year studying with you. Whenever your name comes up with friends and students, I always tell them it was so amazing to study with you! Whether it was improvisation, classical saxophone, doubles, composition, and arranging, there was so much that we covered. So that was an incredible blessing to get to work with you. So, how did you get into music? Was there a family connection? And what brought you to the saxophone?

BM: Well, firstly, I'm flattered and honored that you feel that way. The feeling was very mutual. It was great to work with you. You were so musically inclined from day one. It was inspiring to hear what you were doing and was really a treat for me. In terms of where I started, there were no professional musicians anywhere in my family. I'm told I had a grandmother that played the piano by ear, so that was about it in terms of any connection with music. But as far back as I can remember, I'd say five years old, I was always drawn to hearing music on the television and the radio. I remember there being a piano. We lived above my grandfather's apartment in a two-family house and there was a piano in his apartment. I'd go down there and play, and just explore for hours, and try to play little songs I might hear on TV. I was fascinated by the sound of music, how the notes could be manipulated and put together to form chords, melodies, and progressions and so on.

JG: Where'd you grow up?

BM: Just north of New York City in New Rochelle.

JG: I had a great junior high band director that was very important in my growth and development. Did you have some teachers there that helped you in that way?

BM: I had a couple. I had a private clarinet teacher in elementary school, third, fourth, and fifth grade, who got me started. Junior high was somewhat nondescript. I picked up the saxophone in junior high. They needed a saxophone player for the jazz band there. I was playing guitar at that time and got my first electric guitar in junior high. And really wanted to play guitar. You know, rock and roll and blues. So that happened really before the saxophone. And then in high school, I was probably playing more guitar than anything. But I loved the challenge of learning a new instrument. So, I was playing piano, bass or guitar, clarinet, flute, anything I could get my hands on.

The big shift happened my senior year in high school. I went to Interlochen Arts Academy and I looked around and I saw how much people practiced and what sort of dedication was involved. And that was a big change. I got pretty serious and started spending a lot more time each day in a focused way. You know, I was studying classical clarinet, I was playing saxophone, piano, and bass, still played guitar. Peter Erskine was there, and a bunch of really cracker jack classical players. It was really inspiring and really revealing. And I got out of there and went to Hartt School of Music in Hartford, Connecticut.

JG: Was Jackie McLean there when you were there?

BM: Jackie had just gotten there. That was 1970.

JG: Wow! What was that like?

BM: That was great to hang with him! I was there on a clarinet scholarship. So mainly what I did in school was play in the orchestra, and some chamber music, which was a wonderful experience. And then outside of school I hung out with the local jazz musicians and went to their gigs and eventually started working with them. There wasn't much jazz yet. The jazz program under Jackie's tutelage really developed over time, but he had just arrived. So, I took a history class with him, and a little combo workshop. There weren't a whole lot of jazz players there. It was mostly people interested in education and classical music.

JG: When you were playing jazz at that point, were you playing mostly by ear?

BM: I would say yes. But I was doing a lot of listening. I was listening to recordings all the time. But it was really sort of self-taught. There was nobody to teach me before that about jazz. I would just emulate things I heard on recordings. I learned tunes on piano. I think that was a key element, as far as having an entry into the world of harmony. And with every instrument that I played I tried to mimic the people that played that respective instrument on recordings.

JG: I remember when I studied with you, you said that part of learning to play was emulating and imitating your heroes in the process of learning to play like yourself.

BM: Yeah, and I think that's a misconception that young players sometimes encounter. There's a concern that too much emulation somehow subtracts from finding one's voice, but I think it's the opposite.

JG: Yeah, I agree. I just think it puts an unfair expectation on you. Like, I'm supposed to be a genius, right? There's a lot of craft you have to deal with before you have the opportunity to deal with high levels of creativity. And if you don't deal with that element of craft you just make it much more difficult to get there.

BM: Yes, that's exactly right.

JG: So, I remember seeing videos of you at 7th Ave. South, in the late '70s maybe?

BM: Ahhh, yes. I think 7th Ave. South and that whole scene started around '80, I wanna say.

JG: So, when did you go from classical clarinet to being more in the jazz scene.

BM: Well, I was at Hartt for two and a half years. And then Jackie said, "You need to go to New York 'cause that's where the scene is." I thought that was quite bold of him. I took his advice. I transferred down to Manhattan School of Music and started living on the Upper West Side. I started to meet people on the scene in New York and the lofts were in full swing. People were jamming 24/7. And it became increasingly difficult to get to class obviously. [Laughter]

JG: What were some of the loft jam sessions like?

BM: Yeah, so, one of the ones I went to the most was on Warren Street. That was a large loft. John Abercrombie, Jeff Williams, and Marc—at that time Marc Cohen—lived there. He eventually changed his name to Marc Copland and became a pianist. But when I met him he played saxophone. He was an alto saxophonist, and he played well! So, I was down there a lot. I hooked up with a trumpet player named John D'earth. He took me around, and he knew all these people. And I spent a lot of time on Warren Street in that loft, playing with people like Richie Beirach, who would show up on occasion, Dave Holland, Liebman was down there sometimes, Steve Grossman, Jack DeJohnette came once. He was rehearsing with a band, I think it was called Compost. Then there was another loft on, I wanna say 19th St. There was a German guy there named Chris Braun, and Alex Foster lived over there. And I used to go there and play a lot.

JG: Well it's cool that that scene existed and there were these opportunities to play.

BM: Definitely. I have to say, at that point, very few people were making a living playing jazz. We would play weddings, Bar Mitzvahs, shows, whatever we could. And we'd just jam a lot in the lofts and do the occasional jazz gig. This was pre-Wynton. There wasn't a lot of money to be made in the jazz scene. But to me it was exciting—there was a lot of experimentation, a lot of exchanging of ideas. There was a lot of playing and fraternizing if you will, which felt great. It was sort of the perfect environment to train and grow and develop. In that respect it was very cool. Like, for example, there was a tradition at the Village Vanguard on a Sunday night, whoever was playing there would typically let people sit in on the last set. And that's where I met Art Blakey. I went down there and asked to sit in with his band, and he allowed me to play. And he actually asked me to join his band after that night. I wrote a couple of tunes for one of his records based on that.

JG: Wow!

BM: There seemed to be a more sort of friendly, collaborative thing going on back then. And, well, I mean, I was very lucky. Because as soon as I got out of school I started working with Eumir Deodato. We were traveling the world. I also got onto the Tito Puente Orchestra, and that was a seven night a week gig in town.

JG: Where were you playing?

BM: All over New York City. The other sax players were René McLean and Roger Rosenberg. I took Sal Nistico's place. That was a great learning experience, great band, that was super cool.

JG: It sounds like there were a lot of opportunities to play and grow.

BM: Yeah, most definitely. And there was a lot of live music. Every wedding had a live band, so there were a lot of club dates, as we called them. There was a good deal of recording going on. There was a lot happening.

JG: The studio scene was still really popping then, huh?

BM: Yeah, the studio scene was still really popping then into the mid to late '70s.

JG: Yeah, Milt Hinton, Danny Bank, and Mel and those guys were still doing that, maybe even into the early '80s some. Ken Peplowski told me his first gig in New York was a wedding, with Buddy Tate, Mel Lewis, Milt Hinton, Bucky Pizzarelli, and Dick Katz. And they were all his heroes!

BM: Yeah, yeah.

KP: And he just thought, I can't believe I'm playing somebody's wedding!

BM: Yeah, well all those guys loved to play. I played a wedding with Mel and Ron Carter once.

JG: Ha! Wow!

BM: And this piano player from Mount Vernon, I forget his name. But people liked to play back then. It was just very friendly and relaxed, the whole thing.

JG: Well, you mentioned about the Sunday night tradition. The first the guy I saw do that was Elvin Jones. I later saw Clark Terry do that in '94. But the night with Elvin was maybe '85 or '86. He opened it up at the end of the night on Sunday, and six or seven horn players came up.

And I'd never seen that. I went up and talked with him after the gig, and he said, "Yeah man! And next time I come to town I want *you* to come up and play too!" I never did make it down on one of those Sundays with him, but I wish I had! But that's cool you got an association with Blakey through that. One of the people I wanted to mention that you worked with some is Don Grolnick. I saw you play with him, maybe at Visiones?

BM: At Visiones? We played at Mikell's with Grolnick's band.

JG: OK, maybe that's where it was. He was a guy I really admired and maybe not a lot of people know about, and passed very young. And another guy that was one of my heroes that I know you played with was Jaco Pastorius. How did you meet Jaco and start working with him?

BM: I ran into Jaco at the Vanguard actually, and Mike Brecker had told Jaco about me. Jaco had just left Weather Report and was about to start the Word of Mouth band. He wanted to have Mike and I be the front line. I think I met him in '81. We then did this little hit at 7th Ave. South. It was Mike and I, Don Alias, Peter Erskine, and Jaco. And that's where it started. Then it kind of expanded. Othello Molineaux, this steel drum player was added. We did a big band recording down in Florida. And then after that, Mike left and Randy Brecker took Mike's place in the band. We had a sextet and we did some touring. We did an occasional big band gig, went to Japan, and made a couple recordings there. So, I was involved for most of '81 and '82.

JG: I've seen some great videos of that band with you and Randy out front. And I've heard some great recordings of you and Michael. Man, we all have such respect and admiration for him as a player. Obviously, another person gone way too soon. It's interesting that you said he talked about you. One of the things that impressed me so much about him—not that I got to know him well... I got to be around him a few times—but he was just so generous! What a great guy. What a kind, supportive person.

BM: Yeah. He was a wonderful human being. He always saw something positive, in anyone, you know? He really always looked towards the brighter side of things. It was really refreshing. It was really nice to be around him. And I'm grateful to have known him the way I did. Just a terrific human being.

JG: Another thing that I thought of when you were talking a moment ago. When I got to meet you and work with you, the recordings that I knew were more like the stuff with Jaco or Grolnick. But we did a lot of two-saxophone playing in the lessons. And first of all, you're one of the great saxophone players in the world and an incredible contributor and have been for a long time. But I heard all this history and influences that I didn't know about in you before that, and it was really amazing to get to know you're playing more deeply in that way from hearing you like that. So, who were some of your big influences?

BM: Well, of course all my contemporaries listened to the same guys, pretty much. I mean we were very taken with Coltrane, Joe Henderson, Sonny Rollins, Dexter Gordon, Sonny Stitt, Hank Mobley. And as I matured, I got more into Ben Webster, Lester Young, Coleman Hawkins, Don Byas... I also got into George Coleman. Virtually everyone and anyone. But it's funny, I think the influences that you pay most attention to in your formative years really have an affect. And as you say, based on the work I was doing, either live or in the studios, sort of the current trend back then was... in fact, producers would often say, can you play a solo like Dave Sanborn or Mike Brecker? And just from my association with Mike and hanging out and playing with him, he really had a profound effect on me. I was sounding like him to a large degree for a period of time. I think I moved past that period. You know, I was just checking out all kinds of things, everything really. And really feeling… and being most interested in the older players. Which I think, that really rounds out your playing in a nice way.

JG: It's interesting you say that. When I was 21 I met Jan Gabarek in Oslo and got to hang with him some. I had just checked out this solo saxophone record he did with a wind harp, and a record with a children's choir that's really beautiful. And I asked him, "What inspires you and what do you listen to?" He said, "I get up every day and listen to Johnny Hodges and Ben Webster, and my all-time favorite saxophonist is Eddie Lockjaw Davis."

BM: Check that out.

JG: Right!? But you'd never know that because he's synthesized that in such a personal way. To me, you always sounded like you. I remember you telling me that you and Lawrence Feldman were doing a bunch of gigs with the New York Philharmonic, and that you were playing your Dukoff mouthpiece on those gigs. Most people would think of that as almost a rock kind of mouthpiece. But you sounded to me like you could do anything on it. What were some of the pieces you did with the Philharmonic?

BM: I did Gershwin's *American in Paris*. I did the *Berio Symphonia*. Giuseppe Sinopoli was an opera composer from Italy who'd been commissioned by the Philharmonic to write a piece. And there was a beautiful long tenor solo over muted strings that I got to do three or four times. And some contemporary music that used saxophone as well. There was a series called the *Horizon Series*, I remember playing in that series a number of times. Yeah, it was an interesting period. I was playing in a sax quartet with my mentor at the time, Al Regni. He was really the first call sax guy with the symphony. But he got Lawrence and I to join on some of these things that used multiple saxophone or doublers.

JG: Also, Lawrence was playing lead alto for you on your big band in New York for a number of years around then too, right?

BM: Yeah, absolutely, he's a brilliant lead player.

JG: Yeah, great player.

BM: Actually Dave Sanborn was the first lead alto player in my first big band in '83.

JG: Wow!

BM: That was quite a section. It was Dave, Mike Brecker, me, Roger Rosenberg, and Pete Yellin.

JG: Wow!

MB: It was pretty kickin'!

JG: What a great section!

BM: Yeah… what a place to start, huh?

JG: Oh my god! And that leads me to something else I wanted to ask you about. When did writing for big band become a big part of what you did?

BM: I did my first big band writing on the Buddy Rich band.

JG: What years would that be?

BM: '76, '77, '78. I think I wrote six or seven pieces for him. And then I joined the Thad Jones Mel Lewis band and wrote a couple pieces for them.

JG: Late '70s?

BM: Yeah… '78, '79, I guess up to '80. And then Joe Lovano took over. I was busy doing a million different things, and they wanted someone more steady and they got Joe. But it started on Buddy's band. It was great to have it played by a great band and hear it every night. And Buddy was super encouraging, and said, "Write as much as you want!" And I don't think anybody had written quite like that for the band. Most of the writers and arrangers for that band came out of more of a traditional mold. Particularly some of the rock and funk numbers were of an older style. I was listening to all kinds of music. So, I was writing, just different, I dare say, more adventurous, more contemporary kinda stuff. And Buddy was thrilled. He was just waiting to play on some of that kind of music. So, it was a golden opportunity.

JG: I used to sub with the Vanguard band, and there's a lot of your charts in the book—some Herbie tunes you arranged, "Mr. Fone Bone." When did you write that?

BM: That I wrote for Jaco. Oh, actually, no, I wrote that for my first solo record in 1980, for Canyon Records in Japan. That was one of the songs we did. And then we started playing it with Jaco. Then I did a big band arrangement for Mel.

JG: And when did you do your first big band recording?

BM: Ahh, '83.

JG: Yeah. Because I remember, I had some awareness of that, because by the time I met you a few years later you were known as somebody that was very diverse and making all these different contributions. And that tune to me seemed to be a kind of hit that allowed a lot more people to know about you.

BM: Yeah, well, that tune I think really displays the influence I had from playing with Jaco's group, which didn't include a chordal instrument in the band. There are no chords, I added chords later. So, the idea was to have a melody that outlined harmonic structure without having chords. And that actually is something I've developed over the years, and further influence in that regards comes from J.S. Bach, the *Cello Suites* or the *Violin Partitas*. Just that ability to write a stand-alone melody that sounds like a whole band or orchestra playing. And in fact, I think as an improviser I try to emulate that conception as well.

JG: Yeah, there are certain guys, Sonny Stitt comes to mind, where what they do is so complete and clear.

BM: Yep.

JG: But yeah, that line writing. You mentioned Bach, my god, just kind of an unparalleled genius, whether in the *Cello Suites* or so many other things. It's interesting you mentioned Marc Cohen/Copland before. I took a couple of lessons with him in college and he had me read a book by Ernst Toch called *Shaping Forces in Music*. He wanted me to pay particular attention to the chapter on harmony. Toch's idea was that harmony should return to polyphony, and that the harmony would just be a confluence of the melodies, as opposed to block chords accompanying a melody. Going back to Renaissance music there was some of that in their thinking and that opened up a lot for me. And you look at some of the Bach Chorales, there's some linear motion you don't expect, and all the sudden there are minor 9ths in places. And you're thinking, it doesn't seem like this would be here, but because of the strength of the melodies and linear motion it works. I love that kind of thinking.

BM: Another influence on my writing and early playing was early music. Some Renaissance music and Medieval music. I got to play some of that up at Hartt. Some of it was very far out. Some of the rhythms and contrapuntal writing was very far out. I liken some of it to jazz.

There's a thing I do, where you would have three or four lines and have rhythms that would intersect in such a way that you almost hear every sixteenth note. But it's jumping from line to line. And that's something I picked up from playing early music and carried that over into whatever I'm writing. Whatever you call it… contemporary something… [Laughter] I never know what to call it.

JG: When did you move out to the West Coast?

BM: 2008. I moved out to take a position at the University of Southern California.

JG: Last summer I was invited to come to a session at the Stanford Jazz Camp. I was working at another camp nearby, so I went down. There were a bunch of your recent former students there, teaching.

BM: Yep!

JG: And they all sounded great and raved about working with you and your program. Also, so how long have you been associated with the Yellowjackets?

BM: Thirty years.

JG: Wow! I didn't realize it was that long. Were you one of the founding members of the group?

BM: No, the band is actually forty years old and I joined in 1990. It's been an incredible experience, being in a partnership band with amazing musicians. A band that has an established sound and conception but is also very pliable and has changed over time. Kind of commensurate with who the four members are. So, when I joined the band, I was able to have an influence that eventually shaped the sound and direction of the music. And with each subsequent personnel change, and there haven't been many by the way, but in a partnership band, whoever joins is going to have an impact on the music. It's been exciting and very rewarding to be a part of that.

JG: Do you have another project coming up soon, or some touring coming up?

BM: We tour throughout the year. We did a recording with the WDR Big Band in November, that'll be out in the summer, We're really excited about that. Russ and I arranged some signature Yellowjackets tunes. And we're supposed to do a studio album with that band sometime this year as well. And I'm busy with the WDR. I've been the chief conductor over the past five years. I did my own project there in December. That'll probably be released in 2021. We also did something with Dave Stryker. He's gonna put out a CD of that.

JG: Wow, I didn't know that, that's great! And that's in…?

BM: Cologne. Yeah, it's been really fun.

JG: Beautiful! So how long are you over there each year?

BM: I do three or four productions a year, like a week to ten days each.

JG: Well man, I'd love to hear those projects.

BM: Well, there's a WDR Facebook page with a bunch of video clips of those projects. We did a crazy thing last year. There's a former USC student, Louis Cole, and he's in a band called Knower. We did a project with them in June that was really fun and unusual. Totally different. You might check them out. They've got some different stuff going.

JG: Nice. I'll definitely check that out. Man, Bob, thanks so much for your time!

BK: Yeah! A pleasure.

JG: I could talk to you for hours about your big band writing, and on all the different associations you've had. I just feel like you're one of the musicians I've been around that's making a really important and diverse contribution over the years. And I learned so much from you! I still have notes you gave me on "Iris," and Coltrane changes. So, thanks for all that, and this! I hope we can hang some more in the coming years.

BM: Well, thank you Jon.

JG: Thanks Bob!

Dick Hyman & Lee Konitz

Dizzy's, New York City – July 2018

On a July night in 2018, my quartet was playing at Dizzy's Club at Jazz at Lincoln Center. The band that night, and in recent years, has been Bryn Roberts on piano, Matt Clohesy on bass, and Quincy Davis on drums. We played a short sound check, and then we went to the band room just off the stage to wait for the start of the gig. The marvelous young pianist Aaron Diehl came and hung out with us. We had a couple of hours to wait before the gig, so we ordered dinner and began to talk.

Our conversation somehow led to jazz musicians who played great into their eighties and nineties. I think maybe it was because Dick Hyman had just turned ninety, and I'd recently heard him sounding as great as ever! He'd also recently received an NEA Jazz Masters Award. Dick is a really kind, quiet, decent man, with a somewhat reserved demeanor. When I saw him a few days earlier in the green room at the 92nd St. Y before our gig at the Jazz in July Festival, I said, "Hey Dick, great to see you. Congratulations on the Jazz Masters Award! I was really happy to see that!" He responded in his normal quiet but direct tone, "Oh, thanks... yeah... I'm a... Jazz Master now... [and then, after a beat, even quieter] don't fuck with me...." I cracked up! And so did he! I'm sure I'd never heard him curse before. He has a straight-laced appearance, but a great sense of humor, as he showed with that comment.

We threw out some names that night at Dizzy's, to go along with Dick Hyman. Hank Jones! Benny Waters on saxophone. Doc Cheatham, Benny Carter, Jimmy Cobb, Roy Haynes! It was a fun topic, and inspirational to think about the careers of these amazing musicians.

Our dinner arrived and our talk was just starting to change direction. Then, all of the sudden, I see the door from the club open into our room. Amazingly, Lee Konitz's head appeared at an angle just past the door, and quietly asked, "Is this the band? Are you guys the band?" We all responded, "Yeah! Hey Lee, come on in!" He came in and quietly said, "Hey... I'm Lee..."

I first met Lee Konitz back in the '80s, but I got to talk to him a number of times when he came to Visiones to hear Maria Schneider's band in the '90s. I also used to do quartet gigs with the great pianist Dick Katz, who was a good friend and colleague of Lee's. We played several gigs at the Blue Note, and I saw and spoke with Lee there a bit. He was always very kind and supportive. Now, at ninety, he would often come to Dizzy's and hang out. Sometimes he'd sit in, and on occasion even sing. He'd walk down from his place on the Upper West Side and walk home after. My friend, the great pianist Ted Rosenthal, walked home with him that night.

But the amazing thing about this night, and moment, was the timing of Lee's appearance! I said, "Lee! We were just talking about great jazz musicians who were great into their eighties and nineties! And on cue, you walked through the door!" He gave a kind of faint, quizzical smile, and a shrug, as if to say, "Eh, that and a metro pass'll get me on the subway." Then, after a moment, he sat down and talked with us.

He stayed the whole night, both sets. He sat at a table with old friends Ted Rosenthal and Bill Charlap. We had a good talk at the end of the night and we were honored by his presence.

I just learned today, April 15th, 2020, that Lee passed due to this terrible virus that the country and world are currently fighting. He was one of only four living musicians to have played at the opening of Birdland in 1949. (Along with Dick Hyman, Roy Haynes, and Harry Belafonte.) He was one of the most important voices in the history of the alto saxophone, and of jazz, and he was one of a kind. Thanks Lee....

Leroy Jones

Phone call, NYC/New Orleans – April 2020

JG: Hey Leroy! I think the last time I saw you was at a gig we did with Harry Connick Jr. on Maui in November of 2001.

LJ: Oh my god! Man, that's nineteen years ago.

JG: I can't believe how long it's been! A good friend of mine and his wife went down to New Orleans about five years ago and I told them, keep an eye out for Leroy Jones. He's one of the great musicians anywhere, and particularly in New Orleans. And they were lucky enough to find you and hear you play while they were there, and they raved to me about it when they got back.

LJ: Oh that's great! I'm sure I must've said hello to them. Over the years I've acquired several new fans, because of my colleagues sending visitors to see me, extending their regards. It's made the gigs much more meaningful.

JG: Yeah, and there's certain people that you work with that you feel a sense of comradery with. You're such a special, warm person and your music reflects that. My friend, Pete, that I sent to you came up and said hi to you and said, "My friend Jon Gordon told me to look out for you if I had a chance to catch you here." And he told me you said, "Jon Gordon! Whoo, did you ever see that man eat!? Man could he eat!"

BOTH: [Laughter]

JG: And the funny thing is, him, his family, and all my friend's families that I grew up with used to always joke with me about that. So tell me about growing up in New Orleans and getting into music.

LJ: I grew up in the Seventh Ward of Orleans Parish. I got introduced to a musical instrument when my parents bought me a guitar when I was eight years old. I began to teach myself with books that illustrated chords on the fretboard. By that time, I was already starting to pick up things by ear, what I heard on the radio or the record player. My parents weren't musicians but had a variety of music that they played on the phonograph. They even had some 78s where I got to hear some early recordings of Louis Armstrong, as well as anything that was popular at the time. My folks were avid record buyers. At that time in the early 1960s, I also heard the likes of Donald Byrd, Al Green, Aretha Franklin, and the Motown sound. Even some Herb Albert and the Tijuana Brass was in the mix, along with James Brown, The Temptations, Diana Ross and The Supremes, Bobby "Blue" Bland, Nancy Wilson—whatever was popular at the time I heard it. My parents had it on 45s and LPs, or I listened to it on the radio. During grade school, when I got to the fifth grade, my first instructor was Sister Mary Hilary at St. Leo The Great Elementary School. I was ten years old. All the students in my class were asked if they wanted to play a musical instrument and join the school band. You were offered two choices, so if you picked one and you didn't feel comfortable, you'd have another choice. It was a wind ensemble. That sort of scratched out the guitar. So, I basically put that instrument away and just played it for pleasure. My first choice for the school band was cornet. My second choice was flute. My parents rented a used horn for me. It was a three-month rental. I started taking private lessons with Sister Hilary and made the band. Just as every other young musician during that time I started with the *Belwin Elementary* book. You would go through elementary to intermediate, then progressive. The first page had an illustration of the fingering chart for your instrument. So, I began taking lessons and learning how to decipher notation under the instruction of Sister Hilary. I caught on so quickly, she put me in the concert band, where we performed a variety of musical styles from pop hits of the day to some classical pieces that were geared for beginners to advanced students. Sister Hilary encouraged me and saw how quickly I made progress within those first three months. She also noticed that I could play by ear and that I was doing some things other children my age were not. So, she encouraged my parents to buy me a new instrument. Once I finished that year, in the fifth grade, I had a brand-new trumpet! [Laughter]

JG: Wow!

LJ: My parents bought me a horn, a Selmer Bundy B♭ trumpet. And I'll never forget that. At that time an unused trumpet was like $250! [Laughter]

JG: Yep!

LJ: In 1969 I guess you could say that was a nice taste of bread for a new student model trumpet. I practiced diligently every day, taking more private lessons. Every Saturday I had a lesson with Sister Hilary. I also participated in a lot of the Louisiana Music Educators Association (LMEA) competitions, where you would audition for honor bands and perform solo recitals.

JG: Yes.

LJ: I auditioned, did a recital, played a classical piece, and got a superior rating in eighth grade. By then I'd been playing the trumpet for three years. I also played the baritone horn one year and got a spot in LMEA Symphonic Band. Then I began to set my eyes on high school and continuing to play in band. In New Orleans, we have a very strong marching band tradition.

One of the bands that I admired most and would often see in Carnival parades was the St. Augustine's Marching 100, the Purple Knights. St. Aug. was the high school I wanted to go to. I was inspired when I saw and heard that band! I got a lot of inspiration from the young musicians playing with the Marching 100, who happened to be a bit older—the upperclassmen. I must add, there was so much going on in the neighborhood that I grew up in—this is like 1970–71. I'm around twelve years old, getting ready to go into my freshman year of high school. I met a gentleman named Danny Barker. Unbeknownst to me, Danny was a famous jazz guitarist who'd played with Cab Calloway back in the 1930s, Dizzy Gillespie, Billie Holiday, and his cousin Paul Barbarin, who was also from New Orleans. Actually, I met Mr. Barker before I played an instrument, because he lived around the corner from my house where I grew up. Like some of the other children in the neighborhood, I used to frolic on his front lawn. He and his wife Blue Lu, who was a jazz singer, would treat us very kindly. They loved children.

During that particular time, and just before I got into St. Augustine High School, Mr. Barker and his wife were members of the Fairview Baptist Church. Their pastor was Rev. Andrew Darby Jr. and Rev. Darby knew that Danny Barker was a professional musician. He had an idea to form a youth group at the church, a band, to help keep youngsters like myself off the streets. That youth group was later to be known as the Fairview Baptist Church Christian Marching Band. In 1970, when the band was being formed, the pastor knew he didn't have enough youngsters amongst his congregation playing instruments appropriate for this type of ensemble. But he knew that Mr. Barker had connections within the local music scene. He was already driving around the neighborhood, checking things out, seeing what was going on. I was practicing in my parent's garage at 1316 St. Denis St., which was located about a half of a football field away from Fairview, which was at the corner of St. Denis and Buchanan. Danny Barker lived just a couple blocks away, on Sere Street, which ran parallel to St. Denis. The church was located in between my parents' house and Mr. Barker's. I would practice diligently every day when I came home from school. And often Mr. Barker would drive by the house. He would hear me practicing and one day parked his car, walked up and presented his pastor's proposal. I had the garage door up. I was playing along with LPs on my parents' old stereo. Occasionally some other kids would come by and we would jam. At that time I'd say that at least two out of five children in the neighborhood played a musical instrument in school band.

JG: Hm mmm.

LJ: Mr. Barker told me that the pastor wanted to form this band and asked me if I would be interested. Although I was attending parochial school, primarily raised Catholic, and was not a member of the Fairview Baptist Church as were most of the band members. There were maybe four or five members in the group who were part of the church congregation. But my parents agreed to it and the band was established in 1970. We rehearsed for an hour or so in my garage around 5 p.m. on Monday evenings. The original Fairview Baptist Church Christian Marching Band, later to be known as the Fairview Brass Band, consisted of about ten to twelve youngsters. By 1972–73 the band's personnel increased to about thirty members.

JG: Wow!

LJ: We had enough musicians comprising the band to do as many as three gigs simultaneously in a day. We would do weekend gigs, Second Line parades on Sunday afternoons. Those parades are put on by Social Aid and Pleasure Clubs in New Orleans, African American organizations. We also did the annual Easter Parade for the Fairview Church and occasionally some private functions. I'll never forget one gig we did with the Fairview band. [Laughter] It was the 1971 Celebration of Life Festival, a rock festival in McCrea, Louisiana, near the Atchafalaya River. Perhaps you've heard about it? Sort of like Woodstock. It attracted big names, like Buddy Miles, Stevie Wonder, The Rolling Stones, Chicago, etc. Our brass band was hired to stroll around the grounds and simulate a Second Line atmosphere. Man, the patrons who attended that event were for the most part hippies and 99.9% were in the nude. It was a celebration of life fest! But unfortunately, that weekend the event ended up being canceled due to violence and illegal drug activity.

JG: Oh!

LJ: Through the Fairview band I met Lucien Barbarin, who at the time played snare drum, along with his older brother Charles, who played the bass drum.

JG: Hmm!

LJ: Lucien and Charles were cousins of Danny Barker. Mr. Barker's mother was the sister of Paul Barbarin, of course making Paul Barbarin Danny's uncle. So, Lucien and Charles Barbarin are the great nephews of Paul Barbarin.

JG: Wow. Yeah, I remember hearing about that when we worked with Harry.

LJ: Danny Barker is their second cousin. They grew up in the Sixth Ward. All the kids in the band were from various parts of the city. Herlin Riley was from the Ninth Ward. He played trumpet when I first met him.

JG: Wow, that's amazing!

LJ: Herlin's mother would drop him off at the garage for rehearsals. By 1972 some of the older musicians joined the band, like trumpeter Gregg Stafford, who's been my dear friend for as long as I can remember. Gregg was born in 1953. Clarinetist Joe Torregano was born in 1952. They brought a bit more experience to the band. They weren't in the initial Fairview band, which only consisted of youngsters eighteen and younger. But then we acquired some older guys who were still quite young, like sousaphonist Anthony "Tuba Fats" Lacen, who was 21. That seemed old to us.

JG: Yeah! [Laughter]

LJ: Sometimes Mr. Barker would bring some musicians in to our rehearsals to give us pointers on how to improvise on chord changes and things of that nature. Cats like alto saxophonist Earl Turbinton. Did you ever hear of him?

JG: Yeah, I'm sure I have.

LJ: He's deceased now. But he was friends with Mr. Barker and would sometimes work with him. Another cat, almost your namesake, was Joe Gordon.

JG: Ha!

LJ: He was a clarinetist from New York City who Danny had worked with during his tenure in the Big Apple. Mr. Gordon was a true jazz musician, a real professional. By that time he'd worked with most of the New Orleans cats. He would also come by and give us pointers, play with us and show us the language of improvisation. The tunes we were learning were songs like the ones Louis Armstrong played in Papa Celestin's Tuxedo Brass Band during the early 1900s. Those were hymns, spirituals that they jazzed up, improvised on and were also considered traditional numbers from New Orleans. The Fairview Brass Band's repertoire was quite similar to the older bands, many of which were still in existence at the time. I got to hear some of those bands and received lots of inspiration and understanding from being able to watch them and listen to them play live.

All this was because of Danny Barker. In conjunction with that, I was still taking private lessons and learning from a method book on the weekends. At that time I had moved on to studying from the Arban trumpet book, and later Schlossberg technical studies. I was also playing in St. Augustine's High School bands, the symphonic, stage band, and marching band. St. Aug. was established in 1951 to educate young Black men in the city of New Orleans and to prepare them for higher education. Most of the young men who graduated went on to be academically successful, in business, political science, athletics, creative arts, education, et cetera. You've probably heard of a trumpet player named John Longo?

JG: Yes.

LJ: He went to St. Aug. too and is also from New Orleans. Unfortunately, he passed away some years ago. He was a Purple Knight about a decade or so before I arrived. Longo graduated in the 1960s. He was one of the most gifted trumpet players, and Edward H. Hampton, our band director often recalled him as one of his prime students. With all of that going on, I was involved with music full time. But by the time I was sixteen, I realized that I wanted to pursue music as a profession. I wanted to be a performing artist. I was still playing with the Fairview band. I suppose I was already fulfilling that dream. By the way, my first pro job was the last time Jazz Fest was held in Congo Square, here in New Orleans, before it moved to the Fairgrounds. That was in 1971.

JG: Wow.

LJ: In 1974 Mr. Barker had to cut us loose, so to speak. Because there were some rumors being spread around the city that he was using the youngsters, exploiting us for his own monetary gain, which was a total lie. I believe there were some musicians, his peers, who were jealous of what was going on and what we were doing. And for young kids we sounded pretty good. Strong! Energetic! Playing all the Second Line parades. Nevertheless, we were undercutting the union bands, bands like the Olympia Brass Band, Onward, and Tuxedo—the older cats. Our prices were less than union scale. I was like thirteen, fourteen years old, doing Second Line parades and getting paid $50, sometimes $60 for the day. That's a nice taste of bread for a teenager, especially during the early to mid 1970s! [Laughter]

JG: Oh my god *yes*!

LJ: Yeah! So of course, the professionals were getting paid double that if not more. The Fairview band disbanded in 1974. Later there was a second Fairview band that came about. But I wasn't involved with that group. And then Mr. Barker told us, "Now I'm gonna call you guys the Hurricane Brass Band, because when you come up the street you blow like a storm!"

JG: [Laughter]

LJ: The Leroy Jones Hurricane Brass Band was established in 1974. Some new faces became a part of that band, like Gregory Davis, who was one of the founders of the Dirty Dozen Brass Band. Charles Joseph and his brother Kirk, along with Kevin Harris who were original members of the Dirty Dozen. The Dirty Dozen Brass Band was established circa 1977–78. But the offshoot of the whole brass band thing was, there was this resurgence of brass band awareness that began with the Fairview band. Before Fairview there were no young musicians our age playing that type of music in the city of New Orleans, nor anywhere in the country.

JG: Wow.

LJ: Much of this has already been documented, about the New Orleans brass band renaissance. And it gives Danny Barker credit for rekindling the brass bands in young musicians.

JG: Wow.

LJ: Mr. Barker wasn't consciously trying to revive brass bands. He was just following his pastor's request. And this is what happened. Reverend Darby once said, "Danny Barker didn't move back home from New York to start a band. He moved back because it was too cold." From the Fairview band, to the Hurricane Brass Band to the Dirty Dozen Brass Band, then the Dirty Dozen inspired another generation of musicians, like the Rebirth Brass Band. And bands of that nature began to incorporate modern styles of music within the traditional idiom. Hence the contemporary brass bands of today. The Rebirth Brass Band came about in the early 1980s.

Today there are so many brass bands in the city of New Orleans, young guys, predominantly African American, playing this type of music, I can't even keep up with their names. By the end of the 1960s, beginning of the '70s there was a limited number of brass bands playing that type of music. Rev. Darby and Mr. Barker's actions served a good cause, even if it wasn't intentional. It sparked awareness to an age-old New Orleans tradition.

JG: That's great Leroy. And it's great that you were part of that as a young person, to revitalize that type of band. 'Cause I just remember so many musicians, particularly African-American musicians, that took me under their wing. And one thing they would always say to me was, "I just want people to understand their culture and that this is their heritage, and I don't want that to be taken away from them." And whether it's political, or based in racism, people don't always honor and respect those traditions. But it's just beautiful that the tradition is so strong there and that you were part of the renaissance of it.

LJ: I feel very fortunate to have been around during the time when it happened. After graduating from high school I spent a year at Loyola University. But when my parents broke up in 1976, it affected me in a way where I dropped out of the College of Music, joined the musicians union, and started working in the French Quarter on Bourbon Street with older musicians. I began to learn more about playing with set bands and building a repertoire. I began to understand more about traditional jazz, swing, and bebop. I was drifting away from exclusively doing brass band music. Occasionally I would still do a brass band gig here and there. But by 1978 I was on the musical path to things new and different. I'd also started working on my trumpet playing technique and changed my embouchure. So, from that point I started working at a jazz club on Bourbon St. called the Maison Bourbon. Have you heard of a trumpet player named Jabbo Smith?

JG: Yes.

LJ: Well Jabbo was the trumpeter playing with one particular band at the Maison Bourbon before I landed the gig. Jabbo was living in New Orleans for a little while before he passed away. Of course, he was an older man then, but was still playing and singing quite well. The gig was with clarinetist, Hollis Carmouche. Hollis was from the Baton Rouge area. He'd attended Louisiana State University and obtained a degree in jazz performance. Hollis was a superb musician, with a very individualistic style. He wasn't trying to copy Pete Fountain, although I could say he'd been influenced by him. Not many clarinet players could avoid Fountain's influence around New Orleans during that time.

You could also hear echoes of Benny Goodman and some of the local, great, clarinetists like Willie Humphrey in his playing. Jabbo left the band and started doing this vaudeville show, *One Mo' Time* that originated in New Orleans, then took off in New York City in the late '70s. It became a hit, running for a few years at the Village Gate. The show was so successful, later it even toured through Europe and Australia.

JG: I think I remember that! I saw commercials for that in New York as a kid in the '70s!

LJ: So I took that gig with Hollis. That's when I was encouraged to do some vocalizing. Nobody else in the band sang. The band consisted of Nicholas Payton's father, Walter Payton, on bass, Joe Lambert was the drummer, and a New Orleans piano player who was from the vaudeville era, Frank "Lil' Daddy" Moliere. Lil' Daddy was born in 1911!

JG: Wow.

LJ: I got to work with those type of cats when I was twenty years old. [Laughter]

JG: Yeah!

LJ: At the time, Hollis was about ten years older than me. Walter would've been about 36. During the old days I'll always remember being the youngest one in the band. Nowadays that script has sorta flipped around. [Laughter] I'm usually the elder statesman amongst a group of younger musicians. I guess that's the normal cycle. [Laughter] In those days, when you visited New Orleans, Bourbon Street was the place to hear jazz. There were a lot of great players down there too! Accomplished musicians from out of town had also moved into the city. Preservation Hall was going strong and many of the older local cats who played at the Hall were my age now and younger, though they looked so much older to me 'cause I was just a youngster. Who ever thought I would eventually end up leading a band, playing there myself? But I always knew I would be playing music. Often people have asked me if I got into music because of Danny Barker. Actually, I was playing music before I met Mr. Barker. But the most significant thing that Mr. Barker did for me is introduce me to my cultural heritage. He inspired me to develop a passion for the culture and traditional New Orleans music at an early age.

JG: Yeah.

LJ: Most likely it would've happened later, or maybe not. But it happened then because of Danny Barker, Reverend Darby, and the Fairview Brass Band experience.

JG: Wow. So, you're twenty, you're working on Bourbon Street, and you did one year at Loyola?

LJ: I did a year there in the jazz studies program from fall 1976 until May 1977, while playing with R&B and cover bands on Bourbon St. At that time, you had to be in the union to play at most of the clubs or hotels in the French Quarter. Like I said there were some personal things happening with my folks that affected me in a way that I lost my desire to stay in college. I just wanted to move out of the house and be responsible for myself. It was almost impossible to study full-time and hold down a six night a week gig. Much of my musical knowledge has come from perseverance and self-studying, working with older cats and paying attention to the lessons they expounded.

JG: Well that brings us up to around 1980, and brings in some musicians I know some and that you know very well, and how we got to know each other. In 1998 I got called to do a recording with Harry Connick Jr.'s band. And you and Lucien were just standouts to me when I got there. First of all, you're both very special people and players and musicians. And immediately I got the sense of that history and that lineage that you're a part of in how you played. And one of the first things I came to understand was how much Harry admired and looked up to you guys when he was a young kid coming along. And that was why it was so important for him to have you guys be a part of his band once he became successful and became the big star he became. So, when did you meet Harry?

LJ: Well, Harry's father was the district attorney of New Orleans from 1974 for about 25 years thereafter until his retirement. Prior to his election to that office, my Hurricane Brass Band played for a couple of his campaign rallies. There, at one of them was where I first saw Harry. At that time, I was sixteen and Harry would've been seven years old. We didn't officially meet then, but I saw him and he was hanging out while the band played at the rally. I formed my own quintet in 1980. Lucien played trombone in my band. Some years later, around 1983, I was playing a gig as a sideman in another band on Bourbon St. at the Mahogany Hall, formerly the Paddock Lounge.

One night Harry stopped by and sat in with us. He told me he was getting ready to move up to New York. I hadn't seen him in a while. I was so impressed with how well he was playing the piano, not to mention how much he'd grown up! After that I hadn't heard anything more about Harry. He was going up to New York City to study and pursue his career. A year before that I'd made my first trip to Europe. During the spring of 1982 I toured France with the Louisiana Repertory Jazz Ensemble. Later that same year, during the fall, I brought my own quintet to the Netherlands. The band consisted of Lucien Barbarin on trombone, Shannon Powell on drums, Walter Payton on bass, pianist Richard Knox, and myself. When we returned, I still had my gigs on Bourbon St. and resided in the French Quarter.

In 1985 I got an offer to go to South East Asia with the Camellia Jazz Band, under the leadership of drummer Trevor Richards. This was a traditional New Orleans jazz band. We had a four-piece ensemble, consisting of piano, drums, trumpet, and clarinet. Our initial contract was for three months at a five-star hotel in Singapore. That tenure was such a success, with the New Orleans theme, cuisine, and music, our contract was extended another six months and then six months more! So, I was away for about fifteen months before returning home to New Orleans for a brief visit. The band performed six nights weekly at an exclusive restaurant in the hotel and lived there as well.

JG: Nice.

LJ: From that gig we hooked up with other hotels in the Asia Pacific chain. We performed in Singapore and Malaysia. We did four weeks at a hotel in Kuala Lumpur. Then four weeks in Manila, the Philippines, three months in Jakarta, Indonesia, four weeks in Hong Kong, then on to Taiwan and Thailand for a couple weeks. We performed at a Club Med on Mauritius Islands for six weeks, played in Brunei, then back to Singapore. For a span of about three years or so I was over in Southeast Asia.

During that time, in 1988 I was watching *Dateline with Larry King Live* on CNN International from my hotel room—I saw Harry! They were talking about this Rob Reiner film that had recently been released, *When Harry Met Sally*. Harry also played piano and sang a song from the movie soundtrack, accompanied by bassist Ben Wolfe. I didn't know Ben at the time. I believe they were swinging out on "It Had to Be You." I hadn't seen the movie yet, but I'd heard about it and discovered that Harry was all over the soundtrack. I was so proud! I said, "Wow! My homey has made it to the big time!" I hadn't seen him since that night at Mahogany Hall. This was about two years before he formed his own orchestra and I got the call to join him. I went back to Southeast Asia one more time in 1989 then came back home to New Orleans.

The following year I got a call from Ann Marie Wilkins letting me know that Harry was forming a big band and was interested in having me in his trumpet section. Of course I said yes! Rehearsals commenced in Princeton, New Jersey in June of 1990. After a couple weeks in the shed, we hit the road and the rest is history. The original orchestra was comprised of Lucien Barbarin, Craig Klein, and Mark Mullins in the trombone section. The trumpets were Jeremy Davenport, Dan Miller, Stacy Cole, and myself. The reed section was Brad Leali, Mark Sterbank, Jerry Weldon, Ned Gould, and Dave Schumacher. In the rhythm section, besides Harry, was Russell Malone on guitar, Ben Wolfe on bass, and Shannon Powell on drums. Shortly thereafter Roger Ingram replaced Stacy Cole and Joe Barati was added on bass trombone, along with Louis Ford on the clarinet.

When Harry first started the band almost half the guys were New Orleans cats. In 1994 Harry switched gears and started performing genres that reflect his other New Orleans musical roots and influences. He released an album titled *She*. He also established his own independent record label, NOPTEE Records. I had the honor of being the first artist to record under it, with distribution via Columbia Records, soon after to become Sony Music Inc. My debut was titled *Mo' Cream From The Crop* with a follow up in tribute to Louis Armstrong titled *Props For Pops*, which got some critical acclaim and further established me as a bona fide jazz trumpeter.

JG: Yeah!

LJ: My name and reputation had already been dribbling throughout Europe and Southeast Asia. But because of Harry's generosity and unselfishness I received a lot more visibility in the United States… so did Lucien Barbarin.

JG: Well, I think it was generosity, but I also think it was his love and admiration for you, and the common sense of how great you both played. And what I felt strongly is that appreciation for where he came from. You know, I really had a great time doing those tours. I guess I was there most of the time from '98–'01. But I was very thankful for that and there were a number of things about Harry that I really appreciated. First of all, he was so devoted to guys like you and Lucien, and Jerry Weldon and Ned Goold who are really great players. And you know, people that came up with him in New Orleans, that he knew or looked up to like you guys, or had been with him in the band, or guys he met along the way like Jimmy Greene, that he was very devoted to and supportive of. And I didn't know what kind of talent he was. His ears are as good as anybody I've ever been around. He taught himself how to write for the band, and by the time I got there he was writing beautiful stuff for the band.

LJ: Yeah.

JG: When everything happened with Hurricane Katrina, I admired the way he was so front and center in trying to stand up for and get support for New Orleans. So, I admire those things about him. And a couple of years ago there was something on TV, a group after the big band, with strings and horns. And you guys were playing Mardi Gras in New Orleans. You were there, and Arthur Latin playing drums, and Lucien and Jerry, and it just made me so happy to see that and to feel that vibe and that groove.

LJ: Yeah brother. I reckon that is true. What will also be most memorable to me is getting to meet and play with you, and all the other cats that came through that band—Joe Magnarelli, Derrick Gardner, Jimmy Greene, Jerry Weldon, Dave Schumacher, Will Campbell, and all the cats. Russell Malone was gone by the time you got in the band. Harry wasn't using guitar in the rhythm section anymore, and then we got Arthur Latin. He had gone through a lot of changes with drummers as you recall. Him and Shannon fell out. [Laughter] You know, for a short stint, we had Duffy Jackson holding down the tubs. Even Tain (Jeff Watts) played a couple gigs. As great as these cats play, they just didn't gel with the band. Arthur was a godsend, from Nacogdoches, Texas!

In a way, Harry is like a Duke Ellington of his day. He knew how to use the equipment he had, to make it work. He wrote arrangements that suited each individual musician's personality. Harry's the ultimate musician. I learned a great deal being with him in that big band.

Nowadays I'm writing and arranging. I acquired those skills watching him and watching all you cats. It's like it put my thing into high gear. I'm so thankful for the experience! I had a couple records with distribution on the label. But since then I've produced and released several records. Many musicians are going indie these days. [Laughter]

JG: You mentioned Joe Magnarelli, I just did an interview with him the other day. And when we talked about being on Harry's band together and I mentioned your name, he said, "You know, I didn't get to blow a whole lot on the band. But it never bothered me, because I got to listen to Leroy every night, and for me it was a lesson every night." I felt the same way man.

LJ: Thanks Jon.

JG: So, let me ask you about a couple other people. You were working with Nicholas Payton's dad, Walter. When did you get to know and hear about Nicholas?

LJ: I've known Nicholas since he was a little boy. Walter was leading the band in the musical *One Mo' Time*. When the show opened in New Orleans in 1978, for the matinees on Sundays I would sub for trumpeter Lionel Ferbos, who often did a brunch gig. Before my initial engagement I would go over the routine and rehearse the trumpet parts with Walter. I also rehearsed for other gigs at his house in the Tremé on St. Phillip Street. Perhaps Nicholas would've been around six years old. I believe he is fourteen years younger than me. When I first started subbing for Mr. Ferbos, I was twenty. So Nick was just a kid. I remember him listening in at some of our rehearsals and hanging out. His mother Maria was an accomplished pianist. So, he comes from a musical environment. And his dad was the band director at McDonough No.15 Elementary School. I'd met Nicholas and his brother Darius when they were little boys. So we've known each other a long time. Nick was a prodigy! He's a genius!

JG: Man, I only played with him a couple times. One time was at the Oslo Jazz Festival. I used to play that festival a lot. In fact, that's where I met some of the guys in the Dirty Dozen Brass Band in '89 when I was 22. But this time with Nicholas would've been '02 or '03. On a couple nights I led the jam session at the Grand Hotel. And Nicholas's whole band came and sat in for the whole set, it was great! Nicholas played the drums and played his ass off!

LJ: Yeah!

JG: And everybody in the band came up to me after and said, "*And* he plays the saxophone, *and* he plays the piano, *and* he plays the bass..."

LJ: Yes indeed! Any instrument he touches he plays it with authority and finesse! He also plays the bass like it's his main axe. He's just that type of talent. I've known him and his family for a long time. And you know, he looks up to me. I say, "I look up to you Nick, even though you're shorter than me." I'm quite flattered. [Laughter]

JG: Well, I'm glad you said that. He really admires you. As anyone would that plays this music. But I was very glad to see him give you that shout out, it's very deserved.

LJ: Thanks.

JG: I also wanted to ask you about Terence Blanchard.

LJ: Oh man, Terence Blanchard! He also attended St. Augustine High School. He was one of the gifted students in the special eighth grade class during my last year there as a senior. Normally parochial high schools go from grade nine to grade twelve. Terence was a straight-A student. The senior band members gave me the nickname "Jazz" in my freshman year. When Terence got there, he used to be up under my wing all the time, so they started calling him "Lil' Jazz!" He was also a prodigy. Terence is simply outstanding! His resume speaks for itself. We've known each other for decades, for more than half of our lives. I'm just so thankful that we're still connected. He continues to be an inspiration for me and many other musicians! He's got it all going on and remains quite humble!

JG: Yeah, he's an incredible player and musician!

LJ: There's a documentary film about my life titled *A Man and His Trumpet – The Leroy Jones Story* that will be available soon to the general public. It's been produced and directed by up and coming independent filmmaker, Cameron Washington. He's a big fan of mine, who also happens to play the trumpet. We filmed over the course of a couple years, starting in 2015. There are interviews from Harry Connick Jr., Herlin Riley, Gregg Stafford, Brad Leali, and Terence Blanchard, including live performance footage from yours truly, along with some cultural history about New Orleans. It's supposed to be available via Amazon, Blu-ray and DVD later this year. Unfortunately, the COVID-19 pandemic has slowed things down. There are many things that have been put on hold because of the crisis. But it will be coming soon. Cameron first heard me play on Harry Connick Jr.'s *Blue Light Red Light* album circa 1990–91, when he was a teenager.

JG: And what about the Marsalis family?

LJ: I've been acquainted with the Marsalis family since my high school days. During my senior year Wynton and I played in an honor band together. It was a jazz stage band conducted by guest clinician/trumpeter Mike Vax. Wynton was a freshman from De LaSalle High School. I was at St Aug. Auditions were held and a select group of the best players from various schools around the city made the band. He and his older brother Branford, as well as their younger siblings Delfeayo and Jason, have always been outstanding musicians and great people! Wynton encouraged me to change my embouchure. This was in 1981 and would've been when his debut album for Columbia Records was coming out and after he and his brother moved to New York City. I had come up there to audition for a musical, a stage production on Louis Armstrong's life that was going to be directed by Gene Kelly. He and Branford had just gotten off the road with Art Blakey. They had a little flat in Midtown. I hung out with them for a minute.

JG: Was this the famous dancer Gene Kelly?

LJ: Yep. Wynton was asked to do it. But since he was busy with his debut record release and touring, he told the casting company to call me. So, I came up to New York City and got to hang out a bit with Wynton and Branford.

JG: Yeah.

LJ: It was inspiring and fun, because I hadn't seen them since those days in high school. Apparently the musical never received adequate financial support to commence production. There was a good chance I would have been selected for the part. My audition number was "When It's Sleepy Time Down South." There was a pianist there to accompany everyone, but she didn't really know the tune. So I waved her out and did it solo. Seems like Mr. Kelly, the producers and their associates were impressed. Branford accompanied me to the trials and sat in the orchestra seating area with Gene Kelly and company. The audition was at the theater where the musical *Annie* had run for many years. So that was my first Broadway close encounter, until a two-week run at the Lunt-Fontanne Theatre with Harry Connick Jr. during the fall of 1990. [Laughter]

JG: Well, strangely enough, I was right down the block at Performing Arts High School, which was West 46th Street between Sixth and Seventh Avenues. It's amazing how much stuff can happen in a small area, whether it's New Orleans or Manhattan, where all those famous Broadway plays are.

LJ: Theater Row.

JG: Yeah, so that's amazing man. Had that show not lost its backers you would've been the lead in it!

LJ: I reckon so! That would have been an early break for me. Perhaps it would've been great. But you know everything happens for a reason. If that had happened, maybe I would never have gotten to meet you when I did, and play with Harry's band. Definitely would have changed the course of my life's history.

JG: Oh absolutely! And the reason I asked about the Marsalis family is because I've seen Wynton mention you as someone he's respected and admired. Did you get a chance to know Ellis at all?

LJ: Yes indeed!

JG: Yeah, we just lost him four days ago.

LJ: If our government would have been more proactive once the warnings were out there, perhaps precautions could've been taken for people like Ellis and others who are within the high-risk group for contracting COVID-19. I knew Ellis and Dolores. I'd been to their home, on Hickory St. in the Carrollton area of New Orleans, when I was a teenager to frolic and play music with Branford and Wynton. Ellis even played some gigs with me when the World Fair came to New Orleans in 1984. He would fill in for one of his contemporaries, Edward Frank. Ed was a great pianist and a dear friend from whom I learned a great deal.

My quartet opened the InterContinental Hotel in New Orleans in January 1983. When the Expo started in '84 my band was in demand. There were lots of really good gigs during that time. I was also working on Bourbon St. at Mahogany Hall. Just before heading off to Singapore, I was performing with my quartet in Pete's Pub, five nights a week during the early evening hours at the hotel and playing the Sunday brunch in the Veranda Restaurant. Ed worked with Dave Bartholomew's big band. Whenever he was out of town with Dave I would call Ellis. He was such a humble, down to earth cat! He always agreed to come and play with my band and me! We would play mainstream and New Orleans standards. Ellis could play any and everything! Traditional, modern, ragtime, you name it! Yes, I knew Ellis and can say I had the opportunity to work with him. It was always an inspiration-filled, learning experience! I can say the last time I got to play with Mr. Marsalis was at Dave Bartholomew's ninetieth birthday party. That was ten years ago. Dave was the composer of all the Fats Domino hit songs.

JG: Wow!

LJ: Unlike many musicians, Dave was a good businessman. He managed his publishing, secured copyrights, and ended up becoming quite wealthy. He was born on December 24th 1918 and died on June 23rd 2019.

JG: Wow.

LJ: Allen Toussaint was the master of ceremonies at Dave's ninetieth birthday celebration. It was at the Fairmont Roosevelt Hotel, in the Blue Room. Ellis and I did a duet, and he accompanied me on the classic "Stardust." That was the last time we shared the stage, ten years ago.

JG: Wow... and we just lost Ellis four days ago... and the last time you and I had a little back and forth was when Lucien passed a couple months ago.

LJ: Yeah. Lucien passed away on January 30th 2020. His funeral and going home celebration was held on the fifteenth of February.

JG: Wow... well, one of the reasons I wanted to do this is the kind of musicians that I've been around over the years who are so special. And I wanted to be able to talk with them and pass that on to students. To me you're such a wealth of knowledge, experience, and feeling in the music that you carry forward, so I really appreciate this. Oh and there's one other thing I wanted to ask you about! There used to be two clubs that faced Armstrong Park. One was called the Funky Butt...

LJ: The other one was Donna's, Donna's Bar and Grill.

JG: Yeah! And we sat in there. We had done a gig with Harry. Jimmy Greene and I were at the hotel and somebody said, "Hey, you should come down to Donna's!"

LJ: It could have been me, because on Saturday nights I used to do the late-night jam. Then again it might not have been me, if we were on the road. Most likely I would've been home resting from the tour.

JG: Well, I'm not sure who it was. But Jimmy and I decided to go to the club. I think we walked 'cause it wasn't that far away. So, we go to open the door. And the woman, Donna, who the club is named for, is standing in the doorway when we open it, with two plates of barbecue chicken, BBQ sauce, and white bread, and...

LJ: [Laughter]

JG: As I walk in, she says, "Hi Jon, this is for you!" and hands me the plate of food. And then, "Hi Jimmy, this is for you!" We're not even in the door, and this woman somehow already knows our names, and is feeding us, and I'm like, "This is my kinda situation!"

BOTH: [Laughter]

JG: I don't think it was your gig. But you and Harry were sitting in with whoever's gig it was. But it was just such a beautiful vibe, and you, me, Jimmy, and Harry played on a few tunes. And we sat there and ate. Talk about the hospitality and the vibe… it just made me so happy.

LJ: You know bruh, that was the place! Unfortunately, after Katrina it went down. Donna's opened again for a little while, but then Charlie, Donna's husband, passed away. They didn't own the building. It was leased. It's a pity, because that was the last frontier for a jazz club, a live music venue on North Rampart Street. Some French Quarter residents didn't want live music on Rampart Street. A bar or delicatessen was OK. And of course it was great when the Funky Butt was there too, because people would migrate from Funky Butt to Donna's, and the music was always great. Everyone would pass through, like Nicholas Payton, Branford Marsalis, Allen Toussaint, Dave Bartholomew, Harry Connick Jr., Henry Butler, Hollywood celebrities, famous people. Everyone knew about Donna's. It became a household name.

JG: Yeah.

LJ: Financially, they just couldn't hold on after Katrina. Today the building stands there, empty, just sitting there on the corner, deteriorating. It's funny—the Cahn family owns the building. Photographer Jules L. Cahn has long been dead, but his family owns the building and lots of other property in the French Quarter. Jules produced my first recording in 1975, an album called *Leroy Jones' Hurricane Brass Band*. Is that not ironic? [Laughter]

JG: Wow! Well, listen Leroy, what a great conversation man. I'm so glad we got to talk. And with all the craziness in the world, just stay safe and healthy. I'm hoping we'll get through this as soon as possible and our paths will cross again and we'll get to hang and play again soon.

LJ: Likewise. Thank you for always keeping me in your thoughts and prayers. Katja and I are doing fine. We're raising our two little ones. Luca has just turned three and Aada is four. I'll send you a photo from today, so you can have a look at them. [Laughter]

JG: Oh that'll be great and tell Katja I say hey!

LJ: OK, brother. Be safe up there in New York. Let's stay in touch.

JG: Thanks, man.

Renee Rosnes

Phone call, Brooklyn, NY/West Orange, NJ – March 2020

JG: Hey Renee, it's Jon.

RR: Hey Jon, how are you? Are you in Brooklyn?

JG: Yeah. How are you guys doing?

RR: Thankfully we're all fine. What a bizarre time we're living through!

JG: Yeah… I appreciate you doing this, is now good?

RR: Sure.

JG: Great, so tell me about growing up and getting into music. You grew up in Vancouver, right?

RR: Yes, I grew up on the west coast of British Columbia, in North Vancouver.

JG: And I'm guessing the real estate prices weren't quite as exorbitant then.

RR: [Laughter] No, not in the least. It's become like the San Francisco of Canada!

JG: And how did you get started in music?

RR: I started with classical piano lessons at the age of three, and then also violin lessons at age five. I had two older sisters, and all three of us were adopted. Our parents, though not musicians, were music lovers. They wanted each of their daughters to play a musical instrument. So all of us played the piano and one stringed instrument. I chose the violin, as did my older sister. My middle sister decided on the cello.

JG: So, when did you realize that music was important to you?

RR: You know, I don't remember *not* being a musician. My mother told me the reason I began with lessons so early was because I was getting up on the piano bench trying to copy my sisters. She figured that if I was attempting to play, she might as well get me started. So, I don't really remember a time when I didn't play an instrument. In terms of how important music was to me, it was always a very big part of my life. Our home seemed like a small music school with all of us on a schedule to practice both of our instruments every day! [Laughter] The three of us were also members of the Vancouver Youth Orchestra for many years as well. That was such a wonderful time and I'm so glad I was able to experience several years of playing in an orchestra.

JG: How old were you when you started playing with them?

RR: Oof! Probably about nine or ten.

JG: Wow!

RR: I carried on with both instruments all the way through my teens until I left home to attend the University of Toronto. However, I got introduced to jazz during my high school days. I was very fortunate to have an extraordinary band director named Bob Rebagliati, maybe you've run into him in Canada?

JG: I haven't run into him, but I think he's the teacher there I've heard about that was very impactful for a lot of musicians out there.

RR: Likely that was him. We called him "Mr. Reb" for short. Among his students were singer-pianist-songwriter Laila Biali, composer Darcy James Argue, bassist Brandi Disterheft, and others. So many excellent players came out of his program and went on to become professionals and do great things.

JG: So how old were you when you met Mr. Reb?

RR: He was my teacher for five years, from grade eight through grade twelve. When I entered junior high school, he was aware I was another "Rosnes girl" that played the piano, so he recruited me for the jazz band. I wasn't familiar with jazz at all prior to that point, but I thought it would be a fun experience to play in the big band, or "stage band" as it was called back then. I was used to the idea of playing by ear and would often take pop songs off the radio and enjoyed playing them for my friends—Elton John, Paul McCartney and Wings, Chicago, Stevie Wonder— whatever I heard that appealed to me. So, the aspect of playing by ear wasn't foreign, but the concept of improvising certainly was. The rhythms and harmonies of jazz were a brand-new sound to me. Mr. Reb was important because he would constantly give me albums to take home and listen to, of a wide variety of styles. I immediately understood that jazz was a great American art form with a long and developing history. Of course, at that point I wasn't looking towards being a professional jazz musician, but I was very intrigued with improvisation. The repertoire of the school band was also quite stylistically varied, and I wanted to play every piece well. I listened to the original recordings of the Count Basie Band playing "Hayburner," Horace Silver playing "Song for My Father," Herbie Hancock playing "Chameleon," and Oscar Peterson with the Singers Unlimited performing "Catherine." I remember Mr. Reb asking me to try and take Oscar's solo off from that song. I could actually hear all the notes but didn't have a clue how to notate all the complex rhythms. It was so much fun to work on, I think that's when I really got hooked.

JG: I've been around a few people that have a great ear, or have perfect pitch. I think you have the most incredible ear of anyone I've ever known. Did your teacher Mr. Reb help you to understand that? When did you start to realize how good your ear was?

RR: Well, early on I thought that everyone had that ability. I didn't know it was special, probably because my older sisters also had it growing up. I suppose I also attribute being able to hear to the ear training that my first piano teacher, Miss Patch, provided me. I remember she taught me to identify not only intervals but also individual notes. Ear training was a part of every lesson. It wasn't really until high school that I realized not everyone could distinguish one note from another.

JG: Well, I'd guess that starting at age three, there's some kind of correlation with that and a natural intuiting of things that you're not even conscious of. It's like you're thrown in the pool and you start swimming, and you have muscles there as a result that you don't even know you have.

RR: I think that's a great analogy. That's how it felt… I don't consciously remember learning it. I don't know if this is important to the topic, but I really treasure the Royal Conservatory of Music system of learning that I went through. For every grade level—from beginner to advanced—there is repertoire representing the different historical periods, along with technical requirements, ear training, and sight-reading too. It's quite a successful and comprehensive system of learning to play.

JG: In sometimes talking with Bill[5], and getting to talk some with Richard Rodney Bennett, who I know you knew well… I mean, his mother studied with Gustav Holst! And, I just think he was immersed in that world before he was able to even be conscious of it. I remember with Richard… Bill's friend Darren Motise had asked me to do his grad recital for his master's degree at Juilliard. And we played Richard's soprano saxophone sonata which is one of my favorite pieces for classical saxophone. And from doing that we got to go over to Richard's place a couple times and play for him. I asked him for lessons, and you know how he was. He said, in his erudite British accent, "Oh well, I don't teach, you know."

RR: [Laughter]

JG: But I asked a couple times and eventually he had me come over. There were a couple things that I played for him that he liked, because he couldn't tell where the composition ended and the improvisation began, and he liked that. And then I played him something that I hoped would be the start for a sax quartet, and he listened and said, "Yeees… well… it's not very good now is it? You see what you'd actually like to do is something more like this…" and he wrote out 64 bars of music in under a minute… just a melodic line.

RR: Wonderful.

JG: 32 bars on one page, 32 on the next. He just did it, his hand moved back and forth effortlessly. And I'm looking at this beautiful penmanship, and this brilliant triadic line that's developed, and I'm thinking… oh man! There's so much that's going on here!

RR: Inspiring thing to witness.

JG: Oh, by the way, it's 7:00! I'm hearing people cheer out the window for the health care workers![6]

RR: Oooh how nice! That's a hopeful sound!

JG: Yeah, it's really sweet, God bless them. So, Richard finished, and I thought, just to write something that neat would take me several hours if not days. And I just think that in his case, and yours, there are just things that are naturally ingrained from starting so early perhaps that you don't even know are there and that you just figure, isn't this just how it's done? He was incredibly tactile, as you remember. He used to knit.

RR: Yes, and many other things. Aside from being one of the greatest composers, he quilted, collaged, cooked… you name it.

JG: He said the reason he couldn't tolerate teaching anyone was how sloppy their handwriting was, and I had terrible handwriting! So, I tried not to let him see too much of that in those couple lessons. But I think in spending a little time with him I definitely sensed that innate talent, whether it was something genetic or that came to him very early. Maybe it's a combination of both. But the person that first told me about your ear was Jon Faddis. He said he'd have the whole Carnegie Hall Jazz Band play any note and then you could immediately play them all back, everybody's note, for the audience. And Bill told me you have something beyond perfect pitch that has another name?

RR: Uhhhh… [laughter] well, whatever it is I don't know. You'd have to ask him.

JG: So you were studying with Mr. Reb—were you studying jazz piano with him privately?

RR: No, I just studied with him at the school. But he would give me assignments such as to

---

5   Bill Charlap, Renee Rosnes' husband.

6   During the COVID-19 pandemic of 2020, this became a nightly ritual.

transcribe solos, learn all the blues scales, and he also encouraged me to compose for the school groups. He'd always be turning me on to musicians to listen to and to study. He was definitely my prime mentor in the music. After high school I decided to move to Toronto to attend the Faculty of Music at the University of Toronto. One of the main reasons I wanted to go east was that there was quite an active jazz scene with a lot of great players. The University of Toronto didn't have a jazz degree program at that time. But it did have a big band which I played in, although I was enrolled in the classical performance program. I went out to the clubs as often as I could to hear the local players who were often backing up American jazz artists. During my second year of university, I made the realization that my true passion was jazz, and that's the direction I wanted to pursue. I then quit school and returned to Vancouver and began to gig around the city with my peers, sometimes accompanying players who came through town, such as Joe Farrell and Dave Liebman. During the early '80s there were several clubs that presented great jazz. One was the Plazazz Showroom where I remember hearing Ella, Oscar, Dizzy, Sarah Vaughan, Joe Williams, Toshiko Akiyoshi and Lew Tabackin, and also a young Wynton Marsalis with Branford, Charles Fambrough on bass, Kenny Kirkland, and Jeff "Tain" Watts. Most of the engagements were two weeks long, so I would get to hear the bands more than once. It was an unbelievable time. There was another club called the Sheraton Landmark, where I remember hearing Woody Shaw, and Freddie Hubbard with his band which included a young Billy Childs on piano. There were so many great performances to check out, and at the same time I had a steady trio gig in Vancouver's Hyatt Hotel playing standards.

JG: Oh that's amazing! That's such a blessing to have a gig like that.

RR: It was great. I loved having a salary, and the band managed to keep the gig for three years. It provided me with a strong foundation and I really expanded my knowledge of standards.

JG: Wow. What year was this?

RR: This was about 1982 through '84. I was in my early twenties. There was another place that had a big impact on me… a little dive with a pool table and disco ball, called Basin Street. It was located on Hastings Street, Vancouver's skid row. You'd walk up the block stepping over liquor bottles and garbage. You don't think of Vancouver like that because most of the city is clean. Anyway, this was an after-hours club that I often played at with the drummer Rudy Petschauer. It would open at midnight and be hopping until about 5 a.m. So when visiting musicians finished their gigs they would hear about this place and be skeptical… "Really, an after-hours jazz club? Here?" And they would end up coming over, bringing their horns and jamming with us. Branford, Jeff Watts, Kenny Kirkland, Woody Shaw, Steve Turre, and others came in.

JG: Wow.

RR: I remember when Toshiko's band was playing in town. Walt Weiskopf and Conrad Herwig came to hang at Basin Street. Looking back, I was making new friends and getting acquainted with a lot of the younger generation on the New York jazz scene of that time. Eventually I made the decision to go to New York City, and I applied for and was awarded a Canada Council of the Arts grant. At the end of '85 I made the trek, along with Rudy, to New York. My initial intention was that I would stay a year and then return home. But within that first year, I fell in love with the city's energy, the community of great musicians— both young and old— and all that New York had to offer. It was stimulating and inspiring and I didn't want to pull myself away from it, and I guess I never did.

JG: I remember that time and the scene very well. New York in the '80s, the club scene was amazing. All the different places we could go to for very little money, places you could sit in.

RR: Right.

JG: I used to love to go to Barry Harris' Jazz Cultural Theater.

RR: I would go there too Jon—once a week to check out his masterclass.

JG: Yeah, and Ted Curson ran the late-night jam session at the Blue Note.

RR: I was also a part of that. In fact, that was probably my first real gig in New York. I remember leaving the club at dawn with birds chirping and garbage trucks rolling down Sixth Avenue.

JG: I'm not surprised that you were working right away. I was a part of this thing that Don Sickler put together for the union called Young Sounds, and Bill Charlap, Kevin Hays, Craig Rivers all did it some. And then sometimes Don would put together reading sessions. One time he said there's this great young piano player in town and she's going to play, and it was you. We'd play like James Williams and Donald Brown tunes and things like that. Do you remember that?

RR: I sort of remember doing some playing sessions at Sickler's, but I don't think I did it on a regular basis.

JG: It would've been '85 or '86.

RR: That would've been right about when I got to town.

JG: Well, you've had some of the most amazing side-person associations of anyone I've ever known. So, just walk us through some of that. You come to New York in '85 and you're playing with Ted Curson at the Blue Note jam session right away.

RR: Yeah, I don't remember how I got the gig. I think I sat in one night and he asked if I'd be interested to play the gig some nights and I jumped at the opportunity. I was living in Brooklyn, in a brownstone walk-up. Living above me was the trumpet player Michael Mossman, who had just begun playing with the band Out of the Blue, also known as OTB. It was a Blue Note Records project assembled by the label.

JG: Yeah, and that was a big deal at the time.

RR: The pianist was Harry Pickens. At some point Harry decided to leave New York to pursue another life, and Mossman asked if I'd like to join the band. That was the first gig that introduced me to an international stage. Shortly after that Joe Henderson called and asked if I'd like to tour with him in Europe.

JG: When was that?

RR: That was '86… end of '86. It was within that first full year that things began to happen for me. Joe was assembling an all-women rhythm section. I figured if Joe Henderson wanted me to play, I was going to take the opportunity and learn whatever I could, as well as be happy to know some new players. That group started out with drummer Cindy Blackman—now Blackman-Santana—and bassist Kim Clarke. That was the first version of that band. Shortly thereafter, the drummer Sylvia Cuenca joined as well as a bassist from Chicago named Marlene Rosenberg. So there I was playing with the great Joe Henderson and it was amazing! The level of consistency and imagination that he played with from night to night was astonishing.

JG: Yeah, Joe at that time, that's around the time he was making those *State of The Tenor* records, live at the Vanguard. And I was there some of those nights when they recorded those, it was like '85. He was the first improviser that just totally blew my mind, in terms of what was possible.

RR: Right! [Laughter]

JG: I remember hearing Joe at eighteen, and was like *ohh*!!! Tunes would end and he would just start something else at the end of it, and there was this whole other vibe, and groove, and it was just so deep what he was doing.

RR: Yeah, it was thrilling to be playing with somebody of that caliber. He just never had a bad night, ever, and it was so awe inspiring. It underlined how much work I needed to do, [laughter] not that I didn't know that going in. I soon realized that if I brought in music, you know, pieces he hadn't played in a long time, but great songs from his past repertoire... such as "Punjab," "Afro-Centric," "Power to the People," "Tetragon," "Black Narcissus," "Gazelle"... if he heard us messing around with a something at soundcheck, he would join in and get it under his fingers again. We added a lot of repertoire that way. Much of it was material he hadn't played since he'd recorded it, and he tended toward playing the same book... you know, "Recordame," "Invitation," the blues, etc. So it was a lot of fun to bring in the new "old" tunes.

JG: And how long were you working with him?

RR: Oh, I guess about fifteen years in various contexts. He passed on June 30th, 2001. I recall the year so well because it was two months before 9/11, and I remember having the thought that he wasn't here for that. During the time I worked with him, I really loved the rhythm section with Larry Grenadier and Al Foster, with whom we made some European tours. I think there are some tapes of that band from a Danish radio show. So much fun! Other "Joe" rhythm sections I worked with, included George Mraz, Charlie Haden, Delbert Felix, Ralph Penland, Tootie Heath, and Billy Drummond.

JG: Who are some other folks you worked with back then?

RR: If we're going chronologically, I toured with Wayne Shorter's band in 1988.

JG: Wow.

RR: That was after the releases of *Atlantis, Phantom Navigator,* and *Joy Rider,* so we were doing repertoire from those albums and some older tunes too, such as "Beauty and the Beast," "Diana," and "Footprints."

JG: *Atlantis* is one of my favorite records. That music is so beautiful.

RR: It really is! All the piano parts are through composed, with every bass line and voicing notated. Some of the charts were eight, nine pages long, in his beautiful handwriting.

JG: Yeah, that music is unbelievable. And how long did you work with Wayne's band?

RR: Just that year. When he talked to me about working with him, I remember telling him that I wasn't a synthesizer player. I knew it was important for him to know that, but I also knew how much I wanted the opportunity to play with him. His response—which I loved—was, "It's OK, you can learn on the bandstand."

JG: Wow.

RR: Another thing he asked me during that first phone conversation was, "Have you seen the movie *Alien*?" I thought it was an odd question, and I told him that I hadn't. In his cryptic way, he basically said it was a prerequisite, and then told me not to worry, and that we'd watch it together as a band when we got out to San Francisco to rehearse. So, fast forward to when the famous "chestburster" scene was happening, you know, where the alien dramatically emerges from John Hurt's character's body?

JG: Yeah.

RR: Well, at that moment Wayne clicked the remote to stop the film and said, "You see that?!! That's how I want my band to sound!!!"

JG: [Laughter] Wow! Who else was in the band at the time?

RR: Drummer Terri Lyne Carrington, bassist Keith Jones, and another amazing keyboard player, Bernard Wright.

JG: Well that must've had an effect on the band, I would think.

RR: It was great!

BOTH: [Laughter]

RR: He was trying to convey a sense of drama.

JG: Yes! Well, he embodies that in such a profound way. I've only seen him live a handful of times. What he conveys with one note is unbelievable. I actually stood next to him. There's a video of it at the Monk competition in like 2012 or 2013. It was Josh Redman, Lovano, a bunch of folks, and somebody cut him off and he actually didn't get a chance to solo which was really bizarre. But he leaned over to me with the soprano and was playing "Lester Leaps In" as a background on a blues, so we did that together.

RR: Nice!

JG: And just the fact I got to play that with him, and Herbie was playing, and it was like—*oh my god*! But I remember seeing him play duo with Herbie and, yeah, the ability to create a kind of drama, but one that is actually real and substantive, and not forced or pretentious. It's like a musician like Miles that can invoke a kind of presence and energy.

RR: Absolutely.

JG: It's just astounding.

RR: Well, I would say that those times with him, playing live with him, were some of the most extraordinary moments I've ever had on the bandstand. Not only the level of intensity, but also the perpetual searching. It's truly in-the-moment playing, and Wayne inspires that in everyone around him. His music continues to make a huge impact on me. He opened up my ears to other ways of hearing. It may sound silly now, but it was a big lesson for me back then… not to be so concerned about what a chord is called, or how to interpret a chord based on how it is named. It's much more about what you hear, and the concept that any choices can be valid.

JG: If you hear it you can make it work.

RR: Yeah. I mean, we all know what Miles said—that there are no wrong notes, it's what you do with them—but I was thinking more in terms of chords. One could write a voicing that could technically be called a number of different things depending on how you interpret or view it. But it's not necessary to identify it to be able to play on it.

JG: So you're not yet out of your twenties and you're playing with all these people. Who else did you play with then?

RR: In 1989 I joined James Moody's quartet, with Todd Coolman and Akira Tana, and then drummer Adam Nussbaum. Playing with Moody was always a joy. He knew so much music! In 1991, I became a member of J.J. Johnson's quintet—with Ralph Moore, Rufus Reid, and

Victor Lewis—and worked with him until his last performance in 1996 at William Paterson University's Jazz Room in New Jersey.

JG: What were some of the other associations you had in the '90s?

RR: I played with the Carnegie Hall Jazz Band led by Jon Faddis. Didn't you sub in that band?

JG: No, Faddis called me for some stuff but there was a conflict I couldn't get out of. But I would've loved to have done it some. So, you played in that band.

RR: Yeah, for ten years, 1992–2002. I loved playing with them. There were so many fantastic players—Frank Wess, Jerry Dodgion, Slide Hampton, Earl Gardner, Randy Brecker, Lew Soloff, Doug Purviance, Robin Eubanks, Gary Smulyan, Dick Oatts, Ralph Lalama, John Riley, and more. Every concert, the band presented new arrangements, and the arrangers would come in and work with the band—Jimmy Heath, Jim McNeely, Michael Abene, Frank Foster, Manny Albam, and others. To watch how they rehearsed the band, hear what they had to say, and to learn what was important to each of them was fascinating.

JG: Well, with your ear and your musical IQ, you probably assimilated so much from all these great composers. And you're such a great composer yourself. When did you start focusing on your own music as a leader and your own compositions?

RR: I guess pretty much from the beginning when I started recording my own CDs. I have composed pieces for almost every one of my own albums, except for a few where the focus was something else, such as the trio recording *Black Narcissus* of repertoire that Joe Henderson either wrote or was associated with, or my album with a string orchestra and trio *Without Words* with Buster Williams and Billy Drummond. By the way, Buster is another musician that I've been so fortunate to work with over the years, in his Something More band. I love both his playing and writing.

JG: When was your first album?

RR: It was released by Blue Note Records in 1990. The title was just my name, with Ron Carter and Lewis Nash in the rhythm section. Ralph Bowen and Branford Marsalis played on a few different tracks. There's a two-piano duet with Herbie Hancock that we recorded at Rudy Van Gelder's and a duet of "Diana" with Wayne, that was a recording from a performance on the road. Wayne was very gracious to allow me to use it.

JG : Don't you work with Ron now?

RR: Yes. Actually, since that first CD I had always wanted to have the opportunity to play with him again. So after Mulgrew Miller left the Golden Striker Trio, I subbed for him a few times, and was delighted when Ron asked me to join his Foursight Quartet in 2011. The band just released our first recording, *Live in Stockholm, Vol. 1* taken from a concert in 2018.

JG : What about your second album?

RR: *For the Moment* was released relatively soon after the first in 1992, with Steve Wilson, Ira Coleman, Billy Drummond, and Joe Henderson guesting on all the tracks but one.

JG: I remember hearing and seeing that record at that time. That was the first time I became aware of your music and recordings as a leader, and all that's great.

RR: Thanks very much, I appreciate that. I love composing and feel it's a big part of me—it's one way to find the truth of yourself as a musician.

JG: I agree. What I've found, you learn certain language on your instrument, and then, at least for me, compositions are like—OK, now learn to play on this stuff! 'Cause sometimes the language you have together as an improviser is not consistent with the language you're hearing as a composer, so it's like a signpost, and a new challenge—I gotta figure out how to go this way!

RR: Right, and I think I was very influenced by being around and playing with musicians who were great composers. Being fortunate enough to be around the realm of people like Wayne Shorter, there's a life of inspiration right there. But also, J.J. Johnson and Joe were serious composers too.

JG: Yep.

RR: And then there's Bobby Hutcherson too, who I also played with for many years. As a composer, Bobby was another who would write the voicings out, not being concerned with what you call the chords. He'd come over to the piano and show me a voicing. I knew enough by that time not to ask, "What chord do you think of it as?" [Laughter].

JG: He's another musician that I only saw a few times. But talk about a spiritual presence on the bandstand! Oh my god!

RR: Oh! He was so magical! I loved Bobby! What a positive spirit. He was always in the moment, immersed in the music. I mean, he would just play one note on the vibes and revel in the sound of it, you know?

JG: Yeah.

RR: He had so much fun! He would just intoxicate the bandstand with his joy! I'll tell you just a quick story of one night with Bobby at the Vanguard. We were playing Herbie Hancock's piece "Chan's Song" that was featured in the movie 'Round Midnight. It's real pretty. [Sings melody] Anyway, Bobby would customarily take the first solo. As he got to the end of the head, he didn't go on. I didn't think much of it and just took the first chorus. Bobby went to sit down on the red bench on the other side of the bandstand. I could see him from the piano and noticed that he had a very odd look. I remember thinking, I hope he's feeling OK, as he didn't look like his usual self. After I finished my solo he came back to the vibes, took the song out and ended the set. When we got off the bandstand, I asked him if he was feeling OK. He said in a low voice—and this, I'll never forget—"Renee, I couldn't play because Dexter was standing behind me. I felt the spirit of Dexter on the bandstand, and I knew he was standing right behind me. It moved me so much that I just couldn't play."

JG: Wow.

RR: I didn't quite know what to say. I knew they were very close friends, and that he missed Dexter a lot.

JG: Yeah, I remember when I was at the BMI Composers Workshop, Maria Schneider came in as a guest one time. And she said, "When I wrote "Evanescence" I invited Gil Evans' spirit to come sit next to me at the piano." And I could feel some people in the room pulling back, like, whoa… and I'm very alive to that kind of thinking, you know?

RR: It can happen.

JG: So I just kinda had to interject that I thought that was valid. Because first of all I don't presume to judge anyone else's experience.

RR: Right.

JG: And where else would you experience Dexter's presence but at the Vanguard?

RR: And playing that particular song.

JG: Absolutely. Did Dexter play that song in the movie?

RR: No. Bobby McFerrin sang it, accompanied by Herbie, Ron, and Tony.

JG: Yeah, and Chan was one of Charlie Parker's wives, and the mother of Kim Parker.

RR: Yes.

JG: Well, just to wrap up, I used to sub for Faddis' class at Purchase, and then I took the class for my master's degree. And he'd play us various things and ask us who we thought it was. And he played about thirty seconds of what sounded to me like some Indian music and asked us who we thought it was, and I had no idea. And he told us it was your music.

RR: Oh.

JG: And it's amazing! What's the name of that record?

RR: How nice! The album is *Life on Earth,* and the piece you're referring to is "Empress Afternoon," which featured Christian McBride on bass and the great tabla player, Zakir Hussain.

JG: Well that was really a revelation to me. And that was about the time that you told me about researching your biological parents and finding your mom's family who are from India.

RR: Yeah, it turned out that my maternal relatives are Punjabi and of Sikh heritage. My grandparents were born in India, but my mother is Indo-Canadian. Most of my bio-family live in British Columbia and Alberta. I discovered them in 1994, about eight years prior to that recording project. Regarding that track, I'd always loved Zakir's work and wanted to challenge myself to write something that would work with the tabla. It was thrilling playing with him, and I'm still a huge fan. I love the work he's doing now with Dave Holland and Chris Potter. I've thought about trying to write more in that vein.

You know, another time that was important to me is the six years that I spent with the SFJAZZ Collective. It was—and remains—a really unique experience which enabled me to work with a select group of musicians. We'd spend a couple of weeks each spring workshopping each of our commissioned compositions and other arrangements of pieces by the featured composer of the year, and then go on tour. It was great to have an intense rehearsal period where we had time to really hone the arrangements.

JG: Wow, that must have been great. What years did you do that?

RR: I began as a charter member in 2004 and my last year with the group was 2009. Bobby Hutcherson was there for most of my tenure. The inaugural band was led by Joshua Redman with Miguel Zenon, Nicholas Payton, Josh Roseman, Robert Hurst, and Brian Blade, and then Joe Lovano, Dave Douglas, Robin Eubanks, Matt Penman, and Eric Harland came on board.

JG: Well I'm glad you mentioned that, that's a great group. And hearing you play trio in recent years on the jazz cruise, hearing your group at Smoke, I've just always loved your writing and music and I'm sure that was a great contribution with SFJAZZ. And I think when I heard that piece that Faddis played us, it made me think of your search for your family, that we'd talked about. But that process of you finding your own history, and family… somehow in my own mind I'm piecing these things together, because there's a connection to us both looking for family, and our fathers. I talked with you one time and you had encouraged me to go back on Ancestry.com and do the DNA thing.

RR: Yes.

JG: I'm pretty sure of who he was. So, I just wanted to thank you for you encouraging me to do that. In fact, you and Bill even gave me a year's membership as a gift!

RR: [Laughter] I'm so glad for you.

JG: I just remember talking with you about it, and you said, "Jon, please do the DNA thing. It's really cool." And then you went ahead and did a whole bunch of research and made connections going back generations on my mother's side of the family. It was just so kind, generous, and thoughtful of you to take the time to do that. It really meant a lot, and I just wanted to thank you for that.

RR: Oh, you don't have to thank me for that! I'm as excited about it as you are! [Laughter] You can ask Bill. I love doing that type of research! Maybe it's because as you said, I've been on the same journey as you. I really enjoy discovering family relationships. And you know, it's still entirely possible that more relations are going to pop up for you.

JG: Well, one very odd connection that I found with my background is, when I was eleven, I started going to Alateen meetings on Staten Island. It was just me and this very kind lady, who would come just to sit and read through things with me, at this church on Armstrong Ave. What an angel. But by a bizarre coincidence, the church where we met, which was like a forty-minute bus ride from where I lived, was on the same block where my father and his family had lived and moved away from a couple of years before that.

RR: Wow, what a coincidence!

JG: Yeah. And in the '90s, when I researched this, I found a phone book with a family with the same last name, on that street, and they remembered my father's family being there and moving to Florida about twenty years earlier. And they said, "Oh yeah! We remember them, they moved to Florida. But there was no relation." But it was just a weird coincidence. That's as close as I got. But I just wanted to thank you for your kindness and your generosity. You really helped me with that and thank you for sharing your search with that. So, thank you for that, and thank you for this!

RR: You're most welcome! So... I'm looking at your tree right now...

JG: [Renee then proceeded to show me all kinds of stuff about my family in N.Y.C., Limerick, Ireland, New Orleans, the first governor of Massachusetts, John Endicott, and all kinds of research that she did on my family, and photos going back to the early 1900s that she found and put up for me to see!!!]

JG: [15 minutes later...] Hey! I'm gonna turn off the recording...

BOTH: [Laughter]

RR: Whoops! Oh yeah!

JG: Thanks Renee!

RR: And thank you Jon for inviting me to be a part of this project. It's a real honor.

David Sanborn & Gil Evans

Seventh Ave. South, New York City –1983

In the fall of 1983, in senior year of high school when I was sixteen, I met Margaret D. at a parent/teacher conference at Performing Arts. Margaret was the mother of a friend at school, and a huge jazz fan. When we spoke and she found out that I was a saxophonist and had never been to a jazz club, she said, "You have to come with me some time!" I quickly agreed, and within a week or so we were at Seventh Ave. South, hearing The Art Taylor Quartet, with Clark Terry on trumpet, Branford Marsalis on tenor, Ron Carter on bass, and Art on drums. It was incredible! At the end of the night Clark sang "Mumbles!" I'll never forget it.

The following week, Margaret and I went back to the club to hear Gil Evans' big band. The great trumpet player Lew Soloff came over and said hi to Margaret as he came in. (He got a big kick out of this story when I told it to him, years later when we were playing the Jazz Nativity together.) Hiram Bullock, Howard Johnson, Adam Nussbaum, and so many great players were in the band. Of particular interest to me though was David Sanborn on alto. He was becoming very famous at the time. He had a huge following in the pop/rock and R&B world. But he also sounded great in more straight-ahead contexts. An incredible sound, perfect pitch, a totally original voice, and 10,000-plus alto players tried to sound like him and no one ever did. Dave's just an amazing player!

I introduced myself to Dave on the break after the first set, and he couldn't have been nicer! He spoke to me for about twenty minutes. He asked me where I was from, and who I'd studied with. I spoke to him about practicing classical pieces, Bird solos, and being very inspired by Phil Woods. He told me how much he was inspired by Phil as well.

Then he asked me, "Jon, are you staying for the next set?" I told him I was.

"Do you have your horn with you?"

"Um, yes, I do," I said, somewhat excited and scared at the same time. I was wondering, would he have me sit in?

"Well, listen Jon, can you do me a favor? I need to leave before the next set. Can you finish the gig for me?"

I was shocked! I stammered, "Uh, um… *yeah*! … sure!" Feeling utterly unsure of myself. But what a break! It was the second time I was ever in a jazz club. No one had ever heard me play a note, and I was sixteen. Yet David Sanborn had just asked me to play the last set with Gil Evans' band! I think he thought I was older and more experienced than I was, based on our talk. And I guessed that he might have had an early recording session the next morning and was hoping to get an extra couple hours of sleep.

As he packed up and got ready to leave he said, "Jon, just tell Gil that I had to leave and that I asked you to cover the last set for me, OK?"

"Sure Mr. Sanborn!" I said. "Thank you so much for everything!"

He waived, smiled, and went on his way. I walked over to Margaret and told her what had just happened. She was thrilled! I had my book bag, horn, and coat at the table. It was then that I realized what I was wearing—jeans, sneakers, and a t-shirt. Well, Hiram Bullock played guitar on the gig with his shoes off, and no one was particularly dressed up. So, I thought maybe that would be OK.

I walked over to Gil and introduced myself. I knew I wouldn't have long to explain the situation. But Gil seemed like a nice, sweet, older guy, and smiled at me as I approached him and we shook hands. I tried to be as clear and to the point as I could, and to hopefully seem confident in passing this information on to Gil. "Hi Mr. Evans. My name is Jon Gordon, and I'm an alto player, and David Sanborn just asked me to tell you that he had to leave and that I should play the last set for him." Gil got a strange look on his face as I told him what Dave had said to me. He looked me up and down, from my shoes to my head, and quietly replied, "How can I take a chance on you?" and walked away.

I was disappointed for a minute. But when the music started up, I was just excited to be there again. I used to *love* hearing that band play! I never did get a chance to play with Gil, but I was always thankful that Dave took a chance on me that night.

Coda

In 2013 I met and started working with a student in Winnipeg at the University of Manitoba named Connor Derraugh. Connor had a traumatic brain injury a few years before I met him because of an accident during surgery. Connor's hero was and is Dave Sanborn. While I had only met Dave a few times over the years since, I reached out to Dave through a common friend, and told Dave about Connor when he and his family were planning to drive ten hours to Omaha to see Dave perform. As Dave had lived through paralysis as a result of childhood polio, they had a commonality beyond jazz and the alto saxophone. Dave has had Connor's family as his guests at his gigs ever since then, over the past five years or so, and they've become great friends. He's still the same great guy he always was. And on the topic of stylists, the great Benny Carter told me he thought Dave was truly one of the great stylists in the history of the alto. As a saxophonist I can think of no higher compliment.

Don Sickler

Phone call, Winnipeg, Canada/New York City – February 2020

DS: Hey Jon!

JG: Hey Don! Thanks for doing this. So, what was your start in music? You were born in Washington State, right?

DS: Yeah, in Spokane, Washington. Which is, not Seattle. It's the other side of the world really, a seven-hour drive over the Cascade mountains. A lot of people think, oh yeah, the state of Washington, Seattle, a great city, has some culture. But Spokane is the "inland empire." Hunting and fishing and retirement villages. No artistic value that I could find as a young guy trying to get into music, you know? It was a different kind of lifestyle. I had a lot of free time on my hands and I didn't know what to do 'cause there really wasn't a lot of interest in music, and as a result I really wasn't turned on to it like I got when I came to New York.

JG: When did you start the trumpet?

DS: I started the trumpet in the fourth grade. My parents had the Sickler Accordion Center. My mother taught accordion, which was quite popular in areas like Spokane. My parents have this photo of me with an accordion, at about four years of age. I have no recollection of that photo being taken. I remember from the time I heard the first note out of the accordion I didn't like it.

JG: [Laughter]

DS: I mean, it just had a reedy kind of sound that wasn't appealing to me. We had a piano at home. I played piano, and accordion when it was forced on me. And I was always interested in sports. My parents had this deal, as long as I practiced the piano in the morning before I went to school, then when school was over I could do afterschool sports. But it had nothing to do with the kind of music that turns me on now. It was just playing the piano. My parents published a Sickler Accordion Course, and at the age of four or five I wrote some little piece that they put in one of those books.

JG: Wow.

DS: In other words I was giving Mozart a run at the time.

JG: [Laughter] Well that's pretty impressive!

DS: My mother played piano and organ, and we had an organ in the house. My father fixed accordions, and they had this accordion center that they would go to downtown. I had two great aunts that lived next door to our house; I would come home from school and they would spoil me rotten. They were great, great people.

JG: Well it's just interesting that so many people I talk to say music was a big part of their home life, and it's no different with you though just with accordion.

DS: Yeah, well accordion, like I said, was big in Spokane. And there were several different teachers. They even had, God forbid, accordion orchestras…

JG: [Laughter]

DS: I remember in high school my dad still had the music store. It was primarily accordions, but he also had a half size string bass and small set of vibes in there, both of which I would mess around with. I still have the vibes here in New York and I pull them out into the rehearsal studio for vibes players. That instrument's now been played by all of the great vibists.

Part of my job for my parents was to play bass in their accordion orchestra. In other words, they had a real live string bass, and then twenty accordions simulating flutes, clarinets, etc… it was just a complete nightmare!

JG: [Laughter]

DS: A sonic nightmare! Accordions playing string parts… you know, accordions have all these stops on them. It's bad enough, the sound of it by itself, but then you can falsely imitate all these other instruments.

JG: But what's interesting to me is, you're writing a piece at five, you're playing bass, you're doing all this thinking.

DS: Well, I wasn't really pushing the pencil, I just came up with something at the piano, and my mom liked it well enough to put it in one of her books.

JG: Yeah.

DS: You know, my mother was a good teacher and she taught me theory. And she could swing. She couldn't improvise all that much, though she kinda could. She had a good feeling for music. My parents were completely supportive. After I started playing the trumpet, my dad bought me some Dixieland charts so I could get my friends together to play them. I had a little Dixieland band in like the fifth or sixth grade. My dad actually got us a couple of gigs. It was one of those things, once somebody put some money in my hand to play, my whole attitude toward music took on a different focus. As a kid, I always wanted to have a paper route, for some reason, like all my friends did. You know, get up at 4:00 in the morning and go get the papers and pass 'em out all over. My dad and I fought about this idea, because if I wasn't home to practice before school, there'd be no afterschool sports for me! However, once I started playing a couple of little concerts and I actually got paid for it, I realized what I got paid was like doing two weeks of the paper route for just playing a little concert.

JG: Yeah!

DS: I got interested in the trumpet when they had a thing in fourth grade where you could get an instrument and play in the band. I wanted to play the trombone, at least that's what I remember my parents always saying. But my arms weren't long enough. And I didn't really want to play the flute or the clarinet. But they had a trumpet, so decided I was going to play the trumpet and they gave me that. I was a really competitive young guy. I hated to lose at sports or marbles, I hated to lose at anything. Luckily for me, Spokane had an all-city band program. Every Saturday we would go to a high school on the other side of town; they had a sectional rehearsal, just trumpets, then we'd all go play with the full band. They had five bands, and I started as 55th trumpet in the 5th band—the worst band. In the trumpet sectional, one week we would rehearse the trumpet parts. The teacher would pick one of the pieces that everyone would practice during the next week, and that week they would have a tryout, and that's how you moved up in the band.

So, I got in the band and I'm listening to these guys next to me, and they sound horrible! I realize I've got to practice so I can get out of the back of the trumpet section! I mean, they can't play in tune, or anything! So, I practice my part. And the next week we have a tryout. And then the next week you come back, they place you, and you sit down in the order that they call your name.

Then they give you another piece, and then the week after that you have another tryout. Every other week you have another piece and the following week they put you in your new place, so it was a very competitive thing, which I loved. I started out as like 55th trumpet. And then all of a sudden, the next week I'm 30th trumpet. Everybody's looking at me like, who's this? And I'm thinking, Hmm, this is very interesting. So I worked a little harder the next week, and then I jumped up to 15th trumpet. Soon I'm asked to join the 4th band.

JG: Well, when I was at that age, I wanted to play the saxophone but they always put me in the choir.

DS: Well, our all-city school band was a very hip environment for me, with lots of incentive to practice, and I got to meet great students from all over town. There were like 200 people in every band!

JG: Wow.

DS: You know, the 5th band was a pretty rotten sounding band, and I didn't want to stay there. I just liked this idea that they'd call out my name and everybody would go "Ooh!" And I'd go way up in the band. And I really dug that, so…

JG: Did you have trumpet lessons?

DS: I had a teacher, in fact the guy that was the section leader who did all the tryouts taught at the junior high school near where I lived, so my parents got me lessons with him. He was a really nice guy, but he used a smiling embouchure, which didn't work for me. He really had no chops, and would wear out pretty quickly. From grade school, I went directly to the new high school in town, Shadle Park. My trumpet teacher, Johnny Harris, became the band director at Shadle Park.

In the eighth grade, he asked me if I would come and play a concert with him in the trumpet section of the Spokane Philharmonic Orchestra. The shocker for me was that he was having a lot of endurance problems playing the first part, so the conductor asked me to try the first part, and after that I played the first trumpet parts and he played the second parts. That's when I realized I was in big trouble, trumpet-teacher-wise. He didn't teach about air support and embouchure development. I had to wait until I got to New York to do my master's degree to learn about those techniques. Anyway, Johnny Harris was always very supportive of me, and was always a great guy. After I left Spokane for New York City, he always stayed in touch with me and my parents.

JG: So, you're playing lead in the Spokane Symphony at like thirteen?

DS: Yeah, like in the eighth grade. I mean, I was always an entrepreneurial type of a guy, if that's the right word, and I'd been playing in public since the fifth grade with my little Dixieland band thing. In the seventh grade, my supportive father started buying me stock arrangements, and also made up some nice professional looking band folders for each instrument. Do you remember stock arrangements?

JG: Sure!

DS: The small, octavo size arrangements that you could buy of all the Glenn Miller, Harry James, Dorsey Brothers arrangements, or whatever. I formed a dance band called the Skylarks. It was a nine-piece band, two trumpets, a trombone, two altos and a tenor, and piano, bass, and drums. My dad just kept buying all these stock arrangements. I remember I was in the seventh grade when it really took shape, and I started to look for gigs. The three sax players were in the sixth grade. And we would rehearse, and these kids could all play their parts!

JG: Wow!

DS: I mean, we could play well enough that I started to get college prom gigs with this thing. Got myself deeply in trouble with the musician's union! Because I would play college proms for the same money they could get a professional trio for, but I'd bring a nine-piece band.

JG: Wow.

DS: In the early 1960s, Spokane was not hip like New York City. You still played the music from the '40s big band era for most gigs, "Moonlight Serenade" and "Stompin' At The Savoy"...

JG: Yeah!

DS: But I actually had a band, that actually worked. We actually even went on the road on some weekends and during holiday seasons!

JG: What!?

DS: Meaning that we would go out to other schools in neighboring cities that would want us to come...

JG: When you were in the seventh grade!?

DS: Yeah, in the seventh and eighth grades and then in high school. I had a good little band, OK? Until we were old enough, our parents would drive us to gigs usually.

JG: That's unbelievable!

DS: You know, we'd play "String of Pearls" and I'd play Bobby Hackett's solo [sings], you know.

JG: Yeah, yeah...

DS: And solos were all written in, so you didn't have to be an improvising musician, you know. To keep the band really together, I knew I needed piano parts always played correctly, so often, especially on our road gigs, I'd use my mother. Also, we obviously needed her as a driver as well! This way we also had an adult with us in case alcohol was served...

JG: Gotcha, so you've got a solid piano player and a lift!

DS: Yeah, and my mother, she wouldn't improvise but she could read anything, and she had a good swing feel. She'd do exactly what you'd want. She was always nervous playing, she said. But I was an only child, and my mother and father were totally supportive of me, and my mother was always a sweetheart to everyone.

JG: That's great.

DS: And my dad just kept buying more and more charts. I still have that book. It's probably got over 200 charts in it. And you know, I had made enough money by the time I was sixteen to buy my own Austin Healey Sprite, my own sports car!

JG: Oh my god! [Laughter]

DS: Yeah, so I was a little operator, you know? And eventually I had a couple bands. I was the Lester Lanin of Spokane. I had a couple of bands playing different gigs.

JG: Wow, that's amazing. So, when do you start to learn about improvisation, and did you get a jazz teacher?

DS: Well, I learned about improvisation the hard way. My mother showed me how I could transcribe and notate what I was hearing on music paper. We had a little reel-to-reel tape recorder, so I'd record on it, and I'd transcribe some stuff. And if there wasn't a solo in the part I'd transcribe a solo off one of the old swing band recordings and either play it myself or write it out for one of the sax players to play. Having a good sound on my instrument was always important to me. And people would always compliment me on my sound. So, I was the Kid Trumpet King and Band Leader in Spokane. There were no other trumpet players around who could really play.

Of course, I'd heard Dizzy Gillespie on records and I knew I wasn't anywhere near that level! But if they all wanted to think I was God's gift to the trumpet world in Spokane, fine, I had no problem with that. When I was still in grade school I was invited to play at the Northwest Jazz Festival. They thought I was a young kid who could really play. I could interpret well, but that was about it. And my dad said, "OK, you're going to have to learn some jazz stuff."

I had this record I really liked of a trumpet player named Stu Williamson. His brother Claude Williamson was a well-known pianist and was more widely known than Stu. But anyway, he had this record of… [sings "There Will Never Be Another You"] They wanted me to play a medium up or up tune and a ballad. So, I copied off how Stu played the melody. I then copied off his solo and I learned his two-chorus solo. There was another one, a ballad, "Autumn In New York," and I copied that too. I'm very young and very naïve, as you'll see.

When I went to the festival, I was led into a room where the rhythm section was before we were taken to the stage to play. The pianist asked me, "So what do you want to play?" I said, "There Will Never Be Another You." They say "E flat?" And I say, "Yeah, I guess." And I played the first couple of notes of the melody and they said, "Yeah, that's E flat." Then they asked me, "How do you want us to start out?" and you know, I'm thinking, the only recording of this in the world is Stu Williamson. So I say, "The piano plays the eight-bar introduction, then I'll come in." And the piano player says, "OK, fine." We get up on the stage and the piano player says, "You ready?" "Yeah." "Do you wanna count it off?" I said, "No, you count it off."

BIG MISTAKE! Instead of Stu Williamson's medium up tempo [sings] he plays way faster. And he plays a totally different intro from what I knew from my little record I practiced meticulously with. He played eight bars and I don't come in. He didn't play the intro I was expecting. And he keeps playing another eight, and looks at me and realizes, oh this kid really doesn't know what he's doing. So he cues me to come in, and I come in right. But now I have to play a lot faster! So when I get to the solo, I have not a prayer in hell of playing what Stu Williamson played on the record. I just kinda fell all apart. I played what I could, and faked the rest. I had no idea what I did. I wasn't doing anything. It was just my worst nightmare. I got done, and man, I'm like in tears, and I'm walkin' outside. And then a little later I'm asked to come back and play the ballad. Somehow I got through that. Obviously, again I realized that what they were playing had nothing to do with what the rhythm section played on the recording I had been playing with!

JG: How old were you?

DS: I guess I was like in seventh grade.

JG: Still very young!

DS: Yeah. I had my little band going, but it didn't involve any improvising, you know?

JG: Well it sounds that that was the beginning of your awareness.

DS: Well, right after that, the piano player took me aside and said, "Look, I want you to come back tonight to the festival. We're having a jam session afterwards. And just sit down next to me, and let me just show you a few things." 'Cause I'd never experienced anything like this before. I did that, and they played a blues or something. And I'm watching, and I'm hearing. I knew something about the piano, but I was never that good at transposing what the piano player was playing just by watching his fingers and trying to play it. I could figure out what key he was in, and therefore I thought I should know what key I was in on the trumpet. I'm just looking at what he's doing at the piano. And all of a sudden he says to me, "OK, now you just get up and play a little bit—play whatever you hear." All of a sudden it just snapped in my head. Oh! Play what I hear! Just try to be creative. Don't try to play something you've already learned. And that was the big awakening. Once I did that, I was able to relax, not think about the printed page, and just use my ear.

As I went through high school and into college in Spokane, singers would come through town: Ethel Ennis, Terri Thornton, Sue Raney, you know, great singers. And there were two piano players who lived in the area that I'd try to hook up with, Arnie Carruthers and Joe Kloess. Joe Kloess also played and toured with Julie London and Jack Jones. Both these guys were good jazz piano players. And because they lived in or near Spokane these singers would come and do gigs at the big hotels downtown. They decided that they wanted little arrangements and a little muted trumpet behind them and whatever else, so they would hire me to play. I had limited knowledge of anything. I was having fun just kind of listening to the singer sing, you know? When she takes a breath, then I play a little, you know, accompanying the singer.

JG: Hm mmm.

DS: And I just did it totally by ear. I knew how to stay out of the way of the singer. I remember, one night I'm playing with one of these singers and one of the older, experienced musicians says to me, "Hey, that was unbelievable! How did you play that, man? You had to be in the key of B, they were in A!" And I'm thinking, I was in B? I didn't even think I knew the B major scale!

JG: [Laughter]

DS: I realized, I was just playing what I heard. But that was just really great training, to exercise my ear like that. And then I got good at transcribing, because I would always have to make arrangements of little things, and transcribe solos for people.

My parents were big swing band people. My dad loved and bought me a lot of Harry James and the Dorsey Brothers. and Glen Miller and all that stuff. I'm listening to Harry James and hearing his commercial tracks [sings with big vibrato] and I didn't like that right off the bat. I only had a couple of jazz records. I had one Clifford Brown record—the Pacific Jazz recording with Jack Montrose arrangements—I loved it, but Clifford also scared me to death. I had a Chet Baker record and a Shorty Rogers record, the West Coast guys, you know. And that, with a couple of Stu Williamson records, was about it. I heard Dizzy Gillespie and of course he just scared the hell outta me, you know? I couldn't relate to bebop then.

Everything changed when I was a junior in high school. I'd go to the record store and buy records by singers and always look to see if there was anything that looked like jazz. One day I was in the store and I saw a record by Count Basie, *Chairman of the Board*. I'd heard a little Basie before, but only very early Basie, and some Ellington, but it was more the religious side of Ellington. When I put that *Chairman of the Board* record on and I heard [sings] all this rhythmic stuff! And I just said, *what is that*!?

JG: Right, yeah. [Laughter]

DS: And this rhythm stuff just hit me! I heard Sonny Payne dropping bombs and said *what is that*! And that was it! It was the rhythm thing that turned my head around. My musical life was changed forever. You know, later I got to work a lot with Frank Wess and Benny Powell and Al Grey, the guys who were on that record. It was always such an honor. I used to tell them the story of what that record did for me and I'd always crack Frank Wess up singing him the start of his melody of "Half Moon Street." They'd all laugh like hell as I would carry on, but they also always knew how important it was to me when I first heard it.

JG: Yeah, it's great when we get to meet and work with our heroes, and that you could tell them that. So, where'd you go to college?

DS: Our little stage band at Shadle Park High School was entered in this festival in Bremerton Washington, just outside of Seattle. We went over there and played and I had done a little bit of the arranging. But I really wasn't an arranger. We had some nice charts that you could buy back then. I was the featured soloist. Our band won the competition, and I was given the award as the best soloist, which was a scholarship to the Stan Kenton Music Camp.

JG: Wow.

DS: That gave me a whole new focus. I went to the University of Michigan for a week, then I went to Indiana University and made two weeks of it. These were unbelievable eye-opening experiences for a kid from Spokane. And when I was there, Donald Byrd was my trumpet instructor.

JG: Oh, wow!

DS: So, this was 1961, this was Donald Byrd at the peak of his career, you know? And he was really nice. I don't think I even knew what hard drugs were. I don't think there were even any in Spokane. But he was telling guys don't get involved with drugs. He was just like a big brother. And he invited guys back to where he was staying. He was just like one of the guys. I didn't know that much about Donald before the camps. Once I heard him play, I realized this guy was something else. I also went to arranging classes with Russ Garcia and Johnny Richards. I tried to learn as much as I could, and then I went back to Spokane and tried to share my experiences with my musician friends.

When it was time to apply for college, I sent in applications to Berklee and North Texas State, which were the two big jazz schools at the time. I think I was offered a partial scholarship to both. I was very paranoid, however, and I knew I was very lacking in any real jazz experience so I was afraid of being eaten alive at either of these jazz schools. I'd heard Thad Jones and all these great soloists with the Basie band. And I couldn't play like that. I knew I was not on that level.

Jon Nicholson, a very strong trombonist, had just been hired to head the music department at Gonzaga University in Spokane, and he said he really wanted me to consider going to Gonzaga. But I had a problem, stemming from my early experiences in grade school. My friends and I would always want to play baseball in the nice big park with a nice big baseball diamond that was very close to my house. Practically every day the coach and the students from a nearby Catholic school would invade the baseball diamond and start fights with us. The coach and kids would throw me and my friends off the field. So, me and Catholics didn't get along at all, and Gonzaga was a Catholic school. But Nicholson said, "I'm not Catholic, and Gonzaga University is all run by Jesuit priests." Nicholson knew I was interested in academics, and said, "I want you to come to a couple of classes and check out the teachers, because every Jesuit teacher you're going to be involved with I'm sure has at least two doctoral degrees." I took him up on his offer, and the teachers (mostly priests) were pretty incredible.

JG: Wow.

DS: I'm a little enterprising negotiator. Nicholson said, "If you go out with the head of the school, hang with Father O'Leary, and go out to the Kiwanis club and the Elks club when he goes out to fundraise, and play a little concert for them at each of these events, that's the most important basic thing we need you to do. Of course we need you to play in the orchestra and the concert band and help me start a jazz big band, but you can certainly major in mathematics if you want, or whatever, and we'll give you a full ride to Gonzaga University."

My parents didn't have money to send me away to school. When I went to Gonzaga they paid for everything, and they gave me a room in the music annex building to teach my trumpet students. I'd been teaching trumpet since I was in the sixth or seventh grade. I was teaching at my parents' music store and I was into that, and I got paid for it, you know?

JG: Yeah!

DS: I don't know when you started teaching but I probably started teaching maybe as early as the sixth grade.

JG: Yeah, I started teaching pretty early, and you learn so much when you teach, I find.

DS: Exactly! Teaching gave me more chances to get things together. When I realized other kids couldn't do things, and I'd say, try this. And I'd realize what I could do that other kids couldn't do. By straightening them out, it showed me different exercises to improve myself.

I had my perfect excuse: If anyone would've asked me: "Why didn't you to North Texas State?" "Why didn't you go to Berklee?" I said, "Man, I got too much going here. I got bands working in Spokane, I'm buyin' sports cars, and Gonzaga's giving me a full ride, even more, and I can be a math major at a great school. I'd be crazy to leave Spokane, now."

JG: [Laughter] So during your time at Gonzaga you started as a math major, but you continued to work on music and learn more about jazz. When did you come to New York?

DS: Well, I was a math major for two and a half years. It was straight math, just formulas and stuff, it wasn't physics or anything like that. It was very stimulating for my mind, I really loved working with formulas, but it was very out there, you know? And I realized I couldn't even talk to anybody about what I was doing. My parents had no idea what I was doing. I quit that and went in the opposite direction, and started to become a philosophy major. Because Gonzaga had a great philosophy department, and well-known authors that were priests and philosophers, so I got into that. It actually took me five years to get my bachelor's liberal arts degree.

In my fourth year our Gonzaga big band played in an all-northwest college jazz festival and competition. Donald Byrd was the adjudicator. I won the award as best trumpet player and soloist. Donald had heard me four years before that. So, I knew him to an extent, and he was very complimentary. I invited him to my parent's house for dinner. My parents were really wonderful people, and like I said, totally supportive of me all the way through. Maureen came over too. We were going together; this was just before my last year at school there. Donald was saying, "Don you improved a lot, you're writing now." I said "Yeah, but Spokane's such a drag, man." And I'm just bitchin' and bitchin' about how horrible the environment is. So he listened to me rant and rave, and then he said, "Well, you gotta fix that." And I said "How'm I gonna do that?" "Go back to New York!" "Go back to New York?" "Yeah, come back and do your master's degree at Manhattan School of Music. You should study composition with Ludmila

Ulehla, and orchestration with Nicolas Flagello," and whatever else. He said, "Yeah, you're gonna be doing your fifth year of college. You're gonna get a degree in trumpet." (I didn't want to finish in philosophy or math.) Donald said, "Come back to New York and see if music will really work for you."

This was written up in one *DownBeat* article on me a long time ago. My recollection is, "I said, how am I gonna come to New York? I don't know anybody there. How am I gonna make a living? I got all these bands workin' here." He said, "Look, here's what you do. I'll make a deal with you. I'm in this band with Duke Pearson. We co-lead a band at the Half Note in New York." It was a rehearsal band. It was like the band that happened before the Thad and Mel band. There was no Thad and Mel band yet. And guys like Clark Terry and Bob Brookmeyer would come on Monday nights when they were off, and play with the band. You know?

JG: Wow!...

DS: Just to play, you know? Al Cohn did some arrangements as well, I think. Phil Woods came and did it. All these kinds of people, whoever's in town. He said, "Here's the deal I have for you. Look, the trumpet players, they're great trumpet players. But you've got a nice sound, you play in tune, you got the basic things together. If you come back to New York and you get into Manhattan School of Music, you come down to the Half Note, I'll introduce you to the guys. The more regular guys can't come all the time. We're always needing subs. You could be a sub.

JG: Wow!

DS: I said, "Wow, really!?" Donald knew I was a little business cat, and Donald was that same way too. He sussed me out. And he said, "You come back to New York. First you gotta' get into the school and be serious about getting your degree and getting into the environment of it. And then come down to the club and we'll do this."

JG: Wow!

DS: And that was it. Maureen had one more year of college to go. My parents and her parents wanted her stay to finish college. Maureen wanted to go to New York with me. So, she promised her parents she'd finish college someday, which she eventually did, here in New York at Fordham University. We got married in her home town of Grand Junction, Colorado, in August and then we came back to New York and I started school.

JG: What year was that Don?

DS: 1967. I just missed Coltrane. He died earlier that year. So, a lot of guys I wanted to see I didn't get to see. But I came back and went to school and took it very seriously. I tried to be a composition major. But my counterpoint and things I'd taken at Gonzaga didn't cut the mustard. And when I tried to pass the entrance exam, it was like, OK, you'd be an undergrad second semester junior again. I'd have to do another year and a half of college before I could even get into the master's composition program! But I got to meet Ludmila Ulehla and talked to her and she encouraged me. It was all classical, there was no jazz in those school in those years. But she was a very hip person. Donald said, "They call her the Nadia Boulanger of the U.S." He said, "I studied with Nadia Boulanger as well in France, and I studied with Ludmila Ulehla, and she's fantastic!" And he was absolutely right! She's like an *unbelievable* teacher!

She told me, "You know, you'd do better if you just try to get your master's on trumpet." Because the classical undergrad composition majors had to write the equivalent of a sonata, 30 pages of music, every week. She knew I wasn't that kind of composer. I was laboring over everything. It took me six months to write a brass quintet. So, she said, this isn't going to work for you. Audit my classes, take some of them for credit and just work on your master's degree, just get that."

JG: Well, you told me about her before I went to MSM. I had one semester of composition for non-composition majors with her, and two with Giacomo Braccali. And you told me, "Man, she can sight read an orchestral *score!*"

DS: Yeah, yeah.

JG: And I saw her and Braccali do that, and man, that was unbelievable!

DS: Yeah, and other things… I was in the seminar class, and Chuck Israels was in the seminar class. He was writing for the Duke Pearson big band, writing wild kinds of stuff. And I was trying to stretch out some too. But Ludmila, you'd go into her classes, you'd take your transposed score… and she'd sit at the piano and play your score. And then say, like with my brass quintet, she said, "Oh! Here's where you had some problems." And she said, "And you went this way, but you could have gone like this," and played it, "or like this," and right in my style! She's improvising shit that I could've written!

She was absolutely correct, and found exactly where I started stumbling, and then, in my style, immediately improvised a couple of alternate different ways I could go that would make my composition flow much better. She blew my mind!

JG: [Laughter]

DS: And my mouth is hanging wide open! Same way with Chuck Israels and everybody else. She was just a natural teacher. She could just absorb anything and just give it right back to you! And she was tremendously inspirational, you know?

JG: Wow.

DS: So anyway, I get hooked up into my school and I say, finally, I gotta get down to the Half Note and I gotta make my connections with Donald Byrd, you know? That's what I came to New York for. Though I was there about a month before I ventured downtown. So, I go to the club and I walk in and the band's playing. And the band sounds incredible! I'm looking, but I don't see Donald. But I see the band playing, and it's just like heaven! It's like the records that I loved, Basie and all that stuff. And Duke Pearson's playing, you know. At the intermission, I see a trombone player that looks pretty harmless. And although I was big guns in Spokane I was very timid in New York. I was never one of those guys that put his horn over his shoulder and went and tried to sit in. That just wasn't me. I went up to the trombone player and said, "Hi, I'm here to see Donald Byrd. He told me to come here to see him." He said, "Donald's not here tonight. Wait a second, let me go check this out for you." He goes back to talk to somebody and comes back a minute later and says, "Yeah, Donald took a job at Howard University. He left here like a month ago."

JG: Wow! [Laughter]

DS: I said, *what*!? He said, "Yeah, he's got a full-time teaching job, in DC at Howard University." It took me many years before I was finally able to chase Donald down to tell him my Half Note story. When I finally told him, he laughed like hell, and says, well, it looks like you came out of it all right.

Obviously, I didn't get to sit in and play in the band or do any of that stuff. Guys were going and trying to sit in with Blakey and cop the gig. That just wasn't me. I wasn't in there to try to muscle my way in with these top groups. At MSM there were a lot of guys doing the G.I. Bill that were doing Broadway musicals. So, I got to do a lot of Broadway musical subs. I was playing in show bands, or with like Steve and Eydie Gorme at the Concord Hotel. And I remember doing club dates with the guys that were playing with Chick Corea. When they weren't doing jazz gigs with Chick Corea they were doing club dates. 'Cause there really wasn't much happening in the jazz world in the early '70s.

Before I left Spokane, my father started a music engraving business, making hand-stamped music plates. He asked me to get him work in New York. When I first came to New York to audition at MSM I contacted a publisher and got my father some work. That got me into helping him in the publishing world. Most of the engravers were in Korea or Poland, but Spokane was only 3,000 miles away. Maureen and I did his correction work, to speed up the workflow. And I ended up learning all the editorial marks and everything else and how to work for a publisher.

So I'm doing these club dates, these horrible club dates, and doing some other stuff. I didn't want to really do Latin gigs and bust up my trumpet chops, and I didn't want to go out on the road with Buddy Rich for the same reason. I did get a chance to maybe do that. I saw how tough he was on trumpet players and just thought, I ain't doin' that. And I didn't want to go out on the road.

One day, Bernie Kalban, the head guy of Edward B. Marks Music, called me up, and asked me, when I brought in some more plates and corrections work for my father, if I could meet with him. He wanted to ask me about a guy going to MSM. They wanted to have another editor at Edward B. Marks, and Bernie thought I could tell him something about the guy. So, I went in and I talked to Bernie about him, and this cat was really a gifted guy, but he was really a straight classical guy. And Bernie said, "Well, you know, he'd have to work with these three great Pulitzer Prize-winning composers." They had Roger Sessions, Mario Davidovsky, and Norman Dello Joio, and some other classical composers, that kind of classical thing. They had pop stuff—they really wanted to get into that money-making side of the business—and they also had some jazz commitments, they need to do a transcription book of Paul Horn live at the Taj Mahal. They had Marian McPartland, Dick Hyman, songs that Billie Holiday sang, Eubie Blake material, and some other hip stuff they wanted to put out. They also wanted to do a Marian McPartland transcription book, Bernie said. I said, well this other guy, Joel, I think was the guy's name, he can really handle the classical stuff. But I can't imagine him doing the pop material, or having any experience notating jazz transcriptions. From my Broadway and forced NYC pop experiences, I had experience with that type of music, and I told him his jazz projects looked interesting, and that I'd been already been transcribing some flute things for Hubert Laws, and some lead sheets for Ron Carter, etc.

All of a sudden Bernie says, "Would you be interested in the job? You already know all of the editorial marks, and we like how you've helped us with the final stages of your father's engravings, etc." His offer came out of left field, and I was in total shock. I told him I'd have to discuss it with Maureen, and then get back to him. Maureen was out of town visiting her parents. Every time she's out of town I've gotten into publishing trouble.

JG: [Laughter]

DS: So anyway, I took the job, and then the head editor died! And all of a sudden I became the managing editor at E.B. Marks. I stayed there for two years. I really wanted to learn how this whole music publishing thing worked, and how you marketed things, the full publishing thing.

JG: Hm mmm.

DS: Kalban only wanted me to learn this one job, you know, and be the editor. I wanted to get a full range, but he wouldn't really tell me anything else. So I left that job, and Maureen and I freelanced for several other publishers. And then United Artists asked me to come in. Again, Maureen's out of town...

Their managing editor, who was giving Maureen and I work, wanted me to have a meeting with the VP of publishing, who he said wanted to meet me. So I met with the VP and another one of the top executives. They told me they wanted to create a new position at the company, a Production Manager of the Print Division, and they might be interested in me.

I would have eighteen people working for me, an art director and four artists and all kinds of stuff like that... which I was really not equipped to do. You know, I had no training in any of that kind of stuff. I was recommended by the editor, 'cause he really wanted to retire and he thought I'd end up doing it. They were doing all this pop stuff that you had to make sheet music for, and I just really didn't want to do that. So, I figure I'll talk to Maureen on the phone, she was out in Colorado. We were struggling with our business. We were doing such a good job that we were back loaded with pressure, pressure, job on top of job—and the freelance money wasn't really that good. I just had to somehow get out of that. Maureen said, "They're going to want to know how much you want. So give them a real high price. And they'll just give us some more work and that'll calm things down and you won't get the job." So I said, "OK, good."

I went for the interview and they took me through the whole thing, asked me all these questions.... to tell the truth, I didn't know anything about paper, different paper weights, and they were doing different glossy books with embossed covers and I didn't know about any of that, you know? So they said, "Don't worry about that now, the art director can show you all that stuff. So how much is it gonna cost us to have you here?" By this time I had good credentials, they knew I had been managing editor at E.B. Marks, and they liked all the work Maureen and I had done for them. So I said, "OK, I couldn't consider it for less than..." I don't remember what I said, But the VP says, "Oh well, that's absolutely out of the question. Maybe that could be your salary after a few years..." and the other executive in the meeting says, "Herman, I gotta talk to you." So they leave me there and go into the next office. Turns out he wasn't supposed to do anything like that and make ultimatums. He was supposed to either hire me or not hire me.

JG: Gotcha.

DS: So then all of the sudden the other executive walks back in the room and shakes my hand and says "Congratulations, you're hired." All I could think was, *what*!?

JG: [Laughter]

DS: So I take the position, OK? The guy who was supposed to teach me this whole business is the art director. My first day arrives, and I get in the elevator in the United Artists Building at 729 Seventh Avenue. As the door opens on the publishing floor, Ben Hoagland, Herman Steiger's assistant, is waiting for the down elevator. He grabs my hand and shakes it, and says, "The art director passed away over the weekend, so I've got to handle a whole lot of paperwork. Follow me, and I'll show you where your office is and introduce you to your staff. Your art department is pretty shook up hearing that the art director died."

As we walked into the production room, all Ben said was: "Good morning, this is Don Sickler, your production manager," and to me, "This is your staff," and there were like eighteen people looking at me...

JG: [Laughter]

DS: Fortunately I immediately latched on to one of the staff, my "Girl Friday," who I saw I could immediately relate to. She was kind of a renegade, but a good person, and someone who I knew I could trust. She gave me a person by person run down of the rest of my staff, including the most senior member, who I noticed was looking daggers at me from when I walked into the room. Turned out she applied for my position, and Herman rejected her. I knew she wasn't going to be any help in showing me the ropes. My Girl Friday definitely was my savior for my first few days on the job, telling me what projects were in the works, because I certainly had no idea what to do or assign. I had not a clue what to do!

JG: [Laughter]

DS: And nobody to teach me anything!

JG: So, but you learned the publishing business, much of it, in that position, it sounds like.

DS: In that position, yeah. There was only one guy above me, Herman Steiger, the vice president in charge of publishing. This was back when United Artists was all in one building, 729 Seventh Ave. One floor was movies, a couple of floors handled the record companies. Blue Note was there, and United Artists Records was there, and then there was publishing, and then there was legal.

JG: Wow, well, I just want to jump ahead a little bit. I met you in 1984 when I was seventeen, and you had been hired by the union to put together this group of young jazz players called Young Sounds. And thank God I didn't know who I was around sometimes at your studio. But I remember playing with Renee Rosnes, Ben Riley being there and playing with us. You told us later that Blakey would be there checking us out. And James Williams, and Donald Brown...

DS: And Mobley, did you meet Hank Mobley?

JG: I did! I told that story here in the book where you introduced me to him and played the record he did with Trane and Griff. When you said you were going to put it on he said, "Oh man, those guys kicked my ass so bad!" And you said, "No man, Mobley's a melody player, he played great too!" And that was a real eye-opener for me, to understand that. You introduced us to all this music.

DS: By that time I had become a publisher myself. A lot of the artists knew me as a publishing executive from UA, like Curtis Fuller, who was in the first Philly Joe band that I was in. And those guys didn't like or trust publishers, but they all needed a publisher. That's why they came to me to have me publish their music, you know, because they also saw that I was a player, but also dead serious about the importance of publishing.

JG: Right. Well, just in the years before I met you, I remember seeing those Dameronia records that you were on with Philly Joe Jones. How did you make that association with Philly Joe?

DS: I met Philly Joe when I was still an executive at United Artists. A lot of the guys, they would come into the building for the record company, and they would hear about me and come to meet me. Hubert Laws, Ron Carter, and Cedar knew about me, 'cause I could always transcribe well. I did a couple things for Hubert Laws, transcribed a whole bunch of his flute solos. And he kept saying, "Hey man, they've got this guy up on the sixth floor. You need something transcribed he's not gonna charge you that much. He's really into the jazz thing and he's got the biggest ears in New York!" He was saying stuff like that, you know? So, these guys would come to me and have me do different things. Like Rahsaan Roland Kirk had me transcribe and make lead sheets for him for copyright purposes.

JG: Wow, that's amazing!

DS: So, I was production manager for five years and eventually quit, because they weren't going to let me develop their jazz catalog. They owned Robbins, Feist and Miller, big publishing companies that controlled lots of standards. A lot of Duke Ellington's music was in Robbins Music. They owned Blue Note and Pacific Jazz and their publishing catalogs. "CTA" by Jimmy Heath is in Pacific Jazz. Blue Note had everything.

JG: Yep.

DS: But they wouldn't let me develop their jazz holdings. I was too valuable doing what I was doing. Like, they'd just discovered Barry Manilow. And they were doing Paul McCartney books, and Barbara Streisand movie books. And with jazz, as they told me, "For every one Joe Henderson or Coltrane book I could sell, we can sell 200 Paul McCartney books. So, jazz is great. I know you really love it. Treat it like a hobby. Do whatever you want with the catalog. But I won't give you any time in the office or any staff to do it." That's when I finally quit. I decided I was going to become a jazz publisher, starting my catalog with Rodgers Grant's "Morning Star" that Hubert had recorded and a couple of other things. Maureen was really behind me and said, "Let's just start our own company. You've learned enough about it, we can do it on our own."

JG: And that's what became Second Floor Music, right?

DS: Yes, and we bought the second floor loft where we still are on 28th Street. I named my first company Second Floor Music, that's my BMI company. And I formed Twenty-Eighth Street Music, that's my ASCAP company.

Back to Philly Joe. Philly Joe did two albums on the Galaxy label. Those were the last two records that Blue Mitchell recorded, and then he passed away. And Joe never got the trumpet book back. When I was still at United Artists, Joe asked me to transcribe all the trumpet music on the recommendation of Ron Carter or Cedar or whoever. He was missing a sax part on one thing, and a couple bass parts, so he needed me to transcribe what was missing. They were mostly tough-ass Slide Hampton arrangements of like, "Two Bass Hit." So, I transcribed all the missing music parts and gave it to him. Then I left UA to start my own business.

I'm sitting at home one day, and my belt is tightening. I've got medical and dental expenses and everything. I mean, in the executive world, everything's covered, you know? And now we've got no health insurance of our own. Maureen is helping me, but I was still pretty nervous, they were pretty scary times. One night we're having dinner in the back room and the phone rings and it's Philly Joe. And he says, "Hi, Don, It's Philly Joe. I've got a problem, and I want you to help me, and I know you'll be able to help me. Remember all that music you did for me, putting together those trumpet parts?" I said "Yeah, were they OK?" He said, "I looked them all over and they're great, everything's perfect. And believe it or not I've got a gig coming up next week in New York and I don't have a trumpet player to play these hard charts. And I do know a couple of important things, so just listen to me for a second." He said, "I know that you have a master's degree in legit trumpet from Manhattan School of Music, which is a tough-ass degree program, so you've gotta be able to play your butt off. You know all the music because you transcribed it. The only thing is, I can't find anyone who's heard you play. But that makes no difference to me at all. You've got the other two things, so, I'll see you Monday night at the Syncopation Club. Be there quarter to nine." Bam goes the phone.

All of a sudden I'm hired to play. My saving grace during my heavy executive gig for five years is that every night I would come home and pick up my trumpet and put on my records and just play with them to try to calm down, you know? So, I was always keeping my chops in shape from just doing that. I was always trying to get a good sound, and people always told me I had a good sound, and I knew what that took. I had to just keep that going. So, when Joe asked me to play, although I was scared to death, I knew I at least had a sound and thought I could hopefully play the parts for him. But when I walked into that gig…

Here I was, an experienced executive, I had been working under a real hard-ass guy, having to negotiate with top lawyers— I'm a seasoned guy, you know? I thought, my nerves? I've got nerves of steel! And then I walk in the club: Cedar Walton on piano, Curtis Fuller on one side, the six foot seven inch Harold Vick, an incredible saxophone player, on my other side, and Philly Joe Jones behind me, and I'm going, "Oh my god!" And I can feel my knees start to shake and I'm just scared shitless! You know?

JG: [Laughter]

DS: So, I'm up there, trying to play, putting the charts up, and I can feel my tone kinda going [blahh] and shakin' a little bit, 'cause I'm just scared outta my fuckin' mind, you know!? So, I naturally thought everything I played was horrible. I didn't solo on the first set. There were four horn players in the band and the rhythm section. So, the fact that I didn't solo on the first set, everybody else was ecstatic. Charles Davis was playing baritone on the other end so everybody got to stretch out. We got done with the first set and Joe said I needed to solo on the next set, "I wanna hear you play." Cedar and Curtis knew me from United Artists. Curtis was saying, "Man, I know you transcribed all this stuff, I always wondered how you played." He was all excited to see me there. And I'm sayin', Jesus! I'm a fuckin' nervous wreck!

JG: [Laughter]

DS: So we get into the second set and Joe screams out, "Sickler, solo on the next piece." I'm not gonna burn you with eighth notes, ever. I'm just a lyrical kind of player. I can immediately feel Joe just comping for me, and Cedar too. I'd been playing with Philly Joe and Cedar my whole life, on records, you know, but not with them accompanying me! But when you feel that for the first time, you know, like, I go [sings] and I feel them put in something else to help me and I said, Oh my god! This is *unbelievable*!

JG: [Laughter] Yeah!

DS: By the time I played the second solo on another song, I'm a little more relaxed, but I'm still scared out of my mind. I remember going up, and I hit a big fat wrong note. I just splattered the note and I froze. And Cedar goes up, Wham! and hits my wrong note with the chord and plays, [sings] and just hands it right back to me. And I just said, Damn! Now if this isn't something! You know?

JG: Yeah!

DS: 'Cause I made a mistake and I thought the whole band was gonna stop. But no, Cedar just said—oh, going there? OK! And then he hands to me in a different way.

JG: Yeah, yeah.

DS: After the first night, I had my little speech ready. I was practically in tears. I thought everything was absolutely hopeless. Cedar had a great sense of humor, but if you were nervous, it made him nervous. He told me, "Hey man, you gotta calm down, you're makin' me nervous." That set me off even more. After the gig, Curtis walks back in and says, "Hey, Joe wants to see you." I saw he was starting to take his cymbals down on the bandstand. I got my speech all ready. Don't worry Mr. Jones, you'll never see me again. I'm sorry I really fucked up tonight. You know, I apologize, etc. So I walked out there. And Joe is one of those guys—did you know Philly Joe at all?

JG: No. I never got to know him unfortunately.

DS: Well, he could control the conversation, totally. If he didn't want you to take any time talking you had no way to get anything in. He was a master of that. So, I went out there ready to tell him, don't worry you'll never see me again. He says, "Well, you were a little nervous, but you got a good sound. I hear your tone shakin' a little bit, but you gotta quit that. This is jazz music. This is fun. I can't believe I get paid to have all this fun! We're out there to have fun, and you gotta embrace that. And you gotta go with the flow, you know?"

JG: Hm mm.

DS: "You can't be nervous and neurotic and everything else. You gotta just go with it." And then he takes out the money and tries to hand it to me, and I say, "No, I don't want it." He says "Take this goddamn money! You earned that. You played your butt off tonight!" And I'm still trying to say something to him. He's got his cymbals picked up, he's still talkin', and then he says, "See ya tomorrow night," and then he just walks out the door.

JG: [Laughter] Wow!

DS: And that started five years of working with him. You know, Joe did a lot of all-star gigs and would go to Europe and also go on his own. But whenever he played in New York, and it wasn't just a trio or quartet gig, it was quintet or septet, I was his trumpet player for the last five years of his life. And we did Dameronia, you know. I kept trying to figure why does this guy keep me along with him when there are so many other real good, strong trumpet players?

He got a grant to do the Dameronia thing. He really needed all of Tadd's music transcribed, and he knew I could transcribe. So I ended up transcribing Tadd's nonet and octet music that Joe had played. Then he wanted Tadd's *Mating Call* album, the quartet album with Coltrane. He had me arrange those pieces. Which really was just taking what Tadd played at the piano and orchestrating it, because Tadd was a marvelous comper. I'd never really done arrangements that way. I'd studied classical composition, but that's totally different. I had to just suddenly learn how to arrange by doing it, trial and error, you know. The first record I was on was with Stan Rubin, it was a swing band thing. And the next record was with Philly Joe. It was in New York, myself and Johnny Coles, and Britt Woodman was the trombone player.

JG: Oh, Britt was great.

DS: And then Johnny Coles left the band. Then Britt Woodman left the band. That's when Benny Powell came in the band, he was real close with Frank Wess. We did the second Dameronia record for Uptown Records. The first one was at Nola Studios in NYC; for the second, Joe wanted to go back to record at Rudy's (Rudy Van Gelder's recording studio). On that one, on "If You Could See Me Now," that featured Johnny Griffin, I also played tenor sax. Because, in Spokane, when the club didn't want trumpet, I had to learn something else. My dad had a tenor sax sitting in the music store. I picked that up, and I used a Brilhart metal mouthpiece. I used the German embouchure for the saxophone, don't put my lip over my bottom teeth, you know? I could use exactly the same embouchure for the trumpet that I could use for the tenor. It made it a lot easier. My lower lip, from playing the trumpet, would vibrate against the reed rather than playing against it and wearing it out.

JG: Well basically, from that period on, late '70s, early '80s, you went on to produce…

DS: I was writing arrangements for the Uptown Records label. They'd also want to have me play on some things. I did some two trumpet things with Claudio Roditi and one with Jack Sheldon. And that's how Maureen got involved with Rudy. All those recordings were done at Rudy's.

When I'm in the booth producing, that's great. If I've got to be out in the room and playing my horn, with headphones on, then I don't like to produce. If I have to do it, as I did for Uptown, then I have Maureen come and sit in the control room, where the producer sits, and let me know if the bass player went to the bridge in the wrong place, or whatever. So I had a good set of ears in there. And that's what Rudy picked up on. And that's why Rudy in 1986 hired Maureen when he needed an assistant.

JG: Yeah. I'd love to talk to her at some point about that.

DS: Yeah, well, her first gig was doing a live Tommy Flanagan CD at the Village Vanguard. They wanted Rudy to do it, and Rudy said I'll only do it if I have an assistant. So that was her first job.

JG: Wow!

DS: But look, Maureen is just a super-together person that picks up on anything. As Benny Golson said to me, "You've got one thing that nobody else has. You have a Maureen. If you could clone Maureen I'd be the first person to get one." She can just put it all together, you know?

JG: Oh that's for sure true! Now, you were part of those Freddie Hubbard, Woody Shaw records, right?

DS: Right. I did the arrangements for them. By then I was pretty well known as an arranger. That was for Blue Note. And that was before the Joe Henderson stuff. I actually produced a whole lot of records for Uptown. But those guys treated a producer's credit like in the movies. The producer's the guy with the money, OK? There's no director of recordings, there's a producer of records. So, I actually felt I should have been included as a producer on all of those records. I wrote the arrangements, worked with all the musicians, finished the whole product and everything else. They'd say, arranged by Don Sickler, music coordinator, or whatever they called me, I don't know. I wasn't listed as a producer. But I actually really produced a lot of those things, and that gave me a lot of experience working with musicians.

JG: And didn't you tell me, that those State of the Tenor records by Joe Henderson, that you were a part of that? I was at the Vanguard as a teenager a bunch of nights when they recorded that, which just blew my mind.

DS: I was the music coordinator. I was the one who came up with the music for them to play and did what arranging there was to be done. That was just a trio, tenor, bass, and drums. I remember, one of the thrills for me was in choosing the music. I knew this obscure Sam Rivers song, on *Fuchsia Swing Song*, "Beatrice."

JG: So you're the one that introduced Joe Henderson to "Beatrice."

DS: Yeah. Joe didn't know that song. I had a very delicate phone conversation with him telling him about it. At that time, very few saxophone artists were playing even Wayne Shorter tunes. The major saxophone players weren't playing tunes by other saxophone players.

JG: And you produced a number of great records. I remember loving that great James Williams record, *Alter Ego*.

DS: Yeah, well, again, those guys, I was publishing for them. So I was getting their music together for them or writing arrangements for them. And, whether I really have it together or not, I can always give the appearance that I'm under control in the recording studio, even if sometimes I don't feel that way.

JG: [Laughter]

DS: And look, I love Michael Cuscuna, and a lot of these guys that are producers. But they were never performing musicians. I mean, Michael can wind a stopwatch like very few. But he can't really come and tell you what's exactly wrong. He'll tell you that something's wrong, but they don't know what the problem is. I can tell you what the problem is.

JG: Right.

DS: And I always felt that a musician should be a producer.

JG: Absolutely!

DS: When I was producing Charlie Rouse, I wasn't given that credit. But Rouse could be like a nervous Nellie, you know? I know a lot of it had to do with calming him down to get a good take. You know, if I'd had any idea at Gonzaga of what I would be doing later I would've been doing psychology and getting a law degree rather than math and philosophy.

JG: [Laughter] Now, you've won a number of Grammys, correct?

DS: Yeah, I produced five Grammy Award-winning records. And again, that's just from hard work. The first one was Joe Henderson's *Lush Life* record. All of the young guys, the Young Lions, at the time, were there. Wynton was there also. And they were getting to record with Joe Henderson. They hadn't all worked with that caliber of musician. Joe, and the Charlie Rouses, those guys, once they're calmed down, you have to go for that first take. 'Cause they're gonna give you something on the first take that they're not gonna give you three takes later. That's how they grew up playing. It's either now or never. I mean, Cedar was always so focused for that first take, all the time! I really rehearsed that rhythm section of Stephen Scott, Christian McBride, and Greg Hutchinson, you know? We went through the whole thing and had it all together. So when we sat down with Joe it was just, get it. And they really played their butts off! Still to this day, all three of them, whenever I see them, they say, that's probably one of the best records they ever did. And it really was. Because they all played way ahead of themselves for the limited experience they had at that time.

JG: Well, I just wanna tell you, the career you've had, what you're doing now at Jazzleadsheets.com, the contribution you've made, the things you've accomplished, as a player, arranger, producer and publisher is amazing!

DS: Well, I've always been like this, I think you're like this too. If I don't feel like I learn something new every day I feel cheated in life. I'm always into trying to do things better, and I'm a perfectionist. I really want to lock in and do a professional job, and I want to make musicians feel at ease. I love this music.

A lady friend of ours lost her husband. He was a jazz fan, but never got to Rudy's. She organized a gathering of her husband's friends, and we let them come to the studio to mourn him. I showed them around and talked about Rudy and the studio. They could see the love I have for this music. It's really important to me. The musicians I've worked with understand that, and they all know that I knew enough that I could help them get a project done. I've been lucky to be at the right place at the right time, always. I don't know if it's fate, or what it is. But if it's a chance to do all those Mt. Fuji festivals, who you gonna hire? Well, get Sickler. I put the music together, and I got to work with all these great artists! Why? Because they knew I knew the

Blue Note catalog from being an executive at United Artists, and I know how to work with musicians, you know?

JG: And then the fact that now you and Maureen are running Rudy Van Gelder's studio, and Maureen is the engineer there, it's just amazing!

DS: Yeah, it is. And again, I was a little nervous. I think she was too. But she just said "Let's go for it." The Canadian producer Cory Weeds was just out at the studio. They wanted to have the drums out of the booth in the room for the first time, since (to my knowledge, and Maureen thinks so too) 1983, on the Dameronia record. Philly Joe insisted on being in the room. Joe and Rudy fought like hell, and eventually Rudy let Joe record in the room.

After Rudy had the drum booth built, he liked the drums in the booth. Because that drum booth is magical. And Rudy's a perfectionist. I go nuts if I don't hear the cymbal beat just right and I don't like the drums to be echoey, which they're gonna be of course, out in that big room. Last week, for four sessions in a row, different musicians every day, with, you know, Grant Stewart and guys that can really play, Maureen's out there recording in the room. And they loved it! I didn't like it as much, and Maureen feels the same way. She can't really control the drums as much, but she's still able to get it, you know? You go back and listen to those albums that Rudy did, and how he got the clarity of the drums in that big room, all the time... no matter whether it's Billy Higgins with his soft touch, or Blakey beatin' the shit outta the drums. Still, Rudy got it. He was on a different level. That's why he was Rudy Van Gelder—nobody else could do it like he did it.

JG: Well Don, thanks so much for your time. I hope I'll see you when I'm back in town soon.

DS: Well, talk with Maureen, you get her on the phone. She loves you too. We're thrilled to have guys like you at the studio, and we love helping guys like you get projects done.

JG: Well, I sure appreciate it Don, and thanks so much for all your help with the last CD and over all these years! I'll check in with Maureen, and I'll give you guys a call when I get back in town in a couple weeks.

DS: OK, Thanks Jon.

JG: Thanks Don!

Coda

I asked Maureen to do an interview, but she decided not to do one, or respond to written questions. She's a quiet, shy person, but someone that people should know more about. Rudy Van Gelder would not leave his studio to just anybody! But Maureen did do an interview with PBS Newshour a couple of years ago, as a part of a segment about a newly found recording of Coltrane's, which was great –
pbs.org/newshour/show/lost-recordings-uncover-john-coltranes-timeless-talent

Sean Smith

Phone call, New York City – June 5, 2020

Sean Smith and I have been good friends since early 1984, when as teenagers, we played a gig at Gracie Mansion, for then Mayor Koch. Over the years we've played in many different contexts together. He's as good and decent a person as I've ever known, and he's a wonderful bass player and composer. When I asked him about doing this, he told me he wasn't sure what he wanted to talk about, so I suggested talking about his compositions, which are wonderful, and have been played and recorded by a number of great musicians. So, we went with that, although Sean did have one condition for doing the interview...

JG: Hey Sean, so we'd talked recently about maybe looking at your composing, and how that's developed over the years.

SS: Well, I started composing as a final project while studying at Manhattan School of Music, in the spring of 1990, in David Berger's composition and arranging class. I tried to get out of the assignment of writing a tune and instead wanted to do an arrangement of an existing piece. I'd done some arranging in the class but really wasn't a composer. But David Berger asked me to at least try and write something original, so I did. And I came up with something and enjoyed the process! So, a month later, after I graduated, I sat at the piano and wrote for myself. Up until then I was really mainly an improviser. At that time, the group Square Root was being formed with Bill Charlap, Allen Mezquida, Leon Parker, and myself. It was good timing to have started writing just before then. We were rehearsing a lot. I'd bring in a tune and everyone would seem to like it and seemed to want me to bring in another. I hadn't had a lot of confidence previously. But, the process of writing was a truly satisfying and exciting one, and I couldn't help myself.

JG: How long did that group last?

SS: A year or so.

JG: Where did you play?

SS: We played one week-long engagement at the Village Gate and a few other gigs. But, without the support and enthusiasm and encouragement of my friends, I wouldn't have been able to do it. It enabled me as a shy person to get a decent start in terms of gaining some confidence, and love, quite frankly, because we all need that.

JG: I believe Phil Woods played some of your music.

SS: He did. Jill, his wife, told me one time, "Keep sending Phil your music." Phil originally had asked me to do so and I would send him a couple tunes every so often. Phil was encouraging, but I didn't want to be a pain and bother him. Jill insisted, "Keep sending him tunes, he likes it!" And, two or three ended up in the quintet book. There is a recording, *Phil Woods with the Bill Charlap Trio: Voyage*, and they recorded one of my tunes, "A Smitty Ditty."

JG: Great! I love that piece! Was that one of the pieces in Phil's book?

SS: I don't think so.

JG: What were the tunes in Phil's book?

SS: "Song Without a Lyric," which later became a Mark Murphy tune called "I'll Call You," and "Comedy of Errors."

JG: And what was the tune we recorded on my CD *Witness*?

SS: That was "House of Mirrors."

JG: That's a great tune! So, Mark Murphy put a lyric on your tune and renamed it "I'll Call You"?

SS: Yes, and he recorded that on a vocal record with vocalist Barbara Sfraga.

JG: Mark also recorded other pieces of yours, didn't he?

SS: Yes, "Song for the Geese," which became a very important piece for Mark, because of the subject matter of that tune. It was the title track on the album of the same name in 1997, and was released on RCA/BMG, when that label was around. The album was nominated for a Grammy. And Mark recorded another piece of mine called "Taming of a Rose." He wrote a lyric and recorded it on a CD called *Links*. He wrote lyrics to several others. Many of those were written in the late stage of his life.

JG: Wow. Yeah, Mark was a marvelous singer. It says a lot that he loved your music so much to write lyrics to so many of your pieces, and to have that one be part of a Grammy nomination. Bill Charlap has played and recorded a number of your pieces as well.

SS: Yes, and he's always been very supportive. Early on we made a duo recording, *Bill Charlap & Sean Smith*, and a bunch of my tunes, five or six of them, ended up on it. We were playing a lot of duo then and Bill wanted to record them. A year later there's a recording, "Along with Me," with another duo cut, of a piece of mine, "Has This Song Been Written for You Before?"

JG: Great title.

SS: And on Bill's CD, *Distant Star*, a trio recording with Bill Stewart and myself, we recorded a tune of mine, "'39 Worlds Fair."

JG: Yes, that's another piece of yours that I've played that's great! And what about your own recordings?

SS: I have three CDs as a leader, and there's only one standard on one of them, all the rest are originals. The regular group currently is John Ellis, Nate Radley, and Russell Meissner.

JG: And what about the recent collaborative group you've been a part of?

SS: It's called The Humanity Quartet, and the relatively new album is called *Humanity*. The personnel are Joel Frahm, Peter Bernstein, and Leon Parker. And there are five pieces of mine on the CD.

JG: Great band! Where has the group played?

SS: We've played several weekends at Smalls and some concerts in New York City, Philly, and in the Midwest. We recorded for Cellar Live, Cory Weeds' label. You know, I should also mention that I've been fortunate to have Bill Mays as well as Gene Bertoncini, among others, also play and record some of my music.

JG: That's great! I admire both of those guys a lot, and they've been good to each of us over the years. The great guitarist Peter Leitch is also someone you've played with a lot. Are there some musicians that you've played with that have impacted your writing, or maybe just that you're a fan of that you feel helped shape or influence your writing?

SS: Wayne Shorter, though I didn't play with Wayne. And, I've always loved Tom Harrell's writing and playing. I played early on with Mike Holober and have always really enjoyed his music. I also enjoyed playing Peggy Stern's music with her around that same time period. I love all the great jazz composers and great American songwriters. I myself am not a line writer, I'm more of a melody guy. And, I'm a huge fan of a couple different musical schools in Brazil—Clube da Esquina, Jobim, and many others. Brazil became a big influence for me. And of course, Duke and Strayhorn. Again, I'm not a line writer. You hear very little bebop directly in my music. As an improviser I come out of that, but I don't really improvise like that or write like that. I'm grateful to have had my music played by so many great musicians, peers and beyond. And I'm always excited to hear what different people bring to the music. Things I would have never thought of. I feel very fortunate for all of that.

JG: Well thanks Sean. It's great talking to you, thanks for doing this.

SS: Thank you Jon, good talking with you. And I'm going to hold you to coming over to my apartment to help me vacuum!

JG: Fair enough! A deal's a deal! Thanks Sean!

SS: Thanks!

Sarah Vaughan

Mikell's, Upper West Side, Manhattan – 1986

Mikell's was a jazz club on Columbus Ave. and 97th St. back in the day. I saw Art Farmer, Art Blakey, and other great artists there. I also played there a few times a year during this period of the mid to late '80s. Some time that summer I played there with some friends. The only person I know for sure was on the gig that night was Bill Charlap, though Sean Smith or Andy Eulau was likely on bass, and Justin Page was probably playing drums.

At some point towards the end of the first set, in between tunes, Bill said to me in a breathless and urgent tone, "Do you see who's at the bar!?" I couldn't see the bar very well from where I was, and there was a crowd of people there. I tried to look for whoever he was referring to but couldn't spot anyone I recognized. I looked back at Bill and shrugged my shoulders to silently say, huh? He impatiently waved me off and looked down at the piano and we quickly continued on with the next tune.

At the end of that tune and set, before I had a chance to step off the stage and put my horn away, I saw a woman at the bar, making eye contact with me, slowly walking towards the stage. She had some kind of presence to her that I couldn't quite make out at first. She almost seemed to be floating towards me, and I was captivated by her and just stared at her as she approached me. As she got closer, I started to slowly realize that it was Sarah Vaughan... and was in a kind of shock! When I'd seen her on TV she'd always seemed large, imposing, and regal. But she had something about her that night that made her look to me like a little girl in the body of a woman in her sixties. I stood on the lip of the stage, gawking in disbelief as she walked to about a foot away from me, just off the stage.

She looked up at me, paused a beat, and quietly said in a much higher pitched voice than I expected, "You kids sound beautiful... I didn't know you kids was still playin' tunes... keep doin' what you're doin'." She had an ethereal quality to her—I felt completely captivated, enchanted by her presence, like I was in some slightly altered state of reality. I don't think I said anything other than a kind of mumbled, "Oh... I... uh, OK, uh, thank you, uh..."

Then she said, reaching a hand towards me, "Here, come to the bar and meet Billy." I stepped off the stage in a daze, holding hands with Sarah Vaughan, and walked the fifty feet to the bar. The Billy she mentioned turned out to be Billy Eckstine! She said, "Hey Billy, this is the young saxophone player that was just playin'." Billy Eckstine, who'd been facing forward at the bar with his back to me, turned to his left, partially towards me, not quite far enough around to face me, but enough for me to see his face. He had a drink in his right hand, and he gestured towards me with it as he said, in a gruff, gravelly tone, "Yeah, mgrhr, alrifht, you grham goo yeah..." I literally didn't understand a word he said. But it seemed nice and tough at the same time, so I just slowly nodded my head and said, "Thank you." I looked back to Sarah on my left, who with the same quiet, wide-eyed, vulnerable, almost little girl like manner said, "OK, nice meeting you. You sound beautiful. Just keep doin' what you're doin'." Again, I said something like, "Ahhh, thanks, so much, ah, yeah..." and ambled back towards the bandstand in a daze.

Charlap, still on the stage, saw all this and said to me, even more intensely, "Do you realize who that is!? Do you have *any* idea of who that is!?" I responded dreamily, "She introduced me to Billy Eckstine…" This seemed almost too much for Bill to handle! He threw his hands up and stormed off in an inner huff. Not that he was mad or anything. He seemed to me to be overcome by the level of the people who, we were not only in the presence of, but had also been performing for! As to his question, did I realize who that was? I think it took me a while to start to understand. But I truly felt it in her amazing, transcendent energy.

Derrick Gardner
Winnipeg – June, 2020

Derrick Gardner and I have known each other since the early '90s, and we've worked together at the University of Manitoba, Desautels Faculty of Music for the past seven years, where his office is right next to mine. We've played together hundreds of times in recent years, and it's always a joy. I often hear him working on big band charts next door on his computer. If people are in my office when he does so, I often say, "The Mad Genius is at work!" Because, first of all he's a great jazz musician and an incredible trumpet player who always brings the blues, beautifully, to what he does. Second, he's a brilliant big band composer and arranger. The other reason I call him a "Mad Genius" is because he writes some of the *hardest* parts I've ever seen! He seems to take a quiet joy, and even have a chuckle or two at our struggles to play his music.

A couple of years ago I heard his octet CD, including his brother Vincent Gardner, a brilliant trombonist and a member of the Jazz at Lincoln Center Orchestra. About three tunes in, on a piece of Vincent's, I heard one of the hardest trumpet parts ever! Displaced triplets, tricky articulation, high up on the horn, and *fast*! I saw Derrick the next day and said, "Man, I love the octet CD. But *wow*! That trumpet part that Vincent wrote you on that chart of his was ridiculously hard!" Derrick just shook his head and said, "Man... can you believe it? That my *own brother* would go and do a thing like that to me?" "I said, "Yeah, but you played your ass off on it!" And then it occurred to me, "But hey, now you know how we feel on some of your parts!" We both laughed and I said, "Writing tough charts must run in the family!"

JG: Hey Derrick, I recently saw the Lincoln Center video with you, Vincent, and your dad. Man, that was great! And it was great to hear your dad!

DG: We did that in 2005, for the opening of Rose Hall. They invited family members of players in Lincoln Center Jazz Orchestra to participate. So, it was myself, my dad, and Vincent wrote the arrangement for "Stolen Moments" for four horns. In everybody's estimation Pops cleared the bench! My dad is from Mississippi and moved to Chicago around 1959–'60. Before I was born he went on tour with Ray Charles, when Fathead Newman and Hank Crawford were in the band. After a couple years he said, "Ray's too cheap." He had his music degree and said "I can make more money teaching in public schools and working with cats when they come through town. So, he worked with Basie, Woody Herman—including a couple short tours with Woody—Nancy Wilson, Cannonball Adderley (in a small group!), and Eddie Harris. And then you had all the local Chicago cats that he played with. My mother is a classical pianist, organist, and choir director. She also worked in a couple public schools as a choir director in Chicago. She also worked in a couple churches as an organist and choir director. At one point, my parents went back to school to get their doctoral degrees at Michigan State University. After they finished those, we moved to Virginia, and they both got university jobs there. My dad was at Norfolk State University and my mother was at Hampton. We were living in Virginia Beach, a part of the Tidewater area, encompassing Tidewater and Norfolk. Steve Wilson is also from that area.

JG: Who else did you know from down there?

225

DG: Billy Drummond, Sam Newsome, Alvin Walker (a trombonist with Basie for twenty years or so), James Genus, and some other guys from Richmond.

JG: How did you get into music?

DG: Subliminal suggestion. Music was in the house all the time. My mother would be practicing classical piano upstairs, my dad would be in the basement practicing jazz. My dad was also producing his own records with his own group in Chicago. His brother, my uncle, had one of the main record stores on the south side of Chicago, called Gardner's One Stop Record Shop. My uncle explained to me that the One Stop acted as the middleman between the distributor and all the other record stores. Being the middleman, he was able to get the latest recordings before everybody else. He had a direct line to the distributor. Plus, with my dad producing all his own records through his own label, he would sell them at the store and distribute them as well, throughout Chicago and the Midwest. The group was called Burgess Gardner and the Soul Crusaders.

JG: Great name for a group!

DG: And he just did that until the doctoral degree.

JG: How old were you when you moved?

DG: I was around thirteen.

JG: Who's older, you or Vincent?

DG: Vincent is seven years younger. And I have an older sister as well.

JG: What were some of the things that were important to your growth early on?

DG: I started piano when I was five, and took lessons until I was eight or so. Then I remember taking a break from the piano, I got kinda bored with it, for about a year. But in fifth grade they started a band program. I asked to play trumpet. They said they didn't have one. So I ran home and asked my dad for one, and he got me one so I could play it in the school band. And he didn't just get me any trumpet. I didn't really figure this out until I was a professional. He bought me the same trumpet that Lee Morgan played on *The Procrastinator*, and that Freddie Hubbard played on *First Light*! It was a Conn 8B. And I didn't know any better. I just thought it was a horn. And I *tortured* that horn. [Laughter] I saw new horns that were shinier and looked better. By then I was in Virginia, in the junior high marching band, tossing the horn up in the air and dropping it. And in high school and college too! I really trashed it then!

JG: Do you still have it in your museum in your office?[7]

DG: No! When I got to New York, I went to what I thought was a more professional horn and eventually my tortured and abused Conn was just collecting dust in the closet. Until Kenny Rampton called one day and said, "I'm looking for a Conn 8B, you know anybody that's got one?" I said, "I got one in my closet!" He said, "You wanna sell it?" I told him, "I'd feel bad selling it, I trashed it! It's in such horrible shape. Give me $100 for it." He said "Great!" He had it overhauled and fixed up to brand new. He showed it to me and I said, "This looks great! Why would you put this much money into a student horn?" He said, "What!? This is the horn that Lee and Freddie played on!" And I said, "*What*!? Give my horn back I'll give you your $100 back!"

BOTH: [Laughter]

---

7   He actually has an informal trumpet museum in his office with dozens of horns and mouthpieces!

JG: Well, Kenny's been in the Lincoln Center Jazz Orchestra for some time. Walter Blanding Jr. has been in the band for many years. We knew each other as kids on Staten Island. His dad, Walter Sr. was a bass player, and his mom is an amazing singer! I used to see them perform sometimes when I was in high school.

DG: Oh yeah, man! She's bad! She was on that same concert with me and my dad.

JG: Whenever I see Walter I always ask about his mom, because I was so blown away by her singing. So, where did you go to college?

DG: Where my mom taught, at Hampton University. Both my sister and I went there. Vincent went to Florida A&M. Hampton had a jazz program. It was kind of a shoestring program, that had all the classes covered by one person. That one person was my trumpet teacher, Robert Ransom. We also had adjunct teachers there that were covering other classes, but he was the only full-time faculty representing jazz, and taught both classical and jazz students. He was also assistant director of the marching band. Unfortunately, at the Black schools, HBCUs, their main focus was the marching band. So, I had to march in the marching band the entire four years I was there. In band camp we'd start training in early August, like athletes! So, the first half of the year was marching band. Then we'd start focusing on jazz ensemble in the second half of the year. I wasn't doing nearly as much practicing the first half of the year. Your chops are swollen, you're beat up. In essence, I only got two full years of jazz ensemble when I was there, because of the marching band. But it was a great experience going to Hampton for everything else it had to offer. I had a very well-rounded education, and a meaningful and significant education.

JG: When did you know you wanted to be a jazz musician?

DG: I think I always knew, but I didn't really start going down that path until I went to college.

JG: After Hampton what did you do?

DG: So, after senior year, I thought I'd either go to New York or grad school. And I went to our music library and pulled out a Freddie Hubbard record. I put the needle on the record and listened for about three minutes, and took the needle of the record and said, "OK, I guess I'm going to grad school!" I thought, if I can hang with this I'm going to New York. And three minutes into that record I said, "Ain't no way!" I wasn't ready for New York. So I ended up going to Indiana University, and I got to study with David Baker. He really took me under his wing, because he knew my dad and had worked with him before. And when he found out I was a Hampton grad he was especially drawn to me, because his dad was a Hampton grad. So, he really kinda took me under his wing and showed me the ropes. And I was really able to get a lot of stuff together at Indiana. I was able to continue progressing on the trumpet, continuing the work of Robert Ransom, with other teachers that had a really good philosophy of trumpet playing.

JG: Is that where your composing and arranging started?

DG: That's where I started to focus more on comp and arranging, definitely. From playing David Baker's pieces and taking his composition course. So, then about three quarters of the way through the master's at Indiana, I got recruited in the Basie band. I was there for six years. Five under the leadership of Frank Foster, that last year the band was led by Grover Mitchell. I thought when I left Indiana that I'd stop learning, but that's where the real learning began.

JG: Did you study privately with Frank, or was it just the day to day on the bus?

DG: Both. During the five years we were there I'd be practicing with him damn near every night as we were warming up for the gig. And then as far as arranging was concerned, the Frank Foster era of leadership was the only era, after Basie passed, that there was a significant amount of new pieces added to the Basie book.

JG: Was Dennis Mackrel there when you were there?

DG: No. Bill Hughes was there, who's from Staten Island. He and Eric Dixon, another Basie alum from Staten Island both have streets named for them there. But right after Basie died, Dixon became the interim leader, and then they got Thad Jones, and that's when Dennis was playing drums, through the recommendation of Joe Williams. They were both in Las Vegas at that time.

JG: Was Brian Grice there some? We worked together some in the '90s.

DG: He subbed some when Grover was there. My dad taught Brian Grice in Chicago. My dad had the first Chicago all-city jazz ensemble. And a lot of the competitions were starting up at that time. My dad was writing his own arrangements. Everybody else was doing whatever was published. My dad came in there with his own sound, and he'd take the all-city band in there and just clean house!

JG: What were some of the special experiences you had on the Basie band?

DG: One of the first was when we were at some festival in Florida. I was backstage warming up in a corner. I felt a tap on my shoulder. I turn around, this guy says, "Hey, I really like the way you sound." I say, "Thanks!" I turn around, all the sudden I realize, HOLY SHIT! That's James Moody! So I turned back around and started praising him, as if I was in church! He said, "Let me show you something." He sang this line to me, with his Moody kind of yodeling thing. Go down a major 7th, then up a tritone, then take that down, go through the circle of 5ths, etc. I was like *wow*! I said, "OK, I'm gonna check that out!" He said, "That'll open your ears up. Whenever you learn some shit, just give it away and it'll come back to you tenfold. It'll keep you fresh and keep your mind working."

When we got to the next city I got to a piano and played the chords he mentioned to apply it to and it just fit! Prior to that, I was just playing scalar, serpentine lines—I wasn't dealing with intervallic stuff. I started practicing that every way I could think of. Then I saw him about eight years later in Chicago at the Jazz Showcase. I had my horn. On the break I went up and said hello, and before I could tell him who I was he said, "Gardner... Basie!" I could've just evaporated at that point! I told him, "You showed me something that just changed my life. And I played it for him. He said, "Yeah! That's good! Now add fourths to it!" And that opened my thing up even more.

JG: As I've told you many times over recent years, I think you're one of the most important big band composers and arrangers in Canada. And I know you got a lot from your time with Frank Foster.

DG: Well, with Frank, the thing that really jumpstarted my arranging efforts was playing Frank's arrangements and hearing his sound. So, we're in between cities, on tour. Frank is sitting up in the front of the bus. Everyone has a loose seat assignment. Mine is in the back on the right. Frank would be up front with a big score pad of paper with a black felt tip pen and a ruler. So he'd be up there, he'd have the lead line written, and he'd be voicing it down from the lead line vertically, without a piano, and I'm looking at him thinking, that's amazing! I figured I need to learn some of this from him. So, in the next city I bought a big score pad of paper and pencils and I started to score my own arrangement. I was working without a piano. After a couple weeks I had 8–16 bars done. I went up to the front of the bus and said, "Hey Foss, can you see if I'm on the right track here?" While he's looking at it, he puts the cap on his black felt pen, takes out a red pen, and just annihilates my voicings, one by one. It looked a Picasso by the time he was done. But he wrote all this, instantly revoiced some stuff, gave me instructions, and said, "Here, take this back and work on it." I walked back to my seat, tail between my legs, sad music playing in the background… but when I got to a piano, I saw what he was talking about. After I tried another 8-16 measures or so, I went back to the front of the bus, this time with a more humble demeanor. He did the whole thing with the red pen again. But this time I didn't have as much red ink. So each time I went to the front of the bus I'd have less red ink on my score. And a year and a half later I finally had an arrangement.

JG: Did the band play your chart?

DG: Yeah, it was on "Afternoon in Paris," and we rehearsed a couple of other charts of mine. But that one we performed. After Foss left the band I would go down and study with him, in Chesapeake, Virginia in the Tidewater area. When I went down to visit my mother I'd take arranging lessons with him. This was after he had his stroke. During that period his left side was affected, so he couldn't play anymore, but he was writing his ass off. Finale was his instrument.

JG: So this music he wrote in this period, has it been played by his big band, The Loud Minority, or anyone else?

DG: No, he put together a version of The Loud Minority in Virginia, and he had his New York version as well, that I was a member of. He was still doing a lot of commission work for Carnegie Hall, Lincoln Center, and quite a few singers.

JG: You have all that music?

DG: Yeah. When he passed his family gave me much of his music, maybe half of what was available. The other half went to Duke University.

JG: But to perform and record that music he wrote then would be amazing!

DG: Definitely!

JG: You have a new big band project coming out in July, called "Still I Rise" based on the poem by Maya Angelou. It feels incredibly appropriate, based on what's happening in the world right now and what we were talking about earlier today. I thought what you wrote on Facebook today was great.[8]

DG: Well, I just wrote what I was feeling. This protest feels different from the reactions to other murders, because of what everybody saw happen.

JG: I'm just praying for some healing, some justice and sanity. I think that the message and timing of your CD is needed, for sure. I'm so thankful you've been able to get some grants and do this project, because I think your music needs to be heard and the message is so profound, especially right now.

DG: For the CD, I was able to focus on all original music. There are four dedications—one for Trayvon Martin. I wrote a tune for my dad, "Blues ala Burgess," and another dedication is for the drum professor at Michigan State, Randy Gelispie. In the end I just wanted to create some good music. My hope is that the average person that knows nothing about music can be affected by what I put out. To them it's either good or bad. If I can impress them, I'm OK.

JG: Well, I look forward to hearing it. Thanks Derrick.

DG: Thanks.

---

8   He is referring to the worldwide protests after the killing of George Floyd in May, 2020.

Sylvia Cuenca
Phone call, New York City – June 2020

JG: Hey Sylvia, thanks for doing this. I think we've known each other since the late '80s. We hadn't seen each other in a while, but then we played the San Jose Jazz Festival together last year. It was really great to reconnect with you and play again. So, where did you grow up?

SC: I'm originally from San Jose, California, the San Francisco Bay area.

JG: Was someone in your family a musician?

SC: My father played jazz guitar. My brother played guitar, bass, and mandolin and my mother knew the lyrics to hundreds of songs. They weren't professional musicians, but their love of music allowed me to grow up in a house full of music either from the radio or from my father's jazz record collection.

JG: So did you start playing at home?

SC: My father tried to give me guitar lessons, but I always had my eye on the drum set. When I was eleven or twelve years old I had an opportunity to take a snare drum class in junior high school. I fell in love with the instrument and wanted to learn all I could about it. I worked hard and moved from snare drum to drum set quickly. When I got my first four-piece green sparkle kit I used to practice for hours every day. I was very lucky to have incredibly patient and supportive parents that tolerated me practicing constantly.

JG: Was there a teacher or music program that was really important for you?

SC: Right after I graduated from high school I attended San Jose City College summer jazz program. It was directed by Dave Eshelman, who's a trombonist, composer, and great educator. He was very significant to my musical growth. He instilled a strong work ethic in all of his students. Mr. Eshelman helped me to develop my sight-reading skills and introduced me to different genres of music. He also brought in guest artists to perform with the jazz ensembles. One of them was Joe Henderson. This was the first time I met and performed with Joe. That same summer I also received a scholarship to attend the Stanford Jazz Workshop in Stanford, California. The faculty that year was Stan Getz, pianist Jim McNeely, George Mraz, and the drum instructor was Victor Lewis.

JG: Wow!

SC: I still refer to Victor as my mentor because he had a profound effect on my playing and he was the one who encouraged me to move to New York City to pursue my career. His melodic and tasteful playing still inspires me to this day and I'm proud to call Victor a good friend. In 1988, I received a grant from the National Endowment for the Arts to study with a jazz master for one year. I chose to study with the great drummer and educator Keith Copeland. Keith really helped me to grow! He helped me develop my 4-way independence, time, technique, reading, soloing, comping, and so many other aspects of playing. He also gave me a long list of classic recordings to check out that helped me learn a lot about the lineage of the great jazz drummers. He was always so positive, encouraging, and supportive. He passed away too early and I miss him very much.

230

JG: Wow, you had some great mentors, for sure! Was there a specific moment where you realized you wanted to be a jazz musician?

SC: When I was in high school, I was really involved in sports as well as music. I started having conflicts between scheduling of sporting events and jazz band rehearsals and performances. Finally, my coach told me I had to choose one or the other. It was an easy decision for me to commit my time to pursuing music.

JG: What were some of the recordings or live concerts that you heard when you were coming up that inspired you?

SC: My father's jazz record collection included Wes Montgomery, Dizzy Gillespie, Bird, Sarah Vaughan, James Moody, and Illinois Jacquet. The recording I remember the most was a Max Roach/Clifford Brown record called *Live at Basin Street*. I especially loved how hard Max swung and his melodic soloing. I was intrigued and I started to listen to more jazz recordings and I even started my own record collection. I think it was around this time that I knew I wanted to pursue playing jazz as a career. I also received a lot of inspiration from an amazing local pianist named Smith Dobson. He was the house pianist at a San Jose club called Garden City. He would bring international jazz greats that would be on tour and passing through town. I would always sit right behind the drummer and be completely fascinated. I loved this music and I already knew this would be my life path. Eventually, I started sitting in on some performances and I would always get encouraging words from Smith which meant a lot to me.

JG: What were some of your important early gigs that helped you grow?

SC: My first real jazz gig was with the San Francisco based guitarist (who recently passed) named Eddie Duran. We played at a club called Jazz at Pearls in SF. Bassist Larry Grenadier was also on the gig. We were both very young and just starting out. Around the same time I also belonged to a group called NAYJE which stood for the North Area Youth Jazz Ensemble. It was a big band comprised of select players from the San Francisco Bay Area. We rehearsed regularly and performed challenging charts which helped me to develop my sight-reading chops.

JG: When did you come to New York?

SC: In my junior year at San Jose City College I started feeling like I needed to leave the Bay Area and spread my wings musically, but I wasn't sure where I was going. I applied and got accepted to Long Beach University in Southern California. But in the spring of 1985 I had a chance to visit New York. I went out every night and I was blown away by seeing so many of my heroes playing within a few blocks from each other. I knew that I needed to be here if I wanted to continue to grow as a musician. I went home and told my folks I wanted to try living in New York for a few months.

So, on August 22, 1985, I packed my suitcase and my drums, and boarded a non-stop flight on People's Express Airlines for $99 from San Jose to JFK. My entire family was in the Bay Area and when I moved I only knew two people in New York City. It was a bold move, but in my heart I was following my dream and I just knew it was the right move. Shortly after I got to New York City I went to hear Joe Henderson at the Village Vanguard. After the set I introduced myself to him. He remembered me from San Jose and asked for my number. Three weeks later he called me for a three and a half week European tour.

JG: Wow, great!

SC: It was my first time to Europe and I was so excited to be living my dream. And it confirmed for me that I'd made the right choice by moving to New York.

JG: Absolutely! Amazing to land a gig like that so soon after you'd arrived. So, I know that you played for many years with Clark Terry, one of my all-time favorites and heroes. Can you talk about what it was like playing with Clark?

SC: I first met Clark Terry when I sat in with his band at the Village Vanguard. He asked me for my number and two weeks later he started calling me for gigs with his quintet. I had no idea that sitting in that night would lead to a seventeen-year run which would profoundly change my life. The musicians in the group during the time I was there included Jessie Davis and Dave Glasser on alto, Stantawn Kendrick on tenor, John Campbell, Willie Pickens, Don Friedman and Helen Sung on piano, and Marcus McLaurine on bass. As part of his quintet we traveled extensively and performed at clubs, festivals, and jazz cruises around the world.

Through playing with CT I had the great opportunity to meet and perform with other jazz icons like Jimmy Heath, Frank Wess, Marian McPartland, Billy Taylor, Frank Foster, Al Grey, Red Holloway, Joe Williams, Dianne Reeves and so many others. Clark always believed in me and my playing and he affectionately gave me the nickname "Cuencs." He was kind, supportive, encouraging, and on the bandstand he would often turn around and smile and say, "Yeah, kick 'em in the ass, Cuencs!" Backstage we would usually gather around him while he would tell us his stories about working and traveling with jazz greats. He had a crazy sense of humor and would constantly have us rolling in laughter. I'll never forget those times! I learned so much from Clark on and off the bandstand. On the gig we would never know what tunes we were playing until he called them on the bandstand. But the first tune of every night was always an uptempo burner. Many times we'd rehearse new tunes but then he wouldn't call any of those tunes on the gig. It kept the band on our toes and we quickly learned to spontaneously adjust to all kinds of musical situations.

He'd love it when I would "chop wood" behind his solos. He said it made the time become very clear, like a camera coming into focus. He taught me the "River Boat Shuffle" groove, which was a very distinct groove that drummers would play during the swing era. I loved playing it during the set, especially behind his solos. I was amazed at Clark's level of consistency and how his clear, concise, joyful singing phrases were always locked in. He had such strong time!

JG: Oh, did he ever! He was incredible! There's this solo of Clark's on a Tadd Dameron tune called "Swift as the Wind" that I always play for my students to teach them about time.

SC: Yeah, he was amazing with that! And observing CT off the bandstand, I realized the importance of handling oneself with poise, dignity, and class. He also taught me the importance of staying positive in every situation. He calls it "reaching the plateau of positivity." These are all traits that I've tried to incorporate in my life, and I hope to pass on to future generations. He was generous with his wealth of information and he would reach out to all musicians who were willing to learn. CT was jazz royalty and an extraordinary human being. I've been so incredibly blessed to have had the opportunity to be mentored by and share the bandstand with this remarkable trumpet legend. I'm forever grateful for all he taught me about life and music and it was an honor to call him my dear friend.

JG: Wow, what a blessing to work with someone like Clark for all those years. So, who were some other artists that you worked with that were important to your growth and development?

SC: Definitely getting to play with Joe Henderson. When he asked for my number that time at the Vanguard soon after I got to New York I didn't really think I'd hear from him. A few weeks later some musician friends of mine told me that Joe was looking for me and he was going to call me! Soon after that I got a call. I thought it was a joke, but then I realized it was really was Joe! He called me for that European tour. That was my first time to Europe and it was one of the most incredible experiences of my life. I played with Joe for four years. Some of the sidemen/sidewomen were Renee Rosnes, Kim Clarke, Marlene Rosenberg, Aki Takase, Jim McNeely, Cecil Mcbee, Billy Childs, Tony Dumas, and Herbie Lewis. In a trio setting I played with Joe and Charlie Haden, and later with Joe and George Mraz. It was such a blessing to have had the opportunity to share the bandstand with these amazing artists.

Joe was very soft-spoken and a little shy. I've always thought of him as an introvert/intellectual. He was very worldly and spoke many different languages. After you got to know him, he would literally talk for hours on the phone about a variety of subjects that he was knowledgeable about. In person he would have occasional eye contact during a conversation and he would often look down but he would be listening to you intensely. He wasn't always serious. He had a great sense of humor and loved to joke around, laugh, and tell road stories. We toured and performed at various clubs, concerts, and festivals in the States and around the world. Most of the time he would let us interpret the music as we heard it. He wasn't the type of leader to give a lot of verbal direction, unless it had to do with a specific figure or arrangement. He would say, "Play what you mean and mean what you play!" He made me aware of the importance of playing with conviction. A lot of times he would give you a solo and then the whole band would just leave the stage and let you work out whatever you had to say musically. It was challenging but I felt it helped me to grow as a musician.

He also helped me to be mindful of the form of a song by constantly singing the melody in my head behind solos including my own. By playing with Joe I learned how to be a more sensitive and musical team player in a small group setting. We played a lot of standards on the gigs. But the band would never have a set list and the band never knew what we were going to play next. Sometimes he would have one-word cues for telling the band the next selection. He would just turn around and say "Lady B" for the Sam Rivers tune "Beatrice," or "Jin" for his tune "Jinrikisha," or "Isss" for "Isfahan" by Billy Strayhorn. Out of the tunes Joe wrote we played "Record-a-me," "Y Todavia La Quiero," "Isotope," "Shade of Jade," "Punjab," "Serenity," "Mode for Joe," "Our Thing," "Black Narcissus," "Gazelle," "Inner Urge," and many other great tunes.

JG: Yeah, Joe was so heavy! Just a genius, and one of my heroes. So, what are some of the musical experiences you've been most proud of or inspired by?

SC: In 1992, I was semi-finalist in the International Jazz Drum Competition. The judges that we performed in front of were Alan Dawson, Roy Haynes, Ed Shaughnessy, Jeff "Tain" Watts, and Dave Weckl. Although I didn't make it to the finals, it was still an incredibly inspiring experience. Another time, one night in 2002, I was at home and I got a phone call from trumpet player EJ Allen. He said their drummer didn't show for a Frank Foster Loud Minority Big Band gig and he asked me if I could get down to the Jazz Standard. I said, "Sure, when?" He said, "Now!!!" I said, "I'm on my way!" I loaded my drums in my pickup truck and drove as fast as could to the gig. When I got to the club the whole big band was already on stage and everyone was waiting for me to get set up and play. They handed me the drum book and next thing I know Frank Foster was counting off a tune. Foster was a prolific composer and his charts were extremely challenging and not easy to sight-read. I did my best and it wasn't perfect but I'm proud of the job I did of sight reading under extreme pressure in front of a live audience.

After the first night Foster asked me to stay the rest of the week and be on their live recording on the weekend. I was floored… the great Frank Foster hired me to record a live record with his charts and his Loud Minority Big Band. I learned that you always have to be ready for anything in New York. It was an incredible experience and I'm forever grateful for Mr. Foster putting his trust in me.

JG: Yeah, Frank was amazing, what a great experience!

SC: Yeah, very thankful for that. Another experience that I'm proud of is being asked to play with Albert "Tootie" Heath's four drummer group called The Whole Drum Truth which also featured drum greats Louis Hayes and Joe Saylor. The group consisted of only four drum sets. There were no other musicians on stage with us. We rehearsed the arrangements for several weeks and everyone had a chance to be featured. We performed at Dizzy's Jazz Club and the Kennedy Center in Washington, DC. It was such an honor to be invited to play alongside these accomplished musicians.

One other experience which was very inspiring was being invited by Kenny Barron to tour Korea and Japan with an all-star quartet which included Michael Brecker and Ray Drummond. It was a dream come true to be able to share the stage with some of my jazz heroes. After the gigs in Japan we would often hang out at a club to either have dinner or sit in with some local musicians. One night, Michael Brecker sat in on drums and he was really dealing! He got a great sound and he obviously knew the language on the kit. I had no idea he played so well. I had an amazing time on the road with this band, and they were always very kind and supportive. After this tour Kenny asked me to play the Havana Jazz Festival in Cuba but I was already booked to play Clark Terry's 75th birthday celebration gig. I was so disappointed I didn't make it to Cuba with him. But Kenny respected my loyalty to Clark and he said he would always remember that.

JG: Wow, what a great learning experience. I actually got to play with Michael on drums one time, and yeah, he sounded great! I only got to play with Kenny a couple times, and what a thrill! Such a master. And I went to school with his son Nile. What are some more recent projects that you've done, and what are some upcoming projects?

SC: Last year I was invited to be a featured artist on a tour in Israel. It was my first time to Israel and the project was a tribute to Max Roach, one of my main influences. Alto saxophonist Justin Robinson, pianist Tamir Hendelman, and I collaborated with Israeli musicians including another drummer named Shay Zelman. We played music from the recordings of the Max Roach/Clifford Brown quintet, like "Crackle Hut," "The Scene is Clean," "Gerkin for Perkin," "Parisian Thoroughfare," "Joy Spring," "Daahoud," to name a few. We worked out arrangements for the two-drummer ensemble and figured out how to keep it interesting by alternating comping behind different soloists and included a lot of solo exchanges between both of us. It was such a blast playing these tunes that I've always loved, and it was incredible to get a chance to play them with these exceptional musicians. It was an experience both musically and culturally that I will never forget. I hope to return there in the future.

JG: Yeah, Justin is an old friend and a great player. He and I also went to high school together at Performing Arts.

SC: Recently, I've been leading an organ quartet or quintet in New York City. The trio has been together a long time and includes organist Jared Gold and guitarist Paul Bollenback. The front line changes from time to time, but lately I usually try to get tenor saxophonist Ralph Bowen. And if it's a quintet gig I try to add trumpeter Freddie Hendrix. I was planning on recording the group sometime this year, but now it'll have to be postponed 'til this pandemic is over. My quartet with Bowen just played a weekend at Smalls in New York City in February. Another group I've been working with for a few years now is a trio with guitarist Roni Ben-Hur and bassist Harvie S. We were in the middle of recording a CD right when the pandemic hit. We're planning on completing the recording in the fall.

This trio gives me an outlet to develop my Brazilian playing as well as my straight-ahead playing. I've been listening to Brazilian music for many years now and I've been fortunate to study privately with legendary drummer Portinho. I try to catch him every chance I get in New York. He still continues to inspire me every time I hear him. Like other musicians I had so many gigs that got canceled because of the pandemic. One gig I had in my book was with the great pianist Geoffrey Keezer's group with vocalist Gillian Margot at Bach, at the Dancing and Dynamite Society in Half Moon Bay, California. It's been rescheduled to November and I'm looking forward to playing Geoffrey's beautiful originals and arrangements.

JG: Yeah, Geoff's an amazing musician. And those groups and projects sound great! I look forward to hearing them. Well, hopefully things will be getting back to normal soon and we'll be able to hang and play again soon! Thanks so much for doing this Sylvia!

SC: Thanks, my pleasure.

Harold Mabern & Gene Bertoncini
New York City/New Jersey – January 2019

In late January 2019, I was asked to do some teaching at William Paterson University's jazz program, to sub for my friend Bill Charlap, who's the director of jazz studies there. I was back in New York from Winnipeg for a couple of days so it worked with my schedule. I'd been to the school to play or teach many times in the 25 years or so before. But I'd never taken the bus there. So, I went to the Port Authority Bus terminal, found the area to wait for the bus to take me there, and who do I see sitting there waiting? Harold Mabern! I met and got to know Harold from his support of Bill Mobley's Big Band. From the mid '90s on, Harold would show up at our gigs and clap loudly and shout, "Y'all a bunch a' harmonic geniuses!" at the end of the set. This coming from such an incredible pianist and part of the history of the music! He even had recorded with us and Bill Mobley's band on a couple of projects that featured James Williams, Mulgrew Miller, Donald Brown, Billy Pierce, Harold, and other brilliant musicians and close friends of Mobley's.

Harold had always been friendly, kind, and supportive. He was always that way to everyone! But that day, we got to talk for about two hours, between waiting for the bus, the ride itself, and then walking to the music building. The stories! Memphis, Lee Morgan, the people he'd played with… One of the most striking lessons I took from that day, was that Harold had been doing this commute for almost forty years! Doing this teaching gig had allowed him to pay his bills and have benefits for all that time. And in fact, he lived way out in Brooklyn, and took mass transit to get there. So, it took him 3–4 hours each way to do this! It was a fourteen-plus hour day, at least. But often, after teaching, even into his eighties, he'd go back into Manhattan and hang out and hear music and support musicians he knew. The dedication and humility that he had was so inspiring! I never saw him when he wasn't smiling. I was so thankful to hang with him for those couple of hours.

I taught for several hours that day, and between classes I ran into Gene Bertoncini. Gene is just a gem of a musician and person, and a brilliant and lyrical guitarist. I got to know Gene from playing with him at the Jazz Nativity in the early '90s. We also did a number of other gigs together over the years. He's just the nicest, most laid-back guy, and one of the most tasteful musicians you'd ever want to work with. One other thing about Gene—I noticed that any time he and Ron Carter were around each other Ron would just seem to start cracking up immediately! I saw it happen several times. They must have some great old jokes from various gigs or the studio days, but Gene just had a knack for making Ron laugh! He told me that he taught guitar at City College when Ron was the head of that program, and that Ron got him hired for that.

That day when I ran into Gene in the hallway, he said, "Hey Jon, good to see ya. How ya gettin' back in the city? You wanna lift later?" I said, "Sure Gene, that'd be great, thanks!" So, we ended around the same time, talked with some students at the end of the day, and walked out to the parking lot to his car. He put some music on the car stereo, and we went for a leisurely drive back towards the city. After a few minutes he said, "Hey, you wanna grab a coffee?" I said, "Sure!" We stopped at a cafe somewhere near the school, sat and talked about music, and had a great ninety minutes or so before we were back in New York City. Gene's another one with incredible stories! He talked about how we used to play with Clark Terry at the Jazz Nativity. He also mentioned how he and Clark sat next to each other for two years at the *Tonight Show with Johnny Carson*, before the show moved to L.A. in the early '70s. Gene stayed in New York, because, as he said, "That's where my heart is. That's where the heart of the music is! With guys like Clark, Ron Carter, Grady Tate, what else do you need?"

He talked about doing an album with Nancy Wilson, Hank Jones, Ron Carter, and Grady Tate. He said, "How's that for an afternoon? That was a great album!" He mentioned his days in the New York studio scene and getting to record with guys as diverse as Sonny Stitt, Hubert Laws, and Burt Bacharach among hundreds of others. He told me that he'd gotten a degree in architecture in college, and soon after that he worked for a short time with the architect David Henkin, a protégé of Frank Lloyd Wright. David had designed Rudy Van Gelder's studio. Later when Gene recorded at Rudy's he realized they had a friend in common in David. He also said that he found that the study of architecture was very helpful for his guitar playing. The idea of planning and coming up with a concept was helpful in thinking about music, and the audience, and just thinking with that kind of structure.

Man, between those two guys, on that day, I just felt so blessed to be a part of this music and be around some of that energy, history, and the amazing music that they've been a part of.

Mike LeDonne

New York City – June, 2020

JG: So, Mike, where did you grow up?

ML: Bridgeport, Connecticut.

JG: Is there a family connection for you to music?

ML: Yes, my father, Mickey LeDonne, was a jazz guitarist who was very influenced by the guitarist that played in the Nat Cole trio, Oscar Moore. My dad could also sing and sounded like Nat. He won the *Major Bowes Amateur Hour*, which was a radio version of *America's Got Talent* back in the '30s, when he was seventeen. He got a record deal, moved to New York, and started touring with his trio. They recorded and made film shorts. Then he met my mother, Marion, who didn't like him being away so much, so it all came to an end. But honestly, he never liked the road life either, so they settled in Bridgeport and eventually our house got turned into a music store and teaching studio. LeDonne's Music Box is where I grew up. He would work 9 a.m. to 9 p.m. at the store and then go right to his steady gig to play five nights a week with his trio. He was a local star and everyone in Bridgeport knew and loved him. So the store became a hang for local musicians. There was always a case of beer in the fridge in the back and plenty of guitars and amps set up to try out and jam.

JG: Is that how you got started playing and appreciating music?

ML: Well, when I was five years old I started imitating these boogie-woogie records that my father had, by ear on the piano. After school each day I went to the music store and had access to every instrument there was. I'd spend my day going from one to the other just fooling around and having fun. We also sold records and record players, so I got into listening to the latest 45s. By the time I was ten I had my first band. I played organ and sang along with a guitarist and drummer. We played the R&B hits of the day by James Brown, Marvin Gaye, Wilson Picket, and Sam and Dave. I played the bass lines in my left hand, the horn parts in my right. We'd rehearse down in the basement of the store and keep the windows open so the kids in the neighborhood could come by and dance outside. That's what really hooked me and made me want to play music for the rest of my life. We eventually got good enough so my dad could start booking us some gigs.

JG: What a great start! Was there a teacher that was important for you?

ML: My dad was one of the most important influences on my growth early on. He'd show me chords and we'd play together all the time. Not only was he a great player but he had all the records that I grew up on by Miles Davis, Art Tatum, John Coltrane, Wes Montgomery, and all the cats. Then came Jaki Byard when I went to school at New England Conservatory. I was so blessed to be under his guidance for four full years and learned so much from him. I'm forever indebted to him. What a funny guy and crazy genius he was. He could play anything from stride to bebop and avant-garde, and everything he played swung. Most of all he was a warm and genuine human being who didn't stand for any BS, and I loved him. When I moved to New York City. I used to go to Barry Harris' class and I learned so much from him in only about six classes that it was life changing. To me he found the way to explain the complexities of bebop harmony that was both easy to understand and as undeniable as two plus two equals four. I found myself always thinking "Oh, so *that's* what that is! I still use his general concept of teaching harmony when I teach today.

There was another teacher I had in New York City that was very important to me because, after all my schooling in classical music from both Manhattan School of Music Prep as a teen and New England Conservatory for college, this man really showed me how to play the piano. All of my classical studies up until that point were focused on playing all the notes on the page. But Nicholas "Rod" Rodriguez showed me all the nuance of touch involved in getting the music to come off the page. He wasn't really a jazz pianist like Barry Harris, but he did play in jazz groups with Louis Armstrong, Don Redman, and Benny Carter. He said he was the only pianist ever to sub for Jelly Roll Morton. His parents sent him to America from Panama as a young man to learn dentistry, but he took their money and enrolled in Juilliard. He not only knew how to get all the subtleties of sound out of the instrument but his approach to teaching technique was as clear cut as Barry's approach to teaching harmony and it was a life changer for me. I still use his method as my model when I teach piano technique today.

JG: What were the recordings that were important to you early on?

ML: When I was about eight years old I used to hear a record of my father's called *Miles Davis in Person* which was recorded live at the Blackhawk. It had Hank Mobley, Wynton Kelly, Paul Chambers, and Jimmy Cobb along with Miles on it. He used to play it all the time when we had parties and I found myself always standing right in front of the speakers mesmerized when it would come on. In particular, Wynton Kelly's playing filled me with an electric energy that until then I had only been getting from James Brown. I wasn't big into jazz yet but I knew that I wanted to do what Wynton Kelly was doing and I wanted to get that feeling he got with PC and Jimmy Cobb.

At the same time my older sister happened to have a record of Jimmy Smith's called *Live at The Village Gate* and it had a cool cover that I liked to look at and a tune called "I Got a Woman." That track hooked me because I had never heard anyone get those sounds out of an organ before. By the time I was ten I had an organ and a Leslie speaker, but it wasn't a Hammond. Finally, by the time I was fourteen I found a Hammond B3 and a Leslie speaker for sale as part of a repossession sale in the newspaper and begged my father to buy it. He did and it went right into our basement. I put the record player next to it and got started trying to figure out what those sounds were that Jimmy Smith was getting.

JG: Wow. Yeah, Miles *Live at the Blackhawk* was really important for me too. What were some of your important early gigs that helped you to grow?

ML: Well, there were the R&B gigs I mentioned earlier when I was a kid. They were really monumental in my growth because I got to just really enjoy playing music. But I also had to keep it together because we were playing in front of people. When I was fourteen I met a bunch of older musicians in their twenties that taught at my father's music store. They all lived in the same house together in Bridgeport and invited me over one afternoon. They had all their gear set up in the basement, which included a B3 and a beautiful sounding Fender Rhodes. They were deep into funk and had a Tower of Power style horn band together. I started going there to jam every day and eventually joined the band. That's when I got into the great Chester Thompson who's a great organ player and the greatest funk organ player I ever heard. I got to see him play live with Tower of Power a few times, which were the most exciting concerts I'd ever seen. I spent most of my high school years playing with this funk band in clubs all over the place and it gave me the opportunity to see what it was like to be a professional musician and get my feet firmly planted in funky grooves. Eventually the bass player got an acoustic bass and we started trying to play jazz together and I started to change gears.

JG: When did you come to New York?

ML: A friend of mine named Michael Hashim was playing alto in a ten-piece band, named Widespread Depression, that played music by the Black bands of the big band era like Duke Ellington, Fletcher Henderson, Jimmie Lunceford, Earl Hines, Count Basie, and Louis Jordan. I was about to finish my last year at NEC. They were getting ready to move to New York City and needed a piano player, so I joined and moved with them. It was a great way to move because the bandleader had worked out a way of paying a salary whether the band worked or not. It was only $120 a week but that's what my rent was per month in 1978, so it was perfect! The idea of a big band of young musicians playing music from an older era hadn't really been done before, so we became pretty popular. What we lacked in depth we made up for in spirit. We had so much fun in that band and we worked constantly. It gave me a deep understanding and appreciation of all that music and set me up for many of the experiences that would be coming my way later.

I remember the first time I met Milt Jackson was when he came to hear us one night at a club in the Village. He even sat in with us because we had a vibes player. We used to go to Europe every summer and do the festival circuit, and we had a full week at the Molde Jazz Festival. The MJQ was also there all week and I remember being surprised to see Milt Jackson and John Lewis come in every night to hear us. They just really loved all that music and were excited to see some young musicians really trying to play it. One of the greatest things that ever happened to me was one night at the Wolf Trap Jazz Festival when we opened for the great Count Basie Orchestra. We played our set and went to the dressing room and a man came in asking who the piano player was. I told him it was me and he said Count Basie wanted to speak to me. I followed him out of the dressing room and was shocked to see Count Basie sitting there on his scooter waiting for me. I'll never forget it! He asked me if that was me on the piano, and I said yes. Then he smiled at me, shook my hand and said, "Nice solos." I was dumbfounded and told him I was just trying to sound like him. He said keep it up and drove off on his scooter. I was high on that for weeks.

JG: Wow, amazing! You've been around and played with as many of the masters of this music as anyone I know. Can you talk about that some?

ML: Widespread played opposite a band called Panama Francis and the Savoy Sultans at the Bottom Line one night. Well, the contrast was striking because we were a ten-piece band of young white kids in our twenties and they were a ten-piece band of seasoned Black musicians in their seventies. They kicked our asses, of course, and we couldn't believe how beautiful they sounded and how deep their swing was. The next day my phone rang and it was Panama asking me to join his band. I almost fell over, but, trying to act cool, I said, "Sure!" This band was made up of what you call the real cats. Each musician was part of the history so all the stories they told me were coming right from the horse's mouth. They had a very Basie-like vibe in the rhythm section with a deep swing that sounded very smooth and easy going, but they could also light it up on the fast tempos. I learned a lot from all these wonderful players and people in the six months I stayed with the band. They would do these long stints at the Rainbow Room in Manhattan, which was a very long and grueling society dance gig which I hated so I left. I was playing mostly traditional gigs during this period with older musicians like Roy Eldridge, Ruby Braff, Buddy Tate, Al Grey, Eddie Locke, and Scott Hamilton who was my age. Scott and his band were all close friends of mine and had been playing some dates with Benny Goodman. They told him about me and one morning out of the blue my phone rang, and it was Benny asking me to come right over to his apartment and play for him! I gathered my courage and went. We played for almost two hours. Later that day, his secretary called and said Benny was very excited about my playing and would like me to join his band.

JG: Wow!

ML: So I found myself playing in both his sextet and quartet. Benny was a strange human being and I was never that into him in my youth, until I got to sit right there on the bandstand with him and experience his ferocious abilities up close and personal. I played in his band for a year until he had his aneurysm and had to stop playing for a while. He was a strange bird, but overall he liked me and gave me my first truly big time gig. Everybody knows who Benny Goodman was. In 1988 I got a chance to work in two bands that would establish me in the more contemporary world, the Art Farmer/Clifford Jordan Quintet and the Milt Jackson Quartet. I stayed with Art Farmer for a year and became close with Clifford Jordan who I had a ton of fun with but who also schooled me about how to act on the bandstand. When I first joined the band I would solo until I was done, which could get a little lengthy. One night after the gig Clifford took me aside and told me that some of my solos had been longer than Art's, and since I was only a sideman I should stay aware of that and make sure my solos were shorter than the leader's. I immediately saw his point and learned a lesson that I kept with me for the rest of my life. If we were alone in a room with a piano he'd say, "Go play me some boogie-woogie," which he knew I could do because of my background, but I always thought he was kidding with me.

Then one night we were hanging at his apartment in New York City and he started playing all these old blues records and told me how much he loved that music. That surprised me because to me he was one of the hippest players I ever heard. He explained to me why knowing the history of the music was so important. He was into numerology and he asked me what the most important numbers of all were. He told me zero and one were the most important. To demonstrate why, he pointed out that zero is a circle representing "the whole of something." He said the truth found in zero and one is that the more you know about the "whole" of something the better the one thing you eventually get to will be. This hit me hard because, even though I would have loved to have been playing with Art Blakey and people like that early in my life, my musical journey had been steeped in the history of this music and he helped me realize that I was actually on a great path.

My stay with Milt Jackson was one of the greatest blessings of my life. He, Bob Cranshaw, and Mickey Roker accepted me with open arms and never let go. We truly were a family and we stayed together for eleven years until Milt's passing in 1999. Bags never told me a thing about how or what to play. It was understood that if you weren't able to do the right thing you wouldn't be there. His quartet with Cedar Walton on piano had been my favorite for years, so getting to play in it was my dream come true. Bags had this incredible focus when he played. His head was bent slightly downward and his eyes were fixed on the bars as his arms came down from pretty high up and with a lot of force, but when the mallet struck it produced this relaxed warm beautiful sound. His rhythm came from his whole body, so his arms looked like they were dancing over the vibes, and his rhythm and time were impeccable. Deeply swinging and soulful, Bags would bring down the house with a ballad. Being up there with that level of mastery every night for eleven years does something to you that can't be learned in a school.

At first, I found it hard to talk to him because I was so in awe of him, but after a couple of years we became very close friends. By the end I was the musical director of the band, so I called all the sets and wrote all the arrangements. Never did he not like what I came up with. I got to know him in and out and even though he was a genius he was actually a very simple dude. He loved playing music, he loved the blues, he liked playing cards and pool, and baking pies. He didn't pretend to be anything but who he was and he hated pretentious people. All soul and truth. I always felt honored to get to be that close to a genius like him.

It was because of performing in that band that Oscar Peterson got to hear me one afternoon on a Jazz Cruise dedicated to him. Luckily, I didn't know he was there listening. After the set bassist Milt Hinton came over to me and pointed to the back of the room and told me to go speak to Oscar who was sitting there in his motorized wheelchair. He was so incredibly flattering to me it caught me off guard because I had always heard about what a beast he was on the bandstand. We became good friends and, even though he was undoubtedly a beast on the piano, he was a very kind, gentle, and giving human being.

While playing in Milt Jackson's quintet I received an invitation, through our bass player Bob Cranshaw, to audition for Sonny Rollins. Bob had been with Sonny for decades and was frustrated at not having a pianist for a few years, so he insisted Sonny try out some piano players. I was the first pianist to arrive at S.I.R studios in Manhattan and Sonny was there with his rhythm section ready to play. This was an amazing day because it tied my whole musical experience—up until that point—together in the first five minutes of the audition. Sonny was a man of few words so he just went into a very obscure tune that was also a very old song called "Little Coquette" in D♭. Since I had been through all the traditional gigs I knew the tune well so I came right in and Sonny looked at me and winked while he was playing which put me right at ease. I wound up getting the gig and stayed with Sonny for about four months.

I would have stayed longer but Milt Jackson was working so much in those days I couldn't do both gigs and Sonny wanted someone dedicated to his gig so I bowed out. One thing that I will never forget about Sonny is that he would often warm up by playing Coleman Hawkins solo from "Body and Soul" note for note. He would play it but he wouldn't try to sound like Hawk, he would sound like himself and the amount of expression he put into it showed how deeply affected he was by it. He would really sing out the notes as if he were making it up right there on the spot. That kind of respect for an older master was moving to me and something I did not expect from such a bebop icon. I will never forget being on the bandstand with Sonny. He was the only musician that I played with who actually scared me. Not with his personality but with the passion and sound he played with. He was a very sweet and cool man to talk to but sometimes I could feel my legs actually shaking under the piano from the ferociousness he brought to the bandstand. He would play a ballad and send chills down my spine with his first phrase.

Around this time, I received a call to play in a huge project put together by Slide Hampton that included a big band and a choir. The big band was a who's who of jazz. The rhythm section was Ron Carter on bass and one of my best friends in the world, Kenny Washington. During a break at the rehearsal I wound up talking to this extremely elegant and sweet man who I didn't know, so in the middle of our talk I introduced myself to him and he said, "Mike LeDonne, oh yes, I have your record, you're burning." I thanked him and asked him his name and was shocked when he said, Benny Golson. After the concert he came over to me and said, "I'm going to remember your talent." Then one day about a year later I answered the phone and I hear a voice say, "I told you I'd remember your talent. I want you to record with me in a couple of weeks." It was Benny Golson! Benny Golson is my heart. Right from the start he was so encouraging to me I didn't know if he was putting me on or being for real. His encouragement was meant to give me the confidence to try anything I could think of when we played together. He was always overjoyed to hear something he didn't expect, and it was such a pleasure to be able to make him happy. I was always pushing myself to come up with new things. My first trip to Europe with him also included Curtis Fuller on trombone.

Meeting Curtis was another big blessing in my life. We hit it off right away and remained friends for all these years. We continued working together until a few years ago when his health started to fail. Benny Golson and I have been together for over twenty years now and I have him to thank for opening me up and giving me the confidence to just play. I learned that it didn't matter if I was playing too much or too little or too modern or whatever, just get out of the way and let the music come out. Sometimes I would get self-conscious about possibly having gone too far and I would ask Benny what he thought. He told me that my playing was an expression of who and what I am and as long as I was being true to myself all was good.

While playing with Milt Jackson I got to meet Bobby Hutcherson who was doing a two-vibes gig with us at the Jazz Baltica Festival in Germany. Bobby was another hero of mine so I was nervous about meeting him. To my surprise, he was the one who was nervous when I met him in the lobby before leaving for the gig. He was nervous because he was about to play with his idol, Milt Jackson. He was such a down to earth and funny guy I immediately felt comfortable talking to him. Milt hadn't come downstairs yet, so Bobby and I had a chance to talk about how he was feeling and I remember him looking at me and saying, "Milt Jackson, *wow!*" He told me about discovering Milt in his youth and how it made him feel to hear him play. He put on a big smile and said, "Hearing Bags always made me feel like I had money in my pocket." After Bags passed in 1999 I had the pleasure of getting to work in Bobby's group off and on. Bobby was like Golson, always encouraging and thrilled at what you were doing. These guys made you feel like you were the heavy weight and they were the fans.

I also did a series of trio gigs at Smoke Jazz Club with Ron Carter and Joe Farnsworth over a period of about ten years. I had met Ron during the same gig I met Benny Golson. Not long after that concert I had a weeklong engagement with my quintet at a club in the Village called Sweet Basil and the bass player, Ray Drummond, couldn't make the weekend. Ron had been very nice to me at the concert we did with Slide Hampton, so I thought, let me call Ron and see if he'll do it. Sure enough he was up for it and we began our long relationship of both playing together and being friends. I always loved his playing, as everyone does, but playing with him is a very unique experience. He has all the swing and feeling that place him in the very top level as a bass player, but he also has this uncanny ability to get inside your mind and think right along with you. Just when you play something that may imply a different chord sequence than the original, Ron starts playing the perfect bass notes to make that new sequence sound even hipper. We've recorded together and continue to play together.

My first leader gig at Dizzy's Club a few years back was with Ron Carter and Jimmy Cobb. Only in New York City can you do that. I also started playing with tenor sax giant George Coleman about ten years ago. Big G has become one of my very best friends and I love him to death. George is truly a harmonic genius and he's still coming up with new things all the time. His way of placing fourths into lines is uniquely his own and he has tons of new chord sequences to place over standard tunes. I've played both organ and piano with him and I always start practicing every standard I know through the keys because that's what he's always doing. Any tune in any key at any tempo is a prerequisite for being able to survive a gig with him. He doesn't do it to be mean or hard to work with, it's simply what he does and if he hires you it's because he knows you can do it too. This is how genius raises the level of the musicians around them. It's sink or swim.

There are so many artists that were important to my growth and development. Drummer extraordinaire Eddie Locke. Eddie was truly family to me. We were so close he used to come over to my mother's house in Connecticut for Sunday dinner and my whole family fell in love with him. We met back in my Jimmy Ryan's days in the '80s and we talked to each other almost every day until he passed away in 2009. He was a larger than life personality that was super hip, street smart, and very, very wise. He'd played for years with Roy Eldridge, Coleman Hawkins, and many other jazz greats because of one thing, he could really swing and light the bandstand up. He had a cymbal beat like Kenny Clarke, a shuffle like Art Blakey, and could play brushes like Papa Jo Jones. I was so lucky to get to feel that swing every night for years. But it was his wisdom about life that was also very important to how I developed as a human being. He taught me not to take life so seriously and to be serious about music but above all to enjoy playing. He always preached to me about playing *for* the people and not *at* the people, and above all to be a good human being.

Harold Mabern came into my life a little later during my Bradley's years. He was a giant of music but a truly humble human being. When I was nobody he would come and listen to me all night and always keep yelling "Yeah Donski!" Nobody could rock the house like Mabern. I got addicted to his musical energy and every time he played I would be there getting my dose of that feeling and rhythm. He played a deep kind of blues like Bobby Timmons but also had a modern conception like McCoy Tyner. Getting to actually witness someone playing that kind of modern power piano style all the time had a profound influence on me. He enabled me to see that you could speak that language and not be a clone of McCoy. Mabes and I became the best of friends and I adored him. He was extremely underrated but never bitter. Always "giving it up" to cats that could really play. He would send me video clips of some new young kid playing his butt off and we would talk about music and life all the time. His lack of envy and jealousy was a lesson to everyone around him. I took full advantage of those lessons and I was very lucky to be close with both of these great human beings and musicians.

James Williams and I went way back to my Boston days. I went to New England Conservatory and he was over at Berklee. He was a little older than me and I used to go see him play at local jazz clubs. He was already a great and soulful player with a unique harmonic gift and a talented composer. After I moved to New York, James used to come by my place and we'd hang and listen to records together and talk about music. One day when he was leaving, he told me if he could ever do anything to help me in my career he would. Now, a lot of people say things like that but very, very few ever follow through.

A few years later I got a call from James and he told me he needed a sub to play with Art Farmer and Clifford Jordan. Of course there would be no rehearsal, so he also sent me the music and some tapes of their gigs so I could study up and be prepared, which really touched me. Not only was he handing me this prime opportunity, but he was giving me every chance to succeed. That is not what most people do when they call you to sub. Not too long after that he got in touch again and said he needed me to sub on another gig and this time it was with Milt Jackson! He did the same thing sending me music and tapes of their gigs, and giving me set lists so I could be as prepared as possible.

I already mentioned my tenure with these two great bands and how important they were to me. My time with Milt Jackson's quartet might just be *the* greatest thing to ever happen to me and if it hadn't been for my dear friend James Williams I would have never had that chance. That's the kind of great human being he was and how important he was to my musical life.

JG: Oh man, James was the best! A great musician and such a great person.

ML Yeah. He knew I'd been playing mainly traditional gigs but that my heart was in the kind of music Milt Jackson played, so he opened that door for me and it was life-altering. We stayed good friends until his untimely death in 2004.

I would be remiss if I didn't mention someone who is truly my brother, Kenny Washington. K Wash is not only a true master of the drums, but he has a rare and scholarly knowledge of this music that he didn't learn through studying history books but from a genuine passion for listening to the music. He has both a ridiculous memory and perfect pitch which gives him an encyclopedic knowledge of not only the history but the music itself.

I was introduced to him by Hank Jones one night at the Village Vanguard. Hank was someone I idolized and used to follow around like a puppy dog, so we got to be friendly. I would talk to him during his breaks and one night I was asking him about a recording he was on and he said, "Come with me there's someone I want you to meet." He took me straight over to Kenny and introduced us. Next thing I know I'm going out to Kenny's place in Brooklyn armed with a box of tapes—thirty cassettes in those days. I would arrive at 10 a.m. and leave after dark and every tape would be full of Hank Jones and other masters. Kenny would look at me and say, "Hey man, have you ever heard… ?" I'd say no and he'd pull a nugget of pure gold out of his ridiculous record collection and commit it to tape for me. When I would leave it felt like Christmas morning. We'd be so into listening we wouldn't even talk to each other.

What really impressed me was when he'd start talking about someone's solo and then start singing it. He'd put the record on right afterwards and not only had he sung it note for note but he sang it in the same key as the record! He turned me on to so much incredible music I don't know where I'd be without him. He started to come over to my house and play and we got to be closer friends. He's the one that brought Criss Cross Records owner Gerry Teekens over to hear me play live one night which resulted in my first recording as a leader.

Later we worked in Milt Jackson's quartet together. We'd be playing on location somewhere, like Boston, get up early in the morning, head out the door and be on the bus to the first of many record stores by 10 a.m. All day long Kenny would be pulling out these rare and great recordings by all kinds of people I might have passed right over and he'd say, "Buy this." We'd get back to the hotel about a half hour before hit time with a suitcase full of records. Now I have an incredible record collection thanks to him which is something that not only enriched my ears and my brain but my whole life. Another unique thing about Kenny is that he wouldn't just recommend me for gigs, he'd put on his stank face about everyone else that was mentioned and insist that they hire me.

JG: Ha! I think I know that look!

ML: He's the one that insisted I be the piano player for the Philip Morris world tour I did in '92 which was without a doubt the greatest tour I ever did. Big bucks and first class everything. He was the best man at my wedding and I was the best man at his. Hank Jones really had no idea what a huge favor he did me when he introduced me to Kenny Washington. One of the best friends I ever had or will ever have and one of the greatest drummers I've ever played with.

JG: Yeah, Kenny's such an amazing contributor to the music! And one of the all-time great jazz DJ's! I still miss him on WBGO. We grew up in the same neighborhood on Staten Island, Stapleton, though some years apart. We went to some of the same schools and had some friends in common. And what he did for you, get you on Criss Cross, you did for me! By recommending me to Teekens, and hiring me for the recording "Soulmates" that Kenny produced, by the way. I got to know you through Eddie Locke, and I feel the same way about him as you. And Mabern is one of my favorite musicians that I ever got to meet! Consistently positive, supportive, and inspiring. So, what are some of the musical experiences you've been most proud of or inspired by?

ML: The musical experiences that inspire me are not really about playing big time concerts but about moving people through the music I play no matter where that happens. The kind of communication music creates between complete strangers is what I find most inspiring.

There were many experiences like this throughout my career but one in particular stands out. It was in 1999 after Milt Jackson passed that I asked George Wein if I could produce a memorial concert as part of his New York jazz festival which I think was called the Kool Jazz Festival at the time. He liked the idea and funded the concert to be held at Symphony Space and included Slide Hampton, Jimmy Heath, Jon Faddis, Steve Nelson, Bob Cranshaw, Mickey Roker, Etta Jones, Stanley Turrentine, John Lewis, and yours truly. I wrote out some sextet arrangement of Bags' music for the first half that featured Jimmy Heath, Slide Hampton, Jon Faddis, and Steve Nelson with the rhythm section. John Lewis came out and played a solo piano set and then we closed with Stanley Turrentine and Etta Jones with Bob, Mickey, and me. At the end of that set we played "Bags Groove" and the music went up to the highest level. When Bob and Mickey heard Stanley T. playing on that medium blues the swing went to another level and the whole place started to lift off. Etta Jones is not known for scat singing but next thing I know she's tapping me on the shoulder asking if she could get a piece of this. She went out and started singing and Stanley kept playing and the roof literally lifted off the place. It was a church experience and everyone in that place was charged with the light. I felt like I was elevating off the piano and Mickey and Bob were smiling from ear to ear. I know Bags was there smiling too.

The sad thing is, it was supposed to have been recorded by NPR but at the last minute they decided they needed to record a classical concert instead. I was walking on a cloud for days after that. Weeks after the concert I would be walking on the Upper West Side where Symphony Space is and strangers who had been there would come over to me on the street and tell me they had been there and how heavy it was. That's inspiring!!

JG: Wow! What an amazing night! So, what are some recent projects that you've been involved in, and what are some upcoming projects?

ML: I did a West Coast tour last fall with my organ band, The Groover Quartet with Eric Alexander, Peter Bernstein, and Joe Farnsworth. It's very satisfying that people are reaching out to me to bring this band to festivals all over the world that I really had no access to previously as a leader. It shows me that my conception for the group worked. This is also why I've been able to keep a steady gig in New York City at Smoke for twenty years. The concept was to make people-friendly music that is both soulful and fun to listen to but also challenging and unique. The foundation of the music is swing and blues which may not sound very unique, but in this time of academia-influenced original music made for critics, a band that swings and plays for the people stands out as unique.

I decided early on that I didn't want to only appeal to old jazz fans, but I wanted to bring the music to young people. But I didn't want to do it by adding pop beats to jazz tunes. Instead I added swing to pop tunes which was something I used to hear organist Charles Earland do. I went back into the tunes and bands I grew up with like Stevie Wonder, Earth, Wind & Fire,

The Spinners, and The O'Jays and started looking for tunes that could swing. I rearrange the tunes, find a form and chord changes that challenge the musicians, but have melodies that younger people recognize. The result has been fun and inspiring. As I said I get most inspired when people are moved by, and move to, the music, and The Groover Quartet is made for that. We can play anywhere, whether it's a large concert or a small club, and light a fire because we're a real band that's like a family and it shows. We get to have a ball playing and the people get to hear tunes they know in a way they never heard them before.

As far as new projects, I just released a piano trio recording with Christian McBride and Lewis Nash that we did at Rudy Van Gelder's studio. The three of us were part of a world tour back in 1992 sponsored by Philip Morris. We went out for almost two months and traveled all over Europe, the Middle East, and Asia. We never recorded together after that, so I decided to finally document that trio and the result was a recording that stayed at number one for five weeks. My newest project is a recording that adds a big band to the Groover Quartet. We also did this at Rudy Van Gelder's but, unfortunately, it got stuck in limbo for months because of the coronavirus lockdown. We've finally begun to mix it and I'm very excited about the music. I chose a few originals, some jazz tunes, and Michael Jackson's "Rock with You." My good friend and great drummer and arranger, Dennis Mackrel, wrote the arrangements and he did an outstanding job as I knew he would. I met him years ago when I used to rehearse with his big band over at the musician's union. I couldn't believe how great he not only wrote but orchestrated the music. He's what I consider to be a big band expert so he was the first guy I thought of when I got this opportunity. It should be coming out this fall.

JG: Great! Yeah, Dennis is a great player, composer, and arranger And I'm so glad that Don and Maureen Sickler are keeping Rudy Van Gelder's going. And I can't wait to hear the new CD. Thanks, so much for doing this Mike, really a pleasure!

ML: Thanks Jon.

Essiet Okon Essiet
New York City – June 2020

Essiet and I first met in New York City in the mid to late '80s. But one of the first gigs we did where we got to know each other well was a week at a Club Med in Eleuthera, in the Bahamas in 1990. He and I spent a lot of time snorkeling, so we became known to each other as the "Snorkel Dorks." And honestly, the name just fit. We were out in the water every day for hours, and we had a blast! He's a great person, a great bass player, and an exceptional musician who has had an amazing career.

JG: Hey Essiet! Thanks for doing this, man! It was great to reconnect with you last year at the gig that you and Sylvia Cuenca called me for at the San Jose Jazz Festival. It was great to hear and see you both and to play again. So, where did you grow up? Is there a family connection for you to music?

EE: I grew up all over the USA, Lagos, Nigeria, and London, England. We moved a lot because my dad worked for the U.S. government as a chemist, and we ended up living in Boston, Massachusetts; Stevens Point, Wisconsin; Little Rock, Arkansas; East Lansing, Michigan; Omaha, Nebraska; San Diego, California; Corvallis, Oregon; and Portland, Oregon. My parents didn't play any instruments but my mom loved classical music, and she used to play Nigerian highlife music on the stereo. She wanted me to play the violin so I started at age ten. We had seven kids in the family and most of them also played various instruments.

JG: Were there any teachers that were very important to your growth?

EE: When I started on the violin my family lived in Stevens Point. I took private lessons and I also played in the school orchestra. Four years later I switched to the bass violin in high school and I also started playing the bass guitar at the same time. There was a bassist who was a senior in high school, and he gave me a lesson on the bass when I started then as a freshman in high school at age fourteen. I started getting serious when I switched to the bass while living in Portland, Oregon. My high school teacher was a jazz fan and he introduced me to jazz. His name was Mr. Kerns. Later, some of the local musicians that had a big impact on me were the drummer Mel Brown, a pianist Pat George, and the trumpeter Thara Memory. They were mentors and I learned a great deal from them.

JG: When did you know you wanted to be a jazz musician? What were the recordings and live concerts that were important to you early?

EE: I guess I knew I wanted to be a jazz musician back in my high school days, when my band teacher, Mr. Kerns, gave me some records to listen to, like Don Ellis, The Thad Jones/Mel Lewis Big Band, *Clifford Brown with Strings*, and a Miles Davis record. I was fascinated because I'd never heard jazz before. Mr. Kerns would also use some of the funds from the school to take us to concerts of famous jazz players and bands that were passing through town. I had some rock records, but when I got the jazz bug I started buying as many records as I could. I got Ron Carter's record *All Blues*, Chick Corea's *Light as a Feather*, and many more.

JG: What were some of your important early work opportunities that helped you to grow?

EE: The pianist Pat George, gave me a four month, four night a week gig in Portland at an Italian bistro named Prima Donna playing standards. And that was where I learned the bulk of the standards that I knew at that point.

JG: Yeah, those kinds of gigs can be really important, where you can learn and work on standards like that.

EE: I also played around town with some of the local bands, playing and learning funk, Latin, and rock, as well as jazz. There was a community band leader by the name of Thara Memory that I learned a lot from, and the excellent drummer Mel Brown hired me on some of his projects. Portland had, and has, a rich mix of musicians and bands and they have an excellent jazz festival that brings in many of today's top international musicians. Eventually I moved to LA from Portland because I felt that I needed to expand my horizons. I met some great players there, and one night I met a Dutch pianist named Rene van Helsdingen and he invited me to Holland to play in the summer of 1981. I ended up staying there on and off for five years and started meeting and playing with a number of musicians and bands over that time. Also, when I was in Holland, I met Don Moye of the Art Ensemble of Chicago, Abdullah Ibrahim also known as Dollar Brand, Archie Shepp, and Sam Rivers to name a few.

JG: When did you come to New York?

EE: I first came to New York City in January of 1983 to play at Sweet Basil with the Abdullah Ibrahim Quartet. I was living in Amsterdam then and met Abdullah in Europe where he hired me to do some tours with him in 1982.

JG: I know you played quite a bit with Blakey. Can you talk a bit about getting to play with him, and some of the other artists that you worked with?

EE: When I joined Art's Jazz Messengers it was a bigger group than what he normally had. He had two trumpets, Eddie Allen and Brian Lynch; Frank Lacy on trombone; and two tenors, Javon Jackson and Craig Handy. Vincent Herring was playing alto but Donald Harrison took over soon after because Vincent left to play with Nat Adderley. There was a lesser known bari player named Sam Furnace who played with us some who passed away a few years after that. Benny Green was on piano, and Geoff Keezer joined later. We played at Sweet Basil in the beginning, New Year's Eve week, and soon after that traveled to London to perform at the legendary Ronnie Scott's Jazz Club in early 1989. That's when Donald joined on alto. It was a blast to be in that band for two years! We did Art's seventieth birthday gig in Bayer, Germany with a very impressive big band of Benny Golson, Freddie Hubbard, Wayne Shorter, Jackie McLean, Curtis Fuller, Walter Davis Jr., Roy Haynes, Buster Williams, Michelle Hendricks, Terence Blanchard, Donald Harrison, Brian Lynch, Frank Lacy, Javon Jackson, Geoff Keezer, and myself.

JG: Wow!

EE: There's a video of that concert and group which I think can be found on YouTube. Back in the end of my musical collaboration with Art, he and Dr. John formed a group called Bluesiana Triangle. We made a record back then, around 1990 and the band consisted of Art, Dr. John, Kenny Burrell, and David "Fathead" Newman. Kenny Burrell wasn't on the record, but we did a few gigs including a festival in Seattle called the Bumbershoot Festival. Art passed soon after that and the band continued for a little while longer with Will Calhoun on drums and we recorded a second record the following year. I also got a chance to play a little bit with Bobby Hutcherson at a club named Fat Tuesdays in the early 1990's.

JG: Oh yeah! I remember that club. And Bobby was amazing!

EE: Yeah! The band also had George Cables and Victor Lewis in it. I did a few gigs with Cedar Walton in the '90s and got a chance to play with Freddie Hubbard, mostly in Europe and a little bit around the U.S. for about a year. I joined Bobby Watson's post hard bop ensemble in the mid 1990's and that was a rewarding experience. I also played with Danilo Perez's Motherland Project in the early 2000's. In 1997 I was asked to join an incarnation of the Blue Note All-Stars which included Tim Hagans, Greg Osby, Javon Jackson, Kevin Hays, and Bill Stewart. We toured Canada, the U.S., Europe, and Japan. I've been in separate groups with Pat Martino and Billy Cobham to name a few. And I've been playing lately with the George Cables Trio featuring Victor Lewis, and Eddie Henderson's Quintet. Both bands have recorded CDs.

JG: Yeah, I remember that Blue Note All-Stars group in that period. And what incredible sidemen gigs and associations you developed over the years! What a learning experience playing with all those great musicians!

EE: Yeah. When I think about the '80s and '90s I realize what an amazing musical career I had back then and unfortunately I feel like I took it for granted. But I really am grateful to have experienced that remarkable time.

JG: What are some more recent experiences, bands, recordings that you've done as a leader or sideman. What are some upcoming projects?

EE: I've been in so many bands and groups over the years, but one of my favorites is my own group called IBO. The band mixes West African rhythms with jazz harmonies and I recorded a CD called *Shona* back in 2015.

JG: Wow, that sounds great!

EE: Yeah, I was exposed to a West African style of music called highlife back when I was growing up at home from my parents. They used to play the music on the stereo and my mom would dance to it. West African music is so vast, like any other style of music. King Sunny Adé, Chief Ebenezer Obey are some of the many artists coming out of highlife music. Then there's the folkloric styles from Yoruba to Efik-Ibibio. There's afrobeat like Fela Kuti and Sheena Peters. I'm only scratching the surface of the unlimited amount of music coming out of West Africa. This music seeped into my subconscious and one day my younger brother said to me, "You should mix some of our heritage into the jazz music you play!" So, I started my group IBO back in the '90s. I was living in Brooklyn then and we would rehearse once a week at my place trying out some of the songs I had written mixing the two musical styles. Actually, there were more than two styles being mixed together back then. And we did some performing at Visiones, a club back then, I think you probably remember that place right?

JG: Oh yeah!

EE: A lot of great players used to come over to my place to play. Guys like Jeff "Tain" Watts, Jeff Ballard, Frank Lacy, Mark Feldman, and many others. New York was so open back then. I have such great memories of those days and I miss them.

JG: Man, that project of yours sounds amazing, I'd love to hear that!

EE: Yeah, I'll get you a copy of the CD! I played on a project with Geoffrey Keezer back in 2008 that was Grammy nominated, called *Aurea,* that was a great recording and Geoffrey is an amazing pianist and composer. He went to Peru, and when he came back to the U.S. he wrote music mixing Afro-Peruvian styles with jazz into a rich tapestry of sounds and rhythms. The CD is remarkable and I was honored to be part of the project. Ralph Peterson started the Messenger Legacy group a few years ago and we've toured the U.S. and Europe for a few years.

We recorded a new CD that will be out in a few weeks. The group is an alumni ensemble of Art Blakey's Jazz Messengers from various time periods and we play some of the classics as well as some originals. Lastly, I play with an international band comprised of Freddie Hendrix, Miki Hayama, and Eric Allen. This band is led by the Polish saxophonist Sylwester Ostrowski and we play mostly in Europe and Japan.

JG: Man, that all sounds great! And it's been great catching up. Hopefully we'll get to hang and play again soon. Thanks so much for doing this!

EE: Thanks Jon, my pleasure!

Bill Mays
Pennsylvania – 2020

One of my good friends and mentors over the years is the wonderful pianist Bill Mays. He's a brilliant musician and a great person. I met Bill when I was a teenager. He invited me to play some sessions at his place on West 70th St. when I was around nineteen, which was a great experience for me. Over the years we did some really fun gigs together, and a wonderful recording of his, *Mays in Manhattan*. He'd already had a great career in LA before coming to New York City in the 1980s. I first knew about him from seeing him in a Freddie Hubbard video a few years before I met him. And I saw and heard him many nights with the Gerry Mulligan Quartet, and at Bradley's and The Knickerbocker back in the '80s and '90s. He had wonderful duos with Ray Drummond, Red Mitchell, and others, and several wonderful trios and larger groups over the years.

Some of my fondest memories in my twenties are times with Bill out at his cabin in Pennsylvania, where we'd go for long hikes, bike rides, and swims in nearby Walker Lake. In September of '92, I spent about ten days alone out there, watching his dog Boomerang, while he and his wife were away. I had apples fresh off the tree in the backyard to juice in the morning, and a beautiful Steinway grand piano to play for hours on end. I'd take long hikes in between practicing and composing, and see bears, deer, and even a bobcat once!

Bill's a great musician, composer, arranger, lyricist, and a rough customer at Scrabble! My sons and I went and visited him and his wife Judy (who's a wonderful photographer and artist) some years back. As we hung out at the lake and set up our letters, I warned my kids, "Bill is rough! He can sometimes just come up with a word to start and end the game! He's that good!" My son Shane said, "Huh? How can he do that!?" Next thing we knew, the game started and on Bill's first turn, he said, "Uh... yeah... so that's W-A-L-N-U-T, WALNUT, and WALNUTS, and I'm out of tiles, so guys have to give me all your tiles, and I win." And we all went, "WHAT! How the... ?" and laughed for several minutes at the prescience of my prediction and Shane's doubts quickly being erased!

A few years ago Bill wrote a book called *Stories of the Road, the Studios, Sidemen & Singers: 55 Years in the Music Biz*, which is great and highly recommended! So I thought to ask him if he might want to share a story from the book, and he suggested this one, about his time touring with Phil Woods, from the chapter entitled Strange Venues:

The Phil Woods quintet was booked at a festival in Uruguay. It was held in, of all places, the middle of a cow pasture! The promoter, a jazz-loving rancher, held an annual event on his acreage, out in the middle of nowhere. The stage and audience seats were in the midst of a big grazing field, and the musician's green room was an old converted bunkhouse. During Phil's performance, seated at a gorgeous Steinway grand, I looked up during a tune, and there, just a few feet away, was a huge heifer, simultaneously chewing her cud and taking a leak, looking right at me and seeming to dig every note of "All Bird's Children." Apparently we were swinging 'til the cows came home!

Joe Magnarelli

Phone call, Bay Ridge Brooklyn, NY – April 2020

JG: Hey Joe! Thanks for calling! I was just finishing with a student online. Are you seeing some students online?

JM: Yeah, teaching everybody online through the end of the semester.

JG: How many do you have?

JM: I have eight. But three of them I just keep in touch with 'cause they're in my ensemble. But the other five I see once a week.

JG: Well, we're in a strange time, man. It was good to run into you yesterday.

JM: [Laughter] Sorry, I was in a dark fuckin' mood man... sorry!! [Laughter]

JG: [Laughter] I was too! I'm so conscious of covering my face and staying away from everybody that I didn't recognize you until you were right next to me!

BOTH: [Laughter]

JG: Well, there are so many things we can talk about with this neighborhood and getting to know each other. So, you grew up in Upstate New York, right?

JM: Yeah, Syracuse, I was born in Syracuse.

JG Tell me about your family and what it was like up there.

JM: Well, I grew up in an Italian family on the north side of Syracuse. When I was growing up, sports was a big thing. The New York Giants and basketball. You know, everybody was into basketball. My dad coached and refereed, at the time, when I was real young. And so, my mom was always going to games. Then my sister became a cheerleader. Me and my mom would go to all the high school games when I was a little kid. So that was kinda my childhood, a lot a' sports. And music too, 'cause my dad was in theater. So, I used to go with him to rehearsals, and I would hang out with the musicians. You know... listen to 'em play, hear some great trumpet players play lead. You know, show music and stuff.

JG: What did your dad play?

JM: My dad was an actor. Well, a part-time actor, kind of a comedian kinda... kinda... dude. [Laughter] He was very funny, let's put it that way. He was naturally funny.

JG: Wow, was he involved in theater? Was he on TV at all?

JM: Well, yeah, it was kind of a crazy thing. Like, first of all, he did a theater production every year. But it was a big thing because they did three weekends. They actually did twelve shows. And they'd rehearse for like five months before that. So, it was like half the year he'd be involved with the show. Also, they used to do this thing in downtown Syracuse. They'd make thousands of dollars for the church. And it was a big thing. It was legendary for us in our small little town. And then he also was in politics, which he used to tell me was like being a theater actor.

JG: [Laughter]

JM: And so he was on TV all the time, but he was way serious on TV! He had this really strong voice. So, like, for about four or five years, anything that happened in Syracuse… like for instance my dad was on the Council when they brought cable TV to Syracuse. That was a big thing at the time. He also was the one who orchestrated the building of the Carrier Dome.

JG: Oh my god! That's amazing!

JM: Yeah, because he was the president of the Common Council. So, he was always on TV, but he was always serious on TV. But that made him even funnier on stage!

BOTH: [Laughter]

JM: But then, really what happened with my dad was… his big thing was, he worked for Mario Cuomo. I don't know, '75 or '77? I'm not sure what his first year was, but he was his campaign manager in Central New York. And Mario won Central New York big! So, my dad, the first favor he got from Mario was that he put him on the New York State Council of the Arts.

JG: Wow…

JM: My dad was on that for a few years. That didn't pay any money, but he just wanted to do that. He never made it to New York City, you know. But then, I think that got old after a while. So, Cuomo made him the Commissioner of Parks for New York State.

JG: Oh my god Joe! I can't believe this. I had no idea!

JM: But then while doing that he also had a radio show in Syracuse. He thinks he had about 9,000 fans. It was an Italian hour… but it was three hours.

JG: [Laughter]

JM: He used to do birthdays, and… you know… shout outs, and play Italian music. He had a lot of fans. So, he was doing that shit into his eighties, you know.

JG: Wow…

JM: Yeah, he died when he was 84. He did the show Sunday, he died on Wednesday. [Laughter]

JG: Wow.

JM: Yeah, yeah… that was my old man.

JG: And what was his first name?

JM: Armand.

JG: Armand Magnarelli.

JM: Yeah, yeah.

JG: And how many brothers and sisters do you have?

JM: I have an older brother and an older sister. My older brother, he worked in a kind of accounting. But he was also a basketball referee for about thirty years in college. He did some Division I, but he mostly did Division II and III. And then my sister married an ex-NBA basketball player, Jimmy Lee. So, my whole life, my whole family, is basketball. And they used to live in Syracuse.

JG: Who did Jimmy Lee play for?

JM: He was drafted by the Baltimore Bulls, but he played for Syracuse in college. And actually, they made the Final Four in '75. They were the Cinderella team. They were like the first Cinderella team.

JG: Was Boeheim there already?

JM: No, he was the assistant coach. It was Roy Danforth. And Jimmy averaged 28 points and made the All-Final Four team.

JG: Wow!

JM: Yeah… and he got drafted by the Baltimore Bullets and… you know… he kinda had a cup of coffee. And that was it.

JG: But still, to make the NBA!

JM: Well, he kicked my ass for years, man! I never won a game off him.

JG: [Laughter] When did music and the trumpet become important for you?

JM: My parents bought a piano when I was about eleven. And my dad's best friend was the piano player who led the orchestra for the show. This cat, Mario DeSantis… he just passed away actually. He showed my dad a few chords when he was younger, you know. So, my dad could kinda play 1 3 5 7. And another friend of his, Joe Stagnitta, had a music store down on Salina Street. My dad used to bring home all these fake books. So, he kinda taught me how to play… I don't know. I kinda just had a knack for being able to play a melody. I don't think anybody taught me that. Oh! And then I also started playing guitar when I was twelve. So, I guess that was probably the thing that helped me on the piano. But I took guitar lessons for like four years, I went through all the method books and everything. You know, I played in church in grammar school and early high school.

JG: Wow.

JM: I played piano all the time at home and I would rehearse with my dad. But it was like a disaster. He didn't have good time, you know? He had like, Broadway time. You know what I mean?

JG: Yes! [Laughter]

JM: And then he'd always blame me, so it was like… and then he'd take me out in the backyard and he'd kick my ass in basketball.

JG: [Laughter]

JM: So I was just always getting beaten down when I was a kid! [Laughter]

JG: Nice…

BOTH: [Laughter]

JG: An idyllic childhood…. [Laughter] Well, it sounds like, that part of it aside, it was really amazing. You had a lot of great things happening.

JM: It was great, yeah.

JG: So you were playing piano and guitar. When did you get to the trumpet?

JM: I started playing the trumpet too in sixth grade. A guy named Jack Palmer was my teacher. He was a New York studio musician who came to Syracuse for two years because his wife had cancer, and she wanted to be with her family. But he was a fish out of water. He was the trumpet player on *The Jackie Gleason Show*. He played with Harry James in the '30s. You could look him up. He's definitely in the history books for the big band era. So anyways, his first day of sixth grade was my first day of sixth grade... [Laughter] I mean, you know, as a teacher. And I swear to God, man, this really happened. I had heard trumpet players with my father, you know? And they were real good. But he picked up the trumpet, and it was probably a high C or something, and he shook it! And I thought it just sounded like the greatest thing I'd ever heard in my life man! So that was it, I picked the trumpet that day. But I'd already been playing piano and guitar before that.

JG: Yeah. So, if he was the lead trumpet player on *The Jackie Gleason Show* he played that famous lead on the intro... [sings]

JM: That's it! That's him. That's Jack Palmer.

JG: Wow!

JM: But you know, actually his claim to fame is... I could find it. But there's an advertisement for the Harry James band, featuring Jack Palmer and Frank Sinatra.

JG: Oh my god!

JM: At some theater somewhere.

JG: That's incredible!

JM: Yeah, yeah.

JG: You've probably seen the video with Gleason with Pops where his band is playing and Gleason comes out in his robe and plays one note on the trumpet and gets all happy and runs off the bandstand.

JM: [Laugher] I gotta see that, pretty funny!

JG: There's one with Dizzy and Pops.

JM: Oh, I know that one!

JG: That's the one with the pitter patter and the rain and all that.

JM: Yeah sure. [Laughter]

JG: But man, that's amazing! So, you've got this guy that's a major trumpet player that's played with great people that's your teacher all the sudden in sixth grade.

JM: Yeah, that's why I have no excuse man. I should be a better trumpet player than I am.

JG: [Laughter]

JM: No, I'm just sayin', he taught me the right shit when I was a kid. But I didn't put in the time you know? If I woulda just listened to him I coulda been great when I was in college, you know what I mean? But of course, I was into other shit. So, I never paid it its due, you know?

JG: Well, there's some things there I wanna talk about, regarding the things you were into. Because I know you became an excellent basketball player.

JM: Well... excellent is a strong a word for my career. I would say I was a solid player on good teams. I played on some good teams. And some of them I went through periods where I didn't play that much, and then I went through periods where I played all the time. But the team was already really good. Like, in three years of high school, I played with two guys that became pro basketball players. And my brother-in-law was an ex-pro basketball player. Because of him I used to go up and play, when I was a junior in high school, against the Syracuse basketball players and the alumni players. And there was another college in town, called Le Moyne College. And that was a Division II school and they had good teams. So, I was around these guys all the time. And I'll tell ya a little footnote… Dolph Schayes used to play with us!

JG: Oh my god!!

JM: At the time he was like 51 years old.

JG: But Dolph Schayes is one of the fifty greatest players in NBA history, right!?

JM: Yeah! And we'd play with him with the Syracuse players. He was tough, man! He was real tough… left-handed… he was in good shape.

JG: Wow… that's incredible!

JM: And check this out man… at that same gym… they built a new one but that was a real nice gym… Carmen Basilio was the athletic director.

JG: What!!? The former middleweight champion!?

JM: Yeah! He was the athletic director!

JG: [Laughter]

JM: He used to be up there! And he used to always say, "Hey Mags, what's up?" He liked my father. He used to like to bust my father's balls. And one day he hit me in the fuckin' ribs. He hit me good! He said, "Hey, come here, come here," and he hit me in the ribs! I was suckin' in air for like a minute! I thought I was dead, I thought it was over.

JG: [Laughter]

JM: No really, I didn't wanna cry… but he hit me in the ribs, yeah. But he was a good guy.

JG: How old was he?

JM: He was probably in his sixties. It's hard to tell 'cause I was like fifteen or sixteen.

JG: Well that's incredible, all those associations you had. But you were sixteen and you're playing with grown men, so it's raising your game, right?

JM: I'm playin' with grown men. But my problem was, I didn't have the confidence I shoulda had. 'Cause I wasn't a great athlete. I really worked hard man. I used to run up hills. At the time I did everything you were supposed to do, you know what I mean? So, I made myself the best athlete I could be. But I wasn't a natural. So that always held me back. That's why I developed a good shooting stroke. I was a good passer too. I was all around a good offensive player, actually. Defensively, if the guy was a better athlete than me, I couldn't guard him.

JG: I never played basketball as a kid. But man, we had fun! We knew each other some. But the most time we spent together was on Harry's band. And a lot of guys really liked to play basketball. I started shooting the ball in my neighborhood in Astoria when I was 23, and just played some with kids in my area and tried to learn the game. I just enjoyed it. When we were on the band with Harry, it would be like, you, Ben Wolfe, Ned Goold, Jimmy Greene, a few other folks. And I just remember seeing you and thinking, Joe's a great player!

JM: Can I say something about that? I had lost about 75% of my game at that point, you know? [Laughter] So, you gotta keep that in perspective. [Laughter] I was a lot better man, you know what I mean?

JG: Oh no, I'm sure! You were about 39?

JM: Yeah, I was about 39.

JG: So, you have this guy in sixth grade teaching you who was important to you. You're taking basketball, seriously. But obviously you're taking the trumpet and music seriously too.

JM: Well, kind of. Not in high school so much. By the time I got to high school Jack had left. He moved to Florida. And my high school, C.B.A., it was an all-boys Christian Academy high school and they had Jesuits that taught us. They had a great sports tradition, especially in basketball. They had a great coach—all-boys school—very competitive. I kinda lost my way with the trumpet there, the guitar too. That faded out around tenth grade. Then I just kinda dabbled, you know? I didn't get back to serious practicing on any instrument until I was a junior in college. I did go to Berklee School of Music for one semester in 1980. I sent a tape, I got accepted. Now I realize they accept everybody. [Laughter] But I was there, I was on the lowest grade there on all levels. But I did get more into the piano there, and I did study trumpet with Louis Mucci, which was a great experience actually. That's an important part of my life, especially with teaching. 'Cause he was a great man. He was a great trumpet player and a great person. I studied with him every week for that semester and that was really good. I went from basically hardly any chops, to like… I kinda got a face for a second. Then I went to Fredonia, another college, to play basketball. But after a while I got cut and then after that, that's when I started to take trumpet more seriously, junior year in college.

JG: What was inspiring you at that time, the stuff you worked on with Jack?

JM: Yeah, I think it was mostly that I wanted to go back to that feeling I had with Jack Palmer. The trumpet gave me the greatest feeling. Like the piano… when I grew up, a friend of the family's son was the same age as me, and he was like a piano virtuoso. So, I knew I could never be a great piano player. 'Cause on the piano I was playing tunes like "Hey Jude" [laughter] and on the guitar I was playing Jim Croce tunes. Just a footnote about the guitar—I was on the cutting edge of the new folk sound in the Catholic Church which was guitars in folk music.

JG: Really?

JM: Yeah! Like in seventh, eighth, ninth, tenth grade I played guitar in my church. And the last couple years I was there everybody depended on me. I mean, I was involved in music, but I wasn't listening to Clifford Brown. I didn't even know who Clifford Brown was.

JG: So, latter part of college is when you focused on trumpet and jazz.

JM: Yeah, 'cause I was in Fredonia State.

JG: Was that near Syracuse?

JM: It's near Buffalo. It had a good rep for its music school, which I auditioned for but didn't get in. It just shows you where I was. You know, I came home from Berklee and all those lessons with Louis Mucci and I didn't touch the trumpet for like a month. I just played basketball every day and tried to get back in shape. Oh, and another footnote about Berklee—about a week in I found out they had great games at night at the Huntington Y. And actually, I was just three weeks off my season, man. So, like two weeks earlier I'm playing competitive basketball at this college. I started going to the Y every night from 6–9 playing with Boston University football players and Northeastern athletes. It was heavy games man.

JG: Boston at that time, Larry Bird had just got there, right?

JM: Yeah, Larry Bird's rookie year. I saw him play six times.

JG: That must have been amazing.

JM: That was amazing. I saw Dr. J play twice. I saw him in '77, his second night in the NBA against the Buffalo Braves. I was there. And I saw him in '80 in Boston too.

JG: Wow. So, you're up in Fredonia in the Buffalo area. Did you have any associations with any of those great upstate players, like Nick Brignola?

JM: No, well, actually, what happened in Fredonia was, they had a rich music tradition. But they didn't have a jazz program, the jazz program was student-run. So right away I just naturally became friends with all these musicians. They were all music majors, but I was a liberal arts major and I just started hanging with them. That first year when I got back into the trumpet was when those Aebersolds came out. So, me and this trumpet player, Lee Petruzzi, we started doing Aebersolds. And, after like three or four times I knew that wasn't the shit, and I shouldn't be doing the same part.

When I was at Berklee I got turned on to Clifford Brown, and there were a couple solos I wanted to learn. So, I started going to the old part of the school at Fredonia, where nobody could hear me, where nobody used these practice rooms, and I started working on Clifford Brown solos. So then, I tried out for the big band and I made it, as fifth trumpet player. But I still wasn't practicing trumpet exercises diligently. I just kinda played the trumpet. And I was still playing basketball every day, pretty much. So, you know, that was my life at Fredonia. But I was definitely getting into it though. You know, I was starting to learn stuff, practicing, trying to learn tunes. And then, turns out, my second year at Fredonia I went down to this place called The White Inn, which was this restaurant in the middle of this little small town, and they had a trio playing. These guys were at least in their sixties, all three of them. They played dance music, just tunes, and I knew a lot of tunes from the fake books my father used to bring home. So, I sat in with them. Bro, by December I had the gig! I did it every Saturday night there with them from then on, and I started doing weddings with them. I couldn't play a high C! But I could play tunes.

JG: Wow! Well, just getting to play steady like that, playing tunes, is invaluable. It's so important to your growth.

JM: Yeah, so even though I wasn't really into music, I always was into music. I always had a connection somehow. In high school I played guitar in church. It was really just my senior year in high school that I wasn't as much into music. And you know, I had a really bad experience in high school as a senior. Somebody asked me to play that classical piece you play at the end of graduation. So, I was a big basketball player. I was gonna go up there and play the trumpet at the graduation. Man… I *totally* folded… completely folded. And man, that's what kinda ruined me in college with the trumpet. I got into it for a while with Luis Mucci. But I could never face that fact that I folded at graduation and it fucked me for years.

JG: Well, for one thing, they usually want a tune like that to go on for a long time, to have everybody walk through and…

JM: But bro, first of all ya gotta practice it. I never practiced it! I never got up and played long tones, and tonguing exercises and shit. Seriously. I was playing fuckin' "Hello Dolly" and "Mame"!

BOTH: [Laughter]

JM: I kid you not! You know what I mean? And like right away, I just got the feeling I wasn't gonna make it. 'Cause I made the first passage. But I was just holdin' on for dear life. And it had to be pretty flat I'm sure. And by the second passage it goes higher, you know, like…

[laughter] and it was Splattsville! So man, I just put the horn in the case. I jumped over the railing and joined my other co-eds and we walked out!

BOTH: [Laughter]

JM: I didn't play the other half.

JG: Well, you did enough. And you graduated which is the main thing!

JM: Exactly! You dig? They brought the backgrounds in too early!

BOTH: [Laughter]

JG: Nice!

JM: So I had a lot of negative shit, you know? I had a lot of barriers, man, when I was young.

JG: Well, I would have never known. When we met in the late '80s, I just thought, what a great player! When I heard you with LeDonne at Bradley's, when was that?

JM: Yeah, around that same time.

JG: To me, you're one of my favorite line players, melody players. You hear a melody in your head, and play it through your instrument as well as anybody I know. You've just got a really special thing, So, when did you come to New York City?

JM: Well, I came home from Fredonia in 1982. I'd graduated. I just started practicing trumpet, and I had a couple part-time jobs. I thought I was gonna move to California. I had met a girl in Boston and we'd kept in touch and she invited me out to LA to stay with her. So, I said, OK, I'll try it out. I got out there and I got together with Bobby Shew. And he kinda told me where I was at, which was real good! 'Cause I really respected him. I loved his playing, I'd heard some recordings of him. And he was cool too, such a nice guy. He just said, "Man, just move back to Syracuse, practice, and when you're ready, go to New York. Don't come out here. You wanna play jazz? Go to New York!" So that was what I needed to hear! Boom, just get on a plane and get back to Syracuse, boom. And to my good fortune, J.R. Montrose was playing in Syracuse at the time.

JG: I figured you had to have some contact with those guys up there.

JM: I met him, he was playing, he had a great trumpet player named Sal Amico. These cats played with… Montrose played with Kenny Dorham, he made two records with Kenny Dorham. He was there with Mingus the night Mingus attacked Jackie MacLean, that's how he got the gig with Kenny Dorham. Him and Jackie were tight. He was playing with Sonny Rollins. Sal Amico is just a great trumpet player. Sal Amico, in my opinion, is as good as anybody. Just to put it in perspective about Sal Amico, his ex-wife, who was the mother of his first son, moved back to New York City and he stayed in Utica. And she was Kenny Dorham's girlfriend for like twenty years. So, Sal used to go to New York and see his son and hang with Kenny Dorham. He'd go over to the house, you know what I mean? Plus, he knew Miles' records, you could tell he listened to Miles. Plus, he told me one night he had a gig in New Mexico or Arizona and got high with Bird one night. So, I got immediately into that crowd, you dig?

JG: Yeah.

JM: And they accepted me. I met Nick Brignola shortly after that.

JG: Yeah, Nick was a great player.

JM: Amazing player, but he was a different kinda guy, He was more of a corporate kinda guy. Sal and J.R. were like, let's come over, I'll make ya some lasagna, we'll hang out, smoke some joints, sit and have some greens and beans. Nick was more business in a way. Plus, he never got high. Those guys were high. He was an amazing player though, that's for sure.

JG: Oh man, one of the great baritone players, and sounded great on all the horns.

JM: And I actually saw him stand toe to toe with Phil, man. He's one of those cats who could hang with Phil Woods.

JG: On alto or bari?

JM: On bari, just playin' eighth notes, relentless, in your face, you know?

JG: Yeah, well, Kevin Hays was playing with Nick in the '80s and he'd tell me about nights he pulled out the tenor, the alto, played some doubles too.

JM: Yeah, I remember that. He was a good clarinet player. And he played very good soprano, and great flute.

JG: So, you're spending a lot of time in the '80s playing with these guys Upstate.

JM: That was basically from 1983 to '86.

JG: And when did you move to New York City?

JM: Well, in '85 I auditioned for a road show of *Ain't Misbehavin'* in Rochester and I got the gig with them. We started in the beginning of October and went all the way to the end of February. Then I went back to Syracuse. And May 1st the conductor called me and said, "We're playing in Darien, Connecticut and you got the gig if you want it." This was my chance to move to New York, and I did. I had met Andrew Beales the year before in Aruba. I got hired to play in the house band in the Divi-Divi Hotel and Casino. That lasted like a month or so. They'd just built the dance hall. And when we got there to rehearse, they were finishing it, it was brand new. That was the first two weeks. Then we played like three weeks maybe, so we were there like a month and a half. But I met Andrew Beales and Rob Middleton there. And Andrew had a place to stay in New York, so I came down and moved in with Andrew in '86 and started playing *Ain't Misbehavin'* in Darien.

JG: I auditioned for Lionel Hampton in '87, and you were in the band then, right?

JM: Yeah. The next year, '87, I got with Lionel Hampton. Right after the show closed, I played *A Chorus Line* on the road for another four months. I was home for maybe two weeks. I had met Rob Bargad and we did a thing with John Farnsworth and Joe Farnsworth, because John Farnsworth was the trombone player the first night I played *Ain't Misbehavin'* in Darien. He's the first cat I met from New York. So, he was doing this demo with his brother Joe. They had written this tune, and they won an award from the state of Massachusetts. They gave them some money to put on a concert and make a record. So I'm playing with Joe and John, and Joe's eighteen. And Rob Bargad's playing piano. Rob tells me on the way home there's an audition for Lionel Hampton tomorrow, and that I should go. So, I went and auditioned and got the gig, that was March of 1987.

JG: It's funny, when I did it that must have been a few weeks later.

JM: Were you at the same audition?

JG: I don' think so. I think mine was in April. I just remember, we talked about it on Harry's band on the bus, 'cause Weldon and Schumacher were on the band.

JM: Yeah.

JG: They told me I got the gig before I got there, but then there were a few other alto players there when I got there. We all played. And then Bill Titone came up to me and said, "OK, you got the gig. We're going to Europe. Normally Lionel pays $70 a night. But because he likes you, we're gonna pay you $500 a week!" So, I was gonna get an extra $10 a week… so I said, "Is it $500 for every seven days or $500 for every seven gigs?" He said, "No, no, son, you're not listening to me. It's $500 for every week of gigs." I said, "OK, *so*, is it $500 from Monday to Sunday while we're on the road, or the 5th–14th, when we do our seventh gig?" And he just kept repeating the same thing and never really gave me a straight answer. I was still gonna do it, but I would've had to give up my scholarship at MSM, and I got some advice from some friends that were older and decided not to do it. But how long were you on that band?

JM: I did all of '87. And then summer of '88 they went to Japan and I got fired. It was a whole thing, I don't wanna go into it. And then when they got home I got back on the band somehow. I played probably til the end of '88. By the end of '88 I started playing with Jack McDuff.

JG: Oh man.

JM: Yeah, 'cause Andrew was playing with Jack. And he and Ed Mechechen were on the band, and they were always hanging out in my apartment. So I subbed with Jack for a while, and just around the end of '88, start of '89, I started doing it kinda regular. That was basically two weeks a month, four nights a week. You know it was $60, or sometimes $75. And it was good, good experience, very good experience. You know, just hittin' every night, you know?

JG: I think somewhere in that period of the late '80s was the first time we met.

JM: I was thinking, we had a recording with Mike Holober, with five horns, no?

JG: OK, yeah. I know we did a bunch of stuff with Mike, he's a great musician.

JM: Was Tony Kadleck on that too?

JG: Might have been, yeah.

JM: Was Tim Ries on it?

JG: Probably, yes!

JM: I don't remember if there was trombone on it, probably was.

JG: Listen, we know Tony Kadleck as one of the great lead trumpet players in New York. But when Tony was at Manhattan School of Music in '86, he was a *killer* jazz trumpet player.

JM: Oh yeah, I knew that. I love him.

JG: They started the undergrad jazz program in '86 so that's when I met Tony. And Dave Zalud was the lead player in the band.

JM: Oh, I love him too man!

JG: Tony and I used to go up and play sextet at the Hillside in Waterbury Connecticut with Steve Davis' group. Did you ever play there?

JM: Yeah, I think I might a' gone up there once or twice.

JG: Yeah, Dave Santoro played there and helped bring up Kevin Hays, myself, Joey Calderazzo. Adam Nussbaum would do it sometimes, which was great! Bergonzi played there sometimes. So, it's the late '80s, you played with Hampton…

JM: Yeah, then my main thing was McDuff. By then I was starting to do other gigs, 'cause working with Jack I met some other people. I started to go up and hang out at Showman's on Monday nights and play with Percy France. I was never on the gig.

JG: Man, I don't know if we ever talked about Percy, he was a great player!

JM: He was! He was a great guy too, man.

JG: He was so good to me! I used to play the Saturday gig with Eddie Chamblee at Sweet Basil, and Percy would sub for Eddie sometimes. So, I got to play and hang with him a lot. And Percy knew Bird and had a lot of stories about him. I know he played with that famous organ player, they had a big hit…

JM: Bill Doggett.

JG: Yes! So, how much did you play with Percy?

JM: I used to just go up to the session. Like a year and a half, maybe. But at that time the great thing was Eddie Henderson had just moved back to town.

JG: OK.

JM: Eddie was up there all the time playin' for free. He was just up there blowin'.

JG: Yeah! I remember playing in a couple rehearsal bands with Eddie back then. So, when you were up at Showman's with Percy, was Bobby Forester on organ?

JM: Yeah, Bobby Forester. I can't remember who was playing drums. Sometimes Tootsie Bean or Greg Bandy. But yeah it was always cool. Sometimes on Monday nights there'd be nobody there, but by 10:00 people would come in. And Percy was gracious, man. I was workin' there so I knew how to act. I didn't try to play on every tune. But just enough to work on my shit, you know? So, it was a good scene. So, Showman's was an important place for me at that time.

JG: Yeah.

JM: And after that it was the Village Gate. I'd go to the Sunday brunch there. I started working there in '92, the last three years or so. That was my major hang, along with Augie's, of course.

JG: Yeah, I played a lot at Augie's in the mid '80s to early '90s. And I remember the first time I went when it turned into Smoke, and Tommy met me at the door and said, "It's $25." I looked up smiling and said, "You're joking right?" And he was like "NO!" [Laughter] You know Tommy at Smoke, the bartender?

JM: Sure!

JG: I was like, *really*!? … I never *made* $25 there! We played for tips and a plate of eggs and rice as I recall.

JM: [Laughter] Was that the Peter Mazza days?

JG: I don't know. Did he have a steady night there?

JM: In the '80s I thought. I thought he discovered the place.

JG: Actually, the guy I think discovered it was an old friend of mine, a drummer named Justin Page who lived nearby. We had a different band at the start. But it became me, Justin, Sean Smith, Charlap, and a guitar player named Dan Rochlis. We'd play, and afterwards there was a duo that played the late set with a piano player I used to see at Barry Harris' Jazz Cultural Theater, and Cliff Barbaro on drums. That was 1984. Bill Stewart, Larry Goldings, and Peter Bernstein had a steady night a few years later And I know that Jesse Davis had a steady night for a while, and Scott Wendholt had a steady night.

JM: Well that was later, that was '90s, Thursdays.

JG: And I remember hearing you that night with LeDonne at Bradleys. I knew Mike through

Eddie Locke. He invited me to some sessions, called me for some gigs, got me on my first Criss Cross date as a sideman. He really helped me a lot.

JM: Wow, that's great.

JG: Yeah, he was so great to me. So, what was the '90s like for you?

JM: Well, the '90s was like, before I moved into the Village, from age 30–35, I had like four different apartments. My life was kinda scrambled. I mostly was playin' with Toshiko's band some. She was a little busier back then. McDuff had moved. I guess I was playing down at the Savoy some. I remember I was at the Gate a lot from '92–94.

JG: When did you get that apartment right across the street from the Gate?

JM: Yeah, it was right across the street on Thompson.

JG: And that's right when you were still doing that gig?

JM: No. I moved into that apartment, then two months later the Gate closed.

BOTH: [Laughter]

JM: Yeah, it was pretty depressing. But then Smalls opened up right after that, so it was fine. But I was really practicing a lot. And I started working for Criss Cross and doing recordings for Jerry Teekens, in like '92. I'd say the early '90s is when I started getting called for higher level gigs. I did a Laverne Butler record. That was my first record date in New York. The funny thing is, the other two horn players were Joe Henderson and Jon Faddis. I never saw them, I just made the rehearsal, and then, they didn't wanna come the second day 'cause they wanted more bread. [Laughter] So they fired them and hired me and Chris Potter.

JG Wow.

JM: So I'm on this record. I don't blow, I just played some parts. Criss played a little solo but it's mostly Joe Henderson. Yeah, that was pretty funny. I did this record with McDuff around that time, which was good. I played pretty well on that, I thought. I did two records with Lionel Hampton in that time. And yeah, I just started doing more things like that. Working in New York, mostly big bands.

JG: Well, we saw each other on Maria Schneider's band at Visiones on Mondays.

JM: Yeah, early '90s with Maria, definitely.

JG: Also the Vanguard.

JM: Yeah, that was mostly later for me, my heavy subbing was 2004–2014, 2015.

JG: Then I get a call in '98 and Jimmy Greene and I came on Harry's band to make a record in LA. Were you on that?

JM: No, I came in the next year for the tour.

JG: OK, and then we did that tour in '99 when you joined. We were out that whole summer. That band was a great hang. It was you, me, Leroy Jones, Jimmy...

JM: Also, it's too bad Lucien Barbarin passed away man... right?

JG: Oh man! I was so sorry about that...

JM: Lucien was a good guy.

JG: Yeah, he was great guy. I reached out to Leroy when it happened. It's just heartbreaking. And man, it was so great to get to meet and play with those guys and really feel New Orleans music with these guys that really lived it. I know Lucien had a great uncle, I believe, Paul Barbarin, that played drums with Pops.

JM: Yeah man.

JG: And the guys in that scene take a lot of pride in the history of the music and its meaning, rightfully so. So, that was really a special thing about that gig, and just the hang with you, Leroy, and Jimmy, you know.

JM: I loved it man, I loved it. That was a great time. And Leroy, you know... I wasn't playin' solos. But I didn't care. 'Cause I was listening to Leroy. That shit was a lesson man. I'm not too proud to say, that shit was a lesson. Really. That was an important period in my life, to be around you cats, and hearing Leroy play.

JG: Well, for sure, for me too. I guess I was there from '98 to '01. And then you stayed with the band another couple years, right?

JM: Yeah, I stayed with the band until I went with Ray Barretto, really. I was there 'til the end of 2003. I turned down a tour in the fall of 2003. It's so stupid man. I started playing with Ray in the summer of 2003. And we didn't have any more gigs until 2004. And Ray says, "OK Poppa, we're gonna rehearse a few times in the fall, so I'll call you." And I thought, I don't wanna miss these rehearsals, so I turned down the tour, stupidly. And of course, he never called me for a rehearsal. I didn't hear from him until the next year. But that's alright. That's pretty much when it was over. 'Cause I think I turned down the next tour because I had gigs with Ray. So, when they called me the next time and I couldn't make it they said they were gonna replace me with my sub, but that was cool.

JG: I got to play some with Ray.

JM: He liked you man, he used to talk about you.

JG: Well, he used to bring his son Chris over to my house to study with me.

JM: Yeah, he told me that.

JG: I liked Chris a lot.

JM: Well that shows you what about thought of you bro. 'Cause he was rough, he had very high standards that cat. So, that's a great compliment man.

JG: Well, I was honored that he asked me. And when I think of Ray, it's like when you talked about J.R. Montrose or Sal Amico. He was down home, there was no pretense. And I really enjoyed working with Chris. So, you worked with Ray for how long?

JM: I subbed some early on. But I played from the summer of 2003 until he passed in early 2006.

JG: And was that with Adam Kolker?

JM: No, that was with Myron Walden. Adam Kolker did a few gigs and Chris made the last three gigs. And actually, Ray made a record without trumpet, with Chris, Hilton Ruiz, John Benitez...

JG: Wow.

JM: And the drummer... I can't remember his name, Cuban cat, he was a top guy. He was hot in New York about ten years ago, he used to play at the Zinc Bar every Monday night.

JG: So, that brings us up to 2006. One guy I know you've played with in recent years is Jerry Bergonzi.

JM: Well, I think it was about two years that I seemed to be around him. One was a tour that was put together in Spain by Ramon Jove. That was fun. That was two weeks. And the summer before that we taught at a place in Cadiz together. We did a little tour, some local gigs. We mighta played at The Jamboree there too. There was another thing we did in 2014–2015.

JG: There's also the two-saxophone group with Oatts, who I know you've played with a lot.

JM: [Laughter] Well that's how I got the gig. Oatts couldn't make something and he said to get me. And then we taught at a camp, the three of us. But they sound great together, yeah.

JG: Well, those two guys, any combination of them, with you, would be amazing.

JM: Well, it's very easy for me to play with Oatts, I feel very comfortable. With Jerry, I felt like… I mean, he's a bad motherfucker man. It's almost like playing with George Coleman, or Charles Davis. There's just something there, he's like superior, you know what I'm saying? I never felt like he needed me… to play [Laughter] and he's such a funny guy. He's silly, Jerry.

JG: I don't know that side of him.

JM: And Garzone too. I don't know him well, but he's a bad cat too.

JG: Oh yeah, I love Garzone.

JG: Man, I remember, I was in the car, back in the '90s, and a tune of yours came on the radio, and the name was a woman's name, and I…

JM: "Bella Carolina?"

JG: Yes! And I remember hearing it and thinking, man, what a beautiful record!

JM: Thanks, man.

JG: And you've done so many beautiful recordings as a leader. Some great things with John Swana, all those Criss Cross records. We've done a couple things together. We did that project with Pete Malinverni and his friend who was a singer.

JM: Oh yeah, I remember that.

JG: And you just have such great time, great lines and feel, and a great melodic concept to your playing. And that record with strings you did is incredible!

JM: Oh thanks, man. That was Marty Sheller.

JG: When was that?

JM: That was 2011.

JG: Well, to bring things up to the current day… I was looking for a place in early 2010, and the guitar player Nate Radley told me about these two realtors out here in Bay Ridge. I met them and we were going to look at some things in Sunset Park for like $1600. But before we did they said, "Oh yeah, there's a one bedroom around the corner for a grand." And I said, "Really? Let's look at that!" [Laughter] I can almost afford that!" And that got me in this building here. Then I sent you to them. How long have you been out here?

JM: Since 2011, it'll be nine years this year.

JG: I've loved it out here. One of our favorite things is we're close to the water. There's this restaurant here called Paneantico that we love. And that amazing woman that cooks there, I think her name is Nancy. I call her the Pope of Bay Ridge. Man, I love the food so much I could live there! Just set me up with a cot in sight of the napoleons and the cannoli and I'm good. I'd fall asleep looking at that, get up and have the eggplant parm, you know…

JM: [Laughter]

JG: So we've been out here almost a decade.

JM: Yeah. Thanks to you man, and Dred Scott too.

JG: Yeah, Dred Scott's in your building. Bim Strasberg's out here, Mike Fahie…

JM: Yeah, but you know, to be honest man, in 1993 I met Bim. I used to come out here for sessions. And around '98 he was leaving his apartment and I was thinking about renting his place. It didn't end up happening. But I already had Bay Ridge in my head. So, when you said that, I was like, "Oh man, that's a great idea!" So, you hooked me up with Frank… who then hooked me up with Frank…

JG: Frank and Frankie…

JM: And in the meantime I hung out with Frank Junior. And when we got to see Frank, he was talkin' to his friend Frank…

BOTH: [Laughter]

JG: Exactly!

JM: That's all true, bro!

JG: I know!

BOTH: [Laughter]

JG: It's like a scene outta *Goodfellas* or something! [Laughter]

JM: Oh, it's unbelievable, man! [Laughter]

JG: Dis is Petey ova here… here's Pete Senior. Here's his cousin Little Pete. Here's Pete Junior…

JM: I'll tell you, when my man said, "Hey Frank, I'll see ya later!" to the guy in the car I hadn't met named Frank, I said *oh my god*!

BOTH: [Laughter]

JG: Well, I gotta end this with… you and me are playin' a gig about ten years ago up in Albany…

JM: Uhhh…

JG: We're driving back…

JM: Uhhhh…

JG: [Laughter] And one of my all-time favorite stories is me and Ben Monder playing a wedding in '94. And you know Ben, and he's the most quiet, dead-pan guy. I'm describing us playing the ceremony. I can barely play the flute. Ben doesn't bring the acoustic guitar. He's not wearing a tux, but has like some weird, blue felt suit and black sneakers… we're playing these little Bach and Mozart pieces for like 40 minutes… I'm *destroying* them!

BOTH: [Laughter]

JG: It was just brutal! And we keep thinking, when are we going to play "Here Comes the Bride"? Before the gig, the clergyman says to me, "When you see the small children come up with the flowers and the ring, that's your cue to play "Here Comes the Bride."" So, at one point, the kids come up, and I say to Ben, "Hey, that's our cue." So, he starts playing "Here Comes the Bride," but, like, fast! I said, "Man, slow down!" He does and says, totally deadpan, with Steven Wright-like delivery, "Is that better?" I laughed a little, nodded, and we get into it. [Sings] My flute chops are already just barely hanging on after playing for over 45 minutes… and like five minutes in, we start looking around, but still no bride. Then a couple minutes later the kids go back and sit down! We're like seven or eight minutes into this thing and we're lookin' around desperately… no bride! And Ben and I just sorta looked at each other and didn't know what to do… and the clergyman looked at us like, "I don't know where she is!" And we just didn't stop!

JM: [Laughter]

JG: We just kept playing "Here Comes the Bride"… for like 25 minutes!

JM: Oh, wow… [Laughter]

JG: So, several minutes later, people are yelling, arguing, laughing… on a good day at this point I can barely play the flute. So, by fifteen minutes in I'm severely oxygen deprived… the room is spinning… I'm hangin' on by a thread! And by twenty minutes in, Monder starts to slowly crack up. Probably at least in part from how sad my flute playing was by then. And I'm telling you this story… and your laugh that night in the car…

JM: Ohhh, bro, that's one of the funniest things I ever… I almost died that night…

BOTH: [Laughter]

JM: I started choking from laughing so hard! I thought I was gonna die.

JG: But, you're a big man. And the octave of your laughter was like four octaves higher than your normal speaking voice…

BOTH: [Laughter]

JG: Listening to you laugh like that I lost it and could barely drive coming down the thruway.

BOTH: [Laughter]

JM: Well, can I say something else about that night?

JG: Please!

JM: There's one other element that almost led to my death.

JG: OK.

JM: Because we bought three different pints of Ben and Jerry's man!

JG: Well listen, man!

JM: So we were like… we had all this sugar!

JG: You got your way that you party and I got my way that I party!

BOTH: [Laughter]

JM: Well, I partied with you that night man! I ate as much ice cream as you man! You had to put the clamps on it.

JG: I know man.

JM: You know, so, I mean, really… I was like, *oh my god*! Am I gonna die?

BOTH: [Laughter]

JM: Because I can't fuckin' stop laughing!

BOTH: [Laughter]

JG: Especially if you know Monder… and to just imagine him… in that blue felt suit and black sneakers, playing "Here Comes the Bride"…

BOTH: [Laughter]

JG: And to see the most quiet, reserved guy you know completely lose it…

JM: [Laughter]

JG: And an amazing player! He'd normally play some heavy, personal shit on Maria's music, or these amazing original pieces of his… not a club date guy, to say the least! So, between that, and me trying to pay the flute, and having no chops, and to keep playing non-stop after almost an hour, and then a 25-minute tune… and my upper lip was below my lower lip…

JM: [Laughter]

JG: Just nothing happening. And at about twenty minutes in, I've got nothing. I'm taking these little breaks. And three times, I tried to put the flute to my lips, to reset my chops. And each time I did Ben would start to lose it…

BOTH: [Laughter]

JG: The first time he does that I'm just thinking to myself, "Oh God, please let me get through this!" The second time it happens I'm thinking, "Ben, don't do this to me!" The third time I tried to play, Ben completely lost it! He's laughing, *loudly*! I'm already loopy and oxygen deprived. When I saw him do that, I just fell out of my chair from laughing so hard!

BOTH: [Laughter]

JG: Seeing Ben, of all people, lose it like that… I literally fell out of my chair! Tears streaming down my face from laughter… the people sitting in front of us in the audience are laughing. I'm looking up at Ben from the floor. He's now he's hunched over the guitar, laughing uncontrollably… just strumming quarter notes on open strings, which made it even funnier!

BOTH: [Laughter]

JG: I'm on the ground, I've totally lost it! I look up towards the door at the back of the chapel…. and *there's the bride*!

JM: *Oh my god*!

JG: FUCK! Somehow, I have to get up off the floor, try to get my flute chops together, fast! And we have to try to keep it together to play another three choruses!

JM: Oh my god!

JG: I love that story. But your reaction that night to it was the best part! So Joe, thanks for doing this man.

JM: Hey Jon, this was a pleasure man.

JG: Yeah, one of my favorite people and musicians, I'm really glad we got a chance to do this.

JM: Thanks. Well listen man, let's just keep in touch bro.

JG: Absolutely! Hopefully in a couple months we'll be able to get some lunch at Paneantico!

JM: Yeah, I hope so bro, I hope so.

JG: Yeah, stay safe man.

JM: You too brother. Thanks Jon.

JG: Thanks Joe.

Thanks and Dedication

There are too many people that deserve thanks for their help in this project to name all of them, but they certainly include Annemarie Vance, the faculty and students at the Desautels Faculty of Music jazz program at the University of Manitoba, Loretta Beneducci, The Shanderson family, Tyrone Jackson, Bill and Jacqui Parrott, Brian and Dan Weber, Bill and Denise Dicey, the Echanique family, the Glass family, Bill Charlap, Margaret Davis, the students and faculty at the Purchase Jazz program during my time teaching there from 2002–2013, the faculty and students at the High School for the Performing Arts from 1980–84, and Manhattan School of Music from '84–88, Loren Schoenberg, Jill Goodwin, David Byrne, Joan and Fraser Linklater, Jeff and Lori Derraugh, Bill Kristjanson, Ken and Donna Tugby, Brad Shigeta, Hank O'Neal, Bjorn and Mona Pedersen, Vic Morosco, Caesar DiMauro, T.S. Monk, Larry Laurenzano, Thomas Oberle, Patrick Wolf, Jack Riordan, Mark and Alan Ferber, Stanley and Kathy Ferber, Maryellen Healy, Bryn Roberts, Matt Clohesy, Quincy Davis, Russ Palladino, Gino Moratti, Jimmy Katz, Don and Maureen Sickler, Brian Camelio and ArtistShare, Sarah Fearon, The IAWA, Peter Straub, Malachy McCourt, John Kearns, David Hajdu, Willie Echanique, Bob Athayde, Paul Lucckesi, Isabella Rizzo, Mike Stewart, Mace Francis, and all the musicians mentioned here and their families and estates. Special thanks to David Berger representing the estates of Milt and Mona Hinton.

This book is dedicated to Sue Gordon, Alan J. Barry, Bob Gordon, Steve Gordon, Alana Gordon, Kyle Gordon, Amanda Moyer, Liam Gordon, Shane Gordon, all my teachers and peers that helped and inspired me, and to the next generations of jazz musicians and fans.

About the Author – Jon Gordon

A native New Yorker, saxophonist and composer Jon Gordon was born into a musical family and began playing at age ten.

Jon's love for jazz was sparked after a friend played a Phil Woods record. He attended Performing Arts High School and by senior year was sitting in with Eddie Chamblee at Sweet Basil and studying with Phil Woods.

From 1984–88 he attended Manhattan School of Music. During this time Jon began sitting in with Charles McPherson, Doc Cheatham, Phil Woods, Mike Stern, Percy France, and others. In 1994, Joe Lovano wrote in liner notes for one of Jon's recordings, "Jon is a masterful young altoist with a brilliant future ahead of him." In 1996, Jon won the prestigious Thelonious Monk International Jazz Saxophone Competition.

Jon has played with a who's who of legends and contemporary favorites. He is an accomplished composer and arranger and has an extensive discography as both a leader and sideman. Jon is also an author, writing *For Sue*, a compelling memoir of growing up in an alcoholic family and *Foundations for Improvisers and Further Concepts*, a jazz methods book. Jon is currently Associate Professor of Jazz Saxophone at the University of Manitoba Desautels Faculty of Music. Visit jongordonmusic.com for more information.

"Gordon has embraced the history of his instrument, carrying with it the ability to extend music as a universal language." – Wayne Shorter

"Jon Gordon is someone who is always mindful, discriminating, and attentive to detail. When playing next to him you can feel and hear his focus, energy, and presence... the years of an intimate connection between himself, his instrument and music." – Mark Turner

"Jon is one of the greatest alto players ever." – Phil Woods

"Not only a great soloist, but also possesses a gorgeous tone." – Kenny Washington

"Jon is among that elite few that are truly great alto saxophonists. Not only is he one of my favorite alto and soprano players, he's also a wonderful and very creative composer." – Maria Schneider

Praise for Jazz Dialogues

"Jazz Dialogues is a rarity among books about jazz. It's a book about people—the individual creators who devote their lives to the making of this profoundly individualistic art. It took a writer who's a first-call musician himself to capture the way jazz artists think and feel, on the bandstand and off. From Cab Calloway and Doc Cheatham to Maria Schneider and Steve Wilson, Jon Gordon brings us face to face, mind to mind, heart to heart, with dozens of fascinating musicians. Like a great player in a jazz band, Gordon knows not only how to play, but how to listen." – David Hajdu, author of *Lush Life: A Biography of Billy Strayhorn*

Also by Jon Gordon

For Sue
"An honest, heartbreaking remembrance of an addict and mother. In simple, unadorned prose, each chapter comprises a series of loosely themed recollections. Many highlight his mother's popularity among friends and her universally recognized charisma. The darker material is gripping, if horrifying, and readers are sure to root for the narrator's charming childself. Deftly conjured, this portrait of the author's imperfect mother is neither indictment nor defense; a fine addition to the memoir genre." – Kirkus Reviews

"*For Sue* is an American *Angela's Ashes*." – *Guillermo Echanique, Author & Poet*

"Jon Gordon writes like he plays—with concise structure and graceful human compassion. Bravo Jon!" – Phil Woods, NEA Jazz Master

"Surviving unimaginable hardships, Gordon writes with compassion, poignancy and a keen awareness that the strength of community and the redemptive powers of music helped him not only survive; but achieve great success." – *Marian Fontana, Best-selling author of A Widow's Walk*

"Gordon has written an emotionally honest; in fact, painfully open-hearted account of himself as the loving son of an all but entirely inadequate alcoholic, drug-mesmerized mother who forced him to become more her parent than child. This is a book to cherish." – *Peter Straub, Best-selling, award-winning author 2015 Finalist National Indie Excellence Awards.*

"It doesn't seem fair. Saxophonist Jon Gordon's talents for phrasing and rhythm have translated smoothly onto the pages of his beautifully honest memoir, *For Sue*. Listening to the characters in his life speak is like listening to a fine piece of jazz. As he's proven time and time again, the man's got a great ear." – *Tim O'Mara, author of the Raymond Donne series*

This is a beautiful work: a gripping, tender, raw, account of life on the edge, circumscribed by poverty and his mother's alcoholism. But look at the cover image of his mother that the author has chosen as our entry into their world, and you understand immediately the lens through which he presents their story. It's compassionate without sentimentality or complaint, never shying away from the hard truths, but somehow never losing sight of the human beauty at the core of his world. Or never losing faith. The boy managed to endure and find mentors who helped him, and—especially in alto saxophonist Phil Woods—who recognized and nurtured his tremendous talent. The man who narrates the story, looking back after having developed an admirable career in music, manages to make of it all a tender, melancholy, and ultimately humbly triumphant song. A treasure. – *Nina d'Alessandro - writer, professor*

This is a heart-felt memoir from a man who has come through long periods of hardship in his life, to become an amazing person and true musician. Gordon's story is told with depth and wit, the moments of sadness and pain are brilliantly offset by glimpses of the author's dry sense of humour. An engrossing read that once I started, I found hard to put down. – *Tom Pulford - saxophonist, Adeladie Australia*

Also from Cymbal Press   cymbalpress.com

CYMBAL PRESS

Life in E Flat - The Autobiography of Phil Woods is the life story of the legendary saxophonist, composer, band leader, and National Endowment for the Arts Jazz Master. Look for it in softcover, hardcover, and Kindle at cymbalpress.com.

"*Life in E-Flat* is a gift, a compelling and entertaining memoir by one of the leading alto saxophonists in jazz for 60 years. Phil Woods was a star soloist, influential lead alto player, savvy bandleader, underrated composer-arranger, and consummate studio musician. He was also a charismatic storyteller with a typewriter—literate, funny, insightful, self-aware, with a keen eye and ear for details that reveal character, including his own personal failings. Heroes and colleagues like Charlie Parker, Dizzy Gillespie, Quincy Jones, Benny Carter, and Ben Webster are drawn in quick, astute sketches. Observations about the music business, jazz education, and the vagaries of the jazz life are laced with wisdom and sardonic wit. The book is also an invaluable portrait of world that has vanished: Juilliard at midcentury, the band bus, the bustling post-war bebop academy of the streets, the New York studios of the '60s, the European jazz scene of the early '70s, and the energy and excitement of a remarkable life lived among some of the greatest giants in jazz history." – *Mark Stryker, author of 'Jazz From Detroit'*

"Phil Woods's voice on the page is as raw and lyrical and unmistakable as the sound of his alto. If you want to really know about The Life—the true day-to-day of a working jazz musician, with all its agonies and ecstasies and tedium and the ever-exciting challenge of getting paid something like what you're worth for playing your heart out—look no further. *Life in E Flat* pulls no punches and tells no lies." – *James Kaplan, author of 'Sinatra: The Chairman, Frank: The Voice' and 'Irving Berlin: New York Genius'*

"Someone spotted me fondling the saxophone and misinterpreted my avaricious intent as musical interest…" So Phil Wood's lifelong journey began—a saga he relates with an irreverent, self-deprecating wit, from his earliest days in Western Massachusetts to recording timeless music and traveling the world with jazz legends. Time and again, he sets up a story like a punchline's coming, and often they do. What you always get is history rich in detail and long in feeling and self-honesty—the personal stumbles and the musical triumphs. Phil left us in 2015; this book he left us is a gift that shows how so much of him is still here." – *Ashley Kahn, music historian and author of 'A Love Supreme: The Story of John Coltrane's Signature Album '& 'Kind of Blue: The Making of the Miles Davis Masterpiece'*

"Growing up a New York jazz fan, Phil Woods was always a favorite. He was straight ahead, personal but in control, brimming with ideas: solid in every way. This account of the late jazz man's American journey, assembled with a loving, light touch by the always discerning critic Ted Panken, is like a Woods' gig. Full of the right information, things you thought you knew but didn't (the stories of often being the only white man in the room especially after marrying Charlie Parker's widow are instructive), heartbreaking and triumphant, *Life in E-Flat* is 100% solid." – *Mark Jacobson, author of 'The Lampshade and Pale Horse Rider, former staff writer of the Village Voice and New York Magazine, and contributing editor for Rolling Stone and Esquire*

Made in the USA
Monee, IL
03 September 2021